Dwelling in Possibility

Reading
WOMEN
Writing

a series edited by
Shari Benstock and Celeste Schenck

Reading Women Writing is dedicated to furthering international feminist debate. The series publishes books on all aspects of feminist theory and textual practice. *Reading Women Writing* especially welcomes books that address cultures, histories, and experience beyond first-world academic boundaries. A complete list of titles in the series appears at the end of the book.

Dwelling in Possibility

Women Poets and Critics on Poetry

EDITED BY

Yopie Prins and
Maeera Shreiber

Cornell University Press

ITHACA AND LONDON

First published 1997 by Cornell University Press.
First printing, Cornell Paperbacks, 1997.

Printed in the United States of America

Library of Congress Cataloging-in-Publication Data

Dwelling in possibility : women poets and critics on poetry /
    Yopie Prins and Maeera Shreiber, editors.
        p.   cm. — (Reading women writing)
Includes index
ISBN 0-8014-3199-9 (alk. paper). — ISBN 0-8014-8294-1 (paper : alk. paper)
    1. Feminist literary criticism.   2. Poetry—Women authors—History and criticism.
3. Women and literature.   4.   Gender identity in literature.   I. Prins, Yopie.
II. Shreiber, Maeera, 1956–   .   III. Series.
PN98.W64D88 1997
809.1'0082—dc21   97-25507

Cornell University Press strives to utilize environmentally responsible suppliers and materials to the fullest extent possible in the publishing of its books. Such materials include vegetable-based, low-VOC inks and acid-free papers that are also either recycled, totally chlorine-free, or partly composed of nonwood fibers.

Cloth printing   10   9   8   7   6   5   4   3   2   1
Paperback printing   10   9   8   7   6   5   4   3   2   1

Contents

Acknowledgments   vii

Introduction
Yopie Prins and Maeera Shreiber   1

PART I. QUESTIONING THE SUBJECT

1. When a "Long" Poem Is a "Big" Poem: Self-Authorizing Strategies in Women's Twentieth-Century "Long Poems"
Susan Stanford Friedman   13
2. Female Power and the Devaluation of Renaissance Love Lyrics
Diana E. Henderson   38
3. "Martha's Name," or The Scandal of "The Thorn"
Karen Swann   60
4. Postscripts to Emily Dickinson
Susan Howe   80
5. "Faith in Anatomy": Reading Emily Dickinson
Virginia Jackson   85

PART II. THE VOICE IN QUESTION

6. On Voice
Rita Dove   111
7. Trying Her Tongue
M. Nourbese Philip   116
8. An Interweaving of Worlds
Joy Harjo   126
9. Performing, Not Writing: The Reception of an Irish Woman's Lament
Angela Bourke   132

10. Poetic Subject and Voice as Sites of Struggle: Toward
    a"Postrevisionist" Reading of Stevie Smith's Fairy-Tale Poems
    Romana Huk   147
11. Invading the "Transparent Laberynth": Anne Finch and the
    Poetics of Translation
    Jayne Elizabeth Lewis   166

PART III. CLASSICAL TRANSFORMATIONS

12. On "The Journey"
    Eavan Boland   187
13. A Few Cranky Paragraphs on Form and Content
    Marilyn Hacker   193
14. Genre Development and Gendered Voices in Erinna and
    Nossis
    Kathryn Gutzwiller   202
15. Sappho Shock
    Anne Carson   223
16. Sappho Doubled: Michael Field
    Yopie Prins   229
17. Sappho's Gymnasium
    Olga Broumas and T Begley   252

PART IV. BIBLICAL TRANSFORMATIONS

18. Entering the Tents
    Alicia Ostriker   263
19. In Her Own Images: Lucille Clifton and the Bible
    Akasha (Gloria) Hull   273
20. the woman's mourning song: a poetics of lamentation
    bell hooks   296
21. "Where Are We Moored?": Adrienne Rich, Women's
    Mourning, and the Limits of Lament
    Maeera Shreiber   301
22. Wrestling the Angel of Inscription
    Eleanor Wilner   318
23. Otherhow (and permission to continue)
    Rachel Blau DuPlessis   327

Works Cited   345

About the Contributors   367

Index   371

Acknowledgments

Many conversations have led to the making of this book. We thank all the contributors for conversing with us and with one another over the past few years. Without them *Dwelling in Possibility* would not have been possible. They contributed ideas and questions to shape the collection, they read and commented on various versions of the Introduction, and they helped to refine our thinking about gender and genre in poetry. Through our ongoing exchange the book changed, and changed again, and gradually achieved its present form.

We are deeply grateful to Celeste Schenck for proposing a collection of essays on gender and poetic genres and encouraging us to work together on it. She sustained the project with her enthusiasm and offered invaluable feedback every step of the way. We also appreciate the support and editorial advice of Bernhard Kendler of Cornell University Press, as he patiently guided us through the complexities of a multi-authored collection. For preparation of the manuscript we are grateful to have received faculty research grants from Reed College, Oberlin College, and the University of Michigan, and we give special thanks to Jean Borger and Monika Cassel for their work as research assistants. Many thanks also to Vince Cheng for his help.

For permission to use copyrighted material we thank the following persons and institutions:

The Academy of American Poets, for permission to reprint "A Few Cranky Paragraphs on Form and Content" by Marilyn Hacker, from the Fall 1995 issue of *Poetry Pilot: The Newsletter of The Academy of American Poets*, copyright © 1995 by The Academy of American Poets.

The Amherst College Library, for permission to reproduce parts of Emily Dickinson manuscript no. 828 (Johnson letter 233).

Arion: A Journal of Humanities and the Classics, for permission to reprint excerpts of Anne Carson's "Just for the Thrill: Sycophantizing Aristotle's *Poetics*," 1.1 (1990), copyright © 1990 by Anne Carson.

Lucille Clifton and Curtis Brown, Ltd., for permission to quote from *good news about the earth*, copyright © 1972 by Lucille Clifton; *two-headed woman*, copyright © 1980 by Lucille Clifton; *Next: New Poems*, copyright © 1987 by Lucille Clifton; *quilting poems, 1987–1990*, copyright © 1991 by Lucille Clifton.

Roger L. Conover, Literary Executor, for permission to quote from the poetry of Mina Loy.

Copper Canyon Press, for permission to reprint "Proem" and "Sappho's Gymnasium" from *Sappho's Gymnasium*, Copper Canyon Press, P.O.B. 271, Port Townsend, Washington 98368, copyright © 1994 by Olga Broumas and T Begley.

Rita Dove, for permission to reprint "Ö" from *The Yellow House on the Corner*, copyright © 1980 by Rita Dove; "Shakespeare Say" from *Museum*, copyright © 1983 by Rita Dove; "Gospel" from *Thomas and Beulah*, copyright © 1986 by Rita Dove.

Rita Dove and W. W. Norton & Company, Inc., for permission to reprint "Canary" from *Grace Notes*, copyright © 1989 by Rita Dove.

Rachel Blau DuPlessis, for permission to reprint "Draft 6: Midrush," copyright © 1991 by Rachel Blau DuPlessis, from *Drafts*, Potes & Poets Press, 181 Edgemont Ave., Elmwood, Connecticut 06110. All rights reserved. Additional notes about "Midrush" and *Drafts* made for this volume, copyright © 1996 by Rachel Blau DuPlessis. All rights reserved.

Rachel Blau DuPlessis and Routledge, Chapman & Hall, Inc., for permission to reprint excerpts from "Otherhow" by Rachel Blau DuPlessis, from *The Pink Guitar: Writing as a Feminist Practice*, copyright © 1990 by Rachel Blau DuPlessis.

Gordon and Breach, Science Publishers, for permission to reprint "When a 'Long' Poem is a 'Big' Poem: Self-Authorizing Strategies in Women's Twentieth-Century 'Long Poems,'" by Susan Stanford Friedman, from *LIT* 2 (1990).

Judy Grahn, for permission to quote from *The Queen of Wands*, copyright © 1982 by Judy Grahn.

Graph, for permission to reprint excerpts from "Performing Not Writing: The Reception of an Irish Woman's Lament" by Angela Bourke, from *Graph* 2 (Winter 1991–92): 28–31.

Harlem River Press, for permission to reprint poems from *the woman's mourning song*, copyright © 1993 by bell hooks.

Harvard University Press and the Trustees of Amherst College, for permission to quote from *The Poems of Emily Dickinson*, ed. Thomas H. Johnson (Cambridge: Belknap Press of Harvard University Press), copyright © 1951, 1955, 1979, 1983 by the President and Fellows of Harvard College; and for permission to quote from *The Complete Letters of Emily Dickinson*, ed. Thomas H. Johnson and Theodora Ward (Cambridge: Belknap Press of Harvard University Press), copyright © 1955, 1958 by the President and Fellows of Harvard College.

Johns Hopkins University Press, for permission to reprint "Sappho Doubled: Michael Field" by Yopie Prins, from *Yale Journal of Criticism* 8 (1995): 165–86.

Little, Brown & Company, for permission to reprint poem #657 from *The Complete Poems of Emily Dickinson*.

New Directions Publishing Corporation, for permission to quote and reproduce a drawing from *The Collected Poems of Stevie Smith*, copyright © 1972 by Stevie Smith.

Alicia Suskin Ostriker, for permission to quote from *Nakedness of the Fathers: Biblical Visions and Revisions*, copyright © 1994 by Alicia Suskin Ostriker, and from *The Mother/Child Papers*, copyright © 1980 by Alicia Suskin Ostriker.

M. Nourbese Philip, for permission to reprint "Discourse on the Logic of Language" and excerpts from "The Absence of Writing, or How I Almost Became a Spy" from *She Tries Her Tongue*, copyright © 1989 by M. Nourbese Philip; and for permission to reprint "Ignoring Poetry" by M. Nourbese Philip, from *Women and Performance: A Journal of Feminist Theatre* 14–15, copyright © 1994 by M. Nourbese Philip.

W. W. Norton & Company, Inc., and Carcanet Press, for permission to reprint "The Journey" from *Outside History: Selected Poems, 1980–1990* by Eavan Boland, copyright © 1990 by Eavan Boland.

W. W. Norton & Company, Inc., and Francis Collin, for permission to reprint "A Note Downriver" and "Chiliastic Sapphics" from *Winter Numbers*, copyright © 1994 by Marilyn Hacker.

W. W. Norton & Company, Inc., and the Charlotte Sheedy Literary Agency, for permission to reprint "The Myth of Blackbirds" and "A Post-colonial Tale" from *The Woman Who Fell from the Sky*, copyright © 1994 by Joy Harjo.

University of California Press, for permission to reprint material from *Poetic Garlands: Hellenistic Epigrams in Context* by Kathryn Gutzwiller, copyright © 1998.

University of Pittsburgh Press, for permission to reprint "A Meditation in Seven Days" from *Green Age* by Alicia Suskin Ostriker, copyright © 1989 by Alicia Suskin Ostriker.

University Press of New England, for permission to reprint "Healing Animal" from *In Mad Love and War*, copyright © 1990 by Joy Harjo.

University Press of New England and Wesleyan University Press, for permission to reprint excerpts from Susan Howe's "These Flames and Generosities of the Heart: Emily Dickinson and the Illogic of Sumptuary Values" from *The Birth-mark*, copyright © 1993 by Susan Howe; and for permission to reprint "The Track of Desire" and "The Source of Snow," from *Singularities*, copyright © 1990 by Susan Howe.

Betsy Warland, for permission to quote from *serpent (w)rite: a reader's gloss*, copyright © 1987 by Betsy Warland.

Eleanor Wilner, for permission to reprint "Sarah's Choice" from *Sarah's Choice* (Phoenix Poetry Series, University of Chicago Press), copyright © 1989 by Eleanor Wilner.

Y. P. and M. S.

Dwelling in Possibility

Introduction

YOPIE PRINS AND MAEERA SHREIBER

I dwell in Possibility—
A fairer House than Prose—
More numerous of Windows—
Superior—for Doors—

Dwelling in Possibility opens a space, explores new possibilities, for conversation between critics and poets about the interplay of gender and genre in poetry. What is the place of feminist criticism, where do women poets place themselves in this conversation, and how might we enter poems as a place where the questioning of both gender and genre begins? We take Emily Dickinson's words for the title of our collection, as her famous stanza articulates an alternative that it does not quite name: "Possibility" is not exactly "Poetry," yet it introduces a utopian topos of the poetic—in both its most ideal and most literal definitions—that is the subject on which the following pages dwell. The contributors to this volume read and write poems in order to perform a process of perpetual displacement, to reclaim the wayward etymology of "dwelling" not as a hypothetical house to inhabit but as a verb that also means to go astray, leading us away and unpredictably elsewhere.

Thus, in reading women writing, we find ourselves simultaneously dwelling in possibility and dwelling on impossibility. For feminist thinking within and through poetry, the notion of genre has developed so many windows and doors in it that the structure often seems paper thin; for poets and critics thinking through feminism, assumptions about gender often appear too tenuously constructed to stand for politics. Yet our contributors share Dickinson's optative mode as well as her skeptical one. That poets may disarticulate their own habitation and that critics may themselves depend on poetic structures, that gender may be a hypothetical category and yet a condition of life—these are the claims that this volume takes up and debates.

Many of our contributors understand gender to be inevitably implicated in the historical transformation of poetic genres; this historical approach informs critical essays on Hellenistic women poets, on sonnets written by women in the Renaissance, on the gendering of Romantic lyric, on the feminization of modernism, and on constructions of female authorship from the eighteenth century to the present. Other contributions take the form of poetic meditations by contemporary women poets, demonstrating that questions about gender and genre are also the source of ongoing creative endeavor. By juxtaposing criticism and poetry, this volume presents the possibility of displacing yet another generic distinction, the division between "critical" and "creative" writing; all the contributions are "essays" in their attempt to formulate new feminist perspectives, to put into practice new ways of writing, to experiment with poetry.

There is no critical consensus, of course, regarding the past, present, and future of feminist criticism. Among our contributors there are strong differences of opinion: some insist on the central authority of female experience while others call this assumption into question; some argue that gender determines genre while others argue the reverse; some approach the revision of genres through experimental poetry while others are more interested in revising traditional forms; some align themselves with poststructuralist critiques of the subject while others are interested in reclaiming woman as subject. With *Dwelling in Possibility*, we mean to emphasize many of the disagreements and discontinuities that also characterize this particular moment in feminist literary history.

Contiguity rather than continuity is our principle of organization. This volume offers a multiplication of perspectives rather than a single coherent vision, an invitation to consider how multiple positions modify as well as challenge one another. What kind of exchange takes place, for example, between a politics of self-empowerment and a psychoanalytic reading of woman as lack, between the rhetorical analysis of feminine figures and the study of women poets in specific cultural contexts, between advocating a common women's language and recognizing differences such as race and class? Despite a wide range of theoretical articulations and critical investments in answer to such questions, each contributor here is interested in how a gendered perspective on reading and writing poetry might deepen our understanding of the forms and functions of a poetic response.

Our focus on the intersection of gender and genre reflects contemporary developments within feminist theory, following the trajectory from "feminist critique" to "gynocriticsm" and "gender studies" over the past decade. In *The New Feminist Criticism*, for example, Elaine Showalter defined gynocriticism as the study of "women *as writers*" with special emphasis on "the history, styles, themes, genres, and structures of writing by women" (Showalter 1985a:248). The emphasis on women as a distinct literary group reflects a tendency to categorize gender by analogy to generic categories: one way to define gender is to identify genre, and indeed in the mid-1980s this equivalence served as a functional definition of feminist studies. The analogy appeared less self-evident, however, by the late eighties, as the concept of gender was pluralized, considered less a category than a wide range of shifting alignments along multiple axes. This theoretical shift is evident in the introduction to *Speaking of Gender*, where Showalter announces gender studies as "a new phase in feminist criticism, an investigation of the ways that all reading and writing, by men as well as by women, is marked by gender" (Showalter 1989:2). Increasingly feminist critics have become interested not only in differentiating the genres of women's writing, but in theorizing and historicizing gender itself as a differential structure.

A chronological account of feminist criticism implies continuity from one moment to the next, suggesting coherence where there is contradiction and providing a misleading sense of teleology. In fact, feminist critique, gynocriticism, and gender studies coexist simultaneously, in variously overlapping forms, beside other feminist critical practices that are not yet—or are less readily—identifiable. Further, as Eve Kosofsky Sedgwick points out, while "gender criticism" may in one sense be coextensive with "feminist criticism," in another sense the two are radically discontinuous, when gender studies are taken to mean "not criticism *through* the categories of gender analysis, but criticism *of* them" (Sedgwick 1992:273). The emergence of queer theory in the early nineties has allowed a simultaneous speaking and critiquing of gender, enabling us to question masculinity and femininity as natural categories defined by "likeness" or "kind."

The interrogation of gender within gender studies runs parallel to a shift in genre theory within literary studies. Traditional genre criticism attempted to classify texts according to kind, in the interest of preserving an inherently natural literary order. Such classification systems functioned synchronically by identifying literary characteristics that remain fixed throughout history, or diachronically by tracing the historical evolution of identifiable literary genres, but in both systems the impulse was to taxonomize by analogy to the species of nature. What happens, however, when taxonomies no longer serve to naturalize what they identify, and when the function of genre is no longer taxonomic? This question has been posed over the past two decades by critics of genre (e.g., Hernadi 1972; A. Fowler 1982; Dubrow 1982; Culler 1988; Gerhart 1992; Beebee 1994). Instead of defining a system of ideal categories, genre criticism turns into a self-reflexive critique of the identity of genre—an analytic category that (like gender) proves to be both arbitrary and overdetermined.

With this recognition we have entered into a dialectical use of genre criticism, described by Fredric Jameson as "a new, historically reflexive, way of using categories, such as those of genre, which are so clearly implicated in the literary history and the formal production they were traditionally supposed to classify and neutrally to describe" (Jameson 1981:107). In recent decades, the search for intrinsic genre has given way to the understanding of genres through their historical effects. The reformulation of Anglo-American genre theory has been, at least in part, a reaction against the tendency to focus on texts as decontextualized verbal ojects. New Historicism, in moving beyond the legacies of the New Criticism, has transformed genre studies into an exploration of the poetics of culture, allowing literary genres to be interpreted as "part of the complex network of institutions, practices, beliefs that constitute culture as a whole" (Greenblatt 1982:15). This situational definition of genre emphasizes the mediation between text and context, extending formal analysis into a dialectical analysis of the social formations that simultaneously determine and are determined by genre.

Generic categories, like categories of gender, are therefore not innate but constructed for specific ideological purposes. Feminist criticism has enabled us to analyze such categories from a critical perspective, demonstrating how the very principle of classification produces a hierarchy of masculine over feminine. The will to taxonomize is itself a form of sexual politics, Celeste Schenck argues: "The law of genre, the enforcement of generic purity, the policing of borders, has remained since the classical period a preoccupation of *homo* (properly understood man) *taxonomicus*" (Schenck 1988:281). The task for feminist genre theory is to open the borders—allowing more back-and-forth between categories, demonstrating the transitivity and interdependence of genres marked "masculine" and "feminine," and critiquing the logic of limits—in order to delimit genre itself. Indeed it is possible, as Jacques Derrida has proposed, to read the law of genre in the feminine in order to deconstruct the (masculine) principle of law and order. For if genre enforces its own institutionalization, the logic of the law only asserts itself at the moment of transgression; this transgressive potential of the law, exceeding the very boundaries it presumes to enforce, is what Derrida calls "the law of the law of genre" (Derrida 1980:227). Feminist critics may use this contradiction to their own advantage, to reverse and invert a literary tradition that depends on the regulation of gendered oppositions and hierarchized genres.

Any inquiry into how women writers engage poetic form should therefore take into consideration how gender and genre are being theorized within current critical discourses. *Dwelling in Possibility* seeks to put into practice these theoretical claims, by implicating feminist criticism in the ongoing critique of categories and taxonomies. In taking up this challenge, our contributors show not only how theory may illumine poems but also how poems may speak to theory. Indeed, the relationship between poetry and feminist theory proves to be a matter of mutual implication, and makes our collection possible: connections between gender and genre are elaborated in critical prose and poetry, but not in a relation that implies "theory" versus "practice." If we understand genre theory to be heuristic rather than descriptive or prescriptive—if, as Adena Rosmarin argues,"genre is chosen or defined to fit neither a historical nor a theoretical reality but to serve a pragmatic end" (1985:49–50), which turns out to be our own praxis—then the articles in this volume are as much a form of poetic practice as the poems are a form of critical theorizing.

The contributors to Part I, "Questioning the Subject," conceptualize the relationship between gender and genre by posing a question about the construction of woman as poetic subject. Susan Stanford Friedman begins with the hypothesis that poetic subjectivity is often predicated on the celebration of a masculine self, particularly in epic, a genre from which women have traditionally been excluded. However, in surveying twentieth-century long poems written by women, Friedman discerns various strategies for feminizing the phallic law of genre: by satirical inversion, historical reclamation, interpretive revision, and linguistic experimentalism, women poets are able to write themselves into the position of historical subjects. Diana E. Henderson further explores the problems and the possibilities for claiming a female lyric subject within a masculine lyric tradition; her essay on Petrarchan sonnets by Renaissance women poets calls for a feminist revaluation of the love lyric as a genre that has been devalued precisely because it lends itself to women's writing.

Karen Swann, by contrast, considers the deployment of a woman's story—not as a writing subject, but a historical subject written about—within the lyrical ballads of William Wordsworth. Through his engagement with popular "feminine" plots, she argues, Wordsworth constitutes himself as masculine lyric subject yet also produces the lyrical ballad as a mixed genre, haunted by female figures such as Martha Ray. Corresponding to the construction of male authorship on the model of Wordsworth, the construction of female authorship on the model of Emily Dickinson is the central question posed by the last two contributors in this section. Susan Howe turns to the manuscripts of Dickinson in order to recover an authorial intention obscured by literary history, as well as to discover a precursor for her own experimental poetics; in the "disjunct leaves" of Emily Dickinson, Howe looks for the "understory of another word." Virginia Jackson also takes another look at the material effects of Dickinson's writing, but from a different theoretical and historical perspective, in order to question the assumption of intention and authorial identity within a tradition of subjectivist reading.

Whereas Part I explores the construction, deconstruction, and reconstruction of female subjectivity through various kinds of textual practice, Part II, "The Voice in Question," foregrounds the figure of voice within poetry by women. Feminist criticism has often emphasized the difficulty of coming to voice, or the marginalization of women's voices; yet alongside the resistance *to* voice, voice may also be used *for* resistance in women's poetry. The section begins with three contemporary poets who bring voice into play, in various ways. Rita Dove describes her poetry as a celebration of "language at its most provocative," and in her poems we discover multiple voices, the cadences of gospel and the blues, the reclamation and mediation of song through writing. A different challenge to lyric voice—its explosion or implosion into voices that interrupt and disrupt—is performed by M. Nourbese Philip, as her poetry forces a confrontation between formal English and the Caribbean demotic, between father and mother tongue, between written and spoken language. Joy Harjo allows the patterns of speech to shift into other dimensions; drawing on the tradition of storytelling within Native American culture, Harjo is interested in writing narrative poems with "a lyric overtone"; her interweaving of stories and songs is another instance of generic displacement.

Through the examples of Dove, Philip, and Harjo, we see the importance of situating women's poetry within different cultural contexts and in multiple traditions, oral and written. This argument is further developed by Angela Bourke. Her essay on the reception of Irish poetry by the English literary establishment demonstrates how a famous lament by an Irish woman, taken out of the context of its oral performance, has become a degendered text. Genre theory, she concludes, must take into account a historical tradition of performing as well as writing. In a related argument, Romana Huk points out that women poets must be read dialogically. Although Bakhtin has theorized poetry as a "monologic" genre, Huk offers a feminist revision of Bakhtinian dialogism in her essay on Stevie Smith, whose "double-voicing" is evident in the merging of ballad form with prosaic, lyric, and colloquial language. The decentering of voice in Smith's fairy-tale poems is part of her eccentric modernism, yet as a strategy of disruption it is not unlike the translation of a fable by the eighteenth-century poet Anne Finch. In the critical essay by Jayne Elizabeth Lewis, we see how Finch's conception of translation creates a metaphor for the female voice as it "spoke" in Augustan England. "The Voice in Question" therefore moves from contemporary poems to three essays that historicize and further theorize the assumption of voice by women poets.

Part III, "Classical Transformations," considers the reworking of classical lyric in women's verse, particularly through the figure of the Greek archaic poet Sappho. Placed at the origins of Western lyric, Sappho is often invoked as its originary figure: an exemplary lyric subject who— not unlike Dickinson—is called upon to exemplify a female poetic tradition. In Eavan Boland's poem "The Journey," Sappho defines the vocation of the woman poet by leading her into a vision of other women, whose experience has been excluded from poetic tradition; to bear witness to their truth, however, Boland requires the subversion of inherited forms. In contrast to the Sapphic persona created by Boland, Marilyn Hacker engages Sappho in a purely metrical form. However, in reflecting on her choice to write in sapphic stanzas, Hacker insists on the inseparability of form and content and creates a moving testimonial to historical experience.

Sappho's influence is felt not only in the work of contemporary poets but also in the writing that remains of Hellenistic women poets, who— according to Kathryn Gutzwiller—used Sappho as model for a personalized, feminine voice. Gutzwiller's essay emphasizes the impact of generic renovations by the Greek poets Nossis and Erinna, although their achievement has been rendered almost invisible because of its reincorporation into a masculine poetic tradition. Anne Carson offers another approach to classical scholarship on Sappho. Mediating between ancient Greek and modern English, between philology and poetry, Anne Carson reads the Sapphic fragments in order to reflect on the specularity of lyric as a genre and, in her own poetic imitation of Sappho, she mirrors the disappearance of a lyric subject. A similar question about lyric subjectivity is raised by the Sapphic imitations of Katherine Bradley and Edith Cooper, two Victorian women poets who wrote together as "Michael Field." The essay by Yopie Prins demonstrates how their collaborative writing complicates generic assumptions about the lyric as solitary utterance of a single speaker and enables them to perform the Sapphic signature as plural and lesbian. In our own century, a striking counterpart to "Michael Field" is the collaboration of Olga Broumas and T Begley: they also write on the model of the Sapphic fragments, in order to create a text that refuses "narrative comforts," opening a space for eroticized textual exchange.

By transforming classical tradition, women poets therefore discover new possibilities for writing poetry. The renegotiation of female authorship in relation to the authority of tradition is also in question in Part IV, "Biblical Transformations." Women writers enter biblical texts as a territory that continues to register as somehow forbidden. The interest that the Bible holds for women poets is therefore not merely thematic, for it serves as the ground upon which they interrogate the meaning, the significance, and the legacies of tradition in its most radical sense. The section opens with a poem by Alicia Ostriker, who engages the Hebrew Bible in an effort to excavate a space in which she can dwell as a poet, a woman, a Jew. The Bible also functions as sourcebook for Lucille Clifton, who—as Akasha (Gloria) Hull argues in her essay—successfully transforms a patriarchal text into an Afrocentric, feminist, sexual, and mystical text. We see this spiritual impulse as well in bell hooks, who discovers a poetics of lamentation in biblical writing and uncovers the strong need for women to lament—to express pain, confront death, speak sorrow—in poems that work through grief. The emphasis on women's mourning as a communal enterprise is further elaborated by Maeera Shreiber, in her essay on Adrienne Rich and the tradition of Hebraic lament. However, in observing the vexed relation between feminism and Judaism in Rich's poetry, Shreiber argues that "feminine" lamentation has various implications in the construction of national, ethnic, and religious identities.

Part IV concludes with two longer poetic meditations on the place of the woman poet, as well as her displacements. Eleanor Wilner writes under the aegis of Shekhinah, that feminine aspect of God whose name means "dwelling," in order to dwell on the relationship between poetry and the Bible, poetry and history, poetry and stories. Driven by the necessity of telling not only another story but a better one, Wilner channels the voice of Sarah from the Old Testament, ushering her out of the margins and into a central place, the here and now of our own historical moment. At this same moment it is also possible to conceive of writing, as Rachel Blau DuPlessis does, in terms of a movement away from the center into margins that must forever multiply. The "marginalities" of this textual practice are modeled on the rabbinic tradition of hermeneutics known as *midrash*, which DuPlessis uses as metaphor for her own disjunctive poetics in order to affirm the necessity of placelessness and mobility: in "Draft 6: Midrush" DuPlessis inhabits a discontinuous space to define another way of dwelling in possibility. By way of conclusion, DuPlessis leads us back into the terrain mapped out at the beginning of the collection by Susan Stanford Friedman, whose critical essay describes precisely the crossing of borderlines and undoing of boundaries that the poetry of DuPlessis self-consciously performs.

We hope that readers of this volume will follow a similar logic, by reading not only through but also across and around the categories created by our organization of essays into four groups. There are numerous connections to be found among essays in different sections: on experimental poetics (Friedman, Howe, Philip, Broumas and Begley, DuPlessis), on women in modernism (Friedman, Huk, Hull), on lyric voice (Henderson, Jackson, Gutzwiller, Prins, in addition to Part II), on the gendering of lament (Swann, Bourke, Boland, Hacker, hooks, Shreiber), on love lyrics (Henderson, Howe, Hacker, Prins, Broumas and Begley), on women and translation (Philip, Bourke, Lewis, Carson, Prins), on lesbian poetics (Friedman, Hacker, Prins, Broumas and Begley), on the female body (Swann, Henderson, Jackson, Lewis, Boland, Gutzwiller, Ostriker), on race and ethnicity (Dove, Harjo, Philip, Hull, hooks, Shreiber), on women in colonial discourses (Harjo, Philip, Bourke), on the prose poem (Harjo, Philip, Huk, DuPlessis), and on the role of the poet-critic (Howe, Carson, Ostriker, hooks, DuPlessis).

These and other recurring themes are familiar enough within feminist criticism, and they suggest the ways in which *Dwelling in Possibility* continues the work of several generations of feminist critics. It is a substantial body of work: in addition to the proliferation of numerous anthologies devoted to women poets over the past two decades, several anthologies devoted to feminist essays on poetry have also appeared. Among the earliest and most influential of these critical collections was *Shakespeare's Sisters: Feminist Essays on Women Poets* (1979b), edited by Sandra Gilbert and Susan Gubar to define a distinctively female poetic tradition; it was followed, during the next decade, by various attempts to pluralize their claim to tradition and then by further reflection on the theoretical implications of such a claim (e.g., Moraga and Anzaldúa 1981; Juhasz 1983; Middlebrook and Yalom 1985; Homans 1980, 1986; Ostriker 1986; Montefiore 1987; Berg et al. 1989; Loeffelholz 1991; Yorke 1991; Erkkila 1992). More recently the development of feminist criticism on poetry has been usefully surveyed by Lynn Keller and Cristanne Miller in their introduction to *Feminist Measures: Soundings in Poetry and Theory* (1994), a collection of essays that resonates with our own in approaching poetry as a gendered practice. Such work as well as the contributions in the present volume suggests that this may be a moment in literary criticism and gender studies when poetry marks a horizon of creative collaboration rather than a nostalgic limit, a moment of critical possibility and of new poetical preoccupations.

That insight returns us to Dickinson's poem, which ends with a riddling pun on the "Occupation" of the dweller in Possibility:

> Of Visitors—the fairest—
> For Occupation—This—
> The spreading wide my narrow Hands
> To gather Paradise—
>
> (poem 657)

The stanza collapses occupant and space occupied, poet and poem, gender and genre, so that the lyric "I" seems to become the house she could only ideally inhabit: her occupation proves to be what preoccupies her. Our reading of Dickinson finally points to ways in which "This—" (the occupation of poetry, our occupation as critics and poets) is defined by the hands that, historically, take it up. As Jane Gallop has remarked in *Around 1981*(1992), the expansion of feminist criticism into poetry coincided with the entry of feminist criticism into the academy, and that moment in the early eighties was also marked by the critical revaluation of Dickinson as woman poet. But in the nineties, "the collective feminist critic" postulated by Gallop in her survey of critical collections is not a single unified body. We can no longer read women's poetry—the "fairer House than Prose"—as if it were "A Room of One's Own." But perhaps we can read and write poetry with more narrow claims and with a larger sense of what this occupation may have been, and may yet possibly be.

Part I
Questioning the Subject

When a "Long" Poem is a "Big" Poem: Self-Authorizing Strategies in Women's Twentieth-Century "Long Poems"

SUSAN STANFORD FRIEDMAN

I want to initiate an excursion into and around the long poem by twentieth-century American women poets with a perverse attack on its generic name—"long poem." I distrust the term "long poem"—not that I will propose a new one. For it undoubtedly has "currency" as a new generic category—new, that is, in critical discourse and not, of course, in poetic praxis, where long poems go back several thousand years under a variety of names.[1] But I do want to explore my dis-ease with the term as an entrée into some generalizations about women's status as outsiders in relation to the genre and the self-authorizing strategies in which they have engaged to penetrate and transform its boundaries.

The name "long poem" is deceptively simple and descriptive—neutral, unweighted, unoverdetermined, as if it had achieved a value-free, scientific objectivity or that utopian ideal of what Roland Barthes calls the "innocence" of "writing degree zero" (1953/1968:75). It is also a useful term that appears to define itself. Its virtue lies in its breadth, an inclusiveness that incorporates all poetry that is "long." It is the great umbrella for everything that is not "short." In its seeming neutrality, however, the term may obscure the exclusionary politics inherent in genre categories—especially in the binary "long" and "short" implied in the single category "long poem." In "The Law of Genre," Jacques Der-

This is an expanded and updated version of a paper delivered at the 1987 Modern Language Association convention in San Franscisco and an article published in *Lit* (1990). My thanks to James Justus for asking me to write this chapter; to Nellie McKay, Lynn Keller, Jay Clayton, and Norman Weinstein for references; and to Alicia Ostriker and Rachel Blau DuPlessis for their challenges to my resistance to the term "long poem."

[1] For some discussions of the generic category and debates about terminology, see, for example, Bernstein 1980; Dembo 1965; Friedman 1986, 1994; Kamboureli 1991; Keller 1987, 1993; Miller 1979; Riddell 1978; and Rosenthal and Gall 1981, 1983.

rida offers fair warning. Genre appears to be a *description* of literary types, a taxonomy that borrows from the biological system of classifying species. But *description*, he argues, always implies *prescription*. Like any category, genre likes repetition, not anomaly. "Thus, as soon as genre announces itself," he writes, "one must respect a norm, one must not cross a line of demarcation, one must not risk impurity, anomaly, or monstrosity" (1980:57). Literary taxonomy implicitly prescribes a *law* against "mixing," against the pollution of cross-species or cross-sex miscegenation. As Celeste Schenck writes in her feminist deconstruction of genre, "given that genres are, after all, cultural constructions themselves, they might be more usefully conceived as an overdetermined loci of contention and conflict than as ideal types. . . . Moreover, beneath the western will to taxonomize lies not only a defensive history of exclusions that constitute a political ideology but also a fetishizing of aesthetic purity . . . which has distinctly gendered overtones" (1988:282–83).

And yet, the implicit power and authority of genre is such that we can scarcely read a literary text without some conscious or subliminal set of expectations based on the genre to which the text signals its membership. As Julia Kristeva argues, texts exist within a grid of generic intertexts that shape how we read (1980:36–37).[2] No matter how unusual, a literary text signals its place within a generic category through the use or abuse of the conventions that readers have come to associate with that genre. Even a text that radically departs from those conventions gains its special effect from the absence of what we expect to be present; a generic hybrid acquires its status as anomaly through the tension created by a "mixing" of preexisting "unmixed" genres. These conventions—as well as departures from them—have a politics tied to their manifestation in the sociopolitical domain of history. As Sandra Gilbert and Susan Gubar have led the way in showing, feminist criticism has often demonstrated the gender inflections in the politics of genre—how women's "anxiety of authorship" played itself out in relationship to genre; how the most prestigious genres (like poetry, drama, and epic) erected threatening boundaries against women; how marginal or new genres (like letters, the novel, the gothic) invited women's participation; how genres heavily coded by their masculinist tradition (like the epic, the love lyric, the epithalamium, the elegy) required a fundamental re-vision to function as women's discourses.[3]

[2] See also Culler's discussion of Kristeva and generic expectations in *Structuralist Poetics* (1975:139–40, 145) and his contrasting analysis of Bloomian vs. Barthesian methodologies for intertextual reading in *The Pursuit of Signs* (1981:100–118).

[3] See, for example, Gilbert and Gubar 1979a; Friedman 1986, 1994; Homans 1995; and Keller and Miller 1994.

The descriptive simplicity of the term "long poem"—with its implicit ideology of pure form and value-free aesthetics—represses awareness of this gender-inflected politics with a displacement that substitutes the description "long" for the prescription "big."[4] A long poem is a "big poem," that is, a poem that situates itself within a long tradition of poems that ask very big questions in a very long way—historical, metaphysical, religious, and aesthetic questions. As a "big" poem, a "long" poem has volume—it is a many-sided figure that swells up to take space. As a long sequence, it also takes up time—literally, lots of time to read. In this horizontal-vertical discourse, vast space and cosmic time are the narrative coordinates within which lyric moments occur, the coordinates as well of reality, of history. Big long poems go far, tunnel deep, and fly high. They have scope. They are "potent, important."[5]

This geometry of forms—long poems, big poems—may itself be a displacement for a geography of forms: the territorial imperative of literary history to map literary *landscapes* and *terrains*, chart pathways to *horizons*, canonize *centers*, define *margins*, patronize the *borderline*, and dismiss what is *beyond the pale*—to exercise, in short, the tyranny of categorical *boundaries*, to declare what is inside, what is outside, *us* and *them*.

As poems on the greatest historical-metaphysical-religious-aesthetic questions, big-long-important poems have assumed the authority of the dominant cultural discourses—even when they speak from a position of alienation, like Ezra Pound in *The Cantos* or William Carlos Williams in *Paterson*. The generic grid within which these and other big-long poems are read has been established preeminently by the epic, which has a very big-long history of importance in Western culture. The epic has been the preeminent poetic genre of the public sphere from which women have been excluded. As a narrative of brave men's deeds, the epic often centers on the "destiny" or "formation of a race or nation" (Benet 1965: 317). It reflects a comprehensive sweep of history, a cosmic universality of theme, and an elevated discourse of public ceremony. In Pound's words, the epic is "the speech of a nation through the mouth of one man" (1954/1975:19); it is "a poem containing history" (1910/1968:216). To which we might add—containing philosophy, religion, and aesthetics.[6] These genre codes for the epic intersect with societal gender codes to identify the epic as a preeminently masculine discourse. The "law of

---

[4] For a different view of the significance of length for the "long poem," see Li, who argues that the defining *length* of a "long poem" is not "volume" but "a quality of discourse" (1986:4).

[5] I am echoing H.D.'s "The Master" in *Collected Poems* (1983:460).

[6] For current definitions of the epic, see Yu 1973; Preminger 1974; Maresca 1979; Bernstein 1980; Friedman 1986; and Kamboureli 1991.

genre" prescribed in the practice of the epic is fundamentally phallic.[7] Within the dominant discourses of Western culture, women have been denied the authority to pronounce on history, philosophy, religion, and aesthetics. The epic has consequently been a quintessentially male territory whose boundaries enforce women's status as outsiders on the landscape of poetry.

I am well aware of the considerable debate on whether the term epic can be applied to any long poems after the advent of Romanticism.[8] No longer in a detached, omniscient third person, no longer structured primarily by narrative, Wordsworth's *Prelude* and Whitman's *Song of Myself* introduced the poet's subjectivity into the epic as a major focus. In fragmenting the unitary self and intensifying the lyric as the principle of structure, modernist poets of the long poem further dissolved the authority of the epic bard to be what Thomas Maresca calls "the formulator and preserver of civilization's highest knowledge and belief" (1979:70–71). But these departures from epic convention gain their particular power from being read within the epic grid. The "song of myself" in the "personal epics" of the nineteenth and twentieth centuries is elevated by its epic resonance into a song of the times, of a people. The antiheroes in the antiepics of the modernist and postmodernist poets acquire their ironic nexus of inflation/deflation in reaction to the heroes and epics of the pre-modernist "long poems." As re-scriptions of epic conventions, modern long poems depend for their ultimate effect on our awareness of the epic norms they undo and redo. Rooted in epic tradition, the twentieth-century long poem is an overdetermined discourse whose size, scope, and authority to define history, metaphysics, religion, and aesthetics still erect a wall to keep women outside.

I am arguing therefore that the term *long poem* represses those aspects of the genre that have made it an uninviting form for women writers. Before we can study either the absence or presence of women's writing within this genre, we need to bring to consciousness this "political unconscious." Of the few women who wrote long poems in English before the twentieth-century, not many have survived in critical memory. Mary Tighe's name is known, perhaps because her *Psyche, or the Legend of Love* (1805/1978) influenced Keats. Elizabeth Barrett Browning wrote quite a number of long poems, the most important *Aurora Leigh* (1857/1979), whose epic poetics she defensively justified within the text itself.[9] George

---

[7] See Derrida's conflation of *genre* and *gender* (1980). See also Friedman 1986 for an extended discussion of the gender inflections of epic genre codes.

[8] See, for example, Rosenthal and Gall 1981, 1983; Riddell 1978; Keller 1987, 1993; Bernstein 1980; J. Miller 1979; and Friedman 1986.

[9] See also Barrett Browning's *Battle of Marathon, An Essay on Mind, Prometheus Bound, The Seraphim*, and *The Drama of Exile* in *The Poetical Works* (1974). For a discussion of *Aurora*

Eliot's *Spanish Gypsy* (1868/1899) narrates the dissolution of a romance and the regeneration of a "nation" of outsiders. Frances Watkins Harper's *Moses: A Story of the Nile* (1869) displaces her commitment to black emancipation onto the narrative of Jewish exodus. But as a matrix of historical and literary forces swelled ranks of writing women to a critical mass in this century, more and more women have been writing big-long-important poems exploring vast, cosmic questions of history, metaphysics, religion, and aesthetics. Gertrude Stein, Mina Loy, H.D., and Gwendolyn Brooks were among the first prominent modern writers in English to cross this generic Rubicon, [10] but since 1960, scores of women's long poems have appeared—as different in form and tradition as Ntozake Shange's blues-epic-drama *For colored girls who have considered suicide/when the rainbow is enuf* (1976), Charlotte Mandel's biblical retellings in *The Marriages of Jacob* (1991) and *The Life of Mary* (1988), Diane Glancy's pictographs of personal, familial, and tribal history in *Lone Dog's Winter Court* (1991), Bernadette Mayer's Odyssean wanderings in *Midwinter Day* (1982), Theresa Hak Kyung Cha's diasporic and hybridized *DICTEE* (1982), Susan Howe's linguistic saga of Swift's Stella and Lear's Cordelia in *The Liberties* (1983:64–127), and Rachel Blau DuPlessis' palimpsestic runes and ruminations on history and language in *Drafts* (1991).[11]

As different as these twentieth-century women's long poems are, they share an uneasy position within the generic grid and exhibit a common need to feminize the phallic codes of the genre. One sign of this common

---

Leigh as epic, see Friedman 1986. According to Mary Loeffelholz (in conversation), a number of other nineteenth-century women poets wrote epics, a corpus of forgotten material that she is currently researching.

[10] See for example H.D.'s *Trilogy* (first published, 1944–46), *By Avon River* (1949), *Helen in Egypt* (composed 1952–55, first published 1961), "Sagesse" (composed 1957, published 1972), *Vale Ave* (composed 1957, published 1982), "Winter Love" (composed 1959, published 1972), and "Hermetic Definition" (composed 1960, published 1972); Gertrude Stein's *Tender Buttons* (composed 1911–12, published 1914), *Lifting Belly* (composed 1915–17, published 1953), "Patriarchal Poetry" (composed 1927, published 1953), and *Stanzas in Meditation* (composed 1932, published 1956); Mina Loy's *Anglo-Mongrels and the Rose* (composed 1923–25), never published in toto until 1982 in *The Last Lunar Baedeker*; and Gwendolyn Brooks, "A Street in Brownsville" (1945/1967: 17–41), "The Anniad" (1949/1967: 97–112), and "In the Mecca" (1968). The delayed publication dates for H.D., Loy, and Stein may reflect writers' and readers' anxiety about the coupling of women and the long poem. Edna St. Vincent Millay's *Fatal Interview* (1931), a sequence of fifty-two sonnets organized seasonally, can also be read as a long poem and may have influenced such contemporary sonnetlike sequences as Adrienne Rich's "Twenty-One Love Poems" (1978) and Marilyn Hacker's *Love, Death, and the Changing of the Seasons* (1986).

[11] For discussions of the post-1960 women's long poem, see Friedman 1994; Keller 1992, 1994, n. d. For a developing oeuvre of particular importance to the contemporary long poem, see Susan Howe's *Pythagorian Silence* (1982), "The Liberties" in *Defenestration of Prague* (1983:64–127), *Singularities* (1990), and *The Nonconformist's Memorial* (1993).

dis-ease is the self-conscious intensity of their reflexive textuality. That is, these poems often signal their status as texts, specifically their status as big-long poems whose gender inflections make them somehow different from the dominant examples of the genre. Susan Howe's description of Emily Dickinson's tough-minded intertextuality serves aptly for the women poets writing long poems: "Forcing, abbreviating, pushing, padding, subtracting, riddling, interrogating, re-writing, she pulled text from text" (1985:29). Certainly male poets have also pushed and pulled the texts of their male precursors, as Harold Bloom (1973) and others have argued. But in the psychopolitical "family" history of literary tradition, sons—not daughters—replace fathers. Aware of their absence within the tradition, women poets of the long poem often defensively and defiantly assert their presence. They engage in a feminization of the form—refusing the victim status of woman's objectification in men's texts and making themselves agents in the form's evolution, subjects in its creation.

To feminize the genre, women poets have practiced at least four strategies, each of which deconstructs the opposition of inside/outside that Derrida identifies with the phallogocentrism of "the law of genre."[12] All four, in other words, dismantle the boundaries so as to position themselves *as women* writing inside a tradition in which women have been outsiders. Judy Grahn characterizes this move as "looking at the outside from the inside and at the inside from the outside" (1985:67), while Barbara Christian relates it more specifically to the double consciousness of Afro-American women writers, who "are so often . . . perceived as being on the outside of so many realms, even as we are solidly on the inside" (1987). Not specific to the long poem, these "inside-outside" strategies take form in women's writing in a variety of genres. But their effect in the women's long poem is a distinct demasculinization of the genre that signals an oppositional writing and reading process. Not exclusively used by women, these strategies nonetheless manifest in specifically gendered form as acts of self-authorization.

The first strategy I will discuss is the creation of the discourse of the satiric Other, the outsider who ironically deflates the insider. The second is reclamation of the public domain from which women have been largely excluded through a discourse of history—a (her)story in which the inside is the outside and the outside is the inside. The third is the construction of the discourse of re-vision, in Adrienne Rich's sense of the term, in which the outsider immerses herself in the discourse of the in-

---

[12] See Derrida 1980; see also 1976:27–73. Feminists have also transformed the opposition "inside/outside." See, for example, Judy Grahn in *The Highest Apple*, where she identifies women as both "outsiders" and "insiders" (1985:62–72, 82).

side in order to transform it. And the fourth is the invention of a discourse of linguistic experimentalism, a gynopoetic of the outside that establishes a new inside. I will illustrate these four strategies with brief discussions of four exemplary texts: Mina Loy's *Anglo-Mongrels and the Rose*, written in the 1920s; Alicia Ostriker's *The Mother/Child Papers*, which came out in 1980; Judy Grahn's *Queen of Wands*, published in 1982 as the first volume of her projected tetrology, *The Chronicle of Queens*; and Betsy Warland's *serpent (w)rite (a reader's gloss)*, which appeared in 1987.

The discourse of the satiric Other evokes Virginia Woolf's proverbial "Society of Outsiders" who refuse to join the mad crowd dancing round the mulberry bush of money and war in *Three Guineas* (1938). Like the lecturer in *A Room of One's Own* (1929) who is ultimately grateful that she has been shut out of Oxbridge, the satiric Other revels in her status as outsider, using her wit as a sword that pierces the balloon of the poem's self-important form as a big-long-poem. This means, of course, a comedic mockery of what she cannot possess, a carnivalesque disruption of the authority that the form of the poem itself evokes.

Building on the satiric voice developed in a sequence of poems collected in *The Last Lunar Baedeker* as "Satires: 1914–1923," Mina Loy's three-part, mock-heroic epic *Anglo-Mongrels and the Rose* demonstrates this ironic stance of the outsider in its autobiographical narrative of the poet's development. Acquiring what Jonathan Williams calls "legendary status" among modern writers, *Anglo-Mongrels* appeared only partially, in fragments, and out of chronological order in the avant-garde press from 1923 to 1925. Jerome Rothenberg managed to assemble most of it for his 1974 poetry anthology, enough "to place it beside '& probably not chronologically behind, Pound's early *Cantos* & Eliot's *Waste Land*,' " and called it "one of the lost master-poems of the 20th century" (quoted in Conover 1982:xxvi). In *The Last Lunar Baedeker*, the most complete edition of Loy's poetry to date, the seventy-page text appears in probably complete form, along with Roger Conover's assertion that it is "a missing link in the yet unwritten history of the Long Poem" (Conover 1982:xxvi). This piecemeal publishing history itself represents women's simultaneous absence and presence within the generic tradition and introduces the epic's theme of women's diaspora within the male domain. Loy further acted out this exile in her wanderings. Born in Britain, she moved to New York, became an American citizen, and spent much of her life traveling.[13]

---

[13] Loy's stance as Outsider was so deeply felt that *Anglo-Mongrels* proved to be more of an end point than a beginning of her poetic development. She published occasional poems after Robert McAlmon printed some fifty-eight pages of her mock-epic in 1925, but her creative efforts went increasingly into the visual arts. In the 1940s and 1950s, she lived mostly in New York's Bowery, at home with the winos and "bums" who provided the

Mocking the *Kunstlerroman* tradition of which it is a part, *Anglo-Mongrels and the Rose* narrates the *Bildung* of Ova, the daughter of the Jewish tailor Exodus and the English Gentile Ada. As Melita Schaum argues (1986), the "automythography" is a raw, elliptically brutal satire that adapts Loy's prior alliance with futurism to the violent rupture of bourgeois conventionalism and poetic norms. The mock-epic begins by reviewing the poet's lineage, her patrilineal and matrilineal legacy in the first two parts called "Exodus" and "English Rose." Her father's "exodus" from bondage in Hungary brings him to the promised land of England. But there his freedom is another kind of slavery, a perpetual exile of never belonging, a permanent psychic diaspora. With the satiric playfulness that characterizes the text, Loy dubs him the "wondering Jew" (Loy 1982:117). In an attempt to belong, the "alien" Exodus marries Ada, an English "Rose" whose sexuality has been repressed into "the ap parent impecca bility / of the English"—chaste and without sin (129). She is the "Rose of arrested impulses / self-pruned" and "simpering in her / ideological pink" (121, 124). On the one hand, her "pink paralysis" embodies the privitization of repressed Victorian domesticity, "making a sweetened smell / among a shrivelled collectivity," and on the other hand this "Conservative Rose" signifies "a never-setting-sun / . . . / of British Empire-made pot-pourri / of dry dead men," the "subliminal infection" of compression, and the "dis'armony" of "English Hanthem" (122–30). "And for further information," the poet deadpans, "See *Punch*" (130), an allusion to the prevailing satiric discourse that rules the poem.

Ova's birth to Exodus and Ada in part 3, titled "Mongrel Rose," evokes the scene of Sleeping Beauty's christening, but the godmother's gift of a "Jewish brain" could be the Black Fairy's curse or a good fairy's compensatory promise—we don't know which (132). Ova, "this composite / Anglo-Israelite," is a "Mongrel" Rose, no Sleeping Beauty and never at home with her father's God or her mother's "Gentle Jesus" (132, 148). "Lapped by insensitive maternity," the infant Ova is forced to make do with "Benger's food / for infants" (132). The next section of the poem, "Enter Esau Penfold," contrasts the pampered infancy of Ova's well-off, first husband-to-be, Esau Penfold, with Ova's more lower middle-class surroundings. Esau's mother fêtes his arrival with a book party dedicated to the " 'Infant Aesthete' " (133), while Ova is left alone, "propped upon a chair" (135). Class difference conflates with gender as Esau is petted,

---

inspiration for a series of collages. To a large extent, she exiled herself from the world of the literati, indeed from literary discourse itself. For critical discussion of her work, see Burke 1980, 1985, 1990; Kouidis 1980; Conover 1982; DuPlessis 1992; and Schaum, whose " 'Moon-flowers out of Muck' " (1986) is to date the only essay devoted exclusively to *Anglo-Mongrels and the Rose*.

praised, and posed for a portrait "labelled 'Esau holding an orb' " (133), while Ova is pushed aside and "told to 'Hush' " (134). The poet calls her "the mongrel-girl / of Noman's Land" (143).

Neither Exodus nor Ada can nourish their girl-egg, whose *Bildung* depends upon her developing ability to wander and wonder on her own. Her father deceives her with a worthless gift of money, then expels her from the house. Between her mother and her Nurse, Ova is "jostled / between revolving / armoured towers / . . . / of these / two women's netherbodies" (139). Ova's awakening is all her own. In the poem's fourth section, "Ova Begins to Take Notice," the toddler becomes aware of the wonder of light, color, sound, and words—a scene that mockingly echoes the opening pages of James Joyce's *Portrait of the Artist as a Young Man*. The word she hears is not Stephen's nourishing "moocow," but "irrhea"—diarrhea, the refuse and excrement that disgusts, that must be expelled, that nonetheless contains the mystery of incarnation in the mock-heroics of the epic:

> Sometimes a new word comes to her
> she looks before her
> and watches
> for its materialization
>
>   "iarrhea"
> . . . .
> And in her ear
> a half inaudible   an
> iridescent hush
> forms "iarrhea"
> "It is
> quite green" She hears
>
> The cerebral
> mush   convolving in her skull
> an obsessional
> colour-fetish
>
> veers
> to the souvenir
> of the delirious ball
> . . . .
>
> And instantly
> this fragmentary

> simultaneity
> of ideas
>
> embodies
> the word
>
> (139–41)

Ova's awakening as a child through the agency of refuse and its representation prefigures her teenage revelation in a section called "Jews and
Ragamuffins of Kilburn." Walking through the ghetto of outcasts with her
disapproving nurse, Ova feels at home for the first time. This is, in fact, her
legacy from her father, the one that means the most to her development as
an artist. Structured like an egg, the mock-epic ends with a section on her
father called "The Social Status of Exodus," in which the despised Jew collapses into the category of the despised woman. Like her father, the "mongrel-girl of Noman's Land" is exiled. But as an artist, she exiles herself
from bourgeois "impecca bility"; and as a woman, her body is the sign of
her difference. Echoing, reversing, and satirizing Bloom, Joyce's feminized
Jew in *Ulysses*, Ova becomes the wandering Jew whose wondering cuts
her off from the social practices of proscribed womanhood.[14]

Perhaps because satire is a particularly aggressive and confrontational
discourse, or perhaps because the satiric lance turns ultimately against
the poet herself, not many women writing long poems have engaged in
this strategy. Anne Sexton, whose bitingly ironic slang is a trademark of
her poetic voice, is an exception. Her volume *Transformations* (1971) re-
tells the narratives of *Grimm's Fairy Tales* in the ironic voice of the excluded witch, who is faithful to the given plots, but utterly irreverent in
her tone. Alicia Ostriker's 1971 volume *Once More in Darkness* plays ironically off the epic hero's classic *agon* by juxtaposing irreverent and contemporary colloquialisms alongside lyric enchantments of pregnancy and
birth. More recently, Judy Grahn's "Psychoanalysis of Edward the Dyke"
(1978:26–30) quickly gained the status of an underground classic in its
mock-heroic tale of a lesbian and her analyst, a grand adventure in the
spiritual journey of analysis. *The Queen of Swords*, the second volume of
Grahn's *The Chronicle of Queens*, returns to this satiric mode in configuring the descent of Innana to the underworld as a drama in a lesbian bar.

The second strategy, already implicit in Loy's mock epic of the "wondering Jew," is the (re)constitution of a discourse of history. Conventionally understood, "history" is the diachronic narration of events and

---

[14] Loy met Joyce in 1921 and wrote a double-edged poem titled "Joyce's Ulysses," one
of many poems she wrote about writers that demonstrated her intertextual rewriting of
percursors and contemporaries (Conover 1982:xv–lxxi).

forces at work in the public sphere, precisely the domain from which women have been overwhelmingly excluded, precisely the arena upon which the epic has been predominantly centered.[15] To reclaim "history," women poets have redefined it by breaking down the barriers between the "public" and the "private," the "political" and the "personal." They have historicized the personal and personalized the historical. Like Woolf in *Three Guineas*, some women have shown that "the home"—the institutions of family and sexuality—is no haven in a heartless world, but is rather a contested terrain whose patterns replicate the larger structures of society. What is outside is inside; what is inside is outside—the personal is political in a dynamic whereby no realm is privileged as most important, whereby no site is immune from history. Invisible in or objectified by conventional histories, women poets have devised a discourse of (her)story in which they (re)make "history"—both in the acting and in the telling. Poems that exhibit this strategy in various ways include Adrienne Rich's *Sources* (1983), Shirley Kaufman's *Claims: A Poem* (1984), Irena Klepfisz's *Keeper of Accounts* (1982), Sharon Doubiago's *Hard Country* (1982), Gwendolyn Brooks's *In the Mecca* (1968), Rosellen Brown's *Cora Fry* (1977), Ruth Whitman's *Tamsen Donner: A Woman's Journey* (1977), Rita Dove's *Thomas and Beulah* (1986), Kathleen Spivak's *Jane Poems* (1974), and Ostriker's *Mother/ Child Papers*.[16]

Ostriker's *Mother/Child Papers* is a sequence of discrete lyrics that taken together narrate an epic of motherhood during the 1970s—from the pregnancy and birth of Gabriel in the early seventies, through the period of infancy and dependency with the son and two older daughters, and on to the years of letting go at the end of the decade. Inseparable from this "personal" narration, however, is the "public" story of the Vietnam War, the invasion of Cambodia, the murders at Kent State, the students' protests, the evacuation of Phnom Penh, the rise of feminism. The volume's title—*The Mother/Child Papers*—signals its historical moment by echoing *The Pentagon Papers*. This resonance conflates the domain of the state and the scene of the mother to suggest that the text's "history" is a "leak"

---

[15] See Friedman 1994, for extended discussion of the relation between narrative in women's long poems and the need to reclaim a forbidden historical discourse.

[16] Given this significance of "history" in the cultural definition and evolution of Judaism, it is more than coincidental that many of the poets using this strategy are Jewish. Some—like Rich, Kaufman, and Klepfisz—specifically use this reconstituted historical discourse to explore the meaning of their Jewish legacy. Levertov's long sequence about the death of her sister Olga, *To Stay Alive* (1971) and Plath's "Three Women: A Poem for Three Voices" (1981:176–86) are somewhat more "personal," but their implicit redefinition of women's "personal" struggle as heroic also participates in this "historical" strategy. See also the statements on the cover of Doubiago's *Hard Country* (1982) by Carolyn Forché and by Meridel Le Sueur, who writes: "Doubiago fearlessly enters the labyrinth of our history, our search and danger as woman as human as deep American wanderer. . . . It is a long saga, a woman's history and the history of us all."

that violates the law of the public sphere. Formal aspects of the volume extend the politics of its title. Sharp juxtapositions of "public" and "private" histories, interpenetration of spheres, and alternation of lyric and prosaic discourses inscribe the poet's deconstruction of the binary upon which history writing has been conventionally founded.

The volume opens with a documentary account in prose charting the birth of the poet's son in the countdown of days leading up to and following the National Guard's murder of four students at Kent State. The form combines the factual document with the private journal, concluding the account of the alienating birth with the question: "What does this have to do with Cambodia?" (Ostriker 1980:6). By implication, the poet establishes an analogue of violence between the state in Southeast Asia, the Guard at Kent State, and the doctor who hates women. Having reflected then deconstructed the binary of "public" and "private" in documentary form, the poet repeats the process in lyric form. Liminal, inarticulate speech weaves a cocoon around a more formal elegy that conflates a biblical epic of birth and death:

```
            was dreaming   be
      water was          multiply
      dreaming water   inherit
                  in      earth
```

The Guards kneeled, they raised their weapons, they fired
into the crowd to protect the peace. There was a sharp orange-red
explosion, diminished by the great warm daylight, a match scratching, a
whine, a tender thud, then the sweet tunnel, then nothing.
Then the tunnel again, the immense difficulty, pressure, then the head
finally is liberated, then they pull the body out.

```
      was dreaming
      water was
                  falling and
                  rising all
                        along could
                        not see then
                              a barrier a
                              color red then
                                          cold
   and
   very afraid
```

(9–11)

Against the power of the state that turns sons into cannon fodder, that murders and maims, Ostriker sets up the mother—"the power of a woman / close to a child, riding our tides / into the sand dunes of the public spaces" (44). A mother, a woman who births, has "an opportunity for supreme pleasure and heroism"—in "the final stage of labor," she needs "no drugs because she becomes a goddess" (4–5). Our "first images / of deity come" from "this power" of a mother (44). But in this redefinition of the epic hero-as-mother, Ostriker writes against the conventional valorization of the all-(for)giving Mother of the oedipal son's fantasy by recording in both documentary and lyric form the intensities of a mother's erotic love and hate for her child. On the one hand, she feels:

> but a baby
>   any baby
>   your baby is
>   the
> most perfect human thing you can ever touch
> translucent
> and I want you to think about   touching
> and the pleasure of   touching
> and being touched by this most perfect thing
>   this pear tree blossom
>   this mouth these leafy hands these genitals
>   like petals
>   a warm scalp resting against your cheek
>   fruit's warmth
>   beginning—
>
>   (43)

But on the other hand, she can feel trapped:

> Hour after beastly hour.
>   I swear I try.
> You claw my skin, my nipple.
>   Am a witch. Am dry.
> Cannot endure an existence
>   chained to your cry.
> Incubus.   Leech.   Scream.
>   You confine me. Die.
>
>   (22)

Reversing the narrative pattern of the traditional epic hero, Ostriker's mother must work through her ambivalence not to unite with the beloved but to accept a separation. She must release her children into the world, which might well make them victims. Her son might go to war. Her daughters face a domain in which their gifts might be invisible. This letting go, however, sets her free to (pro)create once again. Egg-shaped like Loy's *Anglo-Mongrel*, Ostriker's volume ends with another history of birth, of a woman—a poet?—who

> crouches over a stool
> > in a green room
>
> she is in labor, she is giving birth
> comfortable, she rides with this work
> for hours, for days
> > > for the duration of this
> > > > dream
> > > > > (62)

Ostriker's revisionist "history" of the 1970s that asserts the centrality of women's (pro)creation suggests the next feminizing strategy: creation of a discourse of re-vision. Rich's hyphenated spelling of the word "re-vision" in her classic 1971 essay "When We Dead Awaken: Writing as Re-Vision" articulates a stance toward the dominant discourses of culture and the forgotten or misread voices of women that characterizes many women writing long poems before and after the term gained currency. By "re-vision," Rich means "the act of looking back, of seeing with fresh eyes, of entering an old text from a new critical direction." This understanding of "the assumptions in which we are drenched" is "for us more than a chapter in cultural history: it is an act of survival" (1979:35). H.D. pioneered this strategy for the feminization of culture in twentieth-century poetry—first in her short gynomythic poems in the twenties, then in her great revisionist epics in the forties and fifties, *Trilogy* (1944–46/1973) and *Helen in Egypt* (1961/1974), and finally in their continuation in a series of long poems "Winter Love" (1972:85–117), "Sagesse" (1972:57–84), *Vale Ave* (1982b), and "Hermetic Definition" (1972:1–56).[17] For H.D., there is a story within a story, the buried voices and visions of women that can be sought and brought to the surface in the very form that repressed it. For example, Homer's *Iliad* can be retold from Helen's perspective in a way that utterly reverses the tradition it evokes. H.D. uses her position as outsider to tunnel deep inside to find what has been repressed in the phallogocentric discourses of patriarchal culture.

---

[17] For a discussion of H.D. as epic poet, see Friedman 1986.

Judy Grahn self-consciously situates her projected quartet *The Chronicle of Queens* in the revisionist tradition H.D. charted—as a re-vision both of the male epic tradition and of H.D.'s *Helen in Egypt*, which seems to presume a classical education and does not incorporate working-class women or Native American narratives in its rescription of male tradition.[18] In "I first met the Queen of Wands," the prose prologue for the three-part sequence of poems in *The Queen of Wands*, Grahn lays out the plan for the whole. A forgotten Babylonian lament for the theft of the queen goddess serves as her buried Ur-text, whose trace the poet uncovers in the shards of the past and in the contemporary world around her: "this theme of a queen who has been stolen, of cities and temples ravaged by soldiers, of people cudgeled in their streets, of lamentation for a female power gone" (1982:xii).

Resonating with and revising modern long poems like T. S. Eliot's *Waste Land*, Grahn's *Queen of Wands* connects the mythic past to the present moment of history by exploring the roots of sterility and the possibility of regeneration. As for Eliot, "tradition"—literary and mythic—is essential in the narrative of the poet's quest for healing. "Nothing begins new," she later explains, "everything has / a mother, a father and a story" (31). But where Eliot uses the myth of the wounded fisher king as a paradigm for modern sterility, Grahn locates the model in the ancient theft of the queen goddess. Like *The Waste Land*, *The Queen of Wands* has footnotes that acknowledge and explain the poet's sources. But where Eliot's notes seemed to signal his membership in an elite community of the highly educated, Grahn's notes (and explanations incorporated into the poetry) are designed to demystify Near Eastern and classical mythology and to make it more accessible to those without an extensive education.[19]

[18] See Grahn 1985 (especially 49–57, 102–10, 135). Grahn further discussed her relationship to H.D.'s poetry in her talk at the Dual Centennial Colloquium on Emily Dickinson and H.D. at San Jose State University, October 1986. Because H.D.'s memoir of her Moravian heritage, *The Gift* (1982a), had not yet been published, Grahn could not also have been aware of how important to H.D. was the mysticism of East Coast Indians who had contact with her ancestors in Bethlehem, Pennsylvania, during the eighteenth century. The Moravians were the first Europeans to construct dictionaries of Indian languages; their relations with the Indians were markedly different from those of many other colonists. Moravianism is not named in but extensively pervades *Helen in Egypt*, which is set in the ancient world. For the importance of race to the formation of H.D.'s modernism, see Friedman 1987. For Grahn's other articulations of "re-vision," see her "She Who" and "A Woman Is Talking to Death" (1978:75–132) and *The Queen of Swords* (1987).

[19] Unlike Grahn, H.D. does not use notes, but she actually employs the technique of incorporated explanation quite extensively. Reference books and a classical education are not necessary to understand the allusions in *Trilogy* and *Helen in Egypt*, where the poet often explains or reflects upon the sources that she uses, a citational strategy that differs markedly from those of Eliot and Pound, whose long poems require a wide-ranging knowledge and recall of literary tradition (Eastern as well as Western) for citations to make much sense.

Grahn's revisionist project also involves breaking down the implicit hierarchy that places Western tradition—especially Greek and Roman culture—at the pinnacle. Extending the marked syncretism of H.D.'s *Trilogy* and *Helen in Egypt* even further, Grahn's "Notes" weave connections among African, Asian, South American, North American, and European traditions back into the lyrics. With its syncretist blend of "high" and "low," epic and folk traditions, *The Queen of Wands* also refuses the generic hierarchy that has in effect excluded the writings of many women, working-class people, and non-Western peoples around the world from the most prestigious canons of literary tradition. *The Queen of Wands* self-consciously and defiantly mixes genres, purifying the epic of its masculinist taint with deliberate and joyful linguistic miscegenations.

Entitled "Gods and Heroes," Part I of the three-part *Queen of Wands* initiates the poet's search for the stolen goddess with a revisionist invocation to the muse, here figured as "webster," the weaver of words:

> Here in the sunrise,
> oh webster, is where,
> intense,
> I hear the singing
> in, and of, the loom.
> (1982:2)

In the prologue, the poet has already explained that her muse is the "spirit" she names the "Spider Webster," which alludes to the "weaving spider," the "female weaver," and the "female possession of the word." "For language," she writes, "is a form of weaving too, a clothing our ideas wear, a glowing flesh they are made of, a heart that beats in them" (xiii). Words and weaving, spirit and flesh are not separate, gender-marked spheres as they are within the dominant Western traditions, but they are rather interpenetrating forms of each other. Later sections of the poem and notes identify this Spider Webster, whose position was usurped by Daniel Webster and Merriam-Webster, with the Grandmother Spider or Thought Woman of the Southwest American Indians. This prototypical weaver or webster who makes stories out of the threads of her own body inspires the poet to reweave the scattered strands of stolen queens into a textual tapestry that restores the queen and the female power she represents to the lands laid waste by the sterile "Foe" (xii–xiii).

In Grahn's revisionist epic, this weaving of "Gods and Heroes" must begin with a reconfiguration of the poet's family constellation. "The land that I grew up on is a rock" is a personal lyric that recovers the mother whom she and her father "locked" out "from our patch of / significant sky . . . / as though she were a sheer wall of will / to be mined / to mill / and to grind and to be there / with or without our care" (4). Finding the stolen queen of mythic tradition means first locating her "theft" within the conventional family and regaining the "mother's brilliance-giving vision, / as the earth, / a rock, a star" (6). Recovery of this personal history makes the poet hunger for mythic history in "History if I could put you," a lyric that paves the way for the discovery of the Babylonian "Tablet of Lamentation" from 2500 B.C.E. (8–10). Its meaning, the poet learns from the Pima woman's parable in the next lyric ("The meanings in the pattern"), has "always been here," "right here," but just not read. The theft of the queen does not mean that she has vanished, but rather that we have been blinded by the traditions that dismiss her: "she always has been, / exactly in place, / and it is we, / we who are mystified, / we who are veiled and without faces" (11–12). The poet will unveil our eyes by retelling one of the many stories of the stolen goddess: the story of the Homeric Helen of Troy, the woman who has remained "veiled" from us by past phallocentric tellings of her story. Unveiled by the poet's lyric meditations, Helen is El-Anna, the Egg of Being, "a poet, / a singer and a weaver," the stolen queen who was deceived, "the Mother of my people" (27).

Part II, titled "Magicians," connects the Greek Helen with other stolen queens, magicians like the "good weef" or "word-wyfe," the Scandinavian Frigga (whose erotic élan is bisexual), and most importantly the defiled and exploited sex goddesses of Hollywood, like Marilyn Monroe, to whom *The Queen of Wands* is dedicated. Used and abused, abandoned when their beauty is gone, the movie stars are the Helens, the stolen queens, of contemporary mass culture. It was her mysterious meeting with an old "crone," one of these desecrated stars, that confirmed the poet's sense of creative destiny, narrated in the lyric "In the tower of the crone," itself a re-vision of the fairy tale "Sleeping Beauty." Like H.D., Grahn revised the story of Helen by having her narrate the tale. But Grahn carried H.D.'s palimpsestic treatment of myth and history one step further by seeing Helen's epic saga repeated in the commodifications of mass culture and in the "little" traditions of fairy tale.

Part III, "Soldiers, Workers, and Gods," narrates in a succession of lyric moments the multiple forms of the stolen queen and announces her return in a rhythmic riddle that borrows its form from folk tradition:

> The egg is always being made
> and making,
> always getting laid
> and laying;
> thread is being spun

> and spinning,
> truth is being found
> and finding,
> being all unsnarled
> and snarling,
> and the Grand Grand
> Mother is returning
>
> (78)

This lullaby-litany that repeats itself for several more stanzas prefigures the poet's recovery of her power in the (her)stories of common women in the final, nine-part lyric sequence entitled "Helen you always were / the factory." "Helen," the Spider says indirectly to the poet, "you always were / the factory / Helen you always were producer" (80). Now, the poet can see and hear the lost queen in the voices of Hannah, the garment worker caught in the flames of the Triangle Fire; Nelda, the black slave whose descendants are "dreaming" a "dance of fire" (85); Nancy, the mother of soldier sons who die in war; and Annie Lee, a secretary whose lipstick tube is her wand, who hears "the singing / of the loom" and sees "the strings of light / like fingers and / the fingers like a web, dancing" (91).[20] The poet's meditative search for the lost goddess whose recovery will bring healing has woven together in a single pattern the stories of queens and factory workers, movie stars and old crones, legendary deities and ordinary mothers.

Re-vision of patriarchal myths and texts concentrates specifically on phallic discourse in the fourth strategy that women have used to feminize the genre: the creation of a linguistically experimental gynopoetic. Feeling exiled from language itself, some women writers of the long poem have tunneled deep inside male discourse—inside the words, syntax, punctuation, rhythm, lineation, and spacing of poetic language—to deconstruct and erase its phallogocentrism. With Emily Dickinson standing behind her, Gertrude Stein is the major twentieth-century pioneer of this strategy, particularly in her prose-poems *Tender Buttons* (1914/1962) and "Patriarchal Poetry" (1927/1980) and lengthy cantos, *Stanzas in Meditation* (1956). Her linguistic experiments in *Tender Buttons*, for example, destroy the conventions of representational reference and domesticate the long poem by focusing on the objects in a house, preeminently female space.[21] As Grahn writes about her, "Stein opened up language itself, the

---

[20] For other poets who use the discourse of re-vision in long poems, see especially Bundez 1984; Clifton 1974, 1976, 1979, 1980; DiPrima 1978; Howe 1982, 1983, 1985, 1990a, 1990b, 1993; DuPlessis 1980, 1987, 1991; Lawrence 1980; Morgan 1976; Rich 1978; Sexton 1971.

[21] For discussion of Stein's experimentation in the context of phallogocentrism, see

very bricks of it, the very of of it, the it of it, the the the of of" (1985:64). Contemporary "language-oriented" poets like Susan Howe, Rachel Blau DuPlessis, Daphne Marlatt, Theresa Hak Kyung Cha, Kathleen Fraser, Beverly Dahlen, Frances Jaffer, and Betsy Warland continue Stein's project, sometimes in short lyrics but often in volume-length "long poems."[22] Some black women poets, for whom the dominant poetic discourse is not only phallic but also white, disrupt the conventional linguistic flow of the long poem with the rhythms and syntax of Black English—like Ntozake Shange in *For colored girls*—or with the colloquialisms, informal speech patterns, and violation of visual conventions used to situate poetic discourse in everyday, "common" life—like Toi Derricotte in *Natural Birth* (1983) and Pat Parker in "Goat Child" and "Womanslaughter" (1983:19–30, 141–57).[23]

This strategy of linguistic experimentation finds its most intense form among those poets whose disruptions attempt to write the female body— to construct a gynopoetic discourse variously named *"écriture féminine"* by Hélène Cixous, *"parler femme"* by Luce Irigaray, "gynogrammar" by Betsy Warland, and "mothertongue" by Daphne Marlatt, or, more generally, the female "erotic" by Audre Lorde. As Cixous's "Laugh of the Medusa" suggests (1974/1980), this gynopoetic involves exploring the shape women's (pro)creativity and eroticism might give to a new poetic discourse.[24] Warland's *serpent (w)rite (a reader's gloss)* writes the female body as an epic whose *agon*—scene of action and struggle—is language itself. Warland engages in a process of "inspiralling" meditations on the

---

DeKoven 1983. For a discussion that links Stein's form in *Tender Buttons* to the politics of genre, see Monroe 1987. For discussion of *Stanzas in Meditation*, see Weinstein (1970:82–99).

[22] The term "language-oriented" is Rachel Blau DuPlessis' designation for contemporary women poets who share a linguistic experimentalism with the "L=A=N=G=U=A=G=E" poets, but who differ from that "school" in their "attitude toward referentiality and meaning" (letter to author, 5 January 1988). DuPlessis's *Tabula Rosa* (1987:3–54) contains a series of lyrics joined in a long poem in process, titled "History of Poetry." In addition to the volumes of these poets, see especially two journals devoted to women's linguistically experimental writing with which these women are associated: the West Coast journal *HOW(ever)* and the Canadian journal *(f.)Lip*, both no longer publishing.

[23] Without using the term, Grahn's introduction to Parker's *Movement in Black* identifies "Goat Child" and "Womanslaughter" as long poems, in spite of their relatively short length. She writes, "*Goat Child* was the first deliberately autobiographical poem by a woman that I had ever heard, although there was no reason (try sexism) why a woman's entire life couldn't be the storyline of a poem, a modern epic. . . . *Womanslaughter* . . . is a major work, a major documentary poem and a feminist statement of commitment for women to defend other women from violent attack" (Grahn 1983:14). See also Brooks's *In the Mecca* (1968).

[24] For long poems that inscribe the epic of pregnancy, childbirth, and lactation with experimental disruptions of poetic discourse, see Ostriker's *The Mother/ Child Papers* (1980) and Derricotte's *Natural Birth* (1983). See also Clifton's Kali sequence (1974:46–61) and Mary sequence (1980:32–47); Plath, "Three Voices" (1981:176–86); and Grahn, "She Who" (1978: 75–110).

problem of language for women, particularly as it is inscribed in the myth of creation in Genesis and reenacted in the current scientific/linguistic battles over women's *wombs* and men's *bombs*. Warland's "gloss" on phallogocentric discourse both thematizes the issue of language and experiments with a form that has what she calls the "scent" of a woman's "sentence," the "fluency" of a woman's "fluids," the "inspiralling" of a woman's inner chambers.[25]

Serpent (w)rite has eight unpaginated sections called "turns," each of which is introduced by a repeated graphic: a spiral shape that looks like the whorl of a shell and rests on wavy lines representing both the sea and the serpent. Each turn circles around the same questions but also moves further into the labyrinthine spiral to provide a sense of narrative. In particular, the story of Adam and Eve in Genesis reappears in each turn as prototypical trope and narrative for the "Fall" into destructive binaries such as "womb" and "bomb." Turn one initiates the quest in a moment of lesbian lovemaking that evokes Irigaray's punning conflation of mouth-lips and vaginal-lips in "When Our Lips Speak Together" (Irigaray 1985b:205–18):

> we lose ourselves in each other
> smell
> a e i o u
> e
> i
> o
> u
> last lest list lost lust
> lest
> list
> lost
> lust
> your smell in / *lists* me
> . . . .
> we are 'lov / hers' of lost
>
> this the lost manuscript
>   (Warland 1987:turn one)

Lost in each other, lost in the erotic vowels of the alphabet, the poet realizes that this moment of paradise is a "lost manuscript," erased by

[25] For Warland's other long poems, see *Proper Deafinitions: Collected Theorograms* (1990) and the double-voiced long poem she wrote with Daphne Marlatt, *Double Negative* (Marlatt and Warland 1988).

the fall into sexual differentiation. In a postlapsarian "wor(l)d," the poet must begin her quest "lost" in the words men have written about women: " 'hold your tongue woman.' " "Confronted with how lost we are narrative begins," she thinks. A full page of empty space surrounds the words "Lost in thought." This moment of negation and confusion is the necessary beginning for the poet's inspiralling meditations on the origins and meaning of language for women. Words are like odors. They can be "read" in the absence of their makers: "eyes smell word sprayed on page" and "smell signal scent / ence" (turn one). Her text is a patchwork of quotations from patriarchal and feminist sources that she glosses by reading their "scent / ence"—their smell, judgment. Thinking about Adam's naming and Eve, she despairs of women's "ventriloquism," their verbal and erotic "lip service" to men:

> Adam's words name
>
> Eve's words repeat
> (lip service)
> she took the words right out of His mouth
>
> this is how we acquired language
> (turn one)

But if "ventriloquism" signifies women's status as object in phallogocentric discourse, it can also represent an emancipatory strategy, as Irigaray demonstrates in *Speculum* (1985a) and theorizes in "The Power of Discourse and the Subordination of the Feminine" (1985b:68–85). "Mimicry," Irigaray writes, allows women to "convert a form of subordination into an affirmation. . . . To play with mimesis is thus, for a woman, to try to recover the place of her exploitation by discourse . . . so as to make 'visible,' by an effect of playful repetition, what was supposed to remain invisible" (1985b:76). Irigaray's principle of mimicry underlies the central narrative of *serpent (w)rite*, which is, as the subtitle explains a "reader's gloss" on phallogocentrism. Much as Irigaray overturns Freud's (and Lacan's) reading of femininity by glossing "Femininity," the narrative "ventriloquism" of *serpent (w)rite* repeats the text of Genesis, a mosaic of multiple cultural texts, and the "text" of language itself, in order "to make 'visible' " what phallogocentrism attempts to repress. Eve as "ventriloquist" becomes the poet's "ventriloquest" (Warland 1987:turn four).

The wordplay of Stein and Mary Daly (especially in *Gyn/Ecology* [1978]) are as much guardian spirits in the poet's "ventriloquest" as is Irigaray. Puns and homonyms become major sources of insight as the poet engages in "circling around words . . . trying to find my way" (turn one). "Phallus? Fell us," the poet muses in turn three. In contrast to the phallic Fall, "Par-a-dice" was "snake eyes!"—the knowing and lucky gaze of the sacred serpent. The phrase "every woman" contains within the prototypical "Eve re woman," and with reverse inflection "country" is "(cunt-tree)" (turn one). Jahann Drucker, the poet notes, said that "the entire historical development of language as a system of representation has always depended upon the grounding of man's subjectivity in the position of woman as object," a statement that the poet glosses with the query "object? / object!" (turn three). Sound play also combines with etymological narratives to uncover the political unconscious repressed in words, as in this inspiralling meditation on "Adam obsessed with surgical solutions":

> *eradication* of female darkness
> *e-, out, from ex- + radix, root*
> womb cut out all traces removed
> hysterectomy
> his-tear-ectomy
> his-to-tear-out-of-me
> his-tear-economy
>
>   (turn four)

Recovery of roots also often accompanies an interrogation of proverbial and idiomatic expressions, whose politics are uncovered through repetition and juxtaposition. *Serpent (w)rite* is punctuated throughout by provocations such as "don't be hysterical," "nip it in the bud," "his ace in the hole," "he's got a lot on the *ball*," "it is a man's wor(l)d," "he's a self-made man," "X marks the spot," and "don't get caught with egg on your face."

The poet's "ventriloquest" becomes what she calls a "gynogrammar spiraling" that holds out the possibility of women's speech. "All we can do is write our way home," the poet says in turn four. This involves on the one hand being lost in complete silence—as when a whole page contains only a question mark or the empty parentheses—"( )"—that signify "an open mouth." On the other hand, it involves forging a speech spun out of women's bodies. "Begin it here/ in our bodies where word begins":

> w(o)rd begins with
> (o)pen m(o)uth with
> w(o)man m(o)ther
>   (turn six)

This language is a kind of "ssss-lang" based in the "fluency" of women's "scent / ence." Its mode of representation is more oral and visual than symbolic, thereby invoking Kristeva's notion of the semiotic register of language that is based in the pre-Oedipal *chora* prior to the child's acquisition of language as a system of signification (Kristeva 1980:124–47, 237–70). Lacan's phallus as the "Transcendental Signifier" is rejected as the "man master / baiting himself into the Transcendental Signifier / of no / body" (Warland 1987:turn three). In place of the "phallus" that "fell us" is the sound of fluidity, which is both amniotic and erotic in origin. " 'And as a mist I covered the earth,' " the poet repeats to invoke the " 'Mother of sap,' " the "mist-ress ('And as a mist . . . ')" which begins the story of creation in Genesis (turn three). Like so much of Stein's experimental writing, sound instead of the sign (signifier/signified) constitutes a new kind of meaning. Visualization also constructs meaning—as in the word "scent / ence"; in the use of parentheses and hyphens—as in the title word "(w)rite; in the presence or absence of punctuation or capitalization; in the explorations and juxtapositions of space; in the erotic coupling of question marks, "¿?"

Serpent (w)rite ends with a quotation from Maria Sabina that sums up the poem's main point about women's enslavement in and liberation through language: "with my hands I catch word after word / that holds us captive set us free wordsmells wombwords wordprints we track endlessly" (turn eight). Women's poetry can be a (w)rite—writing as ritual that undoes and redoes the myths and texts of patriarchy. Like the serpent in Genesis, *serpent (w)rite* offers forbidden knowledge from the tree of life. But this knowledge makes possible the survival of the human race, not its death.

The four self-authorizing strategies that I have sketched in discussions of Loy, Ostriker, Grahn, and Warland can provisionally be called ironist, historicist, re-visionist, and experimentalist. All begin with the recognition that the epic tradition that has established the major grid markers through which we read long poems has been thoroughly overdetermined as a masculine discourse of important quest-ions. Women writing within this tradition consequently often initiate their long poems by feminizing the genre in one form or another so that the big quest-ions they want to ask can be set to the "big" format of the "long" poem. Beginning in a negation of the tradition within which they write, women often break down the boundaries between inside and outside by creating a female space inside a genre that has left women outside.

I do not propose these strategies as discourses that are inherently feminine or available only to women. Certainly many male poets of the long poem have engaged dialogically with the genre by developing ironist, historicist, re-visionist, or experimentalist strategies. Rather, I mean to suggest that these strategies perform feminist cultural work in the long poems of writers whose gender determines an ambivalent and oppositional relationship to the genre within and against which they write. Women's position as outsiders to the kind of masculine authority coded into the genre of the long poem (over)determines the production of gender-inflected forms of these strategies, forms that accomplish a specifically female self-authorization not characteristic of (for example), Eliot's irony, Williams's or Hart Crane's history, Wallace Stevens's supreme fictions, or Pound's experimentalism.[26] Indeed, these strategies in poems like *The Waste Land, Patterson, The Bridge,* and *The Cantos* can be read to affirm a modern subjectivity from which women are excluded. In contrast, these same strategies function in women's long poems to insist upon a gendered subjecticity that is unapolegetically female. Loy's satiric parry is inseparable from her reproductive and erotic tropes. Ostriker's reconstellation of history is marked by a gendered conflation of the "public" and "private." Grahn's revisionist mythography and Warland's experimentalism both construct a gynopoetic.

Moreover, I do not want to suggest that these four strategies are exclusive categories with fixed boundaries. Rather, they have between them the "edgeless boundaries" that Derrida posits for things that are both "inside" and "outside." They are emphatically not useful categories for the classification of poems. Defying the rush to taxonomize, a given text is likely to participate in more than one strategy, and each of the strategies depends on the presence of the other inside itself in order to forward its play with the genre as an outsider. Loy's satire of British "ap parent impecca bility" and paean to "iarrhea" experiment with word, sound, and visualization much as Warland does in *serpent (w)rite.* Ostriker's juxtapositions of the "factual" documentary and the near-inarticulate lyric also disrupt conventional poetics and experiment with space and visualization. Grahn's rhythmic lullaby, punning, and etymological spinnings similarly undo and redo masculine poetic discourse. Conversely, Warland's text is a "re-vision" of Genesis, whose patchwork of quotations from the male and female descendants of Adam and Eve recapitulates the biblical patterns the poet deconstructs. With its interwoven strands of scientific and sacred texts, it also re-visions "history" into (her)story.

I have proposed these strategies, then, as a way into the labyrinth of poetic forms and the cultural work they can perform. As women adapt discourses of irony, history, re-vision, and experimentalism, they unmask

---

[26] These same strategies do appear, however, in Langston Hughes's long poem *Montage of a Dream Deferred* (1951), accomplishing a kind of self-authorization from an African American poet that parallels the function of these strategies in long poems by women.

masculinist forms of "bigness" that inhabit the seemingly neutral space of very "long" poems. In closing, I wonder if this disclosure shouldn't also lead us to discover the strategy of writing very big poems inside very little ones—the volcanic compression of very big questions into a very tight space—poems that are very big, but not long—like Emily Dickinson's oeuvre, which took shape within the little tradition of handmade books and gift-poems and ultimately became a massive body of irreducibly cosmic scope.

2

Female Power and the Devaluation
of Renaissance Love Lyrics

DIANA E. HENDERSON

language has a plastic action upon the real
—Monique Wittig

Trying to make it real—compared to what?
—Gene McDaniels

One of the undeniable advances in literary scholarship during the past twenty years has been the rediscovery of Renaissance women writers, those of "Shakespeare's sisters" whom Virginia Woolf neither imagined nor was able to study as a "common reader." Admittedly those outside the academy, and even outside the field of early modern studies, may not have the same rich if romanticized associations with names such as Lady Mary Wroth and Aemilia Lanyer as they do with Elizabeth Barrett Browning, Christina Rossetti, or Emily Dickinson. Nevertheless, scholars are now reading and studying those earlier writers with equal seriousness and intensity, and new editions and anthologies make the work of early modern women readily available. What remains in question, for both specialists and common readers alike, is *how* we should read their poems, especially as that process raises issues of gender. In no domain are these questions thornier, or more intriguing, than in the genre dubbed "love lyric."

Renaissance women certainly employed masculine traditions of love lyric as sources with which to "negotiate" (in Ann Rosalind Jones's terminology [1990]). But the very adaptability of lyric to "female experience" may have been a mixed blessing, abetting a generic devaluation already rooted in male sonneteers' ambivalence toward their poetic product. Over the subsequent generations, courtly sonneteering underwent a process of trivialization that still makes it difficult to take the love sonnet seriously, and even when we do the legacy of skepticism tends to shape our reading—perhaps with good reason, but with gendered effects. Here I wish to supplement recent critiques of Petrarchan self-enclosure with

Thanks to all who enriched this essay through their insights and advice—most especially Julia Alvarez, Nancy Coiner, Jennie Jackson, and the ever-patient Yopie Prins.

more attention to such lyric's mixed possibilities for female poets. I suggest that the love sonnet, seen within its cultural context, was as fruitful and rich a form for women writers as then existed. Even so—or more likely because it is so—early modern women's lyric poetry raises murky questions about the meaning of female subjectivity and voice.

Secular lyric poetry had a vexed place in the hierarchies of form that constituted much classical and Renaissance literary theory. Not only had Aristotle briskly dismissed lyric in his *Poetics*, but the courtly love tradition had made lyric a form often addressed "To the Ladies" (as George Gascoigne [1910] writes in a preface to *The Posies*). This identification of audience, and often of poetic topic, as female in turn led to a cultural devaluation characteristic of things dubbed "feminine." In "The Anatomie of Absurditie," Thomas Nashe, having dismissed "the blazing of Women's slender praises," proceeds to rail against "our babling Ballets and our new found Songs and Sonets, which every rednose Fidler hath at his fingers end, and every ignorant Ale Knight will breath foorth over the potte, as soone as his braine waxeth hote" (in G. Smith 1904:1. 323, 326). In "A Discourse on English Poesy," William Webbe similarly dismisses sonnets by appealing to standards of quality and elitism, decrying "the uncountable rabble of ryming Ballet makers and compylers of sencelesse sonets, who be most busy to stuffe every stall full of grosse devices and unlearned Pamphlets" (in G. Smith 1904:1. 246). At the same time, the major postclassical lyric form of the Renaissance was the love sonnet, and ancient lyrics were venerated by humanist scholars.

The consequent ambivalence toward love lyric is perhaps best epitomized in Sir Philip Sidney's *Apology for Poetry*, where he will not openly defy the detractors who "say the lyric is larded with passionate sonnets, the elegiac weeps the want of his mistress" (1970:58), yet adds that "it be very hard, sith only man, and no beast hath that gift to discern beauty." His compromise is to distinguish "that lyrical kind of songs and sonnets" which praise "the immortal beauty, the immortal goodness of that God who giveth us hands to write and wits to conceive" (80) from the imitative works of poets who "coldly . . . apply fiery speeches, as men that had rather read lovers' writings, and so caught up certain swelling phrases" (81); the apology thus skirts the issue of generic judgment by turning to a stylistic dismissal of oxymoronic, worldly love poems—that is, Petrarchism.

In Elizabethan England, however, the lyrics of Sidney and his contemporaries not only participated in this Petrarchan tradition but took on an added worldly valence: the queen herself was often figured as the idealized beloved, giving lyric poetry an overtly political meaning. A dramatic disjunction between societal assumptions of female inferiority on the one hand and leadership by a female monarch on the other aggravated conflicting feelings about lyric's status. This paradox found apt expression in oxymoronic love poetry, frequently addressed to Elizabeth, and in the simultaneous emergence of an unusually popular strain of discontented anti-Petrarchan satire. Scholars have long characterized the English sonneteers as more "down to earth," critical, and even quirky in their attitude toward the beloved than were their continental compeers; only recently has this poetic attitude been linked with male rebelliousness against female political authority (rather than seen as a reflection of the bluff and hardy English national character).[1] When juxtaposed with the embarrassing depths to which courtiers stooped in attempts to curry favor, some of the satires look less "realistic" (or flatly misogynistic) and more like compensatory gestures. Envision, for example, a proud would-be king like Robert Dudley crouched behind a bush on his Kenilworth estate voicing his "Deepe Desire" for Elizabeth, only to be rebuffed: "O farewell life, delightfull death farewell, / I dye in heaven, yet live in darksome hell" (Gascoigne 1910:130). Petrarchan oxymora serve quite directly to emphasize Dudley's unfortunate position (physically as well as politically on this occasion) due to Elizabeth's inscrutable marriage policy, reminding us that in this poetic landscape, the beloved did indeed have power over her male "servant."

Incorporation of lyric forms and tropes into Elizabethan drama, narrative sequences, and heroic poetry testifies to the public currency and civic significance of such "love" lyrics. Thus, lyric was not necessarily private and unworldly, or even—as Sir Philip Sidney theoretically wished but in practice denied—a transcendental form rising above the power struggles of court and state. Given the monarch's sex, such struggles were obviously gendered. In their courtly lyrics, male poets confronted not just an abstract feminine madonna but rather the myth *and* reality of female power. One means to resolve the discomfort this caused was to mock the genre of love lyric as unreal, shallow, ineffectual, and "merely" a social performance.

Such critiques also resound in the modern reception history of Elizabethan "dainty delights," and in the twentieth-century primacy of Donne's "strong lines" and what Thomas Carew dubbed his "masculine expression" (in Sylvester 1974:390). During the Renaissance, Ben Jonson

---

[1] Among the more notable studies are those by Forster (1969), McCoy (1979), Montrose (1977), Jones and Stallybrass (1984), and Waller (1979). In the past several years, the study of early modern women has burgeoned; throughout, my essay benefits from that work, including the books by Jones (1990) and Lewalski (1993), and the editions of essays by Ferguson, Quilligan, and Vickers (1986), Haselkorn and Travitsky (1990), Miller and Waller (1991), and Hendricks and Parker (1994), which complement and deepen my discussion of particular poets. I use the term "Petrarchism" to distinguish the tropes typical of those poems written in imitation of Petrarch from Petrarch's own practice.

was characteristically forthright in denigrating through association with the "feminine": "Others there are, that have no composition at all; but a kind of tuneing, and riming fall, in what they write. It runs and slides, and onely makes a sound. Womens-*poets* they are called, as you have womens-*taylors*. 'They write a verse, as smooth, as soft, as cream; / In which there is no torrent, nor scarce streame.' You may sound these wits, and find the depth of them, with your middle finger. They are *creame-bowl*, or but puddle deepe" (*Timbre*, in Herford, Simpson and Simpson 1947:585). Throughout the centuries, adjectival descriptions of poetry have continued to dismiss anything "soft," "sweet," or "effeminate" in preference for the "bold," "muscular," and "manly"; links with gender stereotypes could hardly be more overt. Wordsworth looked for a "manly" style and a "subject of some importance," while Coleridge praised Shakespeare's "will" and "force" (in Holmes, Fussell, and Frazer 1957:202–3, 222). More recently, Yvor Winters (who loved Jonson this side idolatry) avoided the overt gendering of good and bad, but his choice of morally "serious" poems to be praised worked to exclude those directed toward women as audience in favor of those that dismiss them: Sidney's sonnets to Stella show "his incurable tendency to softness in diction" and "charming triviality," but his poems renouncing earthly for heavenly love are the "most serious of his sonnets" and less trivial than the rest (Winters 1967:31–34). Those authors with a "Petrarchan polish," including Spenser, write poetry that "lacks weight," "intellectual substance," and "moral grandeur" (29)—all accusations matching those made in the Renaissance about the nature of women. Current debates about subjectivity and Petrarchan poetics have complicated readings of Renaissance love sonnets, though not always in ways that decenter these assumptions about what constitutes poetic seriousness and worth. Reinterpretations attentive to gender tend to foreground the absence of an active female poetic presence rather than considering the possibilities for female power in the address to and representation of the beloved. More sweepingly, the valid desire to include women's stories in fields other than the romance (the "erotic plot," as Nancy Miller [1986b] and Carolyn Heilbrun [1989] call it) has led to feminist devaluation of conventional love poetry. Still other critics, disappointed by the absence of a distinctively woman-centered correlate or antidote to the male gaze, emphasize the limitations of women's poetry embedded in the poetic traditions of heterosexuality.[2]

[2] A fuller discussion of the history and consequences of the theoretical devaluation of love lyric, and its collisions with female sovereignty in Elizabethan England, will be found in my book (1995). On Petrarchism and its legacy, see especially Freccero 1986; Fineman 1986; Vickers 1982; Patricia Parker 1987:1–7; and Jones 1990. Feminist articles that tend to dismiss Petrarchan and courtly discourse as a given include those by Bono 1986,

And yet while some female poets, like Shakespeare's female impersonators onstage, dismissed "sugared" lyric as a false rhetoric, others recognized that it could be a locus of female influence and voice. Most specifically, Elizabeth's monarchy obviously suggested to women as well as men that the lyric could participate in public realms of discourse, and hence that the erotic and the socially ambitious were not mutually exclusive categories. The number of female-authored tributes to Elizabeth (a woman hardly known for direct support of the "feminine") indicates her historic impact for women seeking a poetic voice—even for those, like Anne Bradstreet, of a later generation who remained in the domestic sphere.[3] That which frustrated and angered male poets provided women writers with a potentially empowering model of discourse, too often dismissed along with the stale self-indulgence of much Petrarchan poetry.

One way to reveal the love sonnet's efficacy is through comparison with other poetic forms and their adaptability to a female voice. If one dismisses the erotic plot and its lyric expression, "good" women in imaginative literature were, if not entirely erased, then most often reduced to ideologically proper silence or removed to religious pedestals far from the earthly realms of social power. Furthermore, the alternative poetic attitudes toward women were often more disturbing than Petrarchan excess; they range from Mercutian mockery to abuse and threats of physical violence. For example, in Shakespeare's *Two Gentlemen of Verona*, Proteus's attempted rape of Sylvia in the woods is presented as the subsequent "strategy" when his courtly wooing (including the arrangement of troubadours to sing "Who Is Sylvia?") fails. To label such voices of masculine aggression as merely the reaction caused by Petrarchan idealization is too simple and often is unsupported by narrative or dramatic context; it resembles contemporary antifeminist arguments blaming the women's movement for backlash and violence against women. Given that these impoverished dichotomies constituted the prevailing attitudes toward "the woman's part" in Renaissance ideology and art, then, Petrarchan lyricism hardly seems the proper object for dismissal when looking at art in its historical context.

Nor did female poets of the time so view it. Among the female authors

---

Eaton 1990, Finke 1990, and Silberman 1986; see Montefiore 1987 for a Lacanian critique. Waller attributes the gaps and melancholy in Wroth to the oppressiveness of Petrarchan lyric per se as a reflection of Court and the "subjection to a language which emphasizes the woman's role as empty, passive, helpless" (1986:268). One might balance this valid hypothesis with D. Cameron's observation: "Men do not control meaning at all. Rather women *elect* to use modes of expression men can understand because that is the best way of getting men to listen" (1985:105).

[3] See, for example, the tributes by Mary Sidney Herbert and Bradstreet anthologized by Gilbert and Gubar (1985:32–35, 63–66); they counter Jardine's dismissiveness of Elizabeth having had any indirect impact (1983:195), as does scholarship in progress by Lisa Gim.

who found the love sonnet an amenable vehicle for their poetic ideas were Vittoria Colonna, Gaspara Stampa, Veronica Gambara, Louise Labé, Les Dames des Roches, Mary Stuart, and Lady Mary Wroth; the last several of these wrote coherent sonnet sequences. In the seventeenth century, lyric poetry remained the form of imaginative literature most often created by women. Because much early modern women's writing has only recently been noticed by scholars, necessarily the first step was to extol these authors for existing, and then to view them as historical forerunners. Now we are examining these authors, especially those who risked public shame by publishing or circulating their poetry, as writers: that is, attending to the tropes and emphases that distinguish their poetic "voices," as well as placing them in historical context and validating them through associative links with other (mostly male) poets.[4] It seems time to pause and examine the actual uses of the sonnet form by women writers before precluding its potential power.

In writing explicitly from a female lover's contemporary perspective (rather than pseudonymously or using an historically removed figure such as Cleopatra or Dido), Wroth, Stuart, Colonna, and Gambara altered the gender of the Petrarchan subject, and thus seem to confront if not enact Virginia Woolf's dictum that "the book has somehow to be adapted to the body" (1929/1957:81). Some of the differences in the works of female lyricists may hardly be discernable to one unfamiliar with reams of Renaissance sonnets (the form and conventions being comparatively rigid), and I do not wish to argue that these differences timelessly define a uniquely feminine poetic. Nevertheless, patterns of variation from male-authored poetic norms do appear and suggest affinities with later female writers—arguably in representations of experience, but more significantly in self-display and attitudes toward the beloved.

Women often employed the sonnet in the same way that female writers still use traditionally "male forms": to take on a masculine role and its powers and/or to modify them so that they capture experiences and values perceived as feminine. Although in academic theorizing these two uses are often schematized as if mutually exclusive, in Renaissance poetry they are not. The examples discussed here illustrate their intersection.

The easiest variations to discern may be those of subject matter and

---

[4] On the Italian and French authors, see Jones 1990; Wilson 1987; Rose 1986; and Phillippy 1989. See Prior 1985 on the genres published by women in the seventeenth century. Mary Burke has work in progress that may refute the common assumption that Mary Stuart's poems constitute a unified sonnet sequence to Bothwell; of course, similar questions arise concerning male-authored sequences such as Shakespeare's, but in Mary's case this will also have considerable impact on how we view her biography. Among the groundbreaking studies that skillfully linked women with male poets were Roberts 1983 and Waller 1979.

the representation of "experience." Women used sonnets to praise what they perceived as explicitly female knowledge and strength, enlarging the notion of a love lyric to include *agape* as well as sexual desire. Vittoria Colonna does so in her sonnet on Mary Magdalene; and Veronica Gambara (who wrote of political topics as well as love) opens her collection of poems with a sonnet not to a male Laura or patron, but to Colonna herself, a model of respectable female strength and authorship. Louise Labé, who seems to have ridden in a tournament during the 1540s, chose the sonnet form as her vehicle for a comparison between herself and Ariosto's woman warrior, Bradamante (see Jeanne Prine's introduction, in Wilson 1987:132–48). Nor was the potential to use Petrarchan tropes and the sonnet for voicing female perspectives confined to the continentals.

However, the complexities of correlating a poetic corpus with a bodily corpse, of "voice" with material "experience," are particularly difficult when the poem is premodern. The poems attributed to Anne Cecil in the 1584 volume *Pandora* provide a particularly vivid case-in-point. These six poems not only refer to the specifically female love-grief of a mother for her dead infant but also use the tropes of traditional "masculine" poetry to proclaim it. In the first of four epitaphs, the speaker compares her grief to that of Venus, converting the goddess of erotic love, the ultimate object of desire (the body of the other), into a maternal figure, a more powerful version of her own body and its creativity.

> Had with the moorning the Gods left their willes undone,
> They had not so soone herited such a soule:
> Or if the mouth, tyme did not glotton up all.
> Nor I, nor the world, were depriv'd of my Sonne,
> Whose brest *Venus*, with a face dolefull and milde,
> Doth washe with golden teares, inveying the skies:
> And when the water of the Goddesses eyes,
> Makes almost alive, the Marble, of my Childe:
> One byds her leave styll, her dollor so extreme,
> Telling her it is not, her young sonne *Papheme*,
> To which she makes aunswer with a voice inflamed,
> (Feeling therewith her venime, to be more bitter)
> As I was of Cupid, even so of it mother:
> "And a womans last chylde, is the most beloved.
>
> (in Moody 1989:164–65)

Ellen Moody, who recalled these poems to our contemporary view, observes that Cecil uses mythology elliptically and metaphorically, not just as allusion, noting moreover that the "learned and mythological texture of the seven sonnets [including as well a sonnet attributed to Queen Elizabeth] is typical of upper-class women Renaissance poets" such as Herbert, Wroth, Gambara, and Colonna (157–58).[5] The speaker specifically appeals to Venus as a mother who will know that "a womans last chylde, is the most beloved" (165). Thwarted by "the gods" in that they took away her child, she nevertheless identifies with that goddess, whose own experience of loss universalizes Anne's plight without denying or diminishing its pain, without a logical consolation; instead, emotional empathy puts Anne "in tune" with the cosmos embodied by classical deities, a recognition of the order of things that neither rebels against fate nor rationalizes her suffering.

Moody observes that the reluctant ending of the following sonnet ("In dolefull wayes I spend the wealth of my time") fits the "elegy form Celeste Schenck has argued is characteristic of women poets, because the poet refuses to accept or to valorize the death of this longed-for baby" (163). This poem transfers the imagery of water and stone from the first poem's portrait of Venus onto the maternal speaker: "And well though mine eies run downe like fountaines here, / The stone wil not speak yet, that doth it inclose." But the association does not help her lessen or mitigate her grief:

> And of this world what shall I hope, since I knoe,
> That in his respect, it can yeeld but mosse:
> Or what should I consume any more in woe,
> When Destins, Gods, and worlds, are all in my losse.
>
> (165–66)

Unlike the epitaphs of Ben Jonson and the anniversary poems of John Donne, and despite the analogy with Venus, Anne Cecil's poem ultimately finds neither transcendence nor compensation in a child's death.

These poems, in their sense of deep regret and loss, implicitly recognize the positive value of the speaker's ability to bear and love a child. In this way, too, the poems call attention to gender. However, perhaps the most intriguing dimension of these poems is their uncertain status as female-authored texts; for here the desire to claim a female subjectivity based on experience confronts the challenges of textual scholarship. While we might expect difficulties in tracking down the women who used pen names or became "Anon," in the early modern period we can-

---

[5] Moody (1989:156–57) quotes Lisle Cecil John's *Elizabethan Sonnet Sequence* (1938), in which he notes the "stiff classical allusions" of the poems, but also that they have "a poignancy unusual in any verse of the century." But see also May 1992, as well as the question of authorship discussed below.

not even trust public attribution when aristocratic women are involved: their class privilege made them attractive patrons for struggling writers who might therefore attribute verses to ladies, as well as write for them, in order to gain prestige by association. Such may be the case of these Cecil poems, which several scholars have attributed to the author of most of the *Pandora* volume, John Soowthern. As Stephen May observes (1992), the uneven metrics match Soowthern's style and imply that he might be imitating a female subject position through *prosopopoeia*. Thus some of the poems with the most overt claims of gendered subjectivity cannot with certainty be deemed a woman's writing. It would seem that long before *Paris Is Burning* and the gender studies of Sue-Ellen Case and Judith Butler, the most authentically feminine voices could be a masquerade.

Whether Cecil's poetic "voice" or only the experience represented within the poems derived directly from the body of Anne Cecil, when female poets complained, they similarly tended to address the experiential differences of women, especially societal ones. They called attention to their lack of education and access to language, and deprecated their ability as a result; however, literary genres per se were not perceived as the sources of inhibition. Even the educated and formally sophisticated writers such as Mary Sidney seldom lamented the limits of generic forms or narratives for female self-expression (though her contorted syntax at times might seem to embody an unvoiced strain). Mary Oxlie of Morpet, for example, notes in praise of William Drummond of Hawthornden's poetry:

> My rustick Muse was rudely fostered,
> And flies too low to reach the double mountaine.
> ....
> Then do not sparkes with your bright Suns compare,
> Perfection in a Womans worke is rare;
> From an untroubled mind should Verses flow;
> My discontents makes mine too muddy show;
> And hoarse encumbrances of houshold care
> Where these remaine, the Muses ne'er repaire.
>
> (in Greer et al. 1988:79)

The conventional gendering of the sun as masculine here serves to illuminate her "muddy" mind by contrast, despite her few "sparks"; Mary Wroth similarly uses these associations to diminish herself when her beloved, the source of light, is absent. While poetic critique is here subordinate to social commentary, Oxlie's juxtaposition of this self-portrait with the idealized blazon of an unspecified "her" in Drummond's poetry accentuates the gap between male authors' display of femininity in Petrarchan poetry and the female poet's sense of her own place.

Obviously, the negotiations between voicing one's emotions and retaining enough respectability to be heard were extraordinarily vexed for early modern women, no matter the poetic form.[6] Yet even as women stooped, they were not silenced. More clearly than in Oxlie's verse, irony pervades Anne Bradstreet's self-deprecation in "The Prologue." There she apologizes for her "obscure lines," "mean pen," and "foolish, broken, blemished Muse." Yet (having illustrated her knowledge of the "great tradition" by alluding to Virgil's epic induction in her first lines), she also blithely pronounces, "Let Greeks be Greeks, and women what they are" (in Gilbert and Gubar 1985:61–62); she has in fact cleared a domestic space for a legitimate female voice. Even as she deprecates her own muse as homely—in both senses—Bradstreet differentiates her poetry as a gendered alternative worthy of reward: "Give thyme or parsley wreaths, I ask no bays," she concludes, reminding those less familiar with the kitchen that many herbs can be flavorful (63).

Within the traditional Petrarchan erotic plot, women similarly modified the speaker's stance to emphasize "feminine virtues," such as constancy, and dilemmas experienced predominantly by women. As Katharina Wilson observes (1987:xiii), Colonna and Gambara altered the tradition by praising married love, an appropriate way for them to retain respectability as women in a world that defined female honor as chastity and fidelity. Thus it is not so surprising (though it remains superficially ironic) that it was almost exclusively this second value, utter constancy, which "true-life" adulterous lovers such as Mary Wroth and Mary Stuart stressed. In the use of specific poetic devices such as oxymora, the Renaissance women poets also diverge from the enclosed Petrarchan tradition of an internally warring self. Lady Mary Wroth, unlike her uncle Philip Sidney, does not portray her central struggle as an internal battle between Reason and Desire; instead, she uses oxymora to stress the opposition between her active desire and externally enforced passivity or powerlessness. Oppositions (day/night, light/dark) render the distance between the self and the beloved more often than a self-contained internal split. "Let me bee darke, since bard of my chiefe light," she laments in a poem (P100) that alludes to stage plays and fiction-making; the associations aptly encourage attention to the pun on "bard" (barred), for it is the beloved's distanced illumination throughout the sequence that allows her to voice a desire for more than her own darkness and silence.[7]

---

[6] See Jones 1990 and Jardine 1983, among many who have contributed to the substantial scholarship on the pressures to conform to Renaissance theories of women as properly "chaste, silent, and obedient."

[7] In citing Roberts's edition (1983), I follow her labeling of Wroth's poems by their num-

Like "ancient fictions" that discern patterns in starlight and create constellations, from the shadows she creates "in my thoughts true forme of love"—and on the page, poetry.

Queen Elizabeth's "On Monsieur's Departure" also highlights the external constraints on a female lover, rather than internal ambivalence about her emotions. In a poem Petrarchan in its oxymora and split self though not formally a sonnet, she points to an acute public/private stress aggravated particularly by her role as a female ruler. No matter how exceptional Elizabeth made herself, she and others couldn't and didn't ever entirely forget her gender as actuality, even as she remained active in the political sphere. She modifies the Petrarchan figure of the oxymoron to express her constrained position, having to hide her "femininity," her passive desire: "I grieve and dare not show my discontent. . . . For I am soft and made of melting snow." The poem explicitly recognizes the power of an external world and another person, even at that moment when her own power splits her in two: "I am and not, I freeze and yet am burned, / Since from myself another self I turned" (in Gilbert and Gubar 1985:29). The subtle mixture of active and passive voices, of multiple internal and narrative conflicts, contrasts with the completely internalized, straightforward frustration of more literal versions of Petrarch (such as Sir Thomas Wyatt's "I fear and hope, I burn and freeze like ice" [in Rollins and Baker 1954:198]).[8] Whereas Wyatt asserts and complains, Elizabeth simultaneously asserts and abnegates.

Positing a female poetics, linked with the poet's subjectivity and poetry's function, is a far more complex task than identifying the representation of female experiences. In Petrarch, John Freccero argues, the laurel is an emblem of a mirror relationship based on "the poetic lady created by the poet, who in turn creates him as poet laureate," and of the circularity that "forecloses all referentiality" with "self-contained dynamism." Corresponding to the sin of idolatry, this poetic strategy makes the reified sign an object of worship; whereas signs are allegorical, pointing to an absence that implies significance yet to come, idols desperately attempt to render presence and evade temporality by realizing significance in the here and now. Freccero maintains that "in order to create an autonomous universe of autoreflexive signs without reference to an anterior logos—the dream of almost every poet since Petrarch—it is necessary that the thematic of such poetry be equally autoreflexive and

---

ber in the publication sequence (P) throughout; Masten 1991, Wall 1993, and others raise valid questions about this ordering, but my argument is not narratively based (either internally or in juxtaposition with *Urania*, both of which may suggest readings that counter or complement mine; see especially Quilligan 1990 and Miller 1996).

[8] Ilona Bell has a work in progress analyzing Elizabeth's poetics in more detail.

self-contained." Moreover, the "idolatrous love for Laura, however self-abasing it may seem, has the effect of creating a thoroughly autonomous portrait of the poet who creates it" (1986:27). For Petrarch, "The exterior quest has become an internal obsession" (28). In contrast, early modern women poets, though wildly idolatrous, do not seem to participate in this dream with such unequivocal intensity. It may be that their conflict is less a struggle of conflicted idolatry, a split attitude directed toward the sign of the beloved, than a struggle of conflicting signs, the sign of the beloved (prompting a voice and desire) set at odds with the signs of convention and society for their sex (prompting silence and passivity). Moreover, just as an elegy does not compensate for Cecil's lost child, the beloved in Mary Wroth's or Mary Stuart's poetry does not become a realized mirror of atemporal consolation. The emphasis is less on self-alienation as the thematics leading to poetic self-creation than on the stressful ambiguity of any self-assertion at all.

Mary Stuart provides a most obvious case of the ironies inherent in such self-representation. Betty Travitsky's anthology rightly emphasizes her as an "exceptional figure" (1989:167), yet in her sonnets to Bothwell (the infamous "casket sonnets," written in French) the queen of Scots abases her "self" in ways typical of women poets. She is obsessive in her claims of constancy and love, "proving" them by proclaiming the absolute primacy of his will:

> I seek but one thing—to make sure of You
> Who are the sole sustainer of my life;
> And if I am presumptuous so to do,
> In spite of all their bitterness and strife,
> It is because your gentle Love's one thought
> Is both to love and serve you loyally,
> To count the worst that fate can do as naught,
> And to make *my* will with *your* will agree.
> Someday you certainly will comprehend
> How steadfast is my purpose, and how real,
> Which is to do you pleasure until death,
> Only to you, being subject: in which faith
> I do indeed most fervently intend
> To live and die. To this I set my seal.
>   (Sonnet X, in Travitsky 1989:197)[9]

Unlike her cousin Elizabeth, Mary appears to dismiss the tension between her public power and private desire; she denies the power entirely,

---

[9] Mary Stuart's poems are complicated by their transmission and historical "framing"

ironically naming her sovereign self "subject" to a man who was her subject and professing to "serve" him by obliterating her independent will (these puns function in the original French of the sonnets, as do others wittily protesting that this is "nulle fiction"). She sets her royal seal to this idolatrous "faith," thus making the poem itself a sign of blasphemy.

It is no surprise that these sonnets became "evidence" at Mary's trial for treason; especially if the verbal wit is suppressed, they can be read as a testament of masochistic folly, conforming to the portrait of royal irresponsibility suggested by anti-Stuart accounts of her several love affairs. Without the ironies of age and sex reversal found in Shakespeare's "willful" abjection as a sonneteer, Mary's sonnets can all too simply be made consonant with the female social position antipathetic to sovereignty. She ends Sonnet VII

> You look upon my words as empty air,
> And think my heart is weak as wax within me;
> You count me a vain woman without sense:
> Yet all you do makes my love more intense.
>
> (196)

Rather than counter his stereotypically misogynist attacks, she concludes that they increase her desire. The French makes this even clearer: after six lines of parallel constructions beginning with "vous" and a verb, emphasizing the beloved's active accusation, the poem simply adds "et tout cela augment mon ardeur." One might theorize that this self-debasing portrait is primarily an elliptical mode of self-assertion, outrageous in its societal parody, but the reiterated abjection and flat diction of the final line, presented as if a counterturn only in English, reads otherwise. The poems certainly functioned otherwise in Mary's life.

Another emphasis in Mary's sonnets, incongruous given her stature as a queen yet consonant with patterns of female representation, is her self-presentation as the "other woman." In so doing, she again diminishes her own power and position, only to argue that this marginality proves her love and constancy:

(that is, they were used as evidence of her treasonous intentions at the trial leading to her execution); moreover, they were written in French. The verse translations here are those in Travitsky 1989, who also includes the originals and further details on the problems surrounding them; more recent literal translations have also elaborated on the biographical context, which remains murky. The crucial referents and tensions, although not all puns and nuances, are the same in both languages.

Not being (to my sore grief), like her, your wife,
But yet in duty I will outdo her still.
Faithful she is, and profits much thereby—
For fine it is to queen it in your house;
Whereas what scandal doth my love arouse;
Albeit she'll never serve you better than I!
. . . .
But against all men's wish I brought you love;
Yet nonetheless you doubt if I be true
And make no question of *her* faith to you.

(Sonnet III, 194)

This translation extends Mary's wit, making the wife the one who "queens" it and calling attention to the word's whorish homonym in English (quean) and the displacement of value from her own royal house to his domestic one; but even in the original French, this is self-conscious self-destruction. Taken out of historical context, one might argue that by making herself the namer and naming her self as the outsider, Mary is a radical challenger of societal notions of propriety. Alternatively, one might stress that she was writing within an adulterous courtly tradition. But either way, as a female her self-placement neither subverts the gendered norms of society nor leads to articulation of alternative powers by the speaker. Moreover, to whatever extent she acted out this fiction, Mary Stuart made destructively literal what for men was merely literary—her life was indeed on the line. Whereas Sir Philip Sidney might write to his "Stella," Penelope Rich, but also marry Frances Walsingham, exclusive choice was demanded for a woman, far more stringently for a queen. Of course, writing itself was another way of violating gendered conventions, though less aggressively; it may be that Mary's self-presentation as a "fallen woman" licensed her assertion of a vivid literary voice as well.[10]

Lady Mary Wroth also violated the cultural absolutes of chastity and silence, participating in an extramarital affair; remarkably, she avoided absolute "ruin" as usually only male courtiers could. Indeed, she seems to have realized the adulterous courtly story and not only retained her voice but literally reproduced it; she had two illegitimate children by her first cousin, the William Herbert to whom Shakespeare's First Folio was codedicated.[11] Both she and Mary Stuart make strong claims for con-

[10] An obvious danger here is simply to reinscribe the Renaissance equation—loose tongue, loose woman—with a different ethical valuation; the social reality of that cultural equation inhibited all the writers under discussion.

[11] Mary Wroth had a son and daughter by William Herbert after her husband's death. Herbert was Wroth's first cousin and had already caused scandal by refusing to marry courtier Mary Fitton after impregnating her. He continued having affairs at court. Quite

stancy, and Wroth at least seems to have been emotionally "faithful" to her lover. Yet in the linkage of common tropes with female experience, in the counterpoint between their sonnet world and their own actions, they become highly unconventional—challenging the standard scripting of female lives and voices. Lady Mary Wroth is especially interesting as an example of a published author of a sonnet sequence (*Pamphilia to Amphilanthus*) working within an erotic lyric tradition not only masculine in the abstract, but identified with her own father Robert as well as her more famous uncle Philip (her aunt Mary, by contrast, appears to have confined herself to translations, pastoral pieces, and psalms).[12] The very specific echoes of her Sidney family models have been emphasized, in part perhaps to "legitimize" *Pamphilia to Amphilanthus* as literary, but also because such ties are clear and numerous. Nevertheless, Wroth also modifies her tradition by drawing specifically on her difference, using the situation of women in society and the place of woman in the Petrarchan tradition to "embody" a female voice—and in the process she reveals the tensions inherent in such an endeavor.[13]

Wroth's poetry displays several traits familiar to readers of women's poetry, most notably the subordination of explicit concern for immortality and fame, together with a self-presentation emphasizing her pain and marginalization as evidence, a textual sign, of love. She begins her sequence with a poem announcing herself as a lover, not with a programmatic sonnet proclaiming the self as writer (as Sidney, Spenser, and Drayton, among many others, do); instead, she makes an elliptical assertion of her Petrarchan literary origin by alluding to the *Trionfe d'Amore* in her dream vision of Venus and Cupid. This beginning exemplifies her adaptation of as well as overt participation in Petrarchan sonneteering. Most of Wroth's poems are not addressed to the beloved, but instead apostrophize grief, night, eyes, shades, and sometimes "love" or Cupid

---

remarkably, a poem by Lord Herbert of Cherbury to Lady Mary Wroth "upon the birth of my Lord of Pembroke's child" praises her—playfully or ironically—for her double abilities as a poet and childbearer; whereas he can add (poetic) feet, she "can, as everybody knows, / Add to those feet fine dainty toes." He concludes with a cryptic indication of society's response to her "illegitimate" powers: "Satyrs add nails, but they are shrews" (Roberts 1983:26). Jones sees this poem as itself satiric. See Waller 1991, as well as fuller discussion in Waller 1979.

[12] Mary Wroth's father was Robert Sidney, whose own sonnet sequence was only rediscovered in the 1970s. Robert was the younger brother of Sir Philip; his sister (and Mary's godmother) Mary Sidney Herbert, Countess of Pembroke, wrote in a number of forms, but not—at least on the basis of extant documentary evidence—the love sonnet. On Wroth's relationship to her aunt, see Hannay and Waller 1991, Hannay 1990, and Miller 1996.

[13] Substantial attention has been devoted to Wroth in recent years; especially important are the essays by Masten 1991; Fienberg 1991; Waller 1991; Quilligan 1990; Naomi Miller on her poetic subjectivity in Miller and Waller 1991; Beilin 1987; Jones 1990; and Lewalski 1993.

(signifying less often the inconstant man than her own emotion). In addressing these external reflections of her own psyche, she participates in the self-enclosed mirroring of Petrarchan poetics, while the attributes of the beloved remain desired, removed, and antithetical to the symbolic extensions of herself.

Wroth participates in the masochistic trope of much love poetry, that the "proof" of her love is her pain. Of course this is not an idea alien to the Petrarchan tradition; yet an unusual stress on her own physical self-display as evidence of that pain links her sonnets more closely with later women's poetry. The poem becomes a bodiless embodiment of her suffering, at times through an association of the poetic landscape with her own—and *not* the beloved's—body. P30 begins "Deare cherish this," eliding the poem and her heart as possible referents for the demonstrative pronoun; not until the second stanza does she specify "this" as "the hart which fled to you." In what seems to be a set of alternative responses suggested for the beloved, the results are similarly destructive for her: he can excuse her, and so she will be pleased, though at least metaphorically dead ("Hartles my lyfe spill"); if he is kind, they can exchange hearts—in which case he will "feed" on her faithful love and see her sacrifices. Thus she posits the poem and her body as symbiotic displays of pain, displays signifying love. In P10 she substitutes her coupling with grief as alternative to "you" who shall remain happy and separate; "Sorrow I'le wed," she declares (rhetorically undermining her own criterion of constancy, as she herself will become "adulterous" in wedding grief and still loving "you"—an imaginative ménage).

Moreover, she would shed her blood at his will, thus overtly destroying her "self" (P15). She "Whom absence power doth from mirth controle" often identifies with the shadow and darkness of night, as opposed to the masculine sun and light of her beloved. In P22, addressing night, she writes her pained body into nature itself, dying (and hence implicitly proving herself a true lover). Punning on "distressed," she embodies herself in the "leafless naked bodies" of trees, whose "dead leaves" create a "hueless carpet"; the common pun on leaves (of poetry, of trees) here overtly equates poetic product with her personal pain, a sign of her own deprivation. The notion of such self-display in one sense builds on the objectification of the female body in the Petrarchan blazon, even as it is complicated by self-voicing of such dehumanization.[14] Wroth plays

[14] The dynamics of this poetry might be linked fruitfully with de Lauretis's work on the complexities of female passivity and desire in film (1984) and with the fictions of Marguerite Duras. See also Montefiore's discussion of masochism (1987:98–115, 125–40); she, like Tilde Sankovitch (1986), sees problems and failure in women's not asserting a unified self. However, a situationally defined or theatricalized self can also be viewed positively as a source of agency. Certainly Wroth's self-dramatization resonates in the wake of postmodern work

with the poem as an extension of her body, as in P48 where she demands attention: "If ever love had force . . . Then looke on me." Her exposed self and her poem become icons of suffering: "I, ame the soule that feeles the greatest smart; / I, ame that hartles trunk of harts depart"; were love not blind, she would "nott have bin made this stage of woe / Wher sad disasters have theyr open showe." Her painful self-display, her poem itself, becomes a substitute for being "seen" by love. Hers is not an active desire to see but a theatrical, voice-blurring desire to be seen.

Many of Wroth's poems dramatize a complicated set of gazes, once more modifying a standard Petrarchan trope of the male gazing upon his beloved. She does not simply reverse this scenario, pleading for a "countergaze" of him; instead, as illustrated above, she seeks to be the object of his sight (usually comparing him to the sun as well, so that his eyes become the condition allowing light and warmth, a source for her flourishing rather than just objectifiers). She lives on his gazing "came-lion-like," an image that ironically acknowledges she is eating air in so doing, feeding herself with emptiness. In P29, she tells her own eyes to "kill all sight, / And looks" with tears, burying her own gaze until "that bright star" (the planet Mars, and her male beloved) reappears: "then by his might bee you redeem'd." The beloved's gaze can bring happiness; the speaker has only the destructive power to efface herself.

As must be obvious by this point, Wroth consistently equates pain with love—not just vice-versa. She concludes P34 by asking the "blessed shades" (with whose darkness and death she often identifies) to "witnes I could love, who soe could grieve." Although the poem may recall her father's Song 19, as Josephine Roberts notes (1983:104), it differs from as much as it resembles Robert Sidney's work, and the differences seem to correlate with larger gendered patterns in Renaissance poetry. Whereas Wroth speaks in the first-person singular and looks for witnesses to confirm her experience, Sidney assumes a generalized experience and is concerned with the immortality, not the present existence, of his love and grief. He looks to a larger audience:

> Mortal in love are joye and pleasure
> The fading frame, wherin love moves
> But greef and anguish are the measure
> That do immortalyze our loves
> (quoted in Roberts 1983:104)

---

on femininity itself as masquerade, though her treatment is so relentlessly characterized by grief and pain that the celebratory, empowering aspects of such performance seem distant indeed.

Sidney makes grief a means to an end, whereas Wroth, in her consistent identification with night (opposed to the desired otherness of male day), stresses grief as a state of being that is equivalent to love (see also P33). For her, "framed words" provide no consolation or removal from the immediacy of pain, even as she recognizes that they are not the source of her sorrow (P45). Words, like the erotic landscape, remain a "labyrinth," and she neither is nor has an Ariadne to provide a thread to freedom. Rather, she repeatedly calls upon her body, especially her heart, to "wittnes canst I love," thus adapting the blazon not to catalogue her beloved but to display herself. The witnessing reveals pain rather than beauty, as she sheds tears and blood, shows fear, grief, pain, and torment, and is racked and pinched (P41). Just as Wroth does not simply reverse the "male gaze" to examine the male beloved, she transforms Petrarchan display of the female body from a seductive *sparagmos*, allowing the man to desire and dominate simultaneously, into a pathetic self-portrait of needy emptiness and positive pain. Sadism, guilt, or mercy (certainly not sensual desire) become the implied incentives motivating the beloved's return.

Wroth, like Mary Stuart, also casts herself as an outsider, displaced by another woman. Even given his infidelity, she will not chastise the beloved or wish him to grieve. Instead, in the hypothetical case that this new "she" does not love him, Wroth wishes to transfer grief to the woman: "And as for mee, she that showes you least scorne, / With all despite, and hate bee her hart torne" (P56). His posited displacement of her as lover is reenacted by the poem's self-displacement; Wroth's grammar marginalizes her speaking self into an extraneous commentator. The deceptive phrase "as for mee" prefaces a profession having nothing to do with herself, except as an oblique testimony to her ineffectual constancy. In representing their "experience" as lovers, Stuart and Wroth (both aristocrats, both at least for a time sexually active with the men figured as distant beloveds in their poems) seem to exaggerate their marginality, or at least to exemplify the difference between a "self" as a voice of historical testimony and one as a psychological construct. Their art supports the observation that many early modern female poets employ Petrarchan tropes in order to represent the struggle to realize any self worthy of being voiced at all: the subject stresses its own liminality and erasure.

At the same time, one can and should also interpret these poems as creative attempts to represent gendered subjectivity.[15] The notable absence of blazons in the sonnets of Wroth and Stuart indicates a less

---

[15] The essays in Miller and Waller 1991, especially those considering the sonnets in the context of the *Urania* narrative, nicely balance my lyric-based analysis with their greater

domineering attitude toward the object of desire, as well as a less self-absorbed stance. Stuart posits a consciousness for the beloved beyond her ken (XI, XII), and Wroth takes on a variety of attitudes in her lengthy sequence, including ones of delight and moral superiority. Wroth did what Virginia Woolf credits Anne Finch with first achieving: "What one would expect to find would be that rather later perhaps [than Shakespeare's time] some great lady would take advantage of her comparative freedom and comfort to publish something with her name on it and risk being thought a monster" (1929/1957:61). Interestingly, the attacks on Wroth as monstrous had less to do with her poetry per se (although that too was vilified) than her topical allusions—which had similarly made trouble for George Gascoigne when he published a collection of poetry and prose narrative forty-five years earlier.[16] Despite a few very angry readers, she succeeded in presenting herself as a valid lyricist.

If Mary Stuart's fate illustrates the omnipresent dangers of female authorship in any form, and especially in the voice of a female outsider refusing to conform to the social order, Lady Mary Wroth's fate both confirms those dangers and reminds us that they were not specifically tied with the sonnet as a problematic genre. Wroth's love poems drew explicit praise from Ben Jonson, who usually extolled potential patrons on the basis of idealized personal attributes rather than the quality of their writing. Coming from one uninclined to literary flattery (especially of women), Jonson's own sonnet bears special notice:

> I that have beene a lover, and could shew it,
> Though not in these, in rithmes not wholly dumbe,
> Since I exscribe your Sonnets, am become
> A better lover, and much better Poet.
> Nor is my Muse, or I asham'd to owe it,
> To those true numerous Graces, whereof some
> But charm the Senses, others over-come
> Both braines and hearts; and mine now best doe know it:
>
> (in Sylvester 1974:96)

---

attention to female agency and self-assertion; genre plays an obvious role in shaping readings here.

[16] Lord Denny did indeed attack her as an "Hermaphrodite in show, in deed a monster" (Roberts 1983:32) after the first part of *Urania* was published—but there is no evidence that the attack was motivated by its poetry (Waller 1986 discounts this in his discussion of the limits of the Petrarchan sequence as a form; but it appears to have been her narrative romance that drew harsh attacks for perceived references to her contemporaries, not her appended sonnet sequence).

Perhaps less noted than Jonson's poem praising Wroth as "a Sidney," this sonnet remains focused on the quality of Wroth's writing rather than resorting to more typical praise of the female author (citing her moral virtues, with the ability to write anything at all as an added spice implying a mind). Moreover, it is one of the very few sonnets Jonson ever published—a unique tribute to Wroth as a model for literary imitation as well as inspiration. This may well be the most unambiguous poem of literary praise to a woman in English before the advent of the professional female author, Aphra Behn.

Several years ago, Carol Thomas Neely suggested we "over-read, . . . read to excess, the possibility of human (especially female) gendered subjectivity, identity and agency, the possibility of women's resistance or even subversion" (1988:15). To continue to pursue a traditional idea of subjectivity as a general reading strategy, however, may no longer be the most fruitful endeavor, given the particular problematics of that concept for women; rather, we need to explore more fully the poetic bodies of these authors, examining not only the appeal of their self-portrayal but also the function of their different practices in context. Thus I have accentuated, more than most recent feminist commentators, the potential troubles and self-destructiveness within the figuration of a female subject in Wroth's and Stuart's poems. Just as George Eliot's novels reveal much about nineteenth-century bourgeois women's lot and the issues involved in female authorship without resorting to simple gestures of resolution, so these Renaissance poems work within the Petrarchan lyric tradition to represent the particular dilemmas as well as strengths of their author's gender within a privileged class. They constitute a poetic corpus that, with more clarity and directness than other genres provide, supplements and qualifies the presentation of courtly women as filtered through male-authored texts.

It is also worth examining further, in light of their emphases and self-assertions, the fact that few women published.[17] Obviously social strictures and class assumptions silenced some and squelched the desire of many others to publish; but additionally, given the poetics of ambivalent self-assertion, the relatively new technology of publishing may not have been as central a concern as the subsequent masculine literary tradition implies. Clearly, the poems of Renaissance men display much more anxiety about immortality and later generations (not to mention the establishment of paternity) than do the women's lyrics I have examined. The incentive to face public scorn may have been less for women because the two implied poetic audiences were not so distinct; that is, the beloved's gender was not at odds with the "serious" male audience targeted in

[17] See Masten 1991 and Wall 1993 on the complexities of gender and publishing.

public circulation. Whereas men held the ambivalent attitudes toward the lyric discussed earlier, love poetry as a genre was not a particularly "abasing" form for women. Indeed, some of these cultural emphases and foci may still have power, given the observations of Adrienne Rich and others about gendered attitudes toward the beloved and poetic immortality.[18]

To take Petrarchan lyric seriously is one way of taking the absence or presence of women in literature seriously, for this was a domain where women counted—in the erotic plot and the lyric mode. Either enshrining or discarding that historical truth won't take us far. If any form could be adopted by women as a means of self-investigation and expression, the examples of Mary Stuart, Mary Wroth, and in some sense even Anne Cecil imply the sonnet sequence was such a form. The rhetoric of sonnets gave women a space in which to work, not only for later putatively "sentimental" poets such as Elizabeth Barrett Browning and Edna St. Vincent Millay, but for those ladies privileged with literacy at the moment when sonnets were comparatively new rather than nostalgic.

For all the fire and ice of male Petrarchan sonneteering, the lady's not for burning. Nor is the sonnet form itself. A gendered perspective can deepen our understanding of the form, its possibilities, and its struggles without reducing all form to a formula, so long as we attend to its multiple functions. As when we discuss "ideology" and other mainstays of current theoretical debate, problems intrude when a monolithic model is constructed at the expense of both spirit and historical evidence to the contrary. Even if one wishes to resist a gendered reading that renders detail feminine (a move that can be pragmatically empowering but easily returns to an essentialist, unspecific philosophy of difference), the details of Renaissance women's lyric reward as much attention as can be mustered before one returns to the distant present. They may spark a serious revaluation of the Petrarchan lyric and its discontents, a new narrative

---

[18] Jones's comments are relevant here (1990): *all* women's discourse was potentially dangerous and debasing, in that open mouths were associated with open sexuality. But given the place of women in culture, love poetry did not "lower" their gaze, as long as the desires posited were conventionally frustrated or sublimated; indeed, women were more likely to be attacked for aspiring up the generic hierarchy to write epic or tragedy, encroaching on exalted male territory. The most famous analogy might be the condescending acceptance of Jane Austen as miniaturist by those who found the Brontës and George Eliot potentially monstrous in their ambition to represent more than the drawing room.

In discussions with contemporary lyricists, I have noted how quickly most men displace the beloved as the object of their love poetry, preferring to see their aim as simply self-titillation or as an attempt to connect with a part of themselves, their creativity, or posterity; some few consciously sought not to write conventional love poetry because of its participation in systems of gendered dominance. By contrast, the female poets have quickly contextualized their love poetry, thinking of and often giving their actual beloved the poem; it became a different sort of fetish.

in which women play a complex part. To judge Renaissance voices as positive only if not vexed would be both ahistorical and utopian, useless in understanding the world as experienced; nor is vexation the sole legacy of these poems. Reviewed contextually, the Renaissance lyric becomes not only a site of male self-involvement and domination, but also a source for an overtly female voice, gendered self-examination, and the exploration of imaginative power.

3

"Martha's Name," or The Scandal of "The Thorn"

KAREN SWANN

For all its antielitism, Wordsworth's 1800 Preface to *Lyrical Ballads* holds firmly to certain class distinctions. In particular it insists that the new "class of Poetry" represented in the volume is *not* to be confused with the literary rabble—"frantic novels, sickly and stupid German Tragedies, and deluges of idle and extravagant stories in verse"—whose appearance on the scene heralded the emergence of what we now call mass literary culture (in Wordsworth and Coleridge 1969:154). Indeed, Wordsworth asserts, his poems would cure the disease that popular sensational literature at once symptomizes and causes, by counteracting the "craving for extraordinary incident" that currently plagues the reading public and returning readers to healthful states of association (160).

For a reader attuned to late-eighteenth-century polemics against sensational fiction, Wordsworth's expressed concern with literary class engages, in a slippery and complex way, issues of gender and social class. While it was not yet the case that specific literary forms and situations were exclusively identified with a mass reading public, still, "feminine" plots, lady scribblers, and female readers had a certain power to focus anxieties about a changing literary marketplace; evoking contemporary attacks on women authors and readers, Wordsworth's charged adjectives—"frantic," "idle," "extravagant"—suggest that what is to be feared is not simply the vitiation but the emasculation of the reading public. In the following pages I connect Wordsworth's efforts to distinguish the lyrical ballad as a literary class or genre to his deployment of gendered poetic form. My test case is "The Thorn." That "The Thorn" troubles the Preface's class distinctions is suggested by Wordsworth's account of the brainstorm that inspired the poem: "Arose out of my observing, on the ridge of Quantock Hill, on a stormy day a thorn which I had often passed in calm and bright weather without noticing it. I said to myself, 'Cannot

I by some invention do as much to make this Thorn an impressive object as the storm has made it to my eyes at this moment'" (138–39). The poem "composed with great rapidity" after this stormy encounter features a speaker who seems to have experienced a similar encounter, and who has made the thorn a permanently impressive object by placing a woman on the spot—and not just any woman, but a sensationally known, possibly infanticidal one. For the speaker, then, the thorn is linked to a lurid and gendered drama, through an association of ideas that reproduces the mise-en-scènes of an extensive class of fictions about thorns and infanticidal mothers popular in the late eighteenth century.

Wordsworth's anecdote thus teasingly suggests the new poet of the age's close engagement with a body of charged feminine plots, without revealing in what spirit he invokes them. I want here to follow the turns that characterize the uneasy and not always palpable difference between "The Thorn" and the literature of sensation—to propose, finally, that we read the discriminatory Preface of 1800 as a defense against the poet's more licentious and exploitative generic practices of 1798. Reading "The Thorn" against its contexts—popular stories of infanticidal mothers, the true story of Martha Ray—allows us to see the poem's narrator as a figure of the literary careerist. I propose that this careerist uses the story of the suffering woman to negotiate his relation to the reading public and even to discriminate among and ascribe values to English reading publics, in a way that redounds to the advantage of a masculine, Romantic poetic identity.

"The Thorn" as Case History

Possibly, the distinctiveness we grant to Wordsworth's lyrical ballads is an effect of the 1800 Preface, which successfully singled out a volume that in 1798 had been received as just one drop in the deluge. Some modern critics have argued that the response of 1798 was not necessarily obtuse, since in terms of content very little distinguished Wordsworth's work from the popular literature of the day: the world of the *Lyrical Ballads*—of vagrants, beggars, huntsmen, Indian women, and, most strikingly, abandoned, suffering, and infanticidal mothers—would have been perfectly familiar to a monthly magazine audience (Mayo 1954). Yet since 1800, anyway, most readers have agreed to see a difference in Wordsworth's poems, not so much in his choice of subject as in his handling of his matter. We expect in the lyrical ballad a certain kind of diction, a certain specificity of locale, and, above all, a certain critical turn.[1] For

---

[1] For a description of critics' insistence on a saving Wordsworthian "turn," see Siskin 1988:19–20.

unlike sensational literature, which merely stimulates, the lyrical ballad reflects on its own operations: it studies as well as provokes emotion. The product of a meditative mind, it traces "the primary laws of our nature: chiefly as far as regards the manner in which we associate ideas in a state of excitement" so that the reader can in turn make sensation the subject of thought (in Wordsworth and Coleridge 1969:156). Or, as Wordsworth states in his Note to "The Thorn," his poetry, like all true poetry, is the "history or science of feeling" (140).

A generic hybrid, a "ballad" made "lyrical" in a way that foregrounds expressive voice, the lyrical ballad reflects on its own telling to what Wordsworth hopes and readers claim is salutary effect. Wordsworth himself often describes the field of his study as the individual human mind. Yet some readers have speculated that the poems also reflect more broadly on the public taste itself, when the often aggressively sensational matter of the lyrical ballads forces the reader to attend to the investments of narrators in lurid events and, by extension, to her own desires for sensational narrative (Sheats 1973; Jacobus 1976; Averill 1980). This interest in "cases" that are pathological yet exemplary, aligning Wordsworth with contemporaries like Erasmus Darwin and locating him in a trajectory extending from Locke and Hartley to Freud, suggests that the new class of poems may have as much in common with another emerging generic hybrid, the scientific case history, as with existing literary forms.[2] Like a case history, Wordsworth's poetry adopts a scientific, speculative relation to passion, studying the pathological cravings that sensational literature merely provokes.

Among the lyrical ballads "The Thorn" has most readily lent itself to an account of the new poetry as case history, particularly since the publication of Stephen Parrish's forceful and influential reading of the poem as a psychological study of an individual mind (Parrish 1957). As his authority, Parrish cites Wordsworth's own 1800 Note to "The Thorn." The Note avoids mention of the poem's sensational and popular subject matter, its embedded story of an abandoned and infanticidal woman, focusing instead on the character of the speaker. Intervening as a scientist of feelings, Wordsworth invites us to imagine this character as a "case"— a representative of a specific "class" of men sharing a certain pathology, a tendency to "superstition":

The character which I have here introduced speaking is sufficiently common. The Reader will perhaps have a general notion of it, if he has ever known a man, a Captain of a small trading vessel for example, who being

---

[2] For an account of the case history in the eighteenth and nineteenth centuries, see Laqueur 1989:176–204.

past the middle age of life, had retired upon an annuity or small independent income to some village or country town of which he was not a native,
or in which he had not been accustomed to live. Such men having little to
do become credulous and talkative from indolence; and from the same
cause, and other predisposing causes by which it is probable that such men
may have been affected, they are prone to superstition. On which account
it appeared to me proper to select a character like this to exhibit some of
the general laws by which superstition acts upon the mind. (in Wordsworth and Coleridge 1969:139)

The Note is itself a tempting subject of analysis, not least because of the
maverick quality of Wordsworth's understanding of the superstitious
character—his surprising demotion of "credulity" to a mere *symptom* of
superstitiousness. Men of superstitious character are afflicted less by a
disposition to believe irrational or unproven things ("credulity") than by
an unusually fraught relation to "ideas" and "words": they possess "adhesive" minds, minds that "cleave to the same ideas," to "words" that
for them are "impregnated with passion" (139–40). It is this pathologi-
cally adhesive relation to representations that the poem would allow us
to "trace": Wordsworth's intention is to "shew the manner in which such
men cleave to the same ideas; and to follow the turns of passion, always
different, yet not palpably different, by which their conversation is
swayed" (139).

Like many of the subjects of the *Lyrical Ballads*, the speaker in "The
Thorn" suffers from a version of the English public's disease—he craves
and sensationalizes a limited set of ideational elements. He's fixated first
of all on a thorn:

I

There is a thorn; it look so old,
In truth you'd find it hard to say,
How it could ever have been young,
It looks so old and grey.
Not higher than a two-years' child,
It stands erect this aged thorn;
No leaves it has, no thorny points;
It is a mass of knotted joints,
A wretched thing forlorn.
It stands erect, and like a stone
With lichens it is overgrown.
(in Wordsworth and Coleridge
1969; ll. 1–11)

Yet oddly, the thorn he's fixated upon seems almost a figure of the pathology of "superstition" as Wordsworth describes it. Knotty symptom of an obscure passion, the wretched thorn is "overgrown" and impregnated with potential and contradictory significances (it's childlike yet ancient, sinister yet victimized, assaulted yet "erect") that become the vectors of an increasingly dilated and sensational plot as the poem unfolds.

The poem's first stanza tests our initial alignment of Wordsworth's new class of poetry with the genre of the case history. The passage illustrates superstitiousness as described in the Note to "The Thorn," and it does, truly if a bit ostentatiously, draw our attention to the turns of passion that produce the turns and returns of the verse to the idea of the thorn. And insofar as it draws our attention to a narrative propensity (typically, a narrative propensity linked to the appetite for sensation that preoccupies Wordsworth in all the experimental lyrical ballads), the poem produces the self-reflex that readers claim distinguishes Wordsworth's poetry from the popular poetry of the day.

Yet in important ways "The Thorn" is of course not a case history. For unlike the Note to the poem, in which the author acts as scientist presenting and explaining to us his pathological subject, "The Thorn" interposes no such mediating consciousness between the reader and its language. In the terms of psychological science, the poem is not a case *history* but a case or analysand, and an analysand of dubious character. For the very adhesiveness of the verse to the overladen figure of the thorn works against the characterization of a distinct dramatic speaker, instead drawing our attention to words operating as poetry—as refrain, as rhyme—in a way that seems eerily detached from identifiable human agency. We become fascinated less with the expressive character of an individual voice than with the formal demands of song. The poem's disturbing foregrounding of poetic structure has led its readers from Wordsworth's day to the present to feel that the speaker of the poem is only precariously dramatized, an impression fostered by Wordsworth's adhesive, constantly turning Note to "The Thorn," which finally turns back to defend poetry's cleavings and adhesions—not now as a function of a pathology (superstitiousness) but of the passions "every man" has for words and of the tendency of "words" to attain a kind of ascendancy over "mind":

Now every man must know that an attempt is rarely made to communicate impassioned feelings without something of an accompanying consciousness of the inadequateness of our own powers, or the deficiencies of language. During such efforts there will be a craving in the mind, and as long as it is unsatisfied the Speaker will cling to the same words, or words of the same character. There are also various other reasons why repetition and apparent tautology are frequently beauties of the highest kind. Among the chief of these reasons is the interest which the mind attaches to words, not only as symbols of the passion, but as *things*, active and efficient, which are of themselves part of the passion. And further, from a spirit of fondness, exultation, and gratitude, the mind luxuriates in the repetition of words which appear successfully to communicate its feelings. (140–41)

For Frances Ferguson, the passage betrays what the poem enacts, that the narrator of "The Thorn" is less a dramatic portrait of a superstitious person than a personification of the poetic figure of repetition (Ferguson 1977:13)—"like" an individual mind only in the sense that the thorn is "like" a stone.

Taking up her suggestive characterization, Jerome Christensen points out that we experience "The Thorn" less as the production of a dramatic speaker than as a "passion" about signs that propagates dramatic situations and events (Christensen 1980). In the world of "The Thorn," words uncannily become things, language tics generate a world: an ominously overdetermined thorn gives rise to a miniaturized and then increasingly dilated "plot"; an apparently rhetorical "you" suddenly starts into speech; an equally anonymous "they" disconcertingly metamorphoses into the homespun company of Farmer Simpson and friends. Finally, during the height of a storm, a blank counter, "as I am a man," thickens into a dramatically traumatized persona:

XVIII

'Twas mist and rain, and storm and rain,
No screen, no fence could I discover,
And then the wind! in faith, it was
A wind full ten times over.
I looked around, I thought I saw
A jutting crag, and off I ran,
Head-foremost, through the driving rain,
The shelter of the crag to gain,
And, as I am a man,
Instead of jutting crag, I found
A woman seated on the ground.

XIX

I did not speak—I saw her face,
Her face it was enough for me;

I turned about and heard her cry,
'O misery! O misery!'

(ll. 188–202)

Amid the tumult a minimally figured passion about signs is born again as an Adam already captivated by his Eve. "The Thorn," then, could be said to generate a narrative machinery that only gradually takes the form of a world of tale producers and consumers; this human world in turn allows our retroactive grounding of poetic passion in a stable if pathological poetic speaker irrevocably bound to an equally stable if overdetermined landscape.

Reading Wordsworth's poem as a case history of an individual mind fails to take into account its unsettling temporal logic. Such a reading discounts the speaker's belatedness, the sense we have that he is not so much a producer as a product of a world of impassionated signs. It also ignores his headlong precipitousness—unremarked, for example, by Stephen Parrish in his important essay on the poem. From the evidence of the poem Parrish reconstructs the speaker's case history, tracing his obsession with the site of thorn, pond, and hill to his traumatic experience on the mountaintop, an experience that Parrish wants to insist results in a moment of *mis*recognition, the speaker's mistaking of the stunted thorn for a woman. His argument marshals contradictions in the speaker's account—for example, the discrepancy between his assurance about seeing the face and his confession that he could see "no object higher than [his] knee"—to propose that the speaker has never seen Martha Ray, but instead saw the thorn and heard the wind's keening cry and, later, "a village superstition about a woman wronged years ago." "In fact," Parrish concludes, "the point of the poem may well be that its central 'event' has no existence outside of the narrator's imagination" (Parrish 1957: 155). This is both reasonable and provocative, but it fails to account for the way the speaker gets ahead of himself—for why, "as [he is] a man," he comes up with the theory that there's a *woman* at the spot, and this *before* he's "heard of Martha's name" or the village superstition about her; or why his theory is then confirmed by a society whose members each and all agree that the spot is indeed haunted by this figment of the narrator's imagination. For Martha's identity and habits are legend, "known to every star / And every wind that blows" (ll. 69–70).

The case "The Thorn" invites us to study is not the "individual mind" but the subject's impossible relation to what is already known. A precipitate from a world of passionately invested signs whose coming to identity is simultaneous with his betrayal into a passionately held theory, a theorizer confirmed in his misrecognition by the world's signifying practices, the narrator of "The Thorn" is caught in a structure of apparent tautology. In 1800 Wordsworth names this epistemological bind "superstition," the laws of which determine how men of deep and adhesive minds produce, cleave to, and exult in the signs that are for them impregnated with passion. But many readers have felt that this account disingenuously seeks to limit to a pathology what Wordsworth suspects is a more general condition—the condition of the poetic imagination, or of readers of Wordsworth's poetry, or even of all users of language. I suggest that what Wordsworth comes to call the laws by which superstition acts on the mind are the laws governing the subject's relation to received cultural materials—to the impregnated words, ideas, and things that constitute the symbolic order. The subject cleaves to impassionated signs that are never adequate to its passions because they preexist the subject, with respect to whom they can only ever be under- or overdetermined—intimating, by their extraordinary opacity, a retroactivity yet to come or gesturing, by their luminous, unexpected significance toward a past and formerly inscrutable promise.

The case history limits to a pathology or case the sensationalism that plagues every subject's relation to the words and ideas that constitute the cultural field. Within the poem, a storm transforms a figure of repetition into a man of science obsessed with the "sad case" of Martha Ray, the woman who embodies the mind's characteristic cleaving to ideas. His effort to contain "sensationalism" by locating its effects in a delimited other site anticipates Wordsworth's in his 1800 Note to "The Thorn," where he figures "superstition" in the case of a hypothetical retired sea captain, and in the Preface, where he locates a problem of sensationalism in a literary class from which his own "class of poems" is to be excluded. In a sense, then, the generic innovations of the lyrical ballad constitute a defense mechanism. The poem's turn on its sensational matter puts distance between the "class of Poems" created by the new poet and a problem of sensationalism: "sensationalism," a charged relation to words or ideas, is thus embodied as a craving for lurid event or story, a passion that can then be studied by the scientist of feeling or the cultural critic.

But "The Thorn" also reflects on these defenses, making a case both of the man who makes a sad case of the woman sensationally fixated on impassionated signs and of the culture that delights in tracing the maternal passions. It invites us to scrutinize the odd cultural consensus around culture's favorite "case"—that of the sensationally known, possibly infanticidal mother whose favorite haunt is a stunted thorn. If the laws by which superstition works on the mind are neutral, superstitions themselves are class- and gender-biased. Thus I turn now from the case of the narrator to the lurid case of his Martha Ray, to trace the laws of superstition as they operate in "The Thorn." What does Wordsworth's poem illuminate about a superstition like misogyny, which, although historically persistent, takes historically specific forms—like the limited yet endlessly modifiable stories of maternal suffering and criminality that so fascinated late-eighteenth-century English culture? These stories haunt the ground on which Wordsworth locates his own Martha Ray and lend a certain lurid light to the poet's reflections on the public taste.

The Case of Martha Ray

An investigation of what "The Thorn" can tell us about cultural credulity regarding the woman might begin with the poem's village culture. The source of its fascination with Martha Ray would seem to lie buried in the past, in an old affront against infancy:

> And some had sworn an oath that she
> Should be to public justice brought;
> And for the little infant's bones
> With spades they would have sought.
>
> (ll. 232–35)

Betraying the familiar indignation of every mothered babe who would attribute old wounds to untoward maternal passions, the villagers' excavationary enthusiasm suggests that Martha Ray suffers for her maternity. Drawing from contemporary psychoanalytic theory, we could speculate that the mother is to blame for the condition Wordsworth describes as a tendency to superstition; some accounts of preoedipal experience suggest that her maternal attentions originally and constitutively wound the child, whose desires are forever after impossible, organized around the desire of the other.[3] The vengeful villagers would seem impelled by this knowledge. Abandoned, pinned to the spot, cleaving to the signifiers of untoward passion, Martha figures and pays for every man's impossible condition, his peculiarly bound and impassioned relation to "words" not his own.

Tracing the passions of the villagers invites us to attribute a cultural dread of the woman to her maternity. But while this hypothesis has explanatory power beyond the world of "The Thorn," it fails to satisfy the narrator, who at the end of the poem dutifully recounts the villagers' stories of a haunted grave and then dismisses them. Focusing on the babe is for the credulous or superstitious, he implies, producing showy

---

[3] See, for example, Jean Laplanche's analysis of Freud's account of the simultaneous emergence of sexuality and representation from the infant's experience of maternal care (Laplanche 1976:chap. 1).

special effects without illumination. He's a wavering and notoriously unreliable figure. But steadier authorities have agreed to impute a cautionary meaning to his account of what "some" say they see in the pond:

> Some say, if to the pond you go,
> And fix on it a steady view,
> The shadow of a babe you trace,
> A baby and a baby's face,
> And that it looks at you,
>
> (ll. 225–29)

Though for the villagers the shimmering image serves as a beacon—the answer to Martha's power lies *here*, in the figure and face of the child— for the narrator and the Wordsworthian reader schooled to habits of reflection it is an ignis fatuus, only delusively promising that the secret of Martha's uncanny power can be brought home to any *heimlich* place.

The narrator is less concerned with what Martha may or may not have *done*—her possible criminality toward her child—than with where she *is*: repeatedly he expresses distrust of any answer to "why" she suffers to dwell on the mere fact of her association with the spot. The arbitrary constellation woman/thorn, not the mother–child dyad, moves and disconcerts him: that, and the apprehension that his highly and personally charged landscape of oddly assorted elements—a woman, a thorn, a mound of moss, a small pond—has in the world the status of an elemental truth. If the villagers naturalize their superstitious dread of Martha Ray by grounding it in a secret of maternity, the narrator would seem to recognize the uncanny force of the arbitrary yet known: in other words, the force of "superstition," an irrational and widely held belief.

The case of the narrator points away from the (perhaps unfathomable) grounds of misogyny and toward the entrenched yet endlessly renewable forms of its cultural expression. For the narrator's experience suggests that the woman's power derives not from her buried crimes but from her extraordinary cultural currency. A notoriously, flamboyantly public figure, Martha Ray is known to "*every* star and *every* wind that blows." But of course *everyone* knows that an infanticidal or abandoned woman belongs at the site of a stunted thorn—that is, everyone familiar with the rich literary context in which "The Thorn" is embedded. The rural culture of "The Thorn" would know traditional ballads on the theme of "The Cruel Mother," in which a thorn is always the setting of an infanticide, or of "William and Margaret," in which a rejected woman returns as a revenant to haunt a stunted thorn and a grave. But even newcomers to village life, like the narrator, or city dwellers, like many of Wordsworth's readers, might know ballads like these from the collections that began to appear during the eighteenth century—David Herd's *Ancient and Modern Scottish Songs* (1769), James Johnson's *Scots Musical Museum* (1787), and of course Thomas Percy's *Reliques of Enqlish Poetry* (1765). There's a good chance Wordsworth would have known these traditional ballads, either from hearing them in the north or from reading them in the collections. But if not, like his narrator and public he would still have been familiar with thorns and infanticidal women from a host of modern poems deploying the same situation—among them, Langhorn's *Country Justice* (1774–77), Merry's *Pains of Memory* (1776), and, most importantly, "The Lass of Fair Wone" (1796), William Taylor's popular translation of Gottfried Burger's "Des Pfarrers Tocher von Taubenheim," a "german" reworking of the traditional English ballads on the cruel mother and an obvious inspiration of "The Thorn" (Jacobus 1976:241).

Moreover, city or country, anyone with access to newspapers or periodicals—or, by 1798, to James Boswell's *Life of Johnson* (1791) or Herbert Croft's *Love and Madness* (1780)—would have "heard of Martha's name" before coming across it Wordsworth's poem. For Martha Ray, mistress of the earl of Sandwich, was the victim in a sensational murder case of 1779, when she was shot outside a London theater by James Hackman, a disappointed lover. The case had not been forgotten by 1798: the 1818 supplement to the Newgate Calendar printed the story of James Hackman as its first entry, and by 1797 Southey was preparing to take Herbert Croft to court over the contents of *Love and Madness*.[4] But few would have been more fully aware of the affair than Wordsworth himself, who was accompanied by the motherless son of Basil Montague, the "natural" child of Martha Ray, when he came across a thorn in a storm and asked himself, "Cannot I by some invention make this thorn as impressive an object as it is to my eyes at this moment?"

The startling consensus about what belongs at the site of a stunted thorn is no mystery. A veritable lightning rod, the thorn merely seeks out whatever charged stories are in the air. Each and all agree to put a woman on the spot because the woman is, quite simply, this culture's favorite case—not for anything she has done, but because she happens to have been notorious in the past. Her prominence is thus arbitrary. But it is not unmotivated; like the laws of public justice, those of superstition work to perpetuate and enforce cultural biases: here, an irrational and prejudicial association of the woman with the scenes of passion.

---

[4] My reconstruction of the murder is indebted to the *Newgate Calendar* (Jackson 1818), to the *Dictionary of National Biography*, s. v. "James Hackman" (Stephen and Lee 1890), and to the notes and text of Reed and Pottle 1977:73–94. Croft's story can be reconstructed from the *Dictionary of National Biography* s. v. "Herbert Croft" (Stephen 1890), and from Cottle 1837:1.256–74. See also Goldberg 1996 for an account of the Croft-Southey affair that sees it turning precisely on questions of literary professionalism and careerism.

What is the relation of Wordsworth's new class of poems to this deluge of sensational stories? Wordsworth's tale of how the poem came to be hints that the new poet may be as caught as his narrator in the workings of superstition. Critics have sometimes found his choice of the name "Martha Ray" scandalously unmotivated—this, I take it, is behind W. J. B. Owen's wondering at Wordsworth's "obtuseness," or behind Boswell's editors' marveling at the poet's "strange lack of taste" in thus taking the name of his friend's notorious mother, a woman who was neither abandoned nor infanticidal, for his protagonist who was both (in Wordsworth and Coleridge 1969:141n; Reed and Pottle 1977:74n). But perhaps the poet who professes to abjure sensation is himself blindly captive in an untoward association of ideas: coming on a thorn in a storm and wanting to convey its lurid lighting by some poetic invention, he merely repeats by apparent tautology a host of lurid, gendered stories he has known—tales of betrayed, treacherous, and dead women that cut across the class lines he attempts to draw in the 1800 Preface between his heralded new writings and popular sensational literature. Like his own narrator, who on the hilltop discovers with the force of revelation what the villagers have known all along, he creates a scene that is powerfully and uncannily uninventive, which seems blindly and mechanically to reproduce the grossly and violently stimulating literature that, Wordsworth charges, substitutes for invention in a superstitious age.

Yet just as plausibly, the self-reflexive poet knowingly chooses the spectacularly known signifier "Martha Ray" in order to intervene into the tautological workings of superstition. For as some readers have complained, "Martha Ray" alludes to events that never touch the manifest content of the poem; it raises expectations that "The Thorn" fails to answer. The name functions flamboyantly, that is, to expose the laws of superstition. If superstition works to domesticate the effects of the sign on the subject by transferring those effects to the "natural" mother, the proper name "Martha Ray" returns the mother to the status of a radically alienated, culturally overdetermined signifier. Unable to read in the manner of the poem's villagers, who see reflected back to them the "face" they expect to see, Wordsworth's public is shocked into analytic reflection on culture's dreamlike production of meaning.

This, anyway, is how the generous modern reader might construe Wordsworth's project, encouraged by the Preface's insistence on his noncompliance with a diseased public taste and a burgeoning literary industry. Neither Wordsworth's blindness nor his knowingness should be underestimated. But the question of the poet's intentions and control— a question that has traditionally preoccupied critics of "The Thorn"— may divert us from other ways of understanding the poet's relation to his narrator and to his literary materials. To tease out these other possibilities, we need to move further into the storm generated by the murder of Martha Ray. For one can argue that this sordid tale's relation to "The Thorn" is not flamboyantly arbitrary at all, but rather guiltily overdetermined; that when read in the proper spirit, the true story of Martha Ray is at once the story of "The Thorn" and the story of the poetic career launched in 1798. In all these stories, "Martha Ray" could be said to function as a screen, invoking a thematics of feminine criminality and fixation in a way that conceals masculine industry and mobility. I turn now to the careers of two literary men, James Boswell and Herbert Croft, who breached decorum, courted scandal, and flirted with criminality in their handling of the case of Martha Ray. Tracing this particular association of ideas brings the narrator of "The Thorn" closer to the literary careerist and invites us to see the latter's use of the woman's scandalous story in a more critical light—neither as a blind and unwilled adhesion to culture's impregnated ideas, nor as a self-reflexive and resistant deployment of prejudicial theory, but as a strategic, vigorous, and interested appropriation of superstitiously invested cultural materials.

The Case of the Literary Man

On 6 April 1779, James Hackman shot Martha Ray through the forehead outside a London performance of *Love in a Village* and then, with his second pistol, attempted to take his own life. London was immediately possessed by the murder, if we judge by the discursive storm it generated—the immediate proliferation of reports in newspapers and periodicals, in eyewitness accounts of the execution, in memoirs of Ray and Hackman. The case attracted such attention in part because of Ray's connection to the powerful and widely disliked earl of Sandwich, but also because it lent itself so well to romance: in contemporary accounts Martha Ray, the poor but honest daughter of a staymaker, apprenticed to a lace-maker at age thirteen, and then discovered and "removed into that higher sphere" by the elderly earl, comes across as a "lass of fair wone"–like character, while Hackman is cast as a young Werther, driven to murder and suicide by desperate and uncontrollable passion.[5] The widely reported trial that followed the murder focused on Hackman's motives and intentions, particularly the latter—did he intend to kill Martha Ray or only himself? The prosecution argued for a verdict of premeditated murder, pointing out that he carried two pistols to the scene of the crime; the defense, pointing to a suicide note found in Hackman's

[5] The description of Martha Ray is from the *Public Advertiser*, 9–10 April 1779, cited in Reed and Pottle 1977:73; my reconstruction of Boswell's activities follows Reed and Pottle.

pocket and addressed to Mr. Booth, his brother-in-law, asking Booth to think well of "her" after he, Hackman, was gone, argued that Hackman at first intended to kill only himself and was only inspired to kill Ray as well in a sudden fit of jealousy. The verdict found Hackman guilty of murder. Hackman responded with a courtroom confession in which he took full responsibility and expressed great regret for the murder, and he was then led to his execution amid one of the largest crowds ever assembled at Tyburn.

The careers of Boswell and Croft take shape against this backdrop of a talking world. Boswell entered the picture immediately, after only one of the protagonists was dead. His attention was drawn to Hackman as he attempted to translate the juridical case into an exemplary case of an individual mind—to press the story of the suffering woman toward one of masculine obsession. He immediately plunged into the case, cultivating the acquaintance first of Booth and then of Hackman, whom he was allowed to see; he then covered the trial for the newspapers so thoroughly that a reader following the case through Boswell's career begins to feel that if the whole world was talking about the sensational crime, it was talking in Boswell's voice. He first published an anonymous report of the trial in the *Public Advertiser*, whose source is a "Mr Boswell, who left the court as soon as sentence was pronounced [and] was the first person who informed [Mr. Booth] of the fate of his relation and friend" (Reed and Pottle 1977: 72, 86). This report was followed by a letter from Mr. Boswell to the editor of the *St. James Chronicle* about the affecting character of Mr. Hackman's speech—a speech that Frederick Pottle speculates may have been drafted by Boswell (Pottle 1965:260). The letter casts Hackman as an exemplary case "of the dreadful effects of the passion of love," for more comment on which Boswell advises the reader to turn to that well-known journal *The Hypochondriack* (by Boswell), from which he cites a passage. In the meantime Boswell was introducing the topic into conversation at social gatherings where Johnson was present, at one point precipitating an explosion between Johnson and Mr. Beauclerk on the subject of the two-pistol defense, which he then recorded in the *Life of Johnson* (Boswell 1964–71:3,383–85). Boswell's manipulation of the drama inevitably brought him too near a connection to criminality when a contemporary account of the execution put him in the carriage with Hackman on the way to Tyburn; upset about his "name" attending Hackman (particularly since it was widely believed that Boswell himself had planted the story) Boswell finally printed a rebuttal in the papers (Reed and Pottle 1977:94).

Collector and purveyor of scandal, catalyst of a talking world, impresario of the lurid drama he purports merely to recount: Boswell has certain affinities with the narrator of "The Thorn" as he might appear in our least flattering accounts of him, for like Boswell the narrator deploys innuendo, hearsay, and eyewitness accounts to influence a "case"—a case less concerned to prove the criminality than the human interest of the marked subject, but one that nonetheless capitalizes on the public taste. We can't be sure what Wordsworth would have known about Boswell's interest in the murder of Martha Ray. But he would surely have been familiar with Sir Herbert Croft, author of *Love and Madness. A story too true. In a series of letters between parties, whose names would perhaps be mentioned were they less known, or less lamented*, a novel comprising a collection of spurious letters between Hackman and Ray (purported to have been acquired through the same Mr. Booth whom Boswell cultivated), which included a memoir of Thomas Chatterton, purportedly by Hackman. The letters are striking for their wooden literariness: each protagonist casts him- or herself as a romantic character, "Mr. H" as a young Werther who periodically bursts out "I shall go mad!" and otherwise tells dark stories of disappointed men who have murdered their lovers, killed themselves or both; "Miss R" as a romantic heroine tragically bound to her May-December romance with the earl, at one point emphasizing her predicament by quoting in full the ballad "Auld Robin Gray," whose young Jenny, still in love with her Jamie gone to sea but married off to Robin Gray, is left to cry "Woe is me." (For a time the ballad becomes the organizing figure of their relationship—she signs herself Jenny and declares her attachment to her Jamie.)

The volume's success (it went quickly into seven editions) makes it probable that Wordsworth would have known of Croft; Croft's connections with Coleridge, Southey, and Cottle, however, make it certain, for as early as 1797 Southey, egged on by Cottle, was preparing to take Croft to court over the latter's theft of Chatterton's papers from the poet's mother and niece. In 1778 Croft had "borrowed" the papers from the two women, ostensibly for an afternoon. Two years later he had published them in *Love and Madness*, the substantial proceeds from which never made it back to Chatterton's impoverished family, and in 1798 he had yet to return the originals to the women (Cottle 1837:1,256–74).

In 1798 Wordsworth would have known that *Love and Madness* was about to become the occasion of a literary storm. But even the uninformed reader can't help noticing that the text itself courts scandal. For the story of Chatterton, awkwardly introduced into the text through one of "Mr. H"'s letters, is only one of many references to forgery or impersonation introduced into the spurious correspondence of Mr. H and Miss R, who between protestations of love and madness are in the habit of discussing matters of literary authenticity and provenance: "Auld Robin Gray" itself, a minor cause célèbre because its authenticity as a traditional ballad was by turns asserted and disputed, is revealed by "Miss

H" to have been in fact written by "Lady A. L.";[6] there are also allusions to James Macpherson's Ossian, to Daniel Defoe's "improvement" of Alexander Selkirk's story in *Robinson Crusoe* (1719), to Chatterton's Rowley, and, with the introduction of Chatterton's life, an elaborate defense by Mr. H of Chatterton's Rowley poems. Where "The Thorn" is relatively decorous in exploring the subject's adhesive relation to words and ideas that it can never quite make its own, *Love and Madness* translates this relation into the strong cultural terms of the gothic revival, which attempts to make the "received" its own, occasionally in lurid and even criminal ways—forgery, charlatanry, the illicit seizure of the property of others.

Popularly construed, the true story of Martha Ray is a tale of love and madness, of a lover's excessive cleaving to a charged idea. This construction, though, masks an equally lurid and fantastic plot involving the weirdly blind yet knowing literary careerist. "Martha Ray" points back to multiple masculine crimes: the literary man's pilfering of literary property, his violation of Bristol's marvelous boy, and his exploitation of female suffering when he turns the woman's story into a matter of public record and the stuff of masculine excitement in order to secure his own place in masculine literary circles and a broader public discourse. It is impossible to tell if his scandalous interventions in the story he pretends merely to repeat are knowing or blind, calculated or driven, but in a sense this doesn't matter, for his self-awareness and madness are equally interested. The stories of Boswell and Croft push the speaker of "The Thorn" in the direction of the literary careerist and the poet in the direction of both, suggesting that despite their critical interventions into the laws of superstition, Wordsworth's new class of poems may also exploit a public interest in sensationally suffering women.

More than this, they may participate in the late-eighteenth-century construction of a reading public addicted to such tales. For what strikes us about the activities of Boswell and Croft is not simply their treatment of a story but their creation of the social context in which it is received, when they ventriloquize both the protagonists of the love plot and a world fixated on tales of love and madness. Both men, that is, display a kind of social imagination that could strike us as Wordsworthian—that could remind us of the way the technical apparatus of "The Thorn" propagates not just a woman and a narrator but also a society obsessed with the tale of Martha Ray, or the way the Preface to *Lyrical Ballads* multiplies "classes" of poems and publics. In all cases, the strategic de-

---

[6] The author of "Auld Robin Gray" was Lady Anne Barnard (Lindsay); for her account of the contestation of the poem's authorship see her letter to Sir Walter Scott in Partington 1930:199–207.

ployment of the woman's story and name enables the literary man to
manage his relation to an increasingly complex social field, and even to
construct that field in a way that is advantageous to a literary career.

The People's Case

We tend to speak of "culture" or "the public" as though these were
monolithic. But by the 1800 Preface, Wordsworth is implicitly discrimi-
nating among the potentially overlapping publics for the classes of fiction
he enumerates: polite literature, popular sensational fiction (a class that
might include both "The Lass of Fair Wone" and the urban legend of
Martha Ray), and "the invaluable works of our elder writers" (including
the "authentic" or traditional ballads sung by people in "common life,"
which by 1800 Wordsworth had discovered and admired in collections
like those by Herd, Johnson, and Percy) (in Wordworth and Coleridge
1969:160). These social groups could potentially make up or be excluded
from the public about to be constituted for the class of poems represented
in the *Lyrical Ballads*, and Wordsworth's representation makes clear
which allegiances this new public is invited to retain and which it must
abandon.

The Preface was an enormously successful document, both in immediate terms, when it made the 1800 *Lyrical Ballads* the focus of attention
and controversy, and of course historically. For its divisive strategy—its
sorting into "classes" a literary field whose boundaries were still in fact
quite fluid—helped establish the terms in which we continue to construct
"the popular," both as a lost authentic culture and as an inauthentic and
alienated mass culture symptomatic of cultural decline. Its account of the
singular author's necessarily alienated and oppositional relation to the
marketplace continues to have force for us today. In "The Thorn" we
can see this relation taking shape, as the poem propagates not one but
two audiences to the tale of Martha Ray—an intimate Wordsworthian
"Reader," figured in the poem by the hysterically reactive "you," and
an unenlightened, sensation-craving popular culture, the "they" who
metamorphose into the villagers. Like the Preface, "The Thorn" splits the
"mass" into an audience of readers who engage the work—whether they
respond to it with hysterical resistance (characteristically prompting a
renewed, prolix display of recalcitrance) or learn to read in it the structure and mechanics of productive passion—and a public depicted as ir-
redeemably bound in the mechanisms of a reductive narrative and
ideological machinery.

Thus "The Thorn" anticipates the Preface's method of constructing
and managing the poet's relation to his public. But it also suggests that

in 1798 Wordsworth may have been more willing to cross and exploit the divisions he creates than he lets on in 1800. The narrator uses the villagers in much the way village culture uses Martha, deriving his tale's more obvious thrills from their hearsay stories while being careful to distance himself from their pathological obsessions for the benefit of "you," his intimate audience. These tactics—which the poem throws into relief for our reflection—clearly resemble Wordsworth's in the 1800 Note to "The Thorn," where he locates "superstition" in the crudely constructed figure of the retired sea captain; more generally, they resemble the tactics of the poet in 1798, when he deploys but does not embrace the sensational appeal of popular literature for the benefit of a public invited to reflect on such tastes. All of these uses of the sensational can look like forms of bad faith, inviting us to charge Wordsworth with a crass though subtle Boswellian or Croftian exploitation of the popular. The narrator of "The Thorn," after all, uses the story of Martha Ray to gain entrance into the culture to which he then condescends in his intimate address to his interlocutor. His case suggests that by a strategic deployment of the woman, the mobile literary careerist can lure the very public he also affects to cast out and thus can have it both ways.

It appears to me that in 1798 Wordsworth was indeed working to accommodate as well as differentiate—to craft a poetry that would at once tap a popular taste and yet distinguish itself from the deluge—and that it was the failure of this strategy sufficiently to distinguish the *Lyrical Ballads* from the mass that prompted the Preface's more defensive and adversarial account of the poet's relation to the reading public and the literary marketplace. But there are multiple ways of understanding this accommodative strategy, only one of which is to see it as simply the crass exploitation of a popular literature and taste—multiple ways of understanding the poem's complex and sometimes self-contradictory figurings of the modern poet's relation to his public, possibilities aborted in 1800 by the Preface's defensive splitting of the literary field into what we now know as mass and elite cultures. For although, like the Preface, Wordsworth's poetry of 1798 plays on distinctions among classes of fictions, it equally calls attention to a kind of generic indiscriminacy. The charged constellation of characters in "The Thorn" conjures willy-nilly a host of stories that cut across the class lines drawn in the 1800 Preface. We can imagine the poet haunted, invaded by the voices of the dead—the dead infants, dead mothers, and dead lovers who make up the rich background of the poem. Or we can point to his knowing, allusive strategy, which invokes a range of sources for the poem, including the texts of the ballad revival and their endlessly variant "originals"—and even, perhaps, the work of Chatterton, Ossian, and the infamous Sir Herbert Croft—to suggest that the authentically popular is only ever retroactively fabricated by the modern. But however we construe the poem's relation to its context, "The Thorn" would seem to bring home to us the common ground occupied by the publics generated by its passionate poetics.

Wordsworth's evocation of the suffering woman would allow poet and public, bound in a vexed relation at the turn of the century, to point to a shared taste and a common literature. I will conclude by exploring this more politically hopeful aspect of Wordsworth's use of Martha Ray and by suggesting that Martha Ray—known to "every star and every wind that blows," who inhabits the traditional ballad, its modern imitation, and the urban legend, and whose keening cry by only apparent tautology sings the burden of a vast literature—shadows forth the liberation of a public voice. This is the implication of the sensational story buried in Wordsworth's Note to "The Thorn," where he cites one "tumultuous and wonderful Poem" from the Bible to illustrate that "repetition and apparent tautology are frequently beauties of the highest kind." Wordsworth quotes from Judges 5:12, 27, and 28:

Awake, awake Deborah: awake, awake, utter a song: Arise Barak, and lead thy captivity captive, thou Son of Aniboam.
At her feet he bowed, he fell, he lay down: at her feet he bowed, he fell; where he bowed there he fell down dead.
Why is his Chariot so long in coming? Why tarry the
Wheels of his Chariot?

(in Wordsworth and Coleridge 1969:140–41)

From the song of Deborah, "a mother in Israel," these verses celebrate the murder of the Gentile general Sisera by the woman Jael. Fleeing the Israelites led by Barak, Sisera sought refuge in Jael's tent, where she nurtured him—fed him milk instead of water, we are told twice—put him to bed, and then, when he was asleep, drove a nail through his skull.

Jael's method of murder recalls that of the mother in "The Lass of Fair Wone," of the cruel mother, and even of Hackman's shooting of Martha Ray. But taking the story as simply another go-round—or possibly an Ur-text—of the tale of the cruel mother overlooks its status as a celebration of the liberation of Israel. The story of Jael and Sisera rises out of the Note to "The Thorn" like the return of repressed political desires. Jael's action triumphs over the power that had divided the Israelites, consigned them to the margins, and blocked their speech, a state of affairs Deborah recalls in the same chapter of Judges (5:6–7):"In the days of Shamgar the son of Anath, in the days of Jael, the highways were unoccupied, and the travellers walked through byways. The inhabitants of the villages ceased, they ceased in Israel, until that I Deborah arose, that I arose a mother in Israel." Sisera's rule has some affinities to the village culture described in "The Thorn," which also secures itself by exclusions. But it is a better portrait of Wordsworth's England during the time of "Adventures on Salisbury Plain" (1795), with its vigorously enforced laws against public gatherings and seditious publication. By 1798 Wordsworth had ceased active protest, opting for the slow education rather than liberation by revolution of the people. But we can speculate that his homage to Deborah's song is linked to an uprising of earlier sympathies. In Judges 5 the mother Deborah rises not in madness but in revolt and finally in prophecy. In that tumultuous and passionate poem, Deborah's voice mingles with Barak's, with that of the third speaker who wakes them both, and even with the lament of Sisera's suffering mother to sing the song of the liberation of the children of Israel by the woman, Jael.

Wordsworth's 1800 Preface to *Lyrical Ballads* premises the emergence of a new national literature on certain discriminatory practices. But Deborah's passionate poetics allow us to see other impulses informing his actual practices of 1798: indiscriminately mingling genders and poetic forms, he created a generic hybrid capacious enough to accommodate the contested and contesting voices of a renewed national culture. Deborah's song bespeaks the new poet of the age's admiration of a poetics that would celebrate popular aims, the vox populi, and the woman's voice.[7]

---

[7] Since this essay was composed, other scholars have written accounts of Wordworth's engagement with "the feminine" in *Lyrical Ballads*. See in particular Pinch 1988 and Wolfson 1994.

4

Postscripts To Emily Dickinson
(Meditations on E. D. excerpted from recent writings)

SUSAN HOWE

An idea of the author Emily Dickinson—her symbolic value and aesthetic function—has been shaped by *The Poems of Emily Dickinson; Including Variant Readings Critically Compared with All Known Manuscripts*, edited by Thomas H. Johnson and first published by the Belknap Press of Harvard University Press in 1951, later digested into a one-volume edition, to which I do not refer because of Johnson's further acknowledged editorial emendations. For a long time I believed that this editor had given us the poems as they looked. Nearly forty years later, *The Manuscript Books of Emily Dickinson*, edited by R.W. Franklin and again published by the Belknap Press of Harvard University Press in 1981, and *The Master Letters of Emily Dickinson*, also edited by R.W. Franklin, in 1986, this time published by the Amherst College Press, show me that in a system of restricted exchange, the subject-creator and her art in its potential gesture were domesticated and occluded by an assumptive privileged Imperative.

Fire May Be Raked Up in the Ashes, Though Not Seen

Words are only frames. No comfortable conclusion. Letters are scrawls, turnabouts, astonishments, strokes, cuts, masks.

These poems are representations. These manuscripts should be understood as visual productions.

The physical act of copying is a mysterious sensuous expression.

Wrapped in the mirror of the word.

Most often these poems were copied onto sheets of stationary previously folded by the manufacturer. The author paid attention to the smallest physical details of the page. Embossed seals in the corner of recto and verso leaves of paper are part of the fictitious real.

Spaces between letters, dashes, apostrophes, commas, crosses, form networks of signs and discontinuities.

"Train up a Heart in the way it should go and as quick as it can twill depart from it."[1]

Mystery is the content. Intractable expression. Deaf to rules of composition.

What is writing but continuing.

Who knows what needs she has?

The greatest trial is trust.

Fire in the heart overcomes fire without

Disjunct Leaves

Emily Dickinson almost never titled a poem.

She titled poems several times.

She drew an ink slash at the end of a poem.

Sometimes she didn't.

She seldom used numbers to show where a word or a poem should go.

She sometimes used numbers to show where a word or line should go.

The poems in packets and sets can be read as a linked series.

The original order of the packets was broken by her friends and first editors so that even R. W. Franklin—the one scholar, apart from the curator of manuscripts, allowed unlimited access to the originals at Harvard University's Houghton Library—can be absolutely sure only of a particular series order for poems on a single folded sheet of stationery.

Maybe the poems in a packet were copied down in random order and the size of letter paper dictated a series; maybe not.

When she sent her first group of poems to T. W. Higginson, she sent them separately but together.

She chose separate poems from the packets to send to friends.

Sometimes letters are poems with a salutation and signature.

Sometimes poems are letters with a salutation and signature.

If limits disappear where will we find bearings?

What were her intentions for these crosses and word lists?

If we could perfectly restore each packet to its original order, her original impulse would be impossible to decipher. The manuscript books and

---

[1] Emily Dickinson, *The Letters of Emily Dickinson*, ed. Thomas H. Johnson and Theodora Ward, 3 vols. (Cambridge: Belknap Press of Harvard University Press, 1958), p. 928.

sets preserve their insubordination. They can be read as events, signals in a pattern, relays, inventions or singular hymn-like stanzas.

T.W. Higginson wrote in his preface to *Poems by Emily Dickinson* (1890): "The verses of Emily Dickinson belong emphatically to what Emerson long since called 'The Poetry of the Portfolio,'—something produced absolutely without the thought of publication, and solely by way of the writer's own mind.... They are here published as they were written, with very few and superficial changes; although it is fair to say the titles have been assigned, almost invariably, by the editors."[2]

But the poet's manuscript books and sets had already been torn open. Their contents had been sifted, translated, titled, then regrouped under categories called, by her two first editor-"friends": "Life," "Love," "Nature," "Time and Eternity."

A Rigorous Line

In 1986 Ralph Franklin sent me a copy of *The Master Letters of Emily Dickinson*, published by the Amherst College Press. Along with *The Manuscript Books*, this is the most important contribution to Dickinson scholarship I know of. In this edition Franklin decided on a correct order for the letters, showed facsimiles, and had them set in type on each facing page, with the line breaks as she made them. I wrote him a letter again suggesting that if he broke the lines here, according to the original text, he might consider doing the same for the poems. He thanked me for my "immodest" compliments and said he had broken the letters line-for-physical-line only to make reference to the facsimiles easier; if he were editing a book of the letters, he would use run-on treatment as there is no expected genre form for prose. He told me there is such a form for poetry and he intended to follow it, rather than accidents of physical line breaks on paper.

As a poet I cannot assert that Dickinson composed in stanzas and was careless about line breaks. In the precinct of Poetry, a word, the space around a word, each letter, every mark, silence, or sound volatizes an inner law of form—moves on a rigorous line.

Singularities

I always think of my work in terms of separate poems in one long poem—that each page (usually it's a page) can stand alone and together:

---

[2] Emily Dickinson, *Poems by Emily Dickinson*, ed. Mabel Loomis Todd and T. W. Higginson (Boston: Roberts Bros., 1890), p. iii.

one reason for calling my book *Singularities*. So although on one level I think the order can't be broken up, on another I mean it to be able to be broken. The following poems have been broken off from the long sequence "Thorow" in *Singularities*.[3]

---

[3] Quoted from private correspondence with the editors.

The Source of Snow
the nearness of Poetry

The Captain of Indians
the cause of Liberty

Mortal particulars
whose shatter we are

A sort of border life
A single group of trees

Sun on our back

Unappropriated land
all the works and redoubts

Young pine in a stand of oak
young oak in a stand of pine

Expectation of Epiphany

Not to look off from it
but to look at it

Original of the Otherside
understory of anotherword

The track of Desire

Must see and and not see

Must not see nothing

Burrow and so burrow

Measuring mastering

When ice breaks up

at the farthest north

of Adirondack peaks

So empty and so empty

Go back for your body
Hindge

5

"Faith in Anatomy":
Reading Emily Dickinson

VIRGINIA JACKSON

Suppose you are sorting through the effects of a woman who has just died and you find in her bedroom a large locked wooden box. You open the box and discover hundreds of sheets of stationery stitched together with string. Other sheets are loose, torn into small pieces, occasionally pinned together; there is writing on a guarantee issued by the German Student Lamp Co., on memo paper advertising the HOME INSURANCE CO. NEW YORK ("Cash Assets, OVER SIX MILLION DOLLARS"), on many split-open envelopes, on a single strip three-quarters of an inch wide by twenty-one inches long, on thin bits of butcher paper. There is writing clustered around a three-cent postage stamp of a steam engine turned on its side, which secures two magazine clippings bearing the names "George Sand" and "Mauprat." Now suppose that you recognize these writings as *poems*. You regret following the writer's instruction to burn her bundles of correspondence upon her death. What remains, you decide, must be published.[1]

Let this brief exercise serve as some measure of what now, a century after the scene in which you have just been asked to place yourself, can and cannot be imagined about reading Emily Dickinson. If my experiment was successful, what the reader may have been able to hold in mind are odd images of the historical details of Dickinson's writing. Do these eccentric materials *matter* to the poetry that has been read off of

---

[1] In a letter to Mrs. C. S. Mack, Dickinson's sister Lavinia wrote, "I found, (the week after her death) a box (locked) containing seven hundred wonderful poems, carefully copied" (17 February 1891) (cited in Bingham 1945:18). I have liberally altered the letter's account by imposing upon it my own experience of discovering the diversity of Dickinson's less carefully copied manuscripts (which may or may not have been in the box that Lavinia Dickinson unlocked) in Amherst College Library's Special Collections. I am grateful to the staff of Special Collections for their generous aid and shared excitement.

them? In some ways, no. The pencil draft of "After a hundred years" (poem 1147), for example, could not be said to refer to the domestic list on the back of the page on which it was written.[2]

> After a hundred years
> Nobody +knows the place
> Agony that enacted there
> Motionless as Peace
>
> Weeds triumphant ranged
> Strangers strolled and spelled
> At the lone Orthography
> Of the Elder Dead
>
> Winds of Summer Fields
> Recollect the way—
> Instinct picking up the Key
> Dropped by memory—
> +knew
>
> [verso]
> Prunes—
> Apple—
> Graham Bread
> Conservatory
> Dough nuts

All that these two texts have in common is paper. After a hundred years, the poem has passed into the cultural memory instituted by literature; the miscellany has been consigned to the scholar's documentary interest. Yet precisely for that reason, it is the latter that may affect us now with some of the uncanny power contained in the poem's central pun on reading. The "Strangers" who discover the traces of the dead are "spelled" from their stroll by stopping to read them; in order to do so, they must "spell" out "the lone Orthography" that indicates the dead's now "Motionless" presence; so spelling, these strollers may fall under the spell of the dead's strangeness. That effect depends on an act of deciphering that is epistemologically incomplete, since it cannot grant

[2] The draft is the only manuscript version of this poem, in the Amherst College Special Collections (envelope 98). Dickinson's poems and letters will be indexed in my pages by their numbers in the Johnson editions (Dickinson 1955, 1958). The variants in the manuscripts will be reprinted here by + symbols that stand for the many kinds of xs that Dickinson used to mark words added in the margins of her texts.

the dead new life: these are strangers, after all, with no direct experience of the past, and the "lone Orthography" does not, in the poem, eventuate in the proper names of "the Elder Dead" (except, perhaps, in the initials E.D.). The readers in and of this poem thus speculate in specular fashion, doubly identified and doubly self-estranged by their interruption by the spirits of "the place." In this place, the pathos of history ("Agony that enacted there") has been reduced to an inscription only "Winds" know how to read—which is to say that no one does. The habits of "memory"—received modes of identifying writing and reference in the person of a living subject—have been displaced by an "Instinct" that hovers between perception and cognition, between the musical "Key" one might hear on the wind and the "Key" to a foreclosed interpretation.

In both of these examples—in my borrowed scenario of the as-yet-unread and in Dickinson's fiction of the no-longer-legible—what is missing is the established literary character that will inevitably influence actual readers who encounter Dickinson's work not in these conjured places but in classrooms, anthologies, and editions. The truth is that we know too much about "Emily Dickinson"—poet, recluse, Myth of Amherst—to be able to imagine her "Orthography" as anything stranger (or more historically distant) than the traces of a subject who will already have been remembered. In this essay, I want both to acknowledge that no current reading of Dickinson can escape this inherited knowledge (mythic as it may be) and at the same time to point to some of the ways in which her writing might escape the tradition of interpretation to which it has been subject. Since two of the distinctions that characterize that tradition also account for the caricature of the poetess in white so widely circulated within it, any discussion of Dickinson's relation to the categories of *gender* and *genre* must itself be circular. It would hardly be an exaggeration to say that the last century's ideas about kinds of persons as well as kinds of poems have been successively personified by Dickinson: by the isolated private genius composing only for herself, by the neglected proto-modernist writing for an audience she had yet to create, by the artist crafting gems of timeless hermetic verse, by the renegade subverting the precepts of her society, by the woman working against the grain of patriarchy, by the writer taking up and forging a women's literary tradition, by the lesbian retreating from and challenging straight norms, by the privileged white woman addressing her familiars from the comfort of her big house. While most serious interpretations of the poetry do not, of course, devolve into such parodies, they do tend to depend upon what Timothy Morris has called "a poetics of presence," which "entails the values of originality, organicism, and monologism" (1995:2). Poststructuralist critiques of these values have gone some way toward unsettling stereotypes of the Dickinsonian poetic presence, and yet the recursive logics of the lyric genre in which Dickinson's work has been received and of the gendered identity that has served to narrate her relation to that genre inevitably implicate the person in the poems. Even if one were to show that Dickinson's writing was largely citational, thoroughly textual, and intricately dialogic, its subject would still "spell" Emily Dickinson.

Recent feminist theory has been vitally concerned with the forms of personal survival available in women's writing—"vitally" so since the rationale of feminism is at stake in them.[3] Despite Judith Butler's assurance that "the category of women does not become useless through deconstruction, but becomes one whose uses are no longer reified as 'referents,' and which stand a chance of coming to signify in ways that none of us can predict in advance" (1993:29), feminists are understandably anxious about the political costs of "opening up" for future use a "category" already layered with historical significance. Recent literary criticism has also worried over the erosion of its founding principles, notably those of genre. The post-Romantic lyric in particular has been a site of critical debate in the wake of the teachings of Paul de Man, who went so far as to claim that "the lyric is not a genre, but one name among several to designate the defensive motion of the understanding, the possibility of a future hermeneutics" (1984:261). Because this hermeneutics issues from the subjectivist tradition that the nineteenth-century lyric's intersubjective structure confirms, identity—not only the lyric "I" but also the reader's "defensive" investment in it—is itself, in every sense, in question in de Man's rhetorical abolition of the genre to which much of his work was devoted (Culler 1988). Yet once gender and genre "are no longer reified as 'referents,' " what are they by other names? Who—or what—comes after the subject?[4]

Dickinson has epitomized assumptions about both literary and personal identity for some of the same reasons that reading her may lead us through—that is, into if not to the other side of —those assumptions. The impulse of the first part of this essay is thus historical, for it attempts

[3] Mary Loeffelholz's question at the end of her book on Dickinson is still the best one for feminist criticism generally, and it has proven far from rhetorical: "What theoretical challenges to the metaphysics of self-presence, what forms of psychic ambivalence, what gaps between revisionary intentions in language and actual linguistic performances, what absences, what distances, what differences (apart from those with a male-authored tradition) can feminist critics entertain with respect to women writers?" (1991:170).

[4] As many readers will recognize, this sentence is an only slightly altered version of the title of a recent collection of philosophical essays by many hands (including those of Blanchot, Derrida, Irigaray, Lacoue-Labarthe, and Nancy) on the status of national, sexual, historical, and written identity for what may be broadly designated as poststructuralism (Cadava, Connor, and Nancy 1991). My citational reiteration of the title's question is not intended to imply that it is the only question one might ask but that it is the one everyone (who is anyone?) seems to be asking.

to trace an arc away from the last hundred years' concentration on the question of subjective reference. Its question might instead be phrased: "How do poems come to be read *as* persons?" For two very different thinkers in Dickinson's immediate intellectual culture, the answer seems to have been that the literal characters of the page—not only those of poetry but those of writing itself—were taken to be instinct with embodiment. In the fantasy of the incarnate letter that emerged in mid-nineteenth-century American thought, reading implicitly became identified with the immediate perception of the human body. If that seems a strange idea, perhaps it is so both because of the difference between Dickinson's historical moment and our own *and* because the referential assumptions of that moment still subtend our own. That, in any case, is the implication of the Dickinson texts I turn to in the second part of the essay. In one fairly minor poem and in the fragment of a private letter, I explore Dickinson's explicit analogies between writing and embodiment as well as her attempts to split the rhetoric of those analogies from within. Since such associations are deeply inscribed in the representative versions of the genre that defined her practice as well as in representations of the gender that defined her person, by employing them Dickinson's writing indeed "opened up" both categories in ways that have yet to be predicted. If we can place ourselves neither before nor after the history of reading Emily Dickinson as a literary subject, in a place "Nobody knows" or *"knew,"* we may still learn to read her with almost as little hermeneutic defensiveness as she read herself. Almost. As Dickinson wrote of another poetic institution, "While Shakespeare remains Literature is firm—An Insect cannot run away with Achilles' Head" (letter 368).

I

In his collection *Women and the Alphabet* (assembled in 1900, though several of the essays were written earlier), Thomas Wentworth Higginson, Dickinson's literary correspondent and posthumous editor, told a story about "the Invisible Lady" who,

> as advertised in all our cities a good many years ago, was a mysterious individual who remained unseen, and had apparently no human organs except a brain and a tongue. You asked questions of her, and she made intelligent answers; but where she was, you could no more discover than you could find the man inside the Automaton Chess-Player. Was she intended as a satire on womankind, or as a sincere representation of what womankind should be? To many men, doubtless, she would have seemed

the ideal of her sex, could only her brain and tongue have disappeared like the rest of her faculties. Such men would have liked her almost as well as that other mysterious personage on the London signboard, labeled "The Good Woman," and represented by a female figure without a head. (Higginson 1900:66–67).

Higginson's interest here, as in his initial feminist argument in "Ought Women to Learn the Alphabet?" forty years earlier, is in the cultural enfranchisement—the cultural presence—of women.[5] It is in the service of enfranchisement that he invokes the prejudice of the "many men" who idealize female obscurity in the public sphere, men who either render "womankind" incorporeal or who prefer their projected "mysterious personage" as a personification without a head. Yet which is it to be? To be all mind or to be all body is to be "invisible" in very different ways. The severed expression of "a brain and a tongue" exerts a personal agency opposite to that of the obscenely decapitated "Good Woman"; indeed, one wonders how the Invisible Lady could be told apart from "the man inside the Automaton Chess Player" except by the advertiser's label required to identify the person within the machine. That the men who mythologized her "would have liked her almost as well" as her exclusively sexualized counterpart reveals less, perhaps, from our perspective, about the misogyny Higginson condemns than it does about his own symptomatic confusion over where to locate (or how to anatomize) the gendered identity for which he assumed advocacy. Talking head or mute body—which would mark woman's characteristic acquisition of the alphabet, which one admit her to the culture of letters that would confer an identifiable written persona, a *literal* figural visibility?

Higginson's point, of course, is that, for the humanist project he has in mind, neither bisection will do. "Ceasing to be an Invisible Lady," the lettered woman "must become a visible force: there is no middle ground" (p.67).Yet the force made visible by the disciplinary power of the alphabet remains entrenched in this middle ground in Higginson's feminist writings. In an essay on Sappho in 1871, for example, Higginson sought to endorse F. G. Welcker's 1816 article "Sappho Vindicated from a Prevailing Prejudice" by enforcing the distinction between autobiographical and dramatic reference in poetry. In response to another

[5] "Ought Women to Learn the Alphabet?" first appeared in the *Atlantic Monthly* for February 1859 (three years before the issue of that journal in which Higginson published "Letter to a Young Contributor," the article to which Dickinson responded by sending him samples of her poems). In a prefatory note to the 1900 volume, Higginson claims that his earlier advocacy has already had "liberal" cultural effects, citing "a report that it was the perusal of this essay which led the late Miss Sophia Smith to the founding of the women's college bearing her name."

German scholar who emphasized Sappho's apparently lesbian eroticism, Higginson thus writes, "He reads [Sappho's] graceful fragments as the sailors in some forecastle might read Juliet's soliloquies, or as a criminal lawyer reads in court the letters of some warm-hearted woman; the shame lying not in the words, but in the tongue" (Higginson 1882:313). The "tongue" that tells Sappho's graceful fragments as dirty jokes is in this case a synecdoche for a perjoratively masculinized representative body (a sailor, a criminal lawyer) that commits the vulgar faux pas of taking literature—and especially poetry—literally. "It is as if one were to cite Browning into court and undertake to convict him, on his own confession, of sharing every mental condition he describes." Yet even as he indicts the becoming-literal of the literary—and the becoming-personal of personae—as a modern corruption more threatening than the sexual "cloud of reproach" it evokes, Higginson ends by displaying Sappho-the-woman as the index of his own civilizing aspirations. Whatever her life may turn out to have been, Higginson writes, "Sappho is gone," and "modern nations must take up again the problem where Athens failed and Lesbos only pointed the way to the solution,—to create a civilization where the highest culture will be extended to woman also. It is not enough that we should dream, with Plato, of a republic where man is free and woman but a serf. The aspirations of modern life culminate, like the greatest of modern poems, in the elevation of womanhood. *Die ewige Weibliche zieht uns hinan*"(324).

Under the sign of modernity, national and gendered identities are married in order to reproduce themselves as "the highest culture," a culture reembodied by the now elevated—because dead—woman and by the characters of a literary language. The idealizing decorporealization of power that Higginson caricatured in "the Invisible Lady" he reads in a sincere register in his citation of Goethe's *Faust*. Unattributed and untranslated at the end of his essay, Higginson's allusion addresses an imagined community of educated readers of belles lettres, readers who are charged with reversing the errors of the sailors and lawyers, who recognize the ideally transcendent (rather than perversely literal) identity between gender and genre. Yet even in the optative temporality into which the greatest of modern poems projects us (*zieht uns hinan*) Higginson's reiteration of the *grammatical* gender of Goethe's "eternal feminine" makes a quite literal slip. While the conceptual referent of *Weibliche* may seem to demand a feminine article, it is in the German language neuter: Goethe's line reads not *Die ewige Weibliche* but *Das ewig-Weibliche*. On the level of the alphabet, then, the difference an article (or three letters) can make enacts the conflation of gender and genre called forth by Higginson's citation. That is, it unwittingly performs the fantasy that grammar, like an anatomy, would not be gendered by arbitrary signs attached to a concatenation of mute bodies but would be subsumed by the eloquent rhetoric of natural law—the law of an embodied writing.

Unfortunately, this is not the occasion to explore the extraordinary complication of Higginson's intertextual examples of the relation between literal and literary womanhood, though they include not only Sappho, Faust, and Browning but also the notoriously public literary personae of Margaret Fuller and George Sand. Before turning to a consideration of writings of the woman poet he introduced into this company in 1890 as one who "habitually concealed her mind, like her person, from all but a very few friends," who "was as invisible to the world as if she had dwelt in a nunnery" (Higginson 1890:iii), I want instead to turn briefly to an unlikely analog to the theory of anatomically scripted reference that Higginson's anecdotes and allusions tended to perform. During the 1860s and 1870s, when Higginson was writing his *Atlantic* essays in Cambridge and Dickinson was writing in Amherst, the philosopher Charles Saunders Peirce was developing in his early lectures at Harvard the semiotic logic that became the basis of American pragmatism. According to this logic, reference is always an emphatically empirical matter: as Peirce has it, "Nothing is assumed [in the semiotic] respecting what is thought which cannot be securely inferred from admissions which the thinker will make concerning external facts" (1982: 518). As Peirce represents these "facts," however, what is most secure about them is that they are, like Higginson's examples, based on the assumption that identity, in order to be empirically indicative, must both be modeled on the principles of natural law and at the same time be susceptible to the abstraction of written representation. Indeed, Peirce's creation of the semiotic appears to have depended upon his presentation of writing as already embodied.

Thus in the lecture entitled "On a Method of Searching for the Categories" (1866), the three aspects of the semiotic—the "ground," the "correlate," and the "interpretant"—all exhibit, in Peirce's illustratively pragmatic examples, the phantasmatic "fact" of the incarnate letter. His remarkable instance of the primary "ground" of referential thought is the proposition "Ink is black." "Here," Peirce writes—in one of many uses of the deictic to express the principle of deixis—"the conception of *ink* is the more immediate; that of *black* the more mediate, which to be predicated of the former must be discriminated from it and considered *in itself* not as applied to an object but simply as embodying a quality, *blackness*. Now this *blackness*, is a pure *species* or abstraction, and its application is entirely hypothetical." Although Peirce's term for "these conceptions between *being* and *substance*" is "*accidents*"(1982:521), there is, I would argue, nothing accidental about his use of a thematics "embodying" writing to describe the process of cognition. In the proposition

"Ink is black," *ink* is the *substance* of the proposition. As such, according to Peirce, it has no *being*, for "to say that *substance* has being is absurd for it must cease to be substance before being or non-being are applicable to it."(1982:518) The definition of a substance is, then, that it can only find "being"—which, for semiosis, must mean *meaning*—only by embodying an apprehensible "quality"; it is this quality, and not the mute substance to which it attaches, that serves as the referential basis for the passage of perception into legibility. "We mean the same thing when we say 'the ink is black,' " Peirce writes, "as when we say 'there is blackness in the ink': *embodying blackness* defines *black*"(521). Because "*embodying blackness* defines *black*," blackness becomes what Peirce calls a "pure abstraction," an elementary conception that can "arise only upon the requirement of experience"(522). We experience blackness; ink embodies this experience; ergo, blackness gives meaning to what defines it *as* a referent. Blackness is what the ink-body means. And it may go without saying that in the United States in 1866, such a structure of meaning naturally (as it were) allows particular bodies to be signed into the cultural semantics of "blackness."[6]

This is to say that the theory of indexical meaning that Peirce developed turns personified abstractions into persons through the agency of the letter already embedded in the nineteenth-century American unconscious. The third, synthesizing stage of the semiotic, the stage of "representation," makes most explicit—and most problematic—the logic that transforms ink into bodies and bodies into ink. Because Peirce sees clearly that referential meaning depends on the structure of a comparison (this he calls the "correlate"), it is his articulation of that structure that bears the weight of his theory. It is also, then, in his representative examples of representation that we find the most complex and revealing description of the mutual implication of anatomized letters and literalized anatomies. What we may also find there, I will suggest, is this implication's potential resistance to a theory that may also serve as a cultural index.

Because both such a complicity and such a resistance may be traced not only in the examples themselves but in the way the logic moves between them—as Peirce would say, in the elementary conceptions entailed in their comparison—I will cite the passage on representation at some length in order to ask my reader to attend to the analogies through

[6] It would be interesting to consider the racist overtones of Peirce's theory of indexical reference in relation to Karen Sanchez-Eppler's work on the complex rhetorical relations between abstract and corporeal personhood in various discourses of antebellum culture (Sanchez-Eppler 1993). Those overtones would also bear consideration in relation to the genealogy of American pragmatism, and particularly to recent empiricist trends in the American literary criticism philosophically indebted to it.

which one substance becomes a quality and again a substance, one letter becomes a body and again a letter:

> Reference to a correlate is clearly justified and made possible solely by comparison. Let us inquire, then, in what comparison consists. Suppose we wish to compare L and Γ; we shall imagine one of these letters to be turned over upon the line on which it is written as an axis; we shall then imagine that it is laid upon the other letter and that it is transparent so that we can see that the two coincide. In this way, we shall form a new image which mediates between the two letters, in as much as it represents one when turned over to be an exact likeness of the other. Suppose, we think of a murderer as being in relation to a murdered person; in this case we conceive the act of the murder, and in this conception it is represented that corresponding to every murderer (as well as to every murder) there is a murdered person; and thus we resort again to a mediating representation which represents the relate as standing for a correlate with which the mediating representation is itself in relation. Suppose, we look out the word *homme* in a French dictionary; we shall find opposite to it the word *man*, which, so placed, represents *homme* as representing the same two-legged creature which *man* itself represents. In a similar way, it will be found that every comparison requires, besides the related thing, the ground and the correlate, also a *mediating representation which represents the relate to be a representation of the same correlate which this mediating representation itself represents.* Such a mediating representation, I call an *interpretant*, because it fulfills the office of an interpreter who says that a foreigner says the same thing which he himself says. (522–23)

A transparent letter L, the act of murder, a two-legged creature, the translation of a foreign language: these are the instances Peirce offers to fulfill "the office" of representation. The story that this sequence itself tells about that office would fill volumes—but let me just point to its cast of characters. First, enter the material letter L and its transposition: this character is "material" because it may be manipulated into a mark that can be *seen* but not read. According to Peirce, in order to turn seeing into "reference" (perception into cognition), we must literally translate—or carry over—one typeface to another: Γ becomes "transparent" to L in this translation, "so that we can see that the two coincide." What is canny about the instruction is that it mimes the interpretive practice that it also determines, thus making the unconditional agency of imagination (invoked by the passage's reiterated imperative, *"Suppose . . ."*) seem "an exact likeness" of a literacy already conditioning these terms. This example makes reading appear an empirical process by challenging the reader not to do it. We are not actually asked to recognize L as a letter of the roman alphabet or to interpret Γ as, say, a Greek capital gamma; we are merely asked to superimpose these shapes by lifting them, in the mind, off the page. The "new image" so lifted "mediates between the two letters" because it seems to simply reflect their anatomy rather than to construct their meaning.

Yet a murderer's relation to a murdered person could hardly be thought analogous to the "transparent" relation between a right-side-up and upside-down letter of the alphabet—or could it? In order to mediate between the terms of this second comparison, "we conceive the act of the murder," an act that acts as the film through which we are to picture—as if empirically—the two as coincidental or the same. The potential violence of the as-if quality of the notion of an empirical identity begins to emerge here as a property not only of the image of murder but also of the image of the letter (and even of the -er suffix that transliterates one into the other). That potential then underwrites, as it were, Peirce's third example, in which he synthesizes in image the imaginary play of the letter and the corpse it may leave in its wake. What unites the French *homme* and the English *man* is not the French dictionary, which merely places one word "opposite" to another, but the idea of a "two-legged creature." The representation produced by the facing-off of the two words in the lexicon (which acts, by the way, like the "new image" in the passage's first example and like the ink in Peirce's earlier proposition, as the mute reflective substance of this apposition, its mirror) has a long history in letters. From Oedipus's riddle to Shakespeare's "bare forked animal," the two-leggedness of the "creature which *man* itself represents" has stood as the problematic figure of the human sacrifice entailed in the semiosis of the human. The potentially tragic consequences of anatomizing h-o-m-m-e or m-a-n *as if* the word were not itself the creature of Western strategies of representation—that is, as if an alphabet could be translated into perception as a transparently self-identified body—may cause Peirce to "sa[y] the same thing which he himself says," and yet to end up writing something different.

The difference inherent in each of Peirce's suppositions is, of course, the subjective agency invoked in and as the very "mediating representation" that is directed to translate them as instances of the same. His description ends up performing exactly the opposite "office" than the one it states as its purpose because he grounds it in the anatomical imaginary his thought implicitly associates with the materiality of writing. Walter Benn Michaels and Michael Fried have argued that such an association characterizes various American texts of the second half of the nineteenth century in which "writing as such becomes an epitome of a notion of identity as difference from itself (in that writing *to be* writing must in some sense be different from the mark that simply materially it is); and that this is important above all because, in those texts and others, the possibility of difference from itself emerges as crucial to a concept of personhood that would distinguish persons from both pure spirit . . . and from pure matter" (Fried 1987:163; see also Michaels 1987:21). If indeed Benn Michaels and Fried are right to point to writing as "an epitome" of mid- to late-nineteenth-century versions of subjectivity, even my brief examples from Higginson and Peirce suggest that they may be cutting off (that is, themselves literally *epitomizing*) half of the analogy's point. The spirit of the person may well have been thought comparable to the spirit of the letter—but what happens to the body thought comparable to the "pure matter" of the letter? In the second half of this essay, I will turn to some of the ways in which Dickinson raised this question from within her culture's rhetorical inscription of personhood. Because the relation between the ideality and materiality of personhood and the ideality and materiality of writing was already embedded in the theory of the genre that defined Dickinson's rhetorical practice, her own linguistic performances often turned a precise and excruciating focus on the role of interpreter who, like Higginson and Peirce, would suppose that letters could refer—even in their differences—to bodies.

II

Consider what the following short poem (probably written around 1864 and sewn into one of the "stitched together" packets found in the locked box) does to the notion of subjective—and anatomically inscribed—lyric reference:

Split the Lark—and you'll find the Music—
Bulb after Bulb, in Silver rolled—
Scantily dealt to the Summer Morning
Saved for your Ear when Lutes be old.

Loose the Flood—you shall find it patent—
Gush after Gush, reserved for you—
Scarlet Experiment! Sceptic Thomas!
Now, do you doubt that your Bird was true?

(poem 861)

To anticipate my argument by stating the obvious: this text stages the act of its own reading in sadomasochistic terms. What is perhaps less obvious about this rather offensive staging is that its terms are drawn from a nineteenth-century discourse already troubled by the approach to written—and particularly literary—representation that Dickinson here parodies. By "perhaps less obvious," I mean that literary critics since 1896, when the poem was first printed, have consistently interpreted it as the poet's lyrical send-up of scientific empiricism, an anonymous reviewer for the October 1896 *Boston Beacon* going so far as to suggest that it be read as the bird's dramatic monologue. "Miss Dickinson rarely falls into another's manner," the reviewer remarks, "but could Browning himself have bettered this?" Such an odd aesthetic apprehension of Dickinson's text may be due in part to the rather odd title given the poem by its first editor, Mabel Loomis Todd: "Loyalty." The literary framing—bound publication, title, critical review—seems to have invited a legacy of the sort of educated response that Higginson (that other reader of Browning) would have counted on. Thus a more recent critic explains that "the poem's real meaning is inverted" so that rather than cooperating with the demand for proof, "this poetic experiment effectively disposes of the empirical approach" (Weisbuch 1972: 160). One sees the point: poetic trope reverses apparent meaning, whether in the Victorian personage of a dramatic speaker or in the New Critical understanding of the artistic function of irony. Either way, the image that mediates between the letters on the page and their "real" meaningful inversion is Literature (and especially Lyric) with a capital L. Yet lyric—or, specifically, the reading of it as indexical cultural identity—may itself be the object of Dickinson's perverse anatomy lesson.

For, suppose you split a lark: what you will find, at least in Dickinson's first stanza, is poetry. Birdsong is Dickinson's figure for poetic writing in (by my last count) over three hundred texts, and it is the subject of her elegies for several other women poets, notably Charlotte Brontë and Elizabeth Barrett Browning. In the beautiful elegy for Brontë (poem 148), the death of the woman is conflated with the death of the literary pseudonym "Currer Bell," which is said to migrate as

> This Bird—observing others
> When frosts too sharp became
> Retire to other latitudes—
> Quietly did the same—
>
> But differed in returning—

The place to which "Currer Bell" differed in returning is, of course, the grave, but it is also the locus of lyric,

Since Yorkshire hills are green—
Yet not in all the nests I meet—
Can Nightingale be seen—

The invisible location of the embodied source of lyric song is the familiar topos of romantic poetics that Dickinson evokes here, for, as we remember from Shelley's figuration of it, the poet is "a nightingale, who sits in darkness and sings to cheer its own solitude with sweet sounds; his auditors are as men entranced by the melody of an unseen musician, who feel that they are moved and softened, but know not whence or why" (1987:223). In the Romantic ideal of lyric affect, bird-poets would have no bodies. In Shelley's "To a Sky-Lark," the object of poetic address is actually the literary dissolution of the body:

Hail to thee, blithe Spirit!
    Bird thou never wert—
That from Heaven, or near it,
    Pourest thy full heart
In profuse strains of unpremeditated art.

"Like an unbodied joy," Shelley's lark bleeds only music. Dickinson's lark, however, produces a bizarrely literal (or "Scarlet") version of Shelley's "profuse strains." Her parody is too strong *not* to be of Shelley, but it is also mediated by yet another nineteenth-century poetic treatment of the Shelleyan lyric ideal, a rather incidental passage in Barrett Browning's *Aurora Leigh* in which the poet Aurora reflects that

The music soars within the little lark,
And the lark soars. It is not thus with men.
We do not make our places with our strains,
Content, while they rise, to remain behind
Alone on earth instead of so in heaven.
                            (3.151–55)[7]

That the difference between real and metaphorical identities should be remarked by a woman poet writing a poem about the career of a woman poet who is writing a poem alluding to Shelley goes some way toward indicating how intimately sexual difference is associated with literary

---

[7] Helen McNeil notes the passage in Barrett Browning (1864:82) in connection with Dickinson's poem, claiming that Barrett Browning's "feminist distinction between womanly song and male song is unmistakable" (1986:96). It seems to me, however, that if "we" are "men," the gendered referents here must be less stable than that.

anatomies in the several birds Dickinson's text (with such violence toward the letter of its sources) begins to splinter. The "Bulb after Bulb, in Silver rolled—" revealed in her first stanza echoes her elegy for Barrett Browning in which she declares that "Silver—perished—with her Tongue—" (poem 312). In the elegy, written perhaps two years earlier than "Split the Lark," the relation between the poet and her aesthetic trace is also cast as consubstantial, nature and artifice having become impossible to tell apart:

> Not on Record—bubbled other,
> Flute—or Woman—
> So divine—

Yet whereas the elegy mourns the mutual passing of "Silver" and Tongue," "Flute—or Woman—," its conclusion also plays upon a way in which writing might alter personhood, and particularly sexual identity, as well as already be inscribed within it: "What, and if, Ourself a Bridegroom— / Put her down—in Italy?" The place in which Barrett Browning made her last strains is here imagined—if only in double hesitation—as a land in which lyric strains would make "our places" different. In the later poem, however, such a utopian possibility is checked by the second stanza's incorporation of a reader who will insist that the lyric subject, in its very ethereal character, remain identifiably corporeal.

To return for a moment, then, in a different strain, to the structure of Peirce's literally anatomized semiotic, what Dickinson's second stanza does is to expose the "ground" of lyric reference as the oxymoron of an embodied abstraction. While Shelley's poem, bent on abstracting embodiment, is addressed to the lark, and Barrett Browning's is addressed to the pathos of such abstraction, Dickinson's addresses "Sceptic Thomas," the type par excellence of the interpreter who demands that cognitive apprehension be secured by the evidence and pathos of physical fact. Christ, we recall, admonishes Thomas for his need for substantiation, but the story of Thomas, told at the end of John, is also the occasion for one of the paradigmatic teachings of the incarnation:

> Now Thomas, one of the twelve, called the Twin, was not with them when Jesus came. So the other disciples told him, "We have seen the Lord." But he said to them, "Unless I see in his hands the print of the nails, and place my finger in the mark of the nails, and place my hand in his side, I will not believe."
> Eight days later, his disciples were again in the house, and Thomas was with them. The doors were shut, but Jesus came and stood among them, and said "Peace be with you." Then he said to Thomas, "Put your finger

here, and see my hands; and put out your hand, and place it in my side;
do not be faithless, but believing." (John 20:24–29, RSV)

Perhaps Thomas should not want to touch Christ's wounds; but as Elaine
Scarry has read this passage, what Thomas finds in Christ's flesh is that
"the Word of God materializes itself in the body of God, thereby locating
voice and body, creator and created, in the same site, no longer stranded
from one another as separate categories, thus also inviting humanity to
recognize themselves as, although created, simultaneously creators"
(1985:217). Thomas's function is thus not only that of the interpreter but,
in Peirce's terms, of the *interpretant*: he is himself a "mediating representation." As such, he performs the creative office of mirroring the spiritual
materiality of the embodied God—yet Dickinson's version of that reflection is rather more disturbing than Scarry's. As Christopher Benfey has
pointed out, Dickinson's "Thomas's doubt and his demand for proof are
as faithless and murderous as the demands of the crucifiers" (Benfey
1984: 94). Murderous, yes. But perhaps Thomas's "demand for proof"
has such tragic consequences in the poem not because of his skepticism
but because he represents the cultural belief that the "patent" poetic
subject—both opened or dilated and published under an official seal—
is not composed of separate categories but is materialized in and as writing.

   That, at least, is the suggestion of another of Dickinson's texts in which
Thomas's demand to touch the word effects a dismemberment of the
identities ascribed to both gender and genre. This text is from one of
Dickinson's infamous "Master" letters—the letters "patent," we might
say, of Dickinson studies, the manuscripts that appear to offer the most
enticing clues to the identity of the woman behind the poems and
therefore to officiate most authoritatively in their interpretation. Preserved in their unaddressed envelopes (they appear to be fair copies),
and left unpublished in their entirety for almost a century, these letters
have come to bear "the burden of proof" (Pollak 1984:90) for the shelves
of narratives generated by Dickinson's writing: her attachment to a married clergyman, her fantasies about a married journalist, her schizophre-
nia, her abortion, her lesbian desire. The creative recognition that these
private letters have invited has indeed located voice and body "in the
same site." The following letter, however, seems in light of our present
discussion (which is to say, because of the story I am now generating
from it) to hint at what remains dangerous about such mutual loca-
tions—not only when, as Higginson would have it, the literal takes the
place of the literary, but when the literary assumes the status of the
literal.

   Here is the opening of the letter:

Master—

If you saw a bullet hit a Bird—and he told you he wasn't shot—you might weep at his courtesy, but you would certainly doubt his word—

One drop more from the gash that stains you Daisy's bosom—then would you *believe?* Thomas' faith in anatomy—was stronger than his faith in faith.[8]

Three discrete representations of the relation between body and voice, sentience and written expression make up this appeal. The first is hypothetical: imagine, reader, that a bird who could talk (a poetic text?) "told you he wasn't shot" when you had seen the wound with your own eyes. As in "Split the Lark," the assumption here is that the wounded body will make the more compelling claim on the imagination. Bullets don't lie. ("Suppose, we think of a murderer as being in relation to a murdered person; in this case we conceive of the act of murder"). But this is a version of substantiation in the frankly fictive conditional. When the representation of the wounded body shifts, so does the *tense* of representation: now witness, reader, "one drop more from the gash that stains your Daisy's bosom." The shift in tense can only be made on the basis of a shift in reference, from fictional "Bird" to a differently fictional "Daisy." The more intimate address of the second figure also depends on a pseudonym, but here it is a more explicitly literary one, since this is the name Dickinson uses for the subject of the Master letters as well as for the subject of many poems on romantic love.[9] The "Daisy," then, bleeds (in catachresis) in the present tense but the question to the reader ("then would you *believe?*") must be phrased in a deictic indicating another conditional: the deferred time of reading. "Thomas' faith in anatomy" is by this point quite explicitly a faith in the written letter *as* an anatomy, a conviction that the "one drop more . . . that stains your Daisy's bosom" is made of ink and that this ink embodies the quality of

[8] The manuscript is number 828 in the Amherst College Library Special Collection, and identified as letter 233 in Johnson's edition, dated (from the handwriting) about 1861. Johnson places it as the second in the series of the three letters to "Master," while R. W. Franklin elaborates an argument on the basis of the handwriting that would place this letter as the final installment (Dickinson 1986). Franklin's edition reproduces the letters in facsimile—going so far as to give the reader the odd mimetic experience of opening the envelope to "discover" these intimate manuscripts.

[9] Some of the "Daisy" poems include (in Johnson's edition) poems 85, 93, 102, 106, 124, 142, 339, 411, 481, 921, and 1232. For an intricate examination of the sexual logic informing these poems, see Homans 1983. On Dickinson's play with the literary pseudonym, see Susan Howe's hyperbolic reading of these letters, particularly her suggestion that in *David Copperfield*, "Master" Davy is "Daisy" to Steerforth and that Little Emily writes "disjointed, pleading letters after eloping with Steerforth, addressed to her family, Ham, and possibly Master Davy/David/Daisy—the recipient is never directly specified, and the letters are unsigned" (1985:118–19).

an identity. Thus this Thomas is said to believe not simply that the imagery of the wounded body may be used to substantiate writing—that is, if I bleed, *then* would you believe me?—but that the materiality of writing may substantiate a body historically subject to the inversions and perversions of reading (e.g., "Put your finger here, and see my hands"). Curiously, it seems to be precisely this latter conviction—so satirically indicted in "Split the Lark" and rather more painfully and intimately exposed in the "Master" letter—that has lately begun to inform the feminist reconstruction of Dickinson as a literary subject.

There is a lot of talk these days about duplicating the poetry *"the way she wrote it,"* about going back to the original manuscripts in order to recover the authentic marks of Dickinson's hand (Bennett 1990:193). One critic has depicted the editorial alteration of these marks—and particularly those of the "Master" letters—as a "mutilation" of Dickinson the person (M. Smith 1992). As sympathetic as we should be to the scholarly project of recovering the manuscripts from the vicissitudes of canon formation and print culture, as I began this essay by suggesting, it may also be important to do so with a view toward the more fundamental problem of identifying writing too transparently with personhood—indeed, of consuming writing *as* personhood. For while Dickinson's writing often aggressively invites such readings, we should attend to the address on the invitation. Just after the lines in the letter on "Thomas's faith in anatomy" we may read (or barely discern, so much of the letter is crossed out, the words typographically bracketed here partially concealed from view; see fig. 1):

> God made me — [Sir] —/ Master —/ I didn't
> be — myself — [He] I don't know how
> it was done — He built the
> heart in me — bye and bye
> it outgrew me — and like
> the little mother — with the
> big child — I got tired
> holding him — I heard of a
> thing called "Redemption" — which
> rested men and women —
> You remember I asked you
> for it — you gave me something
> else — I forgot the Redemption
> [in the Redeemed — I didn't
> tell you for a long time — but
> I knew you had altered me —
> I] /and/ was tired — no more +

And, at the end of the letter, this insertion:

> \+ No Rose, yet felt myself a'bloom,
> No Bird — yet rode in Ether —

Having made the reader complicit in the construction of the subject, and having made jarringly explicit how that complicity shifts the place of the subject from wounded Bird to wounded Daisy to the wounded and risen Christ, the letter now reveals that the wound in identity is the wound *of* identity—a letter already written there. This inscription intensifies as well as undermines Sandra Gilbert and Susan Gubar's claim that in the way Dickinson wrote "the fiction of her life, a wound has become Dickinson's ontological home" (1979a:604). What they aptly term the "hectic rhetoric" (602) of the "Master" letter suggests that the wound is more intimate than feminist criticism generally has imagined: it is not just a theme in the writer's "fiction" but the very condition of ontology, the way the subject is "made" or "built"—or written. This is why the costs of opening it to view may also split it apart. Thus the childishly agrammatical "I didn't be—myself—" may mean both "I did not bring myself into being" and "What I am is not myself" (a pun that would make the line anything but the utterance of a childish persona). In effect, the distance between these two possibilities closes dramatically when "The heart" which is not "my heart" but "the heart in me" acquires its own agency, dwarfing the self of which it becomes much more than a part: "It outgrew me—and like the little mother—with the big child—I got tired holding him." What is built into the self turns out to have been inseminated: as this script is increasingly determined by the reader's "faith in anatomy," the body begins to be placed outside itself, assuming not only disproportionate size but a disproportionate gender. The "thing called 'Redemption'" would, presumably, if it were not in quotation marks, restore the writer to herself, but marked as the word is by its own iteration, it cannot ransom her. She receives instead "something else," is "altered" yet again, and in a way that this time occasions not a switch in gender but in genre: here the only lines of verse that punctuate the Master letters are keyed for insertion. The x that keys Dickinson's variants clearly points to this place in the letter, and yet editors continue to place the lines at the letter's conclusion—as if the final shift in genre could heal the letter's exposure of the wound of gender. "No Rose" and yet "a'bloom," "No Bird" yet "in Ether," the writer momentarily makes her places with her strains.

There is another text that these lines literally repress, however, written in ink and crosshatched in the same pencil with which the verse was written in. After "[I] / and, was tired—no more," we may read,

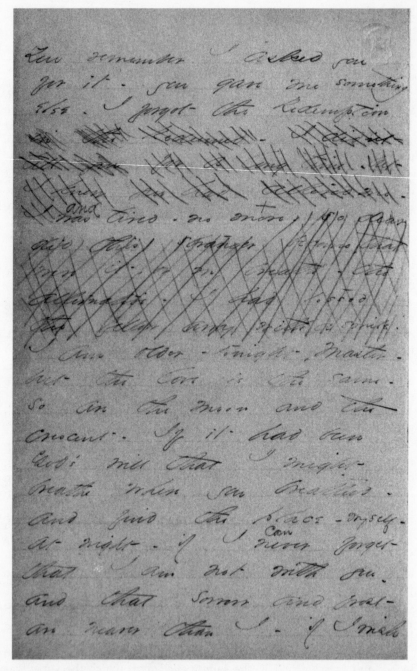

Figure 1. Manuscript no. 828 (Johnson letter 233), reproduced by permission of Amherst College Library.

with a might I cannot
express - that mine were the
Queen's place - the Loss of
the Management - is my one
Apology - to come nearer
than presbyteries - and nearer than
the new Coat - that the Tailor
made - the pranks of the Heart
at play on the Heart - in holy
Holiday - is forbidden me -
Lest make me say it over -
I fear you laugh - when I do
not see - "Chillon" is not
funny - Have you the Heart in
your Breast - Sir - is it set
like mine - a little to the left -
has it the misgiving - if it
wake in the night - perchance -
itself to it - a tune -
these things are [not] Sir,
I touch them - but -

[— so dear
did this stranger become, that
were it, or my breath — the
alternative — I had tossed
the fellow away with a smile,]

This version of redemption differs significantly from that of the lovely verse interpolation. "This stranger" is more closely related to "the big child" grown out of the built-in heart, but it is also the "something else" offered as "Redemption" for the burden of written otherness, the effect of what the addressee reclaims, "the Redeemed." The "it" that has haunted self-inscription from the beginning is at once "dear" and a "stranger," and the strangeness of its dearness becomes evident when "the alternative" of a choice between the two is posed: "Were it, or my breath—the alternative—I had tossed the fellow away with a smile." Does "the fellow" refer to "this stranger" or to "my breath"? The slip of the pen both parallels and unravels the optative verse alternative: the "No . . . yet" syntax occasioned by the shift in genre is an echo of the confusion of desire briefly exposed by the letter's grammatical confusion of gender. The lyric lines do not transcend the anatomical imaginary but repeat it in another key. Even in her inadvertently transgressive moment, the writer finds that sexual, literary identity has already arisen from the act of writing, that she has invoked the strains of "something else" in her place.

In the "Master" letter such displacements seem both tragic and inevitable (or tragic because inevitable), as in part, in the pathos of self-experience the letter represents, they must be. The mock-pathos and mock-tragedy of "Split the Lark" suggest that irony may provide a wedge between the demands of "Sceptic Thomas" and the subject of those demands, and yet the exhibition and dissection of the poetic figure are the costs of addressing the reader's doubt as well as his faith. How might we begin to read Dickinson differently, against rather than along the grain of these appeals? Can Dickinson's writing be said to alter cultural assumptions about the inscription of personal reference in any way *other* than the performance of its costs? The examples invoked at the beginning of this essay were meant to entice the reader with the possibility that other "interpretants," other forms of referential mediation, are indeed central to the conditions of Dickinson's writing—though how the material history of that writing affects interpretation we may yet be too indebted to nineteenth-century Thomases to see.

More apparent in much of Dickinson's extant work is what happens to reference when the scene of writing cannot be recovered—when there are no manuscripts to point to, and the abstractions of genre and gender are lifted off the page in their own hermeneutic spheres. That would certainly be the potential fate of the following two stanzas, taken from a transcript made by Dickinson's first editor, of which no autograph copy is known:

> "Lethe" in my flower,
> Of which they who drink
> In the fadeless orchards
> Hear the bobolink!
>
> Merely flake or petal
> As the Eye beholds
> Jupiter! my father!
> I perceive the rose!
>
> (poem 1730)

It is hard to see how these stanzas *could* be read according to a natural or empirical law of reference, a law that would make reading like perception—and yet on many levels that law is exactly what the stanzas are about. The first is a four-line condensation of Keats's Nightingale Ode (hence the citation of "Lethe" in Dickinson's first line from Keats's fourth), a variation on the play of identification with the poetic figure that we traced in "Split the Lark." Yet the substitution of the homely American "bobolink" for the nightingale's "full-throated ease" and the transference of Keats's "vintage" to the poem itself allow an astonishing shift in the referential layers intrinsic to lyric reading dissected in "Split the Lark." The alien corn in which Keats's subject must stand in relation to the "immortal bird" has been replaced by what "the eye beholds" in Dickinson. In Keats's address to the nightingale, "thy plaintive anthem fades" because it cannot be kept physically near; in Dickinson's poem, "my flower" contains "fadeless orchards" because, though "merely flake or petal," it appears to be *there* to point to. As it probably was. Despite this text's deep immersion in the referential implications of the lyric, Dickinson's habitual practice was to send such poems as letters enclosing a flower—enclosing, that is, a material synecdoche for her commentary on poetics in the context of another genre. Whether "Jupiter" names the masculine addressee (a sort of apotheosis of the "Master"), or a patriarchal principle that collapses myth into immediate perception, is anyone's guess. Half poem, half epistle, these stanzas do not finally point to "Dickinson" but toward something more like history—to a less metaphorical context now faded from view.

We can (and inevitably will) keep reading Emily Dickinson as one of the great examples of a subjectivity committed to the page. Yet the very insistence of that commitment urges us to reconsider our placement of the subject on the page, or within the identifying loops of reading through which she predicted her writing would be mastered.[10] In order to avoid simply repeating the interpretation foretold by that writing, perhaps we need to begin by imagining letters as something stranger than anatomies. One final detail of the "Master" letter manuscript is so strange that I hesitate to call attention to it, but I will end by doing so. In the section of the letter that just follows the passage cited above, Dickinson writes, "if I wish with a might I cannot repress—that mine were the Queen's place—the love of the—Plantagenet is my only apology." What "the Queen's place" might be we can only imagine, and in any case it is not much of an apology. The referent might be part of a discourse familiar to the addressee, or it might be part of the letter's ongoing struggle over the writer's "place." If we were to speculate on the image along these lines, we could refer it to the poet's depiction of herself as "The Queen of Cavalry" (poem 348) and to the desire for a queenly sovereignty that she either refuses or fails to obtain in such poems as "Of Bronze—and Blaze" (poem 290), "I'm ceded—I've stopped being Theirs" (poem 508), "Title divine—is mine" (poem 1072), or "Like Eyes that looked on Wastes" (poem 458). But there is another detail of this letter that, once noticed, might prove distracting to such a broad generic frame of reference. In a tiny frame in the left-hand corner of the stationery on which the letter is written there is the embossed head of a queen poised over the capital letter L. The first stroke of the "w" in "with" ("with a might I cannot repress") just brushes the edge of the boss's frame. The resistance that most readers will feel to any connection between the place of the queen's seal (the Queen of the L, we might say, the Queen of the Letter) and the place to which the writer's desire points may be taken as a measure of just how deeply repressed the historical scene of writing must be when the identity of the writer is prescribed in advance. In order to redeem a version of written identity from the transparency effected by the civilizing aspirations of the nineteenth-century legacy of a faith in anatomy, *what if* an "Orthography" imaged as neither warm and capable of earnest grasping nor as a dissected and speech-producing body *were* brought into view?—See, here it is—I hold it towards you.

---

[10] See, for example, the anatomically literalized reading of this manuscript suggested by William Shurr, who turns Dickinson's tortured figures into the narrative of an affair, pregnancy, and "a painful abortion which left her sick and bedridden" (1983:181).

Part II
The Voice in Question

6

On Voice

RITA DOVE

Something like a trajectory can be traced from my early poems to my current work. *The Yellow House on the Corner* (1980) was largely an apprentice book, one in which I experimented with as many different kinds of poems as possible and in which I tried to find my voice. Hence you have the nineteenth-century diction of the slave narratives, as well as the wistful, contemporary voice of a poem like "Ö." In *Museum* (1983) I was very concerned with presenting a type of antimuseum, a collection of totems that would not be considered "essential" to the canon of Western culture—and to that end I adopted a voice that was distanced, cool, ironic; of all my books, this is the most "European." After *Museum* I felt I had gone away from home and was now able to return, like a prodigal daughter. *Thomas and Beulah* (1986) represents my homecoming, being a book about my grandparents, and, on a subliminal level, a book of reconciliation with my roots. To me, *Grace Notes* (1989) was a book of freedom—having come home again, I was free to fly in whatever direction I chose.

I grew up surrounded by music and to this day study voice and play the viola da gamba. Music suffuses my work in a way that goes beyond or deeper than articulation. I believe that a poem, in some way, "sings"— that is, that the rhythms of a poem affect one as irrevocably as the words and their meanings. In poems such as "Shakespeare Say," "Gospel," and "Canary," I confront music head-on, exploring the lives and the trains of thought of those who make music. In "Shakespeare Say," the blues singer Champion Jack Dupree understands that the circumstances of his life are as much a part of the blues as his music is, that the two are of a piece. In "Gospel," the surging uplift of a gospel song surrounds the speaker of the poem, who feels as overwhelmed by the music as he does at the prospect of the woman who has entranced him. And in "Canary," the singer Billie Holiday builds consciously around herself a myth, at least that's my imagining of it, a myth of herself as "Lady Day"; because she cannot be free as a black, she builds up the myth of herself, her own voice, as a mystery. The remarkable reserve, laced with sorrow, that is so quintessentially Billie Holiday informs the pacing of the language itself. An early poem like "Ö" delights in the very rightness of a single word—in this case a word that is a single letter—and in so doing tries to sing a paean to language at its most provocative.

Ö

Shape the lips to an *o*, say *a*.
That's *island*.

One word of Swedish has changed the whole neighborhood.
When I look up, the yellow house on the corner
is a galleon stranded in flowers. Around it

the wind. Even the high roar of a leaf-mulcher
could be the horn-blast from a ship
as it skirts the misted shoals.

We don't need much more to keep things going.
Families complete themselves
and refuse to budge from the present,
the present extends its glass forehead to sea
(backyard breezes, scattered cardinals)

and if, one evening, the house on the corner
took off over the marshland,
neither I nor my neighbor
would be amazed. Sometimes

a word is found so right it trembles
at the slightest explanation.
You start out with one thing, end
up with another, and nothing's
like it used to be, not even the future.

Shakespeare Say

He drums the piano wood,
crowing.

Champion Jack in love
and in debt,
in a tan walking suit
with a flag on the pocket,
with a red eye
for women, with a
diamond-studded
ear, with sand
in a mouthful of mush—

poor me
poor me
I keep on drifting
like a ship out
on the sea

That afternoon two students
from the Akademie
showed him the town.
Munich was misbehaving,
whipping
his ass to ice
while his shoes
soaked through. His guides
pointed at a clock
in a blue-tiled house.
And tonight

every song he sings
is written by Shakespeare
and his mother-in-law.
I love you, baby,
but it don't mean
a goddam thing.
In trouble
with every woman he's
ever known, all of them
ugly—skinny legs, lie gap
waiting behind the lips
to suck him in.

Going down slow
crooning *Shakespeare say*
man must be
careful what he kiss
when he drunk,
going down
for the third set
past the stragglers
at the bar,
the bourbon in his hand
some bitch's cold
wet heart,
the whole joint

stinking on beer;
in love and winning
now, so even the mistakes
sound like jazz,
poor me, moaning
so no one hears:

my home's in Louisiana,
my voice is wrong,
I'm broke and can't hold
my piss;
my mother told me
there'd be days like this.

Gospel

Swing low so I
can step inside—
a humming ship of voices
big with all

the wrongs done
done them.
No sound this generous
could fail:

ride joy until
it cracks like an egg,
make sorrow
seethe and whisper.

From a fortress
of animal misery
soars the chill voice
of the tenor, enraptured

with sacrifice.
What do I see,
he complains, notes
brightly rising

towards a sky
blank with promise.
Yet how healthy
the single contralto

settling deeper
into her watery furs!
Carry me home,
she cajoles, bearing

down. Candelabras
brim. But he slips
through God's net and swims
heavenward, warbling.

Canary

for Michael S. Harper

Billie Holiday's burned voice
has as many shadows as lights,
a mournful candelabra against a sleek piano,
the gardenia her signature under that ruined face.

(Now you're cooking, drummer to bass,
magic spoon, magic needle.
Take all day if you have to
with your mirror and your bracelet of song.)

Fact is, the invention of women under siege
has been to sharpen love in the service of myth.

If you can't be free, be a mystery.

7

Trying Her Tongue

M. NOURBESE PHILIP

Language of the people. Language for the people. Language by the people, honed and fashioned through a particular history of empire and savagery. A language also nurtured and cherished on the streets of Port-of-Spain, San Fernando, Boissiere Village, and Sangre Grande in the look she dey and leh we go, in the mouths of the calypsonians, Jean and Dinah, Rosita and Clementina, Mama look a boo boo, the cuss buds, the limers, the hos (whores), the jackabats, and the market women. These are the custodians and lovers of this strange wonderful you tink it easy jive ass kickass massa day done Chagaramus is we own ole mass pretty mass pansweet language. A more accurate description of this language would be to call it a demotic variant of English. The Caribbean demotic. The excitement for me as a writer comes in the confrontation between the formal and the demotic within the text itself.

In the absence of any other language by which the past may be repossessed, reclaimed, and its most painful aspects transcended, English in its broadest spectrum must be made to do the job. To say that the experience can be expressed only in standard English (if there is any such thing) or only in the Caribbean demotic (there *is* such a thing) is, in fact, to limit the experience for the African artist working in the Caribbean demotic. It is *in the continuum of expression* from standard to Caribbean English that the veracity of the experience lies.

One can never be less than self-conscious as an African Caribbean writer working in any of the demotic variants of English, whether the demotic variant be a form of standard English or Caribbean English. And for the writer from the Caribbean, language must always present a dilemma. At its most simple, the dilemma can be resolved to an either/or dichotomy: either one writes in a demotic variant of English, or one writes in straight English. Choice of one or the other in this scenario is often seen as a political choice and much bad writing takes place on either side of the divide in the name of linguistic validity. It is not sufficient, however, to write only in dialect, for too often that remains a parallel and closed experience, although a part of the same language. Neither is it sufficient to write only in what we have come to call standard English. The language as we know it has to be dislocated and acted upon—even destroyed—so that it begins to serve our purposes. It is our only language, and while it is our mother tongue, ours is also a father tongue. Some writers—Derek Walcott and Wilson Harris immediately come to mind—have publicly acknowledged their gratitude for the "blessing" conferred on them by the imposition of the English language and have, in fact, refused to acknowledge that there even exists a dilemma; others, like Earl Lovelace, have taken up the challenge that the anguish that is English presents for all African Caribbean people.

The issue is, however, more complex than the either/or dichotomy suggests. The place African Caribbean writers occupy is one that is unique, and one that forces the writer to operate in a language that was used to brutalize and diminish Africans so that they would come to a profound belief in their own lack of humanity. No language can accomplish this—and to a large degree English did accomplish it—without itself being profoundly affected, without itself being tainted. The challenge, therefore, facing the African Caribbean writer who is at all sensitive to language and to the issues that language generates is to use the language in such a way that the historical realities are not erased or obliterated, so that English is revealed as the tainted tongue it truly is. Only in so doing will English be redeemed.

Ignoring Poetry (a work in progress)

Most people ignore most poetry because most poetry ignores most people.
                                                                —Adrian Mitchell

How does one write poetry from the twin realities of being Black and female in the last quarter of the twentieth century? How does one write poetry from a place such as Canada, whose reality for poets such as myself is, more often then not, structured by its absence? How does one write from the perspective of one who has "mastered" a foreign language, yet has never had a mother tongue; one whose father tongue is an English fashioned to exclude, deride and deny the essence of one's be-ing? How does the poet confront and resolve the profound loss and absence of language—a language which can truly be the house of one's being? How does the poet work a language engorged on her many silences? How does she break that silence that is one yet many? Should she? Can she fashion a language that uses silence as a first principle?

This was the first paragraph of a letter covering my manuscripts *She Tries Her Tongue; Her Silence Softly Breaks* and *Looking for Livingstone: An Odyssey of Silence* sent to publishers in 1987. Some seven years, twenty-five rejections, and eventual publication later, the questions answer themselves.

i.

how does one write
poetry
how does one-
poetry from the twin
realities
Black and female

One doesn't. The realities aren't twin. Or even the same.

ii.

how does one
write
poetry from a place
a place structured
                by absence

One doesn't. One learns to read the silence/s.

iii.

how
does one write
poetry
from the perspective
of "mastery" of a mother
tongue—a foreign
language
an anguish

One doesn't. One fashions a tongue
split—two times two times two
into

poly &
multi &
semi
vocalities

iv.

how does the poet
how does the poet

how does the poet
"confront"
how does the poet
"loss and absence"
how does the poet
an absence of language
resolve

She doesn't. She listens to the silence\s—the interstices of time; she listens
again.

v.

how does the poet work
engorged on her many
silences
how does the poet work
her many silences
how does the poet work
a language
engorged
on her many
many silences

Carefully

vi.

How does she
how does she
how does

she
    break
that silence
that silence
       is one
       is many
how does she break
one into many

Loving
ly

vii.

should she
should she what
could she
could she what
should she
could she

Possibly

viii.

can she fashion a language
(what presumption!)
can she fashion
         a language
using silence
can she fashion a language
using silence
as a first principle
can she

she must

All of which brings me to messin with the lyric:

> In "Discourse" by cramping the space traditionally given to the poem itself, by
> forcing it to share its space with something else—an extended image about
> women, words, language, and silence; with the edicts that established the para-

meters of silence for the African in the New World, by giving more space to the descriptions of the physiology of speech, the scientific legacy of racism we have inherited, and by questioning the tongue as organ and concept, poetry is put in its place—both in terms of it taking a less elevated position—moving from centre stage and page and putting it back where it belongs—and locating it in a particular historical sequence of events (each reading of such a poem could become a mini drama). The canon of objectivity and universality is shifted—I hope permanently disturbed.

—Notes from a Working Journal

Black and female—untwinned realities—subversive realities. Is this why I challenge the lyric voice—my lyric voice of authority—authority? Why should anyone care how the "I" that is me feels, or how it recollects my emotions in tranquillity. Without the mantle of authority—who gives me such authority—without the mantle of authority—what gives me such authority—whiteness? maleness? Europeanness? without the mantle of authority what is the lyric voice?

We seldom think of the lyric voice as one of authority—poetry and authority seem strange bedfellows—but it is, with the weight of a tradition behind it, even in its sometimes critical stance against society or the state. The traditional and overwhelming image is of the great man who expresses, in the best possible way, the dreams and aspirations of his people.

Maybe this explains the explosion, or is it implosion, of my lyric voice into many and several—needing others to help in this expression of the many-voiced one of one silence.

And so I mess with the lyric—subverting my own authority—what authority? speaking over my own voice, interrupting and disrupting it, refusing to allow *the* voice, the solo voice, pride of place, center page, center stage—where words are surrounded by and trying to fill all that white space, negative space, blank space—where the silence is and never was silent.

Discourse on the Logic of Language

WHEN IT WAS BORN, THE MOTHER HELD HER NEWBORN CHILD CLOSE: SHE BEGAN THEN TO LICK IT ALL OVER. THE CHILD WHIMPERED A LITTLE, BUT AS THE MOTHER'S TONGUE MOVED FASTER AND STRONGER OVER ITS BODY, IT GREW SILENT – THE MOTHER TURNING IT THIS WAY AND THAT UNDER HER TONGUE, UNTIL SHE HAD TONGUED IT CLEAN OF THE CREAMY WHITE SUBSTANCE COVERING ITS BODY.

English
is my mother tongue.
A mother tongue is not
not a foreign lan lan lang
language
l/anguish
   anguish
– a foreign anguish.

English is
my father tongue.
A father tongue is
a foreign language,
therefore English is
a foreign language
not a mother tongue.

What is my mother
tongue
my mammy tongue
my mummy tongue
my momsy tongue
my modder tongue
my ma tongue?

I have no mother
tongue
no mother to tongue
no tongue to mother
to mother
tongue
me

I must therefore be tongue
dumb
dumb-tongued
dub-tongued
damn dumb
tongue

EDICT I

Every owner of slaves shall, wherever possible, ensure that his slaves belong to as many ethno-linguistic groups as possible. If they cannot speak to each other, they cannot then foment rebellion and revolution.

Those parts of the brain chiefly responsible for speech are named after two learned nineteenth century doctors, the eponymous Doctors Wernicke and Broca respectively.

Dr. Broca believed the size of the brain determined intelligence; he devoted much of his time to "proving" that white males of the Caucasian race had larger brains than, and were therefore superior to, women, Blacks and other peoples of colour.

Understanding and recognition of the spoken word takes place in Wernicke's area – the left temporal lobe, situated next to the auditory cortex; from there relevant information passes to Broca's area – situated in the left frontal cortex – which then forms the response and passes it on to the motor cortex. The motor cortex controls the muscles of speech.

THE MOTHER THEN PUT HER FINGERS INTO HER CHILD'S MOUTH – GENTLY FORCING IT OPEN;
SHE TOUCHES HER TONGUE TO THE CHILD'S TONGUE, AND HOLDING THE TINY MOUTH OPEN,
SHE BLOWS INTO IT – HARD. SHE WAS BLOWING WORDS – HER WORDS, HER MOTHER'S WORDS,
THOSE OF HER MOTHER'S MOTHER, AND ALL THEIR MOTHERS BEFORE – INTO HER
DAUGHTER'S MOUTH.

but I have
a dumb tongue
tongue dumb
father tongue
and english is
my mother tongue
is
my father tongue
is a foreign lan lan lang
language
l/anguish
   anguish
a foreignanguish
is english –
another tongue
my mother
   mammy
   mummy
   moder
   mater
   macer
   moder
tongue
mothertongue
tongue mother
tongue me
mothertongue me
mother me
touch me
with the tongue of your
lan lan lang
language
l/anguish
   anguish
english
is a foreign anguish

EDICT II

Every slave caught speaking his native language shall be severely punished. Where necessary, removal of the tongue is recommended. The offending organ, when removed, should be hung on high in a central place, so that all may see and tremble.

A tapering, blunt-tipped, muscular, soft and fleshy organ describes
(a) the penis.
(b) the tongue.
(c) neither of the above.
(d) both of the above.

In a man the tongue is
(a) the principal organ of taste.
(b) the principal organ of articulate speech.
(c) the principal organ of oppression and exploitation.
(d) all of the above.

The tongue
(a) is an interwoven bundle of striated muscle running in three planes.
(b) is fixed to the jawbone.
(c) has an outer covering of a mucous membrane covered with papillae.
(d) contains ten thousand taste buds, none of which is sensitive to the taste of
      foreign words.

Air is forced out of the lungs up the throat to the larynx where it causes
the vocal cords to vibrate and create sound. The metamorphosis from
sound to intelligible word requires
(a) the lip, tongue and jaw all working together.
(b) the mother tongue.
(c) the overseer's whip.
(d) all of the above or none.

8

An Interweaving of Worlds

I am a poet maneuvering in the field of the English language. Since first writing poetry I have been aware of the English Tradition, for it established the guidelines of what is and isn't poetry in the literary annals of this country. Verse has been defined according to laws that were rather inadvertent in the first place. Why and how was the sonnet invented, or how did iambic pentameter become the rule for measure? Though these invented forms are now etched covenants between the "white poet god" and the formalist poet, they aren't particularly mine. Granted, these rhythms and metrical contracts can give beautiful structural form, but they are not the only reality of poetry. The English language changed especially when used as instrument of colonization, for it was no longer solely in possession of the British. The patterns of speech and the contexts have shifted into other dimensions.

When I write, with the consciousness of being an American, woman, Muscogee Creek, mixed-blood writer in the later part of the twentieth century, I can't separate that consciousness from the act of poetry. My first poems were attempts to stand up as a Native person in the strengthening waves of civil rights in this country. The lines were short, and the poems for the most part rode on one particular image. From there I looked at more traditionally tribal forms, chants, other forms of discourse. These structures are more ceremonial in nature, derived from the tribal cultures around me as well as from my own.

Form is derived from community need, a response to the trials and breakthroughs involved in being human at the end of the twentieth century. We are all changed by the "overculture" (my term for the artificially constructed consumer culture of this age). The discourse of a world constructed primarily by a relationship enforced by the oral is disturbed and changed by a communication developed for buying and selling. The poems in my collection *In Mad Love and War* (1990) demonstrate this disjunctive weave. In "Healing Animal" the outcome isn't jangled but makes a cohesive voice, my attempt to make sense and particular beauty out of the terrible, out of what would destroy all of us. Myth provides the gravity. And the power of words is a respected basic natural law. We cannot separate integrity of the word from our personal lives.

Historically the word was never separated from music or performance. It is only with the advent of the printing press that the word was taken from the community, isolated from performance and thus more easily manipulated. More recently my poetry has been crossing genre lines. In my prose poems, narrative rather than lyric density becomes a primary motivation, though lyric is never abandoned. My work has taken a new direction in which I combine music with the poetry. Here the word resumes multidimensionality, narrative intersects with the lyric, the spoken word with a horn line or bass riff. The prose poems then open in shape, for there's room in the form for improvisation.

"The Myth of Blackbirds" exemplifies what I am after in my poetry, which is an interweaving of worlds. As a biracial and bicultural woman I am aware of two very different cultures informing my reality, my poetry, and there are also other worlds of memory, of future, of past. I am aware of a narrative version of this revelation as well as the lyric overtone. The lyric works as a spiral; it can surround meaning, enter it. The poem/event takes place in Washington—which is a real and immediate location, as well as a place resonant with meaning in the history of the Native peoples in this country. My great-great-grandfather Mohahwee, one of the most remembered leaders of the Muscogee Nation, journeyed there with others of the tribe to speak on behalf of the nation. It's a journey many nations have made. That memory is present in any event in my life connected to the Capital. And then to have an early meeting in that place with my beloved made it all the more poignant and meaningful. There are dense layers in the relationship with my beloved and with loving which make connections to the love that urged Mohahwee to sacrifice for the people. It's all connected, interwoven.

Healing Animal

On this day when you have needed to sleep forever,
to forgive the pained animal kneading
                              your throat,
Sleep, your back curled against my belly.
I will make you something to drink,
                              from a cup of frothy stars
from the *somewhere there is the perfect sound*
called up from the best-told stories
                    of benevolent gods,
who have nothing better to do.
                    And I ask you
what bitter words are ruining your soft-skinned village,
because I want to make a poem that will cup
                    the inside of your throat
like the fire in the palm of a healing animal. Like
the way Coltrane knew love in the fluid shape
of a saxophone
            that could change into the wings of a blue angel.
He tasted the bittersweet roots of this crazy world,
and spit them out into the center of our musical
                              jazzed globe.
Josiah's uncle brought his music
        to the Papago center of the world
                    and music climbed out of his trombone
into the collected heartbeat of his tribe.
They had never heard anything like it,
                but it was the way they had remembered, the way
"Chief" Joe Moore must have known when he sang
                              for the very first time
through the brass-boned monster.
All through the last few nights I have watched you fight for yourself
with the eyes I was warned against opening.
                              You think you are asleep
When you turn off the lights, and we blend into the same
                              hot-skinned sky.
The land called miracle is the daughter you never died for and she
stands at the edge of the bed with her slim hand
                              against your cheek.
Your music is a crystal wall with a thousand mouths, kin to trains and
sounds that haven't yet been invented,
                    and you walk back and forth

through it to know it won't betray you.
And in the last seconds before the breaking light,
when you are nearly broken with the secret antelope
of compassion,
                    when the last guardian angel has flown west to the Pacific
to see someone else through their nightly death,
a homefire is slowly kindled in the village of your body.
And the smoke of dawn turns all your worded enemies
into ashes that will never rise.
Mythic cattle graze in your throat, washing it with milk.
And you will sing forever.

The Myth of Blackbirds

The hours we counted precious were blackbirds in the density of
Washington. Taxis toured the labyrinth with passengers of mist as the myth
of ancient love took the shape of two figures carrying the dawn tenderly on
their shoulders to the shores of the Potomac.

We fled the drama of lit marble in the capitol for a refuge held up by sweet,
everlasting earth. The man from Ghana who wheeled our bags was lonesome
for his homeland, but commerce made it necessary to carry someone else's
burdens. The stars told me how to find us in this disorder of systems.

Washington did not ever sleep that night in the sequence of eternal nights.
There were whirring calculators, computers stealing names, while spirits of
the disappeared drank coffee at an all-night cafe in this city of disturbed
relativity.

Justice is a story by heart in the beloved country where imagination weeps.
The sacred mountains only appear to be asleep. When we finally found the
room in the hall of mirrors and shut the door I could no longer bear the
beauty of scarlet licked with yellow on the wings of blackbirds.

This is the world in which we undressed together. Within it white deer
intersect with the wisdom of the hunter of grace. Horses wheel toward the
morning star. Memory was always more than paper and cannot be broken by
violent history or stolen by thieves of childhood. We cannot be separated in
the loop of mystery between blackbirds and the memory of blackbirds.

And in the predawn when we had slept for centuries in a drenching sweet rain you touched me and the springs of clear water beneath my skin were new knowledge. And I loved you in this city of death.

Through the darkness in the sheer rise of clipped green grass and asphalt our ancestors appear together at the shoreline of the Potomac in their moccasins and pressed suits of discreet armor. They go to the water from the cars of smokey trains, or dismount from horses dusty with fatigue.

See the children who became our grandparents, the old women whose bones fertilized the corn. They form us in our sleep of exhaustion as we make our way through this world of skewed justice, of songs without singers.

I embrace these spirits of relatives who always return to the place of beauty, whatever the outcome of the spiral of power. And I particularly admire the tender construction of your spine which in the gentle dawning is a ladder between the deep in which stars are perfectly stars, and the heavens where we converse with eagles.

I guide your hip home to me with my hand which is more than a hand, rather a river of effervescent water. And I am thankful to the brutal city for the space which outlines your limber beauty. To the man from Ghana who also loves the poetry of the stars. To the ancestors who do not forget us in the concrete and paper illusion. To the blackbirds who are exactly blackbirds. And to you sweetheart as we make our incredible journey.

A Postcolonial Tale

Every day is a reenactment of the creation story. We emerge from
dense unspeakable material, through the shimmering power of
dreaming stuff.

This is the first world, and the last.

Once we abandoned ourselves for television, the box that separates
the dreamer from the dreaming. It was as if we were stolen, put into
a bag carried on the back of a whiteman who pretends to own the
earth and the sky. In the sack were all the people of the world. We
fought until there was a hole in the bag.

When we fell we were not aware of falling. We were driving to
work, or to the mall. The children were in school learning subtrac-
tion with guns, although they appeared to be in classes.

We found ourselves somewhere near the diminishing point of civilization, not far from the trickster's bag of tricks.

Everything was as we imagined it. The earth and stars, every creature and leaf imagined with us.

The imagining needs praise as does any living thing. Stories and
songs are evidence of this praise.

The imagination conversely illumines us, speaks with us, sings with
us.

Stories and songs are like humans who when they laugh are
indestructible.

No story or song will translate the full impact of falling, or the in-
verse power of rising up.

Of rising up.

9

Performing, Not Writing: The Reception
of an Irish Woman's Lament

ANGELA BOURKE

Ireland retains a vibrant oral tradition, especially in Irish, and one that needs no endorsement from the world of written literature to ensure its survival; but the world of writing persists in speaking of and for it, appropriating its materials and often misinterpreting their meanings.[1] The poem known as *Caoineadh Airt Uí Laoghaire* (Ó Tuama 1961), the "Lament for Art O'Leary," was created in the eighteenth century as a woman's oral performance in Irish, but by a triple process of appropriation it has become a degendered literary text in English, versions of which appear in almost all surveys of Irish poetry from major publishing houses (e.g. in Kennelly 1970:78–86).

Unlike most oral poets, the composer of this lament is named. She was Eibhlín Dubh (Dark-haired Eileen) Ní Chonaill, wife of Art O'Leary; but paradoxically, while this very naming marks her as female, it has given her entry to a club whose members are overwhelmingly male, and where questions of gender are therefore beyond discussion. With each successive publication or reference in print, the "Lament for Art O'Leary" has been moved further from its oral origins; the richness of those origins in women's verbal art made more obscure. The reception of Eibhlín's composition by the English-speaking literary establishment illustrates a process whereby assumptions about writing, education, and class have led to misinterpretation of women's traditions, even by feminist scholars.

In oral culture, as Albert Lord pointed out many years ago, composition is part of performance, so that the notion of the author as exclusive owner of a text completed prior to its "publication" breaks down. So too

---

[1] "Irish" is used to refer to the Gaelic language spoken in Ireland as a first language by about ten thousand people, and as a second language by many thousands more. "Gaelic" refers to the wider group that also includes Scottish Gaelic and Manx.

does the claim associated with "high" literary criticism, that great works are new and original from start to finish; for the oral poet or storyteller necessarily makes a new work of verbal art from materials already to hand (Lord 1960). This is what any artist does, but the oral verbal artist, like the maker of Persian carpets, Byzantine icons, or American quilts, has less need to disguise her sources than does the artist in a more metropolitan or privileged medium.

The anxiety of influence in oral culture is finely calibrated: mere imitation is not enough, but without the paper, print, bindings, bookstores, libraries, and other institutions that accord authority to the written word, the oral poet must depend on identifiable pedigree—on participation in something that is clearly traditional—for recognition. Oral verbal art must be understood as in dialogue with what has gone before and will come after *in its own medium*. If it does not make sense within the terms of its tradition it will not be remembered; and if it is not remembered it will die. Originality consists in saying something that is new enough to be arresting and memorable, while remaining true enough to old patterns to be familiar—and memorable (Ong 1982:33–36). Rhyme, meter, alliteration, and formulaic utterance—learned and perfected over a period of years—are among the templates used to fashion experience and thought into poems that can be sung or spoken for generations.

Oral poems presented in literary anthologies (often as the work of Anonymous, who, as Virginia Woolf remarked, was probably a woman), are introduced as having "made it" into literature. In fact they have often been taken over and "made into" literature: appropriated, processed, and packaged as part of literate civilization's colonization of oral culture. This essay argues that while the critical reception of *Caoineadh Airt Uí Laoghaire* has served readers well in providing a magnificent text, it has obscured the artistry that belongs to oral performance. Given the difference in class and status implicit in the encounter between writing culture and oral tradition, the translation into print of an oral composition entails the suppression of much that is not text in what was originally said or sung—and the suppression of what it meant.

When the poetry in question has been translated into English from a lesser-used language, or when women's compositions have been adopted into a male canon, the possibilities for misinterpretation are enormous. Unlike the absent author of a written text, the maker of an oral poem is not assumed by convention to be male. Whole areas of poetic discourse in Irish, notably lament and lullaby, are identified with women's voices; yet so rare are women authors in the canon of writing in Irish that either all poetic utterance is assumed to have male authors, or a woman poet is understood—even by some modern feminists—as engaged in a lonely struggle to be heard by her male peers. The conventions of a kind of poetry (lament), produced in response to a particular social crisis and performance occasion (death), may be interpreted as a purely literary conformation to the requirements of genre.

Printed books may claim to convey the poetry of oral traditions and the production of women within them, but the modern reader who wishes to recover as much as possible of a nonliterate poetic tradition must learn to read through the inscriptions on its apparently clear packaging. The "Lament for Art O'Leary" has been through two separate packaging processes: first by the nationalist romantics of the late nineteenth century, then by twentieth-century scholars of the literature and folklore of the Irish language. This essay is concerned with the stubborn remnants of nineteenth-century wrapping that still cling to the translations currently being anthologized, some shreds of which even underlie critical work in Irish.

I

Art O'Leary was shot dead on horseback in 1773 at the age of twenty-six, and Eibhlín lamented him in the traditional manner known as *caoineadh*, from which the English verb "keen" is derived (see Ó Tuama 1987). This was a ritual lament, led by a close woman relative of the deceased person or by a woman hired for the purpose. Women gathered around the body, swaying back and forth, beating their hands together, and tearing their hair, while the chief keener or *bean chaointe* addressed the dead person in extemporized verse interspersed with rhythmic wailing. An essential part of funeral ritual from early times until the nineteenth century, loud public lamentation of the dead finally disappeared in Ireland only within living memory. Travelers from Giraldus Cambrensis in the twelfth century to Edmund Spenser in the sixteenth and Asenath Nicholson in the nineteenth remarked on the practice, although as outsiders to the society where *caoineadh* had value as poetic discourse, they neither named its composers nor privileged it as art (Ó Muirithe 1978).

In its later years the ritual lament came to be identified with the less privileged strata of society: most examples known to modern scholars were either transcribed as curiosities by nineteenth-century antiquarians or collected as folklore in this century. The immensely valuable insider observations of Irish life made by Ordnance Survey researcher John O'Donovan (1806–61) include the remark that "All decent half-civilized people now laugh at these elegies and hence the better class of farmers have entirely given them up, except in very few instances, where some old female member of the family cannot be restrained from venting her grief in the real old strain of poetry, accompanying it with the howling which seems now to be almost peculiar to the old Irish" (quoted in Ó Muirithe 1978:26).

Born into a prominent, educated, and traveled family two generations before O'Donovan, Eibhlín Ní Chonaill was adept at the "real old strain of poetry," drawing on it when her husband Art was killed. She was apparently one of the last of her class to be expert in the *caoineadh*, and this may have been because although only thirty at the time of Art's death, she had previously been married to a much older man, and widowed while still in her teens. Her mother, Maíre Ní Duibh, was renowned for her quick wit, repartee, and poetry, and tradition states that Eibhlín had participated in the making of a *caoineadh* for her first husband (Ó Tuama 1961:8, 72).

Looking back at Eibhlín's lament performance in the late eighteenth century, we see a chasm opening at her feet: a class divide which grew wider through the nineteenth century and across which bridges are only now being thrown. On one side of that divide stand orality, the Irish language, and poverty; on the other are literacy, English, and all the trappings of patriarchal and colonialist modernity. Eibhlín Ní Chonaill belonged to the class that became modern. Her nephew, the orator and "Liberator" Daniel O'Connell (1775–1847), after whom Dublin's main thoroughfare is named, conscious of the power of the British press, elected to use English rather than Irish in all his public utterances. By the end of the nineteenth century no member of Eibhlín's family knew anything of her lament. But it was not forgotten: on the other side of the class divide, where Irish was still spoken and literacy was less widespread, long passages of it were still quoted, while new laments in the same meter and style were still being composed.

Like other lament poets, Eibhlín used a rhythmic, rhymed meter and a stock of formulas and themes that are associated with women's oral poetry throughout the Gaelic world (Bromwich 1948a, 1948b; Bourke 1988b, 1993). The lines attributed to her and preserved in oral memory (quite probably including later embellishments and additions) over generations make this the longest surviving example of *caoineadh*—almost 400 lines in the standard scholarly edition (Ó Tuama 1961). A lament of this sort is not a song: words matched to a regular melody and capable of being performed by anyone with the skill to sing it. Rather it is a long, ragged rant, rhymed and rhythmic; interspersed with stylized sobs and wailings, chanted, sung or spoken (Ó Madagáin 1982). It is a woman's speech-act: a direct address to a dead person and to others present, a central part of funeral ritual in which women other than the main composer were expected to join.

In most surveys of Irish literature Eibhlín is the only named woman poet for the whole period from medieval times until the nineteenth century. This is largely due to the edition published by Seán Ó Tuama in 1961, which made the lament easily available to translators and whose eloquent introduction placed it in a literary context. It stands out in anthologies as strikingly modern, with its short, terse lines and stanzas of irregular length, its sensuousness, and its vivid, unadorned style. The meter and language are straightforward, not difficult to render into English, and several fine translations exist. Here, however, I offer my own translation of one passage, as a way of illustrating the many-voiced character of this kind of poetry and asserting the primacy of the Irish-language versions over any translation:

> Mo chara thú go daingean!
> Is níor chreideas riamh dod mharbh
> Gur tháinig chugham do chapall
> Is a srianta léi go talamh,
> Is fuil do chroí ar a leacain
> Siar go t'iallait ghreanta
> Mar a mbítheá i do shuí 's id sheasamh.
> Thugas léim go tairsigh,
> An dara léim go geata,
> An triú léim ar do chapall.
>
> Do bhuaileas go luath mo bhasa
> is do bhaineas as na reathaibh
> Chomh maith is bhí sé agam,
> Go bhfuaras romham tú marbh
> Cois toirín íseal aitinn,
> Gan Pápa gan easpag,
> Gan cléireach gan sagart
> Do leífeadh ort an tsailm,
> Ach seanbhean chríonna chaite
> Do leath ort binn dá fallaing—
> Do chuid fola leat 'na sraithibh;
> Is níor fhanas le hí ghlanadh
> Ach í ól suas lem basaibh.[2]
>
> My best-loved friend,
> I didn't credit your death
> till your mare came home,
> with reins trailing down,

2 Ó Tuama 1961:35.

your heart's blood on her cheek
and on the fine saddle
where you sat and stood up.
I took a jump to the threshold,
a second to the gate, and
a third into the saddle.

I struck my hands together
and pressed the mare to gallop
as fast as she could travel,
and found you lying here
by a low furze bush
without pope or bishop,
without priest or cleric
to read a single psalm,
but only one old woman
who spread her cloak across you—
your blood was flowing from you
but I didn't stop to wipe it;
I drank it from my hands.

The *Penguin Book of Irish Verse* devotes nine pages to Frank O'Connor's
translation of the lament, and discusses it extensively in the Introduction.
The editor refers to Eibhlín as one of the poets who "dominated" the eighteenth century, but glosses over the fact that she composed in Irish and
makes no distinction whatever between oral and literary production. The
text is followed in this anthology by another oral poem, attributed to
Anonymous, also translated from Irish by Frank O'Connor. This time it is
a lament song, nine stanzas of four lines each, which can still be heard
sung in Irish: "Donnchadh Bán," or "The Lament for Yellow-haired Don-
ough," prefaced as follows: "An uneducated Connacht girl, or someone
speaking in her name, writes the classic lament, the poem that would have
been understood in the ninth century as it was in the nineteenth by Yeats"
(Kennelly 1970:87). Use of the verb "write" here is symptomatic of the process I discuss in this essay. Describing the composers of "Donnchadh Bán"
and other laments and lament songs as "uneducated" also begs questions
about authorship, originality, gender, and genre.

II

We can best appreciate the extent to which the oral, performance origin
of Eibhlín Dubh Ní Chonaill's poem has been forgotten by examining

the October 1984 inaugural lecture given by Peter Levi as Professor of Poetry at Oxford University. Called "The Lamentation of the Dead," it featured a translation of the "Lament for Art O'Leary" by Eilís Dillon, accompanied by Levi's remark that "I think it is the greatest poem written in these islands in the whole eighteenth century" (Levi 1984:18). The same paper acknowledges that "the true lament is women's poetry" but reveals assumptions about verbal art, literacy, and the male tradition by introducing the "Lament for Art O'Leary" as "composed in Irish at the end of the eighteenth century, and recovered in several different versions from illiterate or scarcely literate countrymen and fishermen in the south of Ireland in the 1890s and later" (11, 18). But of course literacy is of no help to oral memory and almost all the lines as they are now available were transcribed not from countrymen or fishermen, but from women.

Eibhlín Ní Chonaill's poem differs from other published texts of the same period because those other texts were *written* by men, in a tradition reserved for men, while hers was composed orally, in a style practiced almost exclusively by women. The oral lament tradition was a highly sophisticated art, but expertise in it was acquired outside and independently of the system of male education based on writing. Other lament texts survive, and have been published in Irish, but none is as long as Eibhlín's or has captured the English literary imagination in the same way.[3] This may be because Eibhlín's class background made her a credible author for a literary work. She fitted the role of glamorous heroine for nineteenth-century romantics much better than did other makers of laments. The typical lamenter or *bean chaointe* by then was a poor elderly woman who had witnessed many deaths and had time to assimilate all the conventions of the lament tradition,[4] but Eibhlín was scarcely thirty years old, her family was powerful and relatively wealthy, and the man she lamented was not her son or patron but her handsome and headstrong young husband. Laments frequently protest at violence and stinginess, and concern themselves with social as well as personal relations, but Eibhlín's can be and has been read as a love poem, to the exclusion of the other messages it contains (Bourke 1993).

The story of Eibhlín Ní Chonaill and Art O'Leary as told in County Cork and borne out by written sources is ideally suited to romantic in-

---

[3] Bourke 1988b. Cullen 1993 gives a valuable account of the political circumstances surrounding the death of Art Ó Laoghaire and the dissemination of the lament. However, his argument misapprehends the nature of oral poetic composition and the internal evidence that marks this lament as oral. See also Ó Foghludha 1936; Ó Murchadha 1939; Ó Concheanainn 1978.

[4] The lament for Sir James Cotter was made by his old nurse, and that for Diarmaid Mac Cárthaigh by his mother. For descriptions of other lamenters, see Synge 1911:64; Croker 1969:173–74.

terpretation (Ó Tuama 1961: 7–31, 1987). Both came of the native Irish nobility, a class that had suffered severe reversals under English rule.[5] Art O'Leary was headstrong and arrogant. Like many other young Irishmen of his class in that period, he had served for a time in the Hungarian Hussars, under the Catholic empress Maria Theresa.[6] He was twenty-one in 1767 and Eibhlín was a widow in her late twenties. They met and married (to the dismay of her family, who were wary of Art's flamboyance), and settled in County Cork. They had two children, and Eibhlín was pregnant for the third time when Art's history of indiscretion caught up with him. He antagonized a local magistrate, was outlawed, and finally was shot as he fled on horseback, on the night of 4 May 1773.

The earliest published text of the "Lament for Art O'Leary" appeared almost 120 years later as an appendix to *The Last Colonel of the Irish Brigade,* a book about Eibhlín's family by Mrs. Morgan John O'Connell, a gentlewoman writing about her husband's ancestors in 1892 (O'Connell 1892/1977). It was a "corrected" copy of a transcription said to have been made about 1800, but perhaps made as much as forty years later, from Norry Singleton, herself a well-known lamenter who lived just a few miles from where Art was killed (Cullen 1993:34). Mrs. O'Connell's attitude toward the "Lament" is typical of her period and class in its romanticizing of the story of Eibhlín and Art O'Leary. She translates Eibhlín's epithet *Dubh* (black-haired) as "Dark," and refers to her throughout as "Dark Eileen"—a bold stroke in the creation of a romantic heroine. Peter Levi, too, referred to "Dark Eileen" or "Black Eileen" (1984:19), with obvious echoes of James Clarence Mangan's (1803–1819) "Dark Rosaleen" (Kennelly 1970:149–51).

Four years later Osborn Bergin published another version of the same original, with editorial emendation. He wrote: "A rather mutilated edition of this poem has been printed in the appendix to Mrs. M. J. O'Connell's 'Last Colonel of the Irish Brigade.' In its form as now published the poem is yet far from perfect." He further remarked, "It is doubtful if any literature contains so true and powerful an expression of the devotion of a high-minded woman to a noble husband, as shown in her grief after his death" (Bergin 1896:23).

In the last years of the nineteenth century the question of Home Rule

---

[5] Eibhlín's family home was the imposing Derrynane House, in County Kerry, now open to the public as the home of "The Liberator," barrister and member of Parliament Daniel O'Connell, who was her nephew. Her family maintained contacts with the European mainland, but tried to avoid attracting the attention of their English overlords: their aristocratic lifestyle was maintained by keeping a low profile, and by smuggling.

[6] Returning home to County Cork, Art outraged the local colonists by his swaggering bravado: he would stand on top of a rolling barrel all the way down the steep main street of Macroom—making ordinary business impossible—and he wore a sword in public, in defiance of the "Penal" laws that made such signs of independence illegal for Catholics.

for Ireland was being hotly debated. Colonialist rhetoric was at its height
in England, and those who opposed Home Rule habitually denigrated
the Irish—along with Africans, native Americans, and other colonized
peoples—as brutish and ignorant (Curtis 1968, 1971, Foster 1993:171–94;
Bourke 1996). Nationalist Irish scholars and the literati of the Irish Revival were at pains to counter this propaganda, highlighting the aristocratic elements of the texts they edited, translated, and adapted from
medieval manuscripts and contemporary folklore. That the "Lament for
Art O'Leary" could be read as a text of marital devotion among noble
and high-minded Irish people was enough to guarantee it a place in the
canon of Irish literature then being formed.

III

In folklore, anthropology, and Irish-language studies, research on lament poetry has been going on for generations, and recent publications
have led to a considerable reassessment of the published texts in Irish.[7]
However, the makers of poetry anthologies and others who confer the
approval of the English literary tradition on Irish oral poetry have paid
little attention to this work. A single edited text has become standard at
the expense of the many recorded variants. Lines that early editors omitted or relegated to appendices have been silently dropped, and the
uniqueness of Eibhlín's composition has been stressed to such an extent
that her participation in a communal women's performance tradition is
almost forgotten.

Rachel Bromwich in 1948 described the principal themes and conventions of Irish lament poetry, which even include the drinking of the dead
man's blood, as in the lines quoted above, and showed how closely Eibhlín's lament conformed to them. The comprehensive and influential essay
prefaced to Seán Ó Tuama's standard 1961 edition of the Irish text also
recognizes Eibhlín's participation in the tradition of keening, but while
stating that "few poems are as rooted in their background as the 'Lament
for Art O'Leary,'" it paradoxically insists on the transcendent literary artistry of this lament, denigrating all others either directly or by

---

[7] For a short account of lament traditions in different parts of the world, see Leach, 1949:
2.154–57. For studies of lament poetry in particular areas, see on Greece Alexiou 1974,
Chaves 1980, Seremetakis 1987. For other areas see, for example, Honko 1974 on Finland;
Feld 1982 on Papua New Guinea; Finnegan 1970 on Africa; and Tiwary 1978 on northern
India. For the Irish tradition, see Bromwich 1948a, 1948b (includes a translation of the "La-
ment for Art O'Leary"); Ó Coileáin 1988; Bourke 1988a, 1988b, 1993. Studies published in
Irish include a comprehensive introductory essay by Seán Ó Tuama (1961); an article by
Tomás Ó hAilín (1971); and a collection of essays, Ó Madagáin 1978.

implication (Ó Tuama 1961:7–31). Instead of celebrating Eibhlín's poem as the finest surviving realization of a tradition, it presents it as radically different in kind, a unique production.

This interpretation seems to rest on an unspoken assumption of literary romanticism that "folk" poetry cannot be original or passionate and that "the folk" are not capable of consciously reaching the same emotional heights as the upper classes. That assumption, like what Albert Memmi has called "the mark of the plural" in colonial situations—the colonizers' perception of the colonized as an undifferentiated mass, passive and uninteresting—has given rise to a false polarization between "tradition" on the one hand and "inspiration" on the other (Memmi 1965:85).

Two voices speak in the lament for Art O'Leary, according to Ó Tuama's essay: the traditional and the personal. "We" (readers of modern Irish, people of literary sensibility?) "endure the traditional for the sake of the personal and are sometimes even grateful for its soothing monotony, for it is not possible to stay permanently in a state of emotional upheaval."[8] At every point of this critical introduction Eibhlín's emotion is emphasized: "her hot breath can still be felt on the best of her poem [Tá anáil the Eibhlín Dhubh le brath ar an gcuid is fearr de]"(1961:8); and again: "She never departs from the diction of normal speech, but so great is her grief that even the most common words leap into life. Passages of lament flow from her, in floods. The range of her emotion is boundless [Ní théann Eibhlín Dhubh puinn thar chaint an ghnáthchomhrá: ach na focail is comónta féin aici léimeann siad ina mbeatha le teann a dóláis. Ritheann na startha caointeoireachta ina dtuilte uaithi, go taomannach. Tá réim a cuid mothúcháin dotheoranta.]" (1961: 30).

Tradition is presented as a stultifying rather than an enabling force: "Often, unconsciously, Eibhlín made special use of traditional lament themes, stitching them artfully into the pattern of her verse. At other times, by the intensity of her passion, she revived the old clichés completely [Is minic, mar sin i gan fhios di féin, a bhain Eibhlín Dhubh leas speisialta as na téamaí dúchais caointeoireachta: d'fhuaigh si go healaíonta i bpatrún a cuid véarsaíochta iad. Uaireanta eile, áfach, le déine

---

[8] Ó Tuama 1961:21–30. Two voices: "is fíor gur tur linn an guth traidisiúnta i gcomórtas leis an nguth eile. Ach mar sin féin, tá sé le tabhairt faoi deara go mbíonn, uaireanta eile, mar a bheadh sólás is cumhracht gnáthphaidre ag baint le liodán foirmiúil sean-nathanna. Go deimhin is faoiseamh dúinn go minic teacht ar a leithéid i measc véarsaí Eibhlín Dhubh. Ní féidir bheith faoi mhór-chorraí an t-am ar fad" [It is true that we find the traditional voice tiresome by comparison with the other voice. It must be noted, however, that a formal litany of old phrases can sometimes have the consoling sweetness of a familiar prayer. Indeed, we are often relieved to find the like among the Eibhlín Dubh's verses. It is not possible to remain constantly in the grip of strong emotion] (29).

a paisiúin, d'athbheoigh sí na sean-chlichés ó bhonn]" (1961:29). References to the poet's emotional and "unconscious" use of what are termed "clichés" manage to suggest that lament poetry like this is mantic, owing all to affect and nothing to cognition, and that the artist is not herself in full control of her material. But careful study of the work of lament poets demonstrates the discipline with which they handled the various necessary themes of lament within a metrical framework. The lamenter worked like a tragic actor: it was part of her duty and skill to experience and perform strong emotion and to behave in a way that suggested abandonment. In this way she marked funerals as time outside time (Bourke 1993).

Ó Tuama's is the standard edition of the Irish text and is unlikely to be superseded. It is a valuable and elegant work of textual scholarship, produced before Lord's research on oral poetry became widely known, but it is the only authority invoked for the "Lament" by writers of the English literary establishment and its text is the basis for all recent translations. A modern feminist reader cannot help noticing that it relegates lines about marital violence and stinginess to an appendix and appears uncomfortably influenced by English literary romanticism in its echoing of Bergin's sentiments about highmindedness (Bourke 1993).

In spite of having scrupulously gathered evidence about the oral lament tradition, Ó Tuama in 1987 approvingly quoted Peter Levi's pronouncement about the poem's "written" origin (1987:103). In the same essay he seems determined to regard such a fine poem as a product of individual, aristocratic genius, working in opposition to, rather than within, the people's tradition: "While the framework . . . for Eibhlín's lament is the popular extempore keen, it also clearly bears the marks of a literary and aristocratic environment. Throughout her lament one feels the clamour, the spaciousness, the haughtiness of the Gaelic big house in a way that is surprising to find in such a popular-type composition" (109). But the lines quoted in support of this argument are typical of lament poetry, while the waulking songs of Scotland, popular international ballads, and folktale *Märchen* also abound in aristocratic detail. Some of the most sensitive singers of "big" ballads in Scotland have come from the Traveling People, a marginalized and impoverished group who can scarcely be familiar with the environment described in them (Buchan 1972). The *guslars* studied by Milman Parry and Albert Lord in Yugoslavia were poor countrymen, but they sang of noble heroes who rode thoroughbred horses and carried fine weapons (Lord 1960).

Eibhlín's passionate account of her midnight ride to where her dead husband's body lay has been taken as truthful narrative by most commentators, who then present her as being so heroically overwhelmed by grief and of such naturally aristocratic temperament that her poetry must far transcend the "folk" lament tradition. Yet the conventions of that tradition prescribed precisely this kind of heroic transcendence of the ordinary: even to the drinking of blood. Lamenting women are frequently described, or describe themselves, as entering a sort of temporary psychosis on hearing news of a death (Partridge 1980). They are unkempt and barefoot, and oblivious to everything but the fact of death. The Virgin Mary is said to have taken three wild leaps on seeing Christ crucified, and the mother of Diarmaid Mac Cárthaigh, killed in a fall from his horse about 1850, left the cow she was milking and walked twenty miles across the mountains to reach him. She was still carrying the rope she had used to tie her cow when she arrived in the city and began her *caoineadh*. All this behavior, however, is scripted by the tradition: the lamenting woman has license to behave oddly and dramatically—as the central performer in an essential ritual of death she is even required to do so—but she is always in control.

It is of course possible that Eileen, pregnant and responsible for two small children, rushed immediately from her house at night and galloped on horseback through the countryside. We even have good documentary evidence that women did drink the blood of dead relatives as they lamented. But even if Eileen did not, the conventions of *caoineadh* would require her to assert that she did.

In recent years two perceptive critics of Irish literature in English, who are also poets, have written about the "Lament for Art O'Leary" in ways that have prompted me to write this essay. Both Séamus Deane and Eiléan Ní Chuilleanáin, in spite of an active predisposition to read for gender and listen for subaltern voices, seem to have followed the earlier commentators in their treatment of this poem.

In his survey of Irish literature, Deane describes the "Lament for Art O'Leary" and Brian Merriman's *Midnight Court* as "two of the [Irish] language's greatest masterpieces." Acknowledging that the lament reflects an oral tradition, he nevertheless insists on the individual, literary genius of Eibhlín: "['The Lament'] is so much a part of the folk tradition that parts of it may be traditional material from long-rehearsed keenings over the dead. But it is essentially her poem, an outburst of grief at the murder of her husband. . . . Even in translation the passion of her grief is unmistakeable. She remembers everything about him and each memory sharpens the pain. Yet throughout, the poem retains a discipline and measured rhythm; it does not disintegrate into tears, it consistently matches grief with eloquence. There is no greater love poem in Irish" (1986: 250). But this is exactly the skill of the traditional keener: to express powerful emotion with discipline and rhythm and to convey the immediacy of grief without disintegrating into tears (Bourke 1988a). It is worth remarking too that several passages describing conflict with Art are ascribed to Eibhlín in oral tradition. References to violence and stinginess in marriage are common themes of lament poetry, but as such lines appear only in an appendix to the Irish text as edited, they have been omitted from published translations.

Sentimental accounts of the Irish lament argue with the remarkable circularity characteristic of colonial rhetoric that Eibhlín transcended the tradition by composing while in the grip of "real" emotion, unlike peasant keeners who merely repeated formulaic cliches. At the same time, they assert that her true artistry is shown in aristocratic self-control and literary sensibility. A similar circularity underlies the idea that since written poetry is more poetic than oral, a fine oral poem must have a written source or inspiration. *Caoineadh* required the cooperation of several women, and was associated particularly with the less privileged classes, but this poem has come to be regarded as the untrammeled voice of one headstrong and aristocratic individual, working against rather than with the expectations of the people around her.

Irish women lament poets were doubly colonized: they belonged to a society and composed in a language considered inferior and barbarous by those in power, but even within their own society they were an underclass, not taught to write, not admitted to the academy of serious poets, rarely named as authors of their own compositions. The result of all this is that even for a modern feminist reader like Eiléan Ní Chuilleanáin, the artistry of the lament poet as fostered by, rather than smothered by, tradition is largely invisible.

In an essay on "Women as Writers," Ní Chuilleanáin devotes five pages to a discussion of the lament for Art O'Leary, and even refers to Irish as the language Eibhlín Ní Chonaill "writes in" (1985:120). At first she seems to acknowledge the oral tradition as different from the written, describing the destruction of the native, Irish-speaking aristocracy in the seventeenth century, but her assumption that the custom of women keening the dead represents passivity and dull acceptance of the inevitable is disturbing: "The association of women with death . . . [belongs to] the most stultifying traditional views of women, associating them with passivity and surrender to natural forces" (1985:114). Like the male critics, she interprets the vigor and assertiveness of Eibhlín's keen as exceptional: "The death of an individual, the decline of the native aristocracy, can only be countered by this affirmation which transforms the keen, from an instrument of communal acceptance of the inevitable, to an assertion of personal freedom" (1985:119).

But *caoineadh* was always at least potentially an assertion of personal freedom. The texts that survive howl in protest and anger at death and at injustice in the world of the living, and they frequently challenge prestigious persons and institutions (Bourke 1993). Although *caoineadh* was a communal, public activity, all our examples represent the voices of individual women. None of them can be construed as passively accepting of the inevitable—such an interpretation can only have been gathered from the uncomprehending descriptions of unsympathetic colonists who witnessed the Irish *caoineadh* in performance but could not understand the words being spoken.

IV

Publishing women's oral poetry as though it were a literary production contributes to the undervaluing of women's creative output in the Irish tradition—even when the poetry is being celebrated as great art. Rather than show her as a brilliant exponent of a verbal art practiced by many women, literary sources present Eibhlín Ní Chonaill as unique: the exception who proves the rule that great poets are not women. Her achievement is presented as the product of emotion rather than of skill and is characterized as essentially unrepeatable. Her authority as a poet is conditional on her separation from tradition and on her being named, as literary authors are.

Literary culture stands in relation to oral as do colonizers to colonized, or settlers to the nomadic peoples they displace: notions of authority and ownership are differently constructed in the different environments. Sandra Gilbert and Susan Gubar have pointed out that in the written tradition the idea of individual creativity is closely connected to paternity and ownership: "the patriarchal notion that a writer 'fathers' his text . . . has been all-pervasive in Western literary civilization . . . [A writer's] literary creations . . . are his possession, his property. Having defined them in language and thus generated them, he owns them, controls them, and encloses them on the printed page" (1979:4,12). This metaphor of enclosure has powerful implications for the way literary civilization has dealt with oral poetry, for the idea of ownership in orality is much less rigid. So unfamiliar are readers with other ways of authoring verbal art, however, that Walter Ong has devoted a whole chapter of his *Orality and Literacy* to "Print, Space, and Closure" (Ong 1982:117–38).

Any singer or lamenter may add to or edit a song or lament, sing more or less of it, or otherwise vary it, but always within the scope sanctioned by other singers and by the audience. Two singers in the same community may perform very different versions of the "same" song, each maintaining allegiance to the tradition as she has received it, but when one of those versions is enclosed in print, it immediately acquires an authority and primacy not before dreamed of (Partridge 1983: 25–26,

158). When one translation is adopted as standard by editors to the exclusion of all others, it in turn rapidly becomes "the text."

Enclosure suggests a containment of certain words which then become "the text," but it also suggests exclusion: the shutting out of other words and of sounds, gestures and interruptions. In the translated texts of the "Lament for Art O'Leary," everything that is not love poetry has been left out. But other laments, other versions of this lament, and written accounts in Irish and English suggest that the lament poet controlled a far wider range of expression than this (Bourke 1993). Even dependent as we are on written records, an appreciation of the lament as performance would allow us to reintegrate all that "outside" material with what is "inside" the received text and to examine Eibhlín Ní Chonaill's "Lament for Art O'Leary" for what it undoubtedly was: a performance; "an activity which generates transformations" (Sayre 1990:103).

Lamenting the dead was a central and essential part of funeral ritual in Ireland until modern times. The woman who led the *caoineadh* was both poet and performer, taking charge of the community's grief and expressing it in all its complexity by her appearance and behavior, her voice and her poetry (Bourke 1988a, 1993). Eibhlín Dubh Ní Chonaill was an outstanding exponent of the art of *caoineadh*, but far from composing *against* convention, in the modernist, literary manner imagined by editors and commentators, she worked in every detail *within* a tradition. But for the accident of her high birth at a time when the native upper class in Ireland was turning its back on indigenous culture, and the appeal of her poem to Victorian romanticism, modern readers might know nothing of it.

10

Poetic Subject and Voice as Sites of Struggle: Toward A "Postrevisionist" Reading of Stevie Smith's Fairy-Tale Poems

ROMANA HUK

Since the early 1980s, feminist rereadings of literary modernism have illuminated a whole world of women's counterwritings, misread practices, and alternatively modernist strategies. Such revisions of literary history have tended to re-present women of the period as "engaged in a kind of immanent critique, a transvaluation of the very standards which they have been held to epitomize" (Hirsh 1989:15). Accordingly, most figures retrieved for study have been those who seem to write in opposition to T. S. Eliot's canonical vision of tradition and its worthiest modern adherents; the writing of such "oppositional" women writers is characterized by feminist critics as revolutionary "displacements" (voicings of muted femininity in cultural narratives), "delegitimations" of customary conclusions, and radical reclamations of authority—particularly through their revisions of materials instrumental to the processes of socialization, such as fairy tales, folk tales, and classical myth.[1] Yet other women, whose rewritings of such texts are not so clearly subversive, or who perhaps expose their own subjection to the coercions of language, remain unread. This suggests a limitation in feminist readings of women writers excluded from the modernist canon, demonstrating, as Celeste Schenck observes, "the politics of feminist collusion in that exile."[2]

---

[1] T. S. Eliot's notorious image of tradition as a line of literary "monuments," alongside which a modern writer's work should be erected and compared, can be found in his well-known, short 1919 essay, "Tradition and the Individual Talent" (1975:38–39). The terms "displacement" and "delegitimation" used here are borrowed from DuPlessis 1985:108.

[2] This quote is taken from Schenck's introduction to Anna Wickham's poems in Scott 1990:615. Schenck develops her ideas more fully in "Exiled by Genre: Modernism, Canonicity, and the Politics of Exclusion" (1989). She writes in the latter that feminists, by "privileging those female poets who broke form with the boys (even if, as it turned out, they broke form *for* the boys) have reproduced the preferences of dominant critical discourse and extended the hegemony of an exclusive, in this case antigeneric, prejudice which con-

Schenck's work on neglected modern women poets who use traditional forms urges us to interrogate a *feminist* modernist canon that has recently emerged, as well as its version of literary history. Such examination brings still another kind of writer to our attention, one whose experience in language and entrapment in formal and generic imperatives and their contradictions might be understood as being presciently "postmodern"; her work comes into different focus as we learn to read her yet again in a "postrevisionist" fashion, from perspectives obtained at new intersections between feminist, Bakhtinian, and poststructuralist theory.

I

One such writer is "Stevie" (Florence Margaret) Smith, whose first novel became a best-seller in the 1930s and whose poetry won the Queen's Gold Medal shortly before her death in 1971. A prominent if controversial figure in her time, she has been mentioned in only a few of the studies alluded to above, and reread only in one.[3] "Feminists have been slow to acclaim her," as Frances Spalding, her most recent critical biographer, writes (1989:xv); Spalding and others have made it clear that Smith's work has been difficult to appropriate for feminist revisions of literary modernism because her critiques, parodies, and retellings of narratives often resolve themselves in less than clearly alternative terms, and even incorporate what appear to be traditionalist statements about women without employing what we recognize as classic irony. Feminist critics have thus for years tacitly affirmed Sanford Sternlicht's description of Smith as "a conservative . . . suburban middle-class woman, as much a Tory as any stuffy club man . . . [who] could be as hidebound a Victorian as her old aunt . . . [and] not a feminist" (1990:1, 105). This dramatic misreading of Smith's representation of the middle-class, suburban environment which formed her and many of her speakers illustrates, first of all, the persistence even in revisionary criticism of at least two problematic assumptions about subjectivity and essential truth: (1) that statements made, particularly in a woman's works, are representative of her

---

signed most women poets to debased use of tired forms." She even suggests that such revisions of literary history cast both women poets *and* their feminist critics into "collusion with the aesthetic Aryanism of the Modernist canon and . . . [into] enforcement of its exclusionary politics" (230). My own argument depends upon hers and takes it a step further; whereas she focuses on the consequences of neglecting modernist women who wrote radical critiques of power in traditional forms, I attempt to problematize our inability to read anything *but* such "radical" or wholly subversive critiques as being modernist or feminist practice.

[3] The only such reading is in Montefiore 1987:43–49.

own unequivocally held opinions rather than of social discourse as it constructs her and her speakers;[4] (2) that a feminist writer should "correct" the transmissions of oppressive, inculcated, ideological media like fairy-tales and myth, on the assumption that she enjoys the very kind of "transcendent" or privileged detachment long criticized in male modernists' work. But Smith demonstrates an alternative way of discovering her own agency and voice in a language that she, like Gertrude Stein, recognized to be "speaking her"; her work demands that we perform a different reading act, one that focuses on traditional literary forms and cultural discourse as the subject(ivity) of the work and as the arena for struggle with "self-centered," or internalized, inscriptions and contradictions rather than bold new truths or radical revisions.

Some feminist critics have found it helpful to borrow certain ideas from sociolinguist M. M. Bakhtin as they attempt to find ways of speaking about such agency and its operations at the root of such struggle without resorting to essentialist arguments. Bakhtin's conception of "dialogism" as a response to what he would call the relativization of language—the recognition that words do not innocently refer to the world but compete to define things, and that reality, identity, and subjectivity itself are constructed by words—makes new ways of reading women's textual awakenings possible. Patricia Yaeger, for example, in her readings of "emancipatory strategies" in nineteenth- and twentieth-century women's fiction and contemporary poetry (1988), has significantly drawn upon Bakhtin's theory to suggest that "hybridized utterances" (ones that mix discourses, or demonstrate "multivoicedness") allow for "intimate contact" between often contradictory sociolinguistic views, enabling the emergence of "new 'internal forms' for perceiving the world in words."[5] Casting traditional and otherwise internalized forms of social and literary discourse into dialogue with oppositional others is a way for modern women writers like Stevie Smith, who are particularly aware of their imprisonment in patriarchal language, also to act from their position within it—in Yaeger's words, to "open a self-enclosed discourse to the collision of other points of view" in order to shift textual perspectives and thereby "change their sociohistorical fate."

That poetry (which Bakhtin all but banished as the "monologic" genre)

---

[4] See Millard 1989 for a discussion of the historical tendency for women's poetry to "attract biographical speculation" rather than close reading, as well as the continued tendency on the part of critics to read women's poetry as "a form of disclosure, rather than composition" (65).

[5] This and the following quotation by Patricia Yaeger are from an unpublished essay, "Bakhtin and Ye Ma Jah: Dominant Discourse and the African Name"; she draws her quoted fragment from Bakhtin (1981:360).

can indeed function dialogically in this fashion is an assertion that has been made numerous times in the last decade; it seems hardly possible, at any rate, given our evolving definitions of subjectivity, that we could continue to *read* any genre as the vehicle for "unified utterance"—"a voice . . . completely alone with its own discourse" (Bakhtin 1981:328).[6] Whatever one's views may be with regard to Bakhtin's famous generic distinctions, Smith's poems are ones that must be read dialogically as "novelized" forms because they do indeed *represent* utterance as novels do—particularly the "internal stratification of language" (Bakhtin 1981: 264)—rather than attempting unified self-expression in lyric, or creating a transparent narrative in fairy-tale mode. One might even say, given the tendency of Smith's poems to break rhythm into flat, prosaic lines, that they turn into Bakhtinian "prose," as Bakhtin defines it: "As soon as another's voice, another's accent, the possibility of another's point of view breaks through this [unifying] play of the symbol, the poetic plane is destroyed and the symbol is translated onto the plane of prose" (Bakhtin 1981:328). Here "double-voicedness" replaces the conventional sort of ambiguity he associates with modern poetry.

But there is an established tradition of attributing "double-voicedness" to all genres of women's work in the modern age. A direct line can be traced from Virginia Woolf's famous celebration of a woman's status as outsider to later theories concerning her "double consciousness," or an internal split between "critic and inheritor" (Du-Plessis 1985:41); more recently, critics have emphasized woman's awareness of her gendered position of powerlessness *within* language, as well as her constitution by an internal "heteroglossia" reflective of and effectively controlled by dominating discourses in her historical context. Yet even to this date women poets have generally not been read as exhibiting a public political voice; perhaps there is a "glass ceiling" in the hierarchy of poetry or a lingering desire on the part of feminist readers to keep alive hope of the essentially female lyric voice, sought like a buried treasure. Women poets are usually understood to be expressing a self rather than representing social discourse, and they have been misread by those "critic[s] on a quest for personal relevance, rather than the play of intertextualities" (Millard 1989:65). Our latest phase in

---

[6] Too many to name have argued against poetry's monologism; however, one might look for recent, relevant examples in readings of women poets by Patricia Yaeger (1988) and Lynn Shakinovsky (1990). As Michael Holquist suggests, the "dialogic imperative, mandated by the pre-existence of the language world relative to any of its current inhabitants, insures that there can be no actual monologue" (Bakhtin 1981:426); every word is fraught with an intersection of discourses that causes it to slip out of the writer's hands into the language that formed her or him—though Bakhtinian, unlike many versions of poststructuralist, theory remains deeply interested in the specificity of each "location" (or subject, with its surpluses and limits of inflection) from which utterances issue.

reading history, marked as it is by pluralized approaches and intersections between poststructuralist, feminist, and sociolinguistic theory, now
allows us to see that the two are one—that the public/political practice
of a writer like Smith is conducted through the expression of self as the
play of intertextualities, accomplished through the representation of social discourse as it constitutes subjectivity. It allows us to make new
connections between "modernists," such as Stevie Smith and Emily
Dickinson, two poets associated with one another for decades because
of their spinsterhood, "eccentricity," and obsessions with death, but related more significantly by their internally dialogic and thus socially in-
teractive methods of writing. Like Dickinson, Smith's language
"relativizes itself" by splitting off into many voices, or "linguistic consciousnesses" (Bakhtin 1981:359) that join or retreat from introduced
speakers, as well as respond to "hidden listeners" with silence or uncomfortable, shifting discourse (Shakinovsky 1990:199). Both writers
have been noted for the strange disingenuousness of their simplicity,
which, within the present framework, might be read as their presentation of the impossibility of speaking in an unmediated way, or "straight
from the heart."

Smith's poems differ, however, both from Dickinson's word-by-word
dissonances and from Gertrude Stein's microlinguistic dissections and
repetitions, in that she works in great swatches of familiar discursive
modes and poetic forms that often veer out of control as they mix. Thus
her work demonstrates an unusual and fierce interest in the influence of
familiar generic rhythms on the successful propagation or internalization
of ideas that couch themselves, for example, within the easy resolve of
hymn movements, the tendentious weight of formal meter and closure,
or the memorable, addictive, and sometimes terrifying flights of the fairy
tale, a mode that will be the focus of this essay. Smith casts her unconventional, disunified speakers into conversations with the conventional
sorts of discourse resident in such forms, as well as with echoes of those
who have left their mark there: Herbert, Crashaw, Blake, Tennyson, the
brothers Grimm, and others. Rather than proving "influence" or adherence to traditional values relayed through such forms, echoes such as
these (continually interpreted as homage by even her most recent critics)
draw attention instead to the destabilizing dialogue that Smith com-
mences by dispersing her narrator's own among such voices, all of which
are found in varying degrees of opposition to one another even as they
remain distinct from what the reader might assume the narrator's own
stance *should* be. Although most of the feminist poets read by critics or
gathered together in anthologies have avoided traditional forms, con-
ceiving of them as the historical vehicles of patriarchal order, Smith's
work both acknowledges her inescapable construction by that dominant,

centralized order and, by bringing other "ex-centric" voices into play, acts to hybridize or change it along with our very conception *and valuation* of the stable, balanced, and therefore "right-thinking" subject as it has evolved from classical models.[7] As Clair Wills writes, "it is only by bringing the excluded and carnivalesque into the official realm in a single text that the concept of public discourse may be altered" (1989:132); likewise, it is only by bringing the official realm into the subject's intimate sphere that the concept of "private" discourse may be altered. Smith does both; and by exposing contradictions between the discursive constituents of a single subjectivity, she not only jeopardizes their coherence and therefore their authority, but she also foils those forces that would "preserve," as Felicity Nussbaum writes, "existing subject positions . . . [by discouraging attention] to the ways in which the discourses are incongruent" (1989:33).

Of course the line in recent poststructuralist theory between preserving existing subject positions (and therefore the illusion of their elected integrity, so crucial to maintaining culture's status quo) and erasing the subject altogether is quickly crossed; and such erasure, with its dehistoricizations and deferrals, has been accused of compromising feminist agency. The apparent need at present is to retrieve some discussion of the disunified gendered subject operant *in discursive history* (and not as extradiscursive essence, force, or abyss); I would suggest that a possibility for the beginning of such discussion may exist at the crossroads between an "historicized poststructuralism" and a "gendered Bakhtinianism." For example, Yaeger's reading strategies, combined with those of Anne Herrmann, Laurie Finke, Clair Wills, Nancy Glazener, Dale Bauer, and others, have worked to politicize the poststructuralist approaches upon which they depend, to varying degrees, by bringing Bakhtinian alterity into play—but with a *difference*: by theorizing "a process through which power relations among *gendered* subjects are deconstructed" (Thomson 1989:153; my emphasis). Thus they introduce into Bakhtin's somewhat utopian descriptions of dialogue unequal relationships between discourses, as well as the possibility of suppressions within the dialogic community, by focusing on *the figure* of "voice"—or "multivoicedness"—with gender-motivated questions; even more important is the fact that they do so *without* fetishizing or essentializing repressed, "carnivalesque" forces as the "diffusively subversive Other,

---

[7] Smith's suspicion of feminist anthologies of poetry won her no friends among her feminist contemporaries. But her objections had to do with the withdrawal from dialogue that such projects implied; as she wrote in her partially negative review of one such book, *Without Adam: The Femina Anthology of Poetry*, compiled by Joan Murray Simpson, "Why have poems by women only? Or any group poems, come to that . . ." (*Observer*, 19 May 1968; reprinted in S. Smith 1981:180).

which parts of Bakhtin's work and certain strains of feminist theory have endorsed" (Glazener 1989:111).

Such reading strategies help us begin again with Smith's poetry, where there is no clearly subversive force operating from either below or outside the discursive thoroughfare, though several of her more recent critics have attempted to locate it as emanating from one or another of the recurrent players and places in her work—from women, from children, from animals, from fantasy.[8] Rather, all of her subjects are either infiltrated by competing discourses or helplessly constructed by them; "voice" becomes, in other words, the *site*, always gendered, always historically specific, at which the struggles of language take *place*. Bakhtin's emphasis on the "situationality" not only of each speaker but of each utterance functions—as do Smith's continual, if spare and often hauntingly inappropriate, insertions of autobiographical material into her poems—as a helpful reminder that generalizations about genre as the product of larger, slippery (con)textual forces at work might lead to new, sweeping cultural narratives, if they are formed without heed of the complex pivot that is the discursive subject, the *gendered* subject, different in each historical instance of generic inscription. Somewhere in between the essential feminine voice and the erased subject that swiftly succeeded it is a struggle that is not *for* identity, for it *is* identity in Smith's work; much is revealed about the construction of gender through that dynamic in her poetry, but its locality and historical specificity—in other words, its admitted limitations—also work to ensure that no transcendent resolution or subversion can emerge from it in any final, unified, or unambiguous way.

In short, these recent theoretical developments enable us to reread what many have called Smith's "uncomfortable" poems. They are differently dialogic rather than "revisionary" in our present sense of the term, demonstrating her anachronistic conception of identity as a disjunctive conversation between selves and informed by competing cultural discourses. This disjunction is exemplified by the genre of the fairy tale, offering "constructive" yet often contradictory advice aimed at children during their formative years. Smith's retrieval of the fairy tale as a genre does not involve its reversal or redefinition, for as Nancy Glazener writes in her reconsideration of Stein, women's "problematizations of discourses [are] not usually governed by classic irony" (1989:

---

[8] This reference is made specifically to Martin Pumphrey's work. Though this is arguably one of the most valuable of writings to date on Smith, my own argument nevertheless takes issue with it because he "divi[des] Smith's poetry between the stable authoritarian, restrictive world of adults and the linked, fluid worlds of play and fairy land that are inhabited by children, animals, supernatural characters, women, poets and the muse" (Pumphrey 1991:103).

121). In other words, rather than overturning dominant perspectives from the purview of a stable counterperspective or moral imperative, Smith's texts, like Stein's, disrupt without redefining. Smith even counterpoints any and all emergent statements produced in her poems with what she considered to be their necessary partners: her much misunderstood, amateurish, cartoonlike drawings fraught with misery and subversive laughter—her gestural "codas" struggling toward even further qualification of both tradition *and* her critique.[9] This is feminist inquiry of a sort we are only now learning to appreciate and validate; it is one in which, as Janet Wolff describes it in the work of Sandra Harding, "there are 'no true stories' [but] a feminist intervention which, in true post-modern terms, operates the destabilization of thought, recognizing at the same time 'the permanent partiality of feminist inquiry' " (Wolff 1990:80; quoting Harding 1986:194). Smith's rewritings of cultural "stories" in her fairy-tale poems likewise destabilize by hybridizing or pluralizing each of her speakers' languages to expose their collusive contradiction in the telling; these poems often "resolve" in estrangement from all languages available to a discomfited persona. Such discomfiture becomes, in Smith's fairy tales, "disenchantment"—a state redefined in this present reading as prerequisite to the death that Smith so ardently longs for throughout her *Collected Poems*. For Smith, as for Sylvia Plath (who once wrote that she was a "desperate Smith-addict"; Spalding 1989: 256), death becomes the as yet unimaginable possibility beyond imprisoning language, the space against which words and identities take definition, the darkly desired Lacanian "real" glimpsed when the symbolic (or linguistic) and "imaginary" worlds collide; it is the night or blankness into which Smith's speakers often run or ride as they attempt to escape from their own discursively constructed selves in her fairy-tale poems. As she writes in one comic address to a kindred beast of symbolic burden, "The Donkey" (a dialogue with Yeats's vision of eternal themes and glad wisdom carved in enduring stone, in "Lapis Lazuli"):

> . . . the thought that keeps my heart up
> That at last, in Death's odder anarchy,
> Our pattern will be broken all up.
> Though precious we are momentarily, donkey,
> I aspire to be broken up.
>
> (S. Smith 1983:535)

---

[9] For an expanded discussion of her sketches and their significance see Barbera 1985 or my own reconsiderations of their relevance in Huk 1993 and *Stevie Smith* (London: Macmillan, forthcoming).

II

When our thoughts turn specifically to women's reinterpretations of fairy tales, most of us find it difficult *not* to think simultaneously of Sandra Gilbert, Susan Gubar, and their now famous rereading of "Snow White" as patriarchy's story of how "woman has internalized the King's rules" (1979a:38). Critical studies since theirs have offered readings of contemporary women writers/poets, too, "re-view[ing], revis[ing], and reinvent[ing fairy tales] 'in the service of women,' " even "find[ing] true images of [them]selves" (Rose 1986:211) and "telling their own authentic stories" (Montefiore 1987:42). Jan Montefiore, the only feminist rereader of modern women poets to discuss Smith's fairy-tale poems, inadvertently demonstrates the problems that arise when we try to read Smith's work in this way. She attempts to use poems such as "The Frog Prince" and "I rode with my darling . . ." as examples of how "women poets invoke the fairy tale in order to counter its proverbial 'experience' with their own axioms . . . [yet] avoid those 'explanations' which kill the memorable simplicity and wisdom of true storytelling" (43). But Montefiore illustrates only the latter achievement in these poems by telling us that Smith leaves it up to the reader "to decide what the moral is," preserving "the simplicity and strangeness of storytelling as [Walter] Benjamin defines it" (44–45). By thus implying that there has been some kind of "axiomatic" feminist revision in Smith's fairy-tale poems despite their refusal to give up such wisdom, this kind of analysis links Smith's very different use of ambiguity with the manipulations of traditional storytelling. However, Smith is precisely writing against the "simplicity" and "strangeness" of stories that gesture mysteriously toward their own wise, underlying "counsel." Her use of the fairy-tale mode is entirely demystifying—not only with regard to generic suppositions about "wisdom in simplicity" but also with regard to its narration by the anonymous or detached voice of "true storytelling." Her speakers locate themselves instead through their inflections in the discourses that arise in the narratives; in other words, they situate themselves among the contradictory and even violent clashes of cultural/textual trajectories that contribute to fairy tale's notorious ambiguity and lurking strains of cruelty—a nexus that in some ways mirrors what we might think of as discursive subjectivity, or at least binds this socializing genre *en face* to the "self."

In "The Frog Prince" Smith does, of course, as Montefiore writes, retell part of this apparently simple story of love's transformation of life from a view "inside the story," and even from inside an actor not usually developed in the story: the frog. But this alone constitutes no immediately apparent political or feminist commentary, particularly as the frog represents the male's point of view. What is remarkable in this poem is the clash of internalized languages, which conflict without finally jeopardizing the frog's decision to act exactly as he is "fated" in the story, presenting himself for the princess's kiss; this clash causes us to imagine how incongruous discourses can fuse coercively in order to construct gender and gendered expectations (here out of froggish ambiguity, or "amphibiousness") and can influence arguments between "selves" in the act of misdefining present situations and future scenarios. There is nothing mysterious about the "very English mixture" of discourses that entraps this frog in his destiny;[10] each one is culturally or historically specific to Smith's own linguistic horizon—from the childlike rhythm, rhyme, and diction of the fairy-tale genre to what must be read as the repertoire of Smith's own unmistakably English suburbanite complacency,[11] to the politicized, heroic, and gradually all but evangelistic rhetoric of persuasion with its incitative repetition, which Smith had heard much of during the British "Red Thirties" to what finally pales into echoes of idle if effusive social chatter in the repeated adjective *"heavenly."* We hear their contradictory but ultimately collusive interplay as the frog squats at his crossroads, considering his own attitude toward his apparent options: continued froghood or "disenchantment," a state extolled by fairy-tale tradition but rendered suspect in the course of his internal dialogue:

> I am a frog
> I live under a spell
> I live at the bottom
> Of a green well
> ....
>
> I am happy, I like the life,
> Can swim for many a mile
> (When I have hopped to the river)
> And am for ever agile.

[10] Spalding 1989:260; Smith apparently demonstrated her awareness of her art's specific circumscription within its cultural text by expressing concern as to whether an American audience could possibly understand its "very English mixture."

[11] Smith was so well known as a suburbanite who wrote self-reflexively and usually complicitously about her own site's hypocrisies—in, for example, "Syler's Green," a BBC Third Programme essay (1947), numerous short stories and poems read on either radio or her poetry reading circuits, as well as her best selling novel of the 1930s, *Novel on Yellow Paper* (1936)—that it becomes difficult to imagine this as anything but an insertion of "locating" autobiography, reminding the reader that the narrator of this text is, like her frog, similarly circumscribed within it.

And the quietness,
Yes, I like to be quiet
I am habituated
To a quiet life,

But always when I think these thoughts
As I sit in my well
Another thought comes to me and says:
It is part of the spell

To be happy
To work up contentment
To make much of being a frog
To fear disenchantment

Says, It will be *heavenly*
To be set free,
Cries, *Heavenly* the girl who disenchants
And the royal times, *heavenly*,
And I think it will be.

Come then, royal girl and royal times,
Come quickly,
I can be happy until you come
But I cannot be heavenly,
Only disenchanted people
Can be heavenly.
                    (S. Smith 1983:406–7)

As her drawing of an unbalanced-looking frog (fig. 2) suggests, our speaker decides how he feels while reeling between several "enchanting" discourses—first, "habituat[ion] / To a quiet life" in the "green well" of London's suburbs, perhaps even Smith's own Palmers Green (which, we get the feeling, doesn't *often* involve "hopp[ling] to the river" and thus the freedom to get about). Intimately connected with such ordinary settings, albeit contradictory, are the influential tones of fairy tale's ubiquitous but misleading dreamlands, described as freedom in "her father's palace." Through such description, the poem forecasts for unwitting frogs (culture's "toadies") another kind of circumscription within another kind of spellbinding—but this time human and thus patriarchally ruled—domestic text. He affirms the latter enthusiastically by an internalized, rhetorical, coercive voice that first pummels his "false con-

Figure 2. Stevie Smith's Frog Prince. Reproduced by permission of New Directions Publishing Corporation.

sciousness"—his being "happy," "content[ed]," in frogdom—with the instigatory rhythms of revolutionary propaganda; the voice then modulates into an unlikely blend of heroic and salvational tones in order to celebrate love and marriage as the "heavenly" alternative, located in fairy tale's "ever after."

Critics who analyze this poem often cite Smith's own brief introduction, when she described it as a "religious poem" at poetry readings in the 1960s, a poem about a too-contented being who "nearly missed the chance at that great happiness" (Barbera and McBrien 1985:257; Spalding 1989:273). But Smith was an admirer and practitioner of satire, whose aim was often leveled at Christianity's constructions of afterlife—a bit of biography momentarily put aside in such simplified readings. The dialogic nature of the poem itself is enough to destabilize both such an introduction and the poem's apparently unproblematic resolution, which the genre's coercively simple form and tone urge us to accept. The hybridization of the emphasized word "heavenly" alone, as it resonates in each of its fairy-tale, moral/spiritual, and superficially social modes ("such a *heavenly* party"), scatters and problematizes the advice of the frog's internal voice, demonstrating its construction by contradictory discourses infiltrating both fact and fantasy. All of these discourses are found here to collude in the propagation of dominant (English) social patterns: marriage, domestication, and "royal," filial obeisance to centralized standards and values. Even the rhetoric of political radicalism and its generated energies are co-opted here, as they are in Smith's novels, toward such conservative ends; the uncertainty of disintegrated selfhood seems easily locked into a cycle of choosing clear purpose and radical breakout, already inscribed with the telos of the dominant cultural myth. As a consequence, verbal irony gathers in her potential prince's wishful use of the word "disenchanted," whose alternative denotative meaning is, of course, "disillusioned"—which is indeed what the frog may become if his union resembles what his equally idealistic young readers will experience. Yet the ironies in this poem obtain from such complex sets of slippages between signs and intended or imminent meanings that no simple reassignments of value are possible: there is no positive relocation of that heavenly state. Rather than espousing either the "heavenliness" beyond or the frog's "quiet life," Smith leaves her readers reeling drunkenly between discourses and selves, like the frog; but unlike him we are also cognizant of the impossibility of going forward without being "under the influence" of words, images, and rhetorics inculcated throughout childhood. Thus one might finally say, with reversed irony, that the only surely valuable experience awaiting our frog prince is that necessary and painful disenchantment which, as he cannot yet realize, will mean freedom but by another definition. It will come only in the form of an awareness of his own constructed nature; it will be, in other words, the *jouissance* or "coming" he longs for, but only in that it will provide a glimpse of himself between discourses (the desired "real," if one likes, in all its Lacanian unnameableness). Metaphorical "death" is achieved momentarily through exile from the symbolic order that fetched him there.

Such disenchantment, becoming dead to the influence of discursive and cultural patterns, is more clearly the dream-outcome or the "beyond" actively sought in Smith's other fairy-tale poems. The characters who, unlike the frog prince, go knowingly and willingly into the disenchanting darkness or blankness are, invariably, the women—not because they enjoy any special powers but rather because they *don't*. Their experience is an even more oppressive entrapment within dominating discursivity than their male counterparts ever come to know. In these narratives, the inflections of fairy-tale form and its informing discourses, along with insertions of material from Smith's own life, do much to outline (as do Smith's sparely drawn sketches) a specifically located, gendered agent constructed by and working within the text. And yet the chosen fates of the characters never contrast in any simple way with, or manage to transcend, their alternatives—theirs never become "new stories" assigned greater value in relative terms.

For example, in "I rode with my darling . . . ," one such woman, heading off toward the fulfillment of her dreams with her potential male hero, parts ways with him in order to stay in the dark wood with an "angel burning bright." Like Blake's "tyger" of experience, this herald signals ambiguous disaster for other dimensions of her innocence (though the value of the latter becomes destabilized by the end of the poem):

I rode with my darling in the dark wood at night
And suddenly there was an angel burning bright
Come with me or go far away he said
But do not stay alone in the dark wood at night.

My darling grew pale he was responsible
He said we should go back it was reasonable
But I wished to stay with the angel in the dark wood at night.

My darling said goodbye and rode off angrily
And suddenly I rode after him and came to a cornfield
Where had my darling gone and where was the angel now?
The wind bent the corn and drew it along the ground
And the corn said, Do not go alone in the dark wood.

Then the wind drew more strongly and the black clouds
      (covered the moon)
And I rode into the dark wood at night.

                    (S. Smith 1983:260)

Here, in the first part of the poem, the speaker's departure from her initial, "innocent" self and conventional role is accomplished through disobedience; her "darling" is the one who obviously assumes himself "responsible" both for their actions and for deciding what is "reasonable." His diction slips humorously out of fairy-tale mode into the recognizable tones of male dominance in everyday life; such slippage calls attention to the reinforcement of culture's power structures and values in even the most fantastic and anarchic of narrative genres. Smith revises this familiar fairy-tale event to the extent that she refocuses it upon the female figure, who decides not once but twice to do the "unreasonable," breaking the form and rhythm of the poem as well as its expected story line both in the seventh line and, more emphatically, in the fourth stanza above.

But the second half of the poem becomes more difficult to read because it bears no clear evaluation or judgment of her action and its outcome. It even seems to elicit from our speaker a dismissal of the women as well as the man in her life, a dismissal that has presented a formidable stumbling block to feminist critics:

There was a light burning in the trees but it was not the angel
And in the pale light stood a tall tower without windows
And a mean rain fell and the voice of the tower spoke,
Do not stay alone in the dark wood at night.

The walls of the pale tower were heavy, in a heavy mood
The great stones stood as if resisting without belief.
Oh how sad sighed the wind, how disconsolately,
Do not ride alone in the dark wood at night.

Loved I once my darling? I love him not now.
Had I a mother beloved? She lies far away.
A sister, a loving heart? My aunt a noble lady?
All all is silent in the dark wood at night.

Smith's speaker finds herself in a situation much like that of Robert
Browning's hero in "Childe Roland to the Dark Tower Came," a work
whose images often surface beneath the experience of female characters
in her poems and novels. She once explained her admiration for Browning's particular version of Roland's story—for the latter's bleak last stand
at the desolate dark tower against all those who had come before him,
all those lost "adventurers [his] peers" (in Buckler 1973: 288)—by writing
that "that whole poem is so full of the feeling of courage without hope
and resistance without belief" (quoted in Spalding 1989:61). The key
phrase, "resistance without belief," repeated in the second line of the
penultimate stanza above, helps us to reread not only this poem's "resolution" but Smith's dialogic strategies as they take form in all of her
work. They involve, first of all, bringing her speakers into disenchanting
confrontation, like Roland's, with "all all" that have gone before them
or have had a dominant hand in constructing their stories, including
sympathetic but complicit, instructing figures like mothers and sisters
and aunts (or those who filled Smith's own "house of female habitation").[12] Resistance without belief indeed occurs, in slightly different
fashion, in her poems as they resist simple destabilization in order to
conduct a dialogue with such voices, without belief in the rightness of
their story or any other one might construct. It is certainly a bleak but
courageous view, and the end of this poem conveys it along with the
repeated presence of its counteroption in the Dylan Thomas-esque line:
"Do not go/stay/ride alone in the dark wood at night." If one does not
venture, then one does not (as our speaker *does*) approach that strange

---

[12] See the first line of Smith's autobiographical poem, "A House of Mercy": "It was a
house of female habitation" (S. Smith 1983:410). Smith wrote repeatedly about her family
nucleus, which included a frail mother left by her young husband, a schoolteacher sister,
and a "Lion Aunt"—a stalwart spinster Smith associated with the backbone (both strong
and unflexible) of Britain. Among them they exhibited not only all of the supportive loyalty
and courage that Smith more or less celebrates in this poem but also a continuum of cultural
biases and conservative feminine practices that exercised such contradictory power over
Smith's formation of her own self-image.

periphery of "disenchantment," where the many influential voices that fed her identity become distant, are perceived to "lie," by double entendre, "far away," and finally fall "silent"; this poem arguably ends in metaphorical death at the cessation of discourse, her patterns finally, as in "The Donkey" (quoted earlier), "all broken up." Death in Smith's translation is not like the state that Thomas's speaker urges his father to rage against in "Do Not Go Gentle into That Good Night," but it is one almost as desperately and universally avoided; whether or not it *should* be is the "argument" of the poem (redefined to read "dialogue"), with echoes of Thomas on one side and the will of our speaker on the other. At the very least, one can say that the poem's interactions with Thomas, as well as with Blake, Browning, and the covert masculinist voice in this fairy tale, introduce an(other) gendered perspective into their precincts, causing a destabilizing "angel" to burn within images of destruction and desolation—the tyger and dark tower—in order to hybridize the connotative definitions of "darkness" and "death" while putting no certain value on choices made in the poem. The final interrogatives—each one difficult and by no means rhetorical—produce no new story; they only leave us with a speaker in dialogue with herself, at an estranged intersection of discourses and with no arrows home.

All of Smith's fairy-tale subjects seem to be presented to us at one of three stages: immersed, like our frog prince, in influential discourses; cast, like our rider above, onto the periphery of awareness with regard to her own construction by such languages; or finally, as in the case of Mary in "Cool as a Cucumber," flown beyond the ken of both ourselves as readers and the formerly influential voices in her life who speak the poem. Mary was once, as the title tells us through a familiar expression, "cool as a cucumber," a phrase that conjures up images of smooth, well-integrated self-possession. The poem dismantles this former view of Mary, as her story is retold by the many fragmentary but recognizable voices that owned her:

> Cool as a cucumber calm as a mill pond sound as a bell
> Was Mary
> When she went to the Wishing Well.

> But a fairy came up out of the well
> And cursed her up hill and down dale
> And cursed her from midnight to morning hail.

> And now she gets worse and worse
> Ever since she listened to the fairy's curse

She is nervy grim and bold
Looks over her left shoulder and does not do as she is told.

She is quite unfit for marriage
Of course
Since she listened to the fairy's curse
She grows worse and worse.

Starts off by herself each day
In a most unusual way
But nobody seems to know which way.

She looks pale, really unhealthy,
And moves so queerly, rather stealthy.

Mary come back to me,
Cried one who loved her.
He is the miller's son.

And when she heard him she broke into a run.

She has not been seen since then.
If you ask me she'll not be seen again.

                              (S. Smith 1983:240)

"Cool as a cucumber" comes to mean several different things in the course of the poem. Instead of evoking "self-possession" it stays closer to its referent, becoming an image of well-cultivated, vegetable conformity that Mary "broke" out of, running—perhaps in the way that the second line of the poem breaks out of the first line's gridlocked compilation of tired, objectifying similes, whose tendency is to obscure rather than to describe. Her fate is to become differently "cool" and unreadable after choosing flight from the discursive options that did (and in this poem still try to) compose her—coolly suicidal, in either the real or metaphorical sense, or in both. Whether she is "bewitched," as Frances Spalding has called her (1989:200), or "debewitched"—disenchanted with bewitching discourse—is of course unknowable, since Mary herself is no longer in evidence here. If one believes the first voice, which tells us that Mary must have been "cursed" because she is now "nervy grim and bold, and does not do as she is told," then the former is true. But if one finds the model of obedience with which she conformed to be *more* trancelike or deathlike—when "cool" and "calm" and "sound" she did as she was told, did not go off alone, and made herself fit for marriage—

then it becomes difficult to discern which bewitching is which. As always, Smith increases that difficulty by destabilizing the meanings and historicizing the values of words like "cursed" and "fit," making us aware that they are both specific to, and ironically not in the possession of, her speakers. For example, the familiarity of the unattributed pronouncement "She is quite unfit for marriage" would seem to alert us to the fact that this is fairy tale's timeless "wisdom" speaking; however, it is spoken amid intersecting discourses on manners signaled as specifically English through their idiomatic usages such as "nervy." The words thus open instead the *textuality* of conventional wisdom to historical critiques of the traditional and religious ideas and fears (such as Christianity's fear of feminine independence and power) that inform it. The concept of the fairy tale as a narrative issuing from the faceless source of collective wisdom is therefore transformed into a narration by language itself: a kind of recognizable discourse not requiring an individual speaker because it belongs to the spell of culture. Yet just in case we begin to feel comfortable with the kinds of historical critiques we might produce from our distanced perspective on such discourse, Smith inserts yet another stumbling block into the poem in the form of a "me" (an unannounced subject) who emerges in the last line. This suddenly reminds us that Smith often spoke of *herself* as being "unfit for marriage," reproducing this text yet again in new light as an internal dialogue from Smith's very specific point of construction within it. Dangerously bound and attracted to each voice in the poem, like the English folk lyric lament spoken here by "the miller's son" (whose father in old British balladry abuses the drowned body of one of "The Two Sisters"), Smith can jolt her own poem out of such dark seductions only by casting them into dialogue with the condemnatory social gossip that infiltrates the surrounding stanzas. She allows these voices to become refracted alongside the spectral, hegemonic cultural text that, for all its multivoicedness and constitutive contradictions, works to mold Mary into a single-minded product it can recognize as its own.

We might tentatively say that the slow breakdown and fragmentation of the form of the poem suggests that Mary's "enchantment" by her contextual voices is likewise losing hold of her; in this case the "curse" she received at the Wishing Well might be seen as empowering rather than bewitching. In her novel *The Holiday*, Smith's central character Celia also becomes "nervy bold and grim" just before she begins to quote verbatim from Dostoevsky's *Notes from the Underground*, adopting his "grim" tone of self-castigation and confession of complicity in his world's self-delusive and deceitful discourses (S. Smith 1979:192–93). The "fairy" who cursed Mary "up hill and down dale / And cursed her from midnight to morning hail" may have been of the same internal origin as the one that pursues Dostoevsky's memoir writer; in any event, their disenchantment with social/textual influences seems to leave them in the same state: "We don't know ourselves. . . . Why, we do not even know where we are to find real life, or what it is, or what it is called. Leave us alone without any books, and we shall at once get confused, lose ourselves in a maze, we shall not know what to cling to, what to love and what to hate, what to respect and what to despise" (Dostoevsky 1968:376–77). Going off alone, running from what she should love, Mary slips out between the lines of this fairy-tale poem without articulating what she thinks or envisions, perhaps because she has found herself suddenly between texts and looking to remain there without knowing "what it is called." The last lines of the poem suggest, with their dismissive finality and rhymed couplet snapped shut, that Mary's choice is death, the only permanent removal from her discursive world. But Smith never attempts to narrate a journey into that space beyond the social and poetic discourses where her fairy tales and poems, in testimony to our imprisonment, remain locked. While Mary's flight may be into a fairyland of Smith's own wishing, a much-desired place beyond encircling or self-centered constructions, these poems bring us only to the window of such possibility, in order to begin new dialogues with other "outside" perspectives on our own special sort of solitary confinement.

If Smith's poetry is "uncomfortable," a word often used by her critics, the discomfort derives from its dialogic rather than prescriptive nature. In the poems discussed above, the merging of simple fairy-tale diction and ballad form with the simultaneous appearances of many other kinds of prosaic, lyric, and colloquial languages, as well as prismatic points of view, showcases the multiplicity as well as the complicity of any discourse. By separating out the many voices latent in the fairy tale and forcing them to speak up, Smith dramatizes the collusion of discursive codes in the imagination of identity, while also demonstrating several strategies of her own for "resistance without belief." Although her postmodern tactics have gone largely unread within certain inhospitable frameworks of contemporary criticism, new developments in our own reading strategies have made at least some aspects of her radical renegotiation of language and poetic subjectivity leap to view. Our attempts to investigate the partial exclusion of other writers like Smith from the newly developing canon of women modernists will undoubtedly "discomfit" us, as well as destabilizing some of the valuable work done to date in constructing new histories. But unending disenchantment with new constructions of cultural narratives might be learned from such investigations and might become itself invaluable both to our rereading of modernism and to the necessary, continual rereading of reading.

11

Invading the "Transparent Laberynth": Anne Finch and the Poetics of Translation

JAYNE ELIZABETH LEWIS

> A real translation is transparent; it does not cover the original, does not block its light, but allows the pure language, as though reinforced by its own medium, to shine upon the original all the more fully. This may be achieved, above all, by a literal rendering of the syntax which proves words rather than sentences to be the primary element of the translator. For if the sentence is the wall before the language of the original, literalness is the arcade.
>
> —Walter Benjamin, "The Task of the Translator"

> On a rich Pallace at the first they light
> Where pleas'd Arachne dazzl'd with the sight
> In a conspiccuous corner of a Room
> The hanging Frett work makes her active Loom.
> . . . .
> [But] with extended Broom th'unpitying Maid
> Does the transparent Laberynth invade.
> Back stroke and fore the battering Engin went
> Broke evry Cord and quite unhing'd the Tent.
> —Anne Finch "The Goute and Spider:
> A Fable imitated from Monsr de la Fontaine"

As translator of a fable by Jean de la Fontaine, Anne Finch offers a spellbinding textual metaphor for the female voice as it 'spoke' in Augustan England. In her early-seventeenth-century translation of "La goutte et l'araignée" (1668), Finch's voice is figured in a "transparent Laberynth" that is at once her own and stolen property: writing from the boundaries of English, along the border of its blending into French, Finch also writes at the boundaries of gender, where male and female authors mingle souls. Translation is not of course a genre in and of itself, but it does press on questions of form's integrity and of form's fate in the scenes of its own reading and transcription. In this essay I want to view from a historical and textual perspective some of these theoretical questions identifying female voice with the boundaries of gender and genre.

When Walter Benjamin declared that "a real translation is transparent" and that it becomes so by forsaking "sentences" in order to cleave to the "pure" verbal elements of its "original," he probably did not have Anne Finch in mind (1969:79).[1] Yet in translating La Fontaine, Finch figures the failure of translation in precisely the terms Benjamin uses to represent its triumph. Since these are also the terms in which Finch's own contemporaries cast the task of the translator, the plot of "The Goute and Spider" repays closer attention. In La Fontaine's fable, but far more graphically in Finch's rendering of it, an ambitious spider sets about weaving her web in the "conspiccuous corner" of an elegant drawing room. When she tries to make the "hanging Frett work" her own "active Loom," however, she only woos the brutal attentions of the housemaid's broom—which instrument, as it rends the spider's "transparent Laberynth," also drives home the moral of the story: "each [should] his propper Station learn to know."[2] The sentence plunges Finch's own poem from the public and visible realm of translation to the more obscure domain of household panegyric; imitating the spider's unhappy trajectory from "rich Pallace" to obscure hovel, the poem ends in a domestic environment utterly foreign to the original text, for its last lines rest content to praise Finch's husband and the "happy Nuptial state" she shares with him.

Perhaps "a real translation is transparent," but "The Goute and Spider" is factitious and opaque. It shirks the bonds of revelation and correspondence that we, like Benjamin, expect translations to forge with their originals, choosing instead to move from a set of purely verbal correspondences to the web of historical and personal relations that, it insists, frames all linguistic activity. At the same time, however, Finch's translation is not altogether unfaithful, for it finds those relations already incipient in the original text: the task of translation is implicit in the spider's "transparent Laberynth," just as translation's frustration is built into the maid's "battering Engin." Both the web and the broom emerge less as figures that Finch replicates than as modes of symbolic action that writing absorbs and reproduces in its own rhetorical processes. In other words, Finch's conspicuously impure rendering of La Fontaine's fable interprets it as an allegory of translation—an allegory whose constitutive figures can then grow into literal features of her own work. That work in turn achieves transparency—illuminating coherence with its original—through its own exemplary failure, as well as through its submission to the very "sentences" that "real translation" should avoid as it disentan-

---

[1] For a valuable critique of Benjamin's argument, see Jacobs 1975.

[2] Anne Finch, "The Goute and Spider: A Fable Imitated from Monsr de la Fontaine," l. 50 in Finch 1903. All citations of Finch's work are from this edition; hence for the line and page references appear in the text.

gles itself from the cultural and historical fibers that spoil the play of pure language.

Because it illuminates its original through its liberties and errors rather than by means of a simple transposition of terms, Finch's poem finds a fitting emblem in the "transparent Laberynth" at its center. Indeed, the labyrinth summarizes Finch's conception of translation—devious, inward-turning, embodied—at the same time that it leads us out away from the poem into the cultural climate which the same poem at once replicates and reproaches. Primarily, of course, the "transparent Laberynth" is an organic transcription of La Fontaine's "toile tissue," a device that transforms the "Frett work" of his poem into Finch's own "active Loom."[3] Spun by a "pleas'd Arachne," however, the labyrinth also feminizes her habitat. It incorporates both material and mythic dimensions of women's art (weaving) so that even as the text turns into textile, it also gestures toward the fables of Arachne and Ariadne.[4] These fables in turn not only recall the continuity of women's art with the desiring female body but also foretell the inevitable conclusion of that art in fragmentation and despair. Thus just as Finch's poem as a whole imagines new modes of translation—new relationships between languages—only to register their defeat, so her transparent labyrinth holds the center of the poem in critical tension between poles of possibility and futility. If we were to try to picture it, we would find that a transparent labyrinth can only be an oxymoron that compensates for the material obstructions of the maze with the dangerous pleasures of an unimpeded gaze.

In my reading, Finch's "Laberynth" embodies a constitutive contradiction in English women's relationship to neoclassical poetics, and particularly in their relationship to contemporary theory and practice of translation. Because English writers of the late seventeenth and early

---

[3] La Fontaine's description of the spider's web tells us only that
"L'Aragne . . . se campe en un lambris,
Comme si de ces lieux celle eut fait bail a vie;
Travaille a demeurer: voila sa toile ourdie;
Voila des moucherons de pris.
Une servante vient balayer tout l'ouvrage
Autre toile tissue, autre coup de balai:
Le pauvre Bestion tous les jours démenage."
See La Fontaine, "La goutte et l'araignée," ll. 20–27, in La Fontaine 1668–92/1967.

[4] For excellent discussions of the relationship between weaving and women's art, see Joplin 1984 and N. Miller 1986a. The stories of Ariadne and Arachne, which Miller analyzes in detail, may be found in Book 6 of Ovid's *Metamorphoses*, where Ariadne spins the thread that leads Theseus out of the labyrinth and is then abandoned by him; at the end of the same book, the gifted but mortal Arachne wins a weaving contest with Athena, who immediately transforms her into a spider.

eighteenth centuries saw all written language as intrinsically translatable, they created ways for women to enter entrenched cultural discourses; but at the same time they also reinforced old obstacles to genuine transformation. For instance, although by 1711 La Fontaine had "come more into Vogue than any other Author of our Times" (Addison 1711/1965: 220), and although Finch—the most prolific and eminent woman poet of her day—was one of the first to turn some of his fables into English, "The Goute and Spider" remained unpublished in her lifetime.[5] Like much of her work, it stayed handwritten until the twentieth century, locked between the covers of a manuscript folio circulated among close friends. Finch's poetry needs to be read in the context of contemporary obsession with translation for two reasons. First, neoclassical writers perceived translation as an essential and potentially exemplary cultural activity; thus, in interpreting the task of the translator, Finch engaged, and ultimately dismantled, long-established linguistic assumptions. Second, conceptions of translation are really conceptions of the relationship between authoritative and disadvantaged languages. Therefore, understanding how those conceptions work can help us make out the voices of those who, like Augustan women in England, speak from linguistic positions always on the verge of obscurity.

Ambivalent Amities: Neoclassical Translation
Theory and the Question of Eve

Finch's dates (1661–1720) place her in one of the most volatile phases of English political history. Born just after the Restoration, she came of age in the court of James II, where as a maid of honor to Mary of Modena she belonged to a glittering literary circle whose female members, including Anne Killigrew, were actively encouraged and supported by the queen.[6] The Revolution of 1688 forced Finch to leave the court for the obscurity of her husband's Kent estate; she spent the last thirty-two years of her life there, producing translations, imitations, and "occasion'd" verses as well as the lyrical and polemical poems that would later be noted by William Wordsworth and Virginia Woolf respectively.[7] Like "The Goute and Spi-

[5] Before Finch, the two most notable translators of La Fontaine were the critic John Dennis (as part of his *Miscellany Poems*, 1692) and the physician and satirist Bernard Mandeville (in his highly selective *Fables after the Easie and Familiar Method of Monsieur de la Fontaine* of 1703 and its expansion, *Aesop Dress'd*, 1704).

[6] The standard biographical discussions of Finch herself may be found in Myra Reynolds's introduction to Finch 1903:xvii–cxxxiv and Rogers's 1979:vix–xxiv. See also Hinnant 1994; McGovern 1992; and Salvaggio 1988.

[7] Woolf's discussion of Finch's work marks a critical point in *A Room of One's Own* (1929: 59–63); Wordsworth selected some of Finch's poems for inclusion in a nineteenth-century

der," much of Finch's poetry retraces her fall from the public center to the private periphery—a fall whose metaphorical possibilities she, an attentive reader of Milton, expanded in poetry that often protests against women's limited access to the symbolic centers of English culture.

The political traumas that structured Finch's own life also molded the literary conventions of her day. Late- seventeenth- and early- eighteenth-century English poetry is perhaps more consciously committed to the construction of a stable symbolic community than that of any other age. Rocked by civil war and repeated revolutions within a putatively restored political order, English writers sought methods whereby language itself—and particularly written language—could ameliorate confict and draw contentious English speakers together into a single refined and coherent linguistic group. Many of the notoriously "neoclassical" preoccupations of the period—with genre, with public voice, with poetry that makes its own discursive strategies apparent—are motivated by the perceived necessity of constructing a culture unified by convergent literary values, improved through its exposure to other, more polished languages, and secured by openly rhetorical linguistic process.

Because it found so many of these ideals within reach, translation emerges as one of the most coherent, visible, and urgent literary activities of the neoclassical period. Works like John Dryden's *Aeneid* (1695), Alexander Pope's *Iliad* (1715–20), Thomas Creech's rendering of Lucretius's *De rerum natura* (*The Epicurean Philosopher*, 1682) and Samuel Garth's *Metamorphoses* (the joint labor of "several Hands," 1717) made classical literature part of the English poetic tradition. Likewise, a torrent of translations from contemporary French writers simultaneously refined the estate of English letters and extended its boundaries. In the preface to his own influential collection of translations from Ovid, Boccaccio, and others, *Fables, Ancient and Modern* (1700), Dryden thus pronounces himself "studious to promote the Honour of my Native Country" (in Dryden 1700/1968:4.1445). Translation is a public service motivated by the sense that the mother tongue is insufficient, even savage. Until the translator proves it otherwise, suggested one seventeenth-century poet, it will lie coated with "ancient Rust," desperately "want[ing] one who license could restrain, / Make Civil Laws o're *Barbarous* Usage reign."[8]

The muscular tone of most neoclassical constructions of translation suggests that something more than the promotion of national honor might be stake here. At first glance, translation appears to have been a

---

miscellany. While admiring her poems about nature, he decided "that Lady Winchilsea was unfortunate in her models—*Pindarics* and *Fables*." See Wordsworth to Alexander Dyce, 10 May 1830, in Wordsworth 1939:1.477.

[8] Knightley Chetwood, "To the Earl of Roscomon on His Excellent Poem," Dillon 1684.

site of competition with previous cultures, a method of self-assertion that lets English writers, fortified with "manly Sweetness," "on equal terms with ancient wit ingage."[9] The commendatory verses Dryden prefaced to the earl of Roscommon's influential "Essay on Translated Verse" (1684) go on to enjoin the modern translator "nor mighty Homer fear, nor sacred Virgil's page," thereby portraying translated verse as a transhistorical, transcultural, and explicitly masculine battleground where "Men" grapple with men. But the space of translation is more deeply conciliatory: potential opponents suddenly find themselves "on equal terms," their relationships no longer mediated by "fear" or awe but rather by writing itself, which, as its mechanisms become transparent and thus demonstrably universal, works as a kind of adhesive to secure male bonding. As a good translation derives its authority from its amicable transparency with respect to its original, it even simulates male friendship; Roscommon encourages the translator to

> Chuse an *Author* as you chuse a *Friend*,
> United by this *Sympathetick Bond*,
> You grow *Familiar*, Intimate, and *Fond*,
> Your *Thoughts*, your *Words*, your *Stiles*, your *Souls* agree,
> No longer his *Interpreter*, but *He*.
>
> (Dillon 1684:7)

The task of the neoclassical translator is to suppress opposition (here linked with interpretation) by subordinating every possible difference to the field of distinctions that regulates all languages. Thus for Roscommon the ideal translator is Milton's Raphael, who could represent the War in Heaven (a "conflict 'twixt Host and Host") in a way that exemplifies that conflict's submission to "the great Ensign of Messiah"—that is, to visible signs themselves. Under these signs' presumably impartial jurisdiction, perfect convergence with an original text is possible: "Consult your *Author*, with *Himself* compar'd," Roscommon advises the would-be translator. "While in your *Thoughts* you find the least debate, / You may *Confound*, but *never* can *Translate*" (Dillon 1684, 12-13). Dryden similarly declares that a translator should make "his Author appear as charming as possibly he can, provided he maintains his Character, and makes him not unlike himself" (Dryden 1685:A3r). Garth felt that translation in general "cannot be too exact," but when a translation has to deal with an unfinished work "dark through a hasty Brevity," the "translator may be excus'd for doing what the Author upon revising would have done himself" (Garth 1717:xix).

[9] John Dryden, "To the Earl of Roscomon on His Excellent Poem," ibid.

Neoclassical theory expected exact translation to prove language's powers of analogy, its continuity with the material world of sympathy and personality, and thus its potential to build a coherent, and virile, practical culture. But while translation may demonstrate language's ties to the real as it moves toward the "familiar" and against conspicuous interpretation, it also discourages explicit resistance. English translators often did bend the translated text to please contemporary tastes, to address current issues, or to elide what might be morally offensive to their readers, but they normally did so while asserting an essential bonhomie with the original author. It is only in erasing all signs of resistance to its original that a translation becomes powerful, allowing English letters to "their ancient Rites restore, / And be, what Rome or Athens were before" (Dillon 1684).

Once we see that in neoclassical theory good translation demonstrates language's power as a mechanism of cultural reproduction only to the extent that it routs "barbarous usage" and other real differences, its significance for women becomes immediately apparent. It is no accident that Roscommon likens the bad translator to a bad midwife, for the former fails to manage the isomorphism between languages that permits stable, and stabilizing, meaning to pass between them.[10] Roscommon's bizarre obstetrics, moreover, raise the question of what happens when real neoclassical women undertake the task of translation. After all, they seem to figure in metaphors of translation only as bad examples: good translators are friendly men eager to reinforce the irenic and transparent elements of written language, and thereby to found pure and lawful linguistic communities. Yet translation accounts for a good part of women's private and professional writing from the end of the seventeenth century forward. Aphra Behn actually managed to support herself in the last years of her life by translating from French texts, while aristocratic women took advantage of translation's reputation as a polite pastime through which to practice submission to established authority.

When women translate, however, they can also challenge the structures of authority that neoclassical translation theory assumes. For one thing, translation was often occasioned by a newly literate female reading audience, one with access to written English but unlikely to know the work's original language. As translation's implied readers, neoclassical women introduce the dimensions of reading and interpretation—hence of potential resistance from positions outside culturally sanctioned uses of language language—that contemporary translation theory tried to

---

[10] Roscommon's bad translator is "a *Quack*" who "by *Man-Midwifry*, got *Wealth* and *Fame*." Roscomon imagines language as a "*Lab'ring Wife*" who, "as if *Lucina* had forgot her trade," mistakenly "invoks his Surer aid" (Dillon 1684:16).

mask if not altogether to suppress. Women trouble translation's constitutive assumptions about linguistic stability in other ways as well. For one thing, women readers unfamiliar with the original versions of the translations before them might read differently from better-educated male readers. For them, a translation could usurp the authority of the original; therefore their reading, precisely because of the linguistic inadequacy that motivates it, reminds us that language displays and disrupts as easily as it harmonizes.

Furthermore, women translators themselves consciously brought nonlinguistic experience to bear upon their work, weaving the material, the occasional, and the apparently extraneous into translations already more explicitly marked with the traces of reading than they "should" have been. When "The Goute and Spider" frames "La goutte et l'araignée" in a web of social and personal relationships, it retraces a pattern already woven into women's translations of the period. For example, translating Fontenelle's *Plurality of Worlds*, Behn says that she "naturalize[s his] words."[11] Mary Evelyn's contribution to her husband's 1651 translation of Lucretius was a frontispiece worth a thousand words.[12] Lucy Hutchinson undertook her own late-seventeenth-century translation of *De rerum natura* "in a roome where my children practizd the severall qualities they were taught, . . . & I numbred the sillables of my translation by the threds of the canvas I wrought in, & sett them downe with a pen and inke that stoode by them." Hutchinson also resisted the original text as "ridiculous, impious, execrable," and found it impossible to produce an amicable translation of it; in the end she pronounced her effort a hopeless failure—"not worthy either of review or correction, the whole work being one fault" (dedication to her translation, in Greer et al. 1988:215–16).

Hutchinson's conviction that she has botched the task of translation literalizes (transposes to the field of letters) contemporary myths of female identity—myths which link women with just the rebellious, indeterminate, and congenitally incorrect elements of language that translation is supposed to eradicate. Most obviously, born into public view in 1667, Milton's Eve is properly regarded as an archetype of the late seventeenth-century woman. In *Paradise Lost*, she is also born at one remove from God, thus from the word and from law. Already an image of impure transcription ("Hee for God only, shee for God in him" [Milton 1667/1983:4.299]), she asks that Adam communicate with her in words mixed with "grateful digressions" and "conjugal caresses" (8.55–

[11] Built on the example of her own translation, Behn's argument is that the English translations of French writers, like her own, not only "naturalize their words, but words they steal from other languages" (Behn 1688:A7r).

[12] For a brilliant discussion of Mary Evelyn's frontispiece to John Evelyn's 1656 translation of Lucretius, see Kroll 1991.

56). In the end, Eve is seduced by the serpent in very large part because of her reverence for the ties that bind senses and signs. In fact, Eve emerges as a sign not just of the desire for translation but also of the ways in which desire, sensuality, and subjectivity can beguile and deform symbolic action. It is thus appropriate that from the beginning Eve's relationship to herself is mediated through a false transparency: upon her creation, she hangs over her own reflection in a "smooth lake," materially "stay[ed]" from herself by the very clear surface that makes her visible to her own eyes (4.45, 470). Eve always enters the world as a reader of the most dangerous kind—one whose physical intimacy with signs feeds her growing consciousness that they deprive her of authority.

Postlapsarian women living in literate culture—that is, post-Miltonic women reading Eve—reproduce her irregular relationship to symbolic authority in their own potentially transgressive negotiations with written signs.[13] Their work is dangerous because of what it insinuates about the way morals and meanings are transmitted. And what it insinuates is not just that discursive systems can be disrupted or blocked but, far more scandalously, that cultural paradigms can be transmitted in and through their very disruption. Moreover, like myths of errant womanhood, even contemporary constructions of female perfection link women with doctrines of translatability. Dryden, for example, included among his translated *Fables* an original poem whose presence there is otherwise enigmatic. An inscription to the recently departed Mary Frampton, the poem eulogizes her as "A Fair Maiden Lady, who dy'd at Bath, and is there Interr'd." It goes on to "inscrib[e]" the female body with the same ideals of transparency and unobstructed transmission that motivate the task of translation:

> Her Limbs were form'd with such harmonious Grace;
> So faultless was the Frame, as if the Whole
> Had been an Emanation of the Soul;
> Which her own inward Symmetry reveal'd,
> And like a Picture shone, in Glass anneal'd;
> Or like the Sun eclips'd, with shaded Light,
> Too piercing else, to be sustain'd by Sight.
> Each Thought was visible that rowl'd within;
> As through a Crystal Case, the figur'd Hours are seen.
> And Heav'n did this transparent veil provide,
> Because she had no guilty Thought to hide.
> (ll. 8–18, in Dryden 1700/1958:4.1740)

[13] See also Froula 1983.

Like Eve, Mary Frampton exemplifies linguistic process. As familiar ideals of transparency are brought to bear upon it, her body demonstrates the possibility of flawless correspondence between "inward Symmetry" and outward "Frame"; the "transparent Veil" of her flesh reconciles inner and the outer. She also makes visible the system of analogy that at once integrates Dryden's own poem and relates it to the outer world of its referents. "Crystal Case," "transparent veil," "Glass anneal'd"—the woman's skin embodies an ideal of representation in which Dryden's own poem may also participate through analogy and approximation. But under the inspection it invites, the integrity of Mary Frampton's body— its ability to transmit meaning reliably—turns on an absence at the center, something she does not possess: "she had no guilty Thought to hide." And indeed, as analogies multiply, the same body begins to look less and less like a secure system of cross-references, and more and more like an inconclusive maze. No wonder it is finally "too piercing . . . to be sustained by sight."

Dryden's "Fair Maiden Lady" mirrors—reflects and reverses—Milton's Eve, and with her figures a perceived threat to neoclassical assumptions about linguistic transparency and stability. Far from being exiled from the translative properties of language, women would seem to belong all too securely within them. They reveal that the analogical patterns that seem to make meaning transferable across boundaries go hand in hand with obstruction, exclusion, and indeterminacy. Finch's "transparent Laberynth," then, addresses a linguistic predicament that women, women's writing, and especially translations by women absorb at their own expense throughout the neoclassical period.

"(By Our Seducement Wrought)": Obstruction as Performance

When Virginia Woolf read Anne Finch, she found her poetry "harassed and distracted by hates and grievances." But before she put Finch back on the shelf, Woolf quoted some of her work as an important example of bad writing, using its putative failure to build her own argument that women's oppression and subsequent rage create abrasions and ruptures which forbid their poetry to "consume all impediments and become incandescent" (1929:62). What Woolf's own rhetorical dependence on Finch kept her from seeing was not only that harassment and distraction may themselves be deliberate and even constructive rhetorical modes but also that many of Finch's poems—those about translation, and the translations themselves—*do* consume their impediments. Instead of assimilating them, however, these poems make those very obstructions exemplary threads in their own verbal fabric. When, in lines Woolf did praise, Finch vowed that she would never "in faded Silks compose / Faintly th'inimitable *Rose*," she meant it ("The Spleen," ll. 85–86).

Of course, the sheer number of imitations that Finch produced throughout her creative life can make it seem that she didn't. Her imitations can seem slavish, derivative, or at best trial runs in preparation for her "serious" verse. And while in contemporary eyes Finch's imitations would have shared the prestige of the independent pieces with which some of them are mingled in the only published volume of her work, *Miscellany Poems* (1713), Finch's choice of original texts can still appear erratic and the translations themselves abortive and feeble. The originals include a French version of Petrarch's Sonnet 188, a verse ("The Song of the Cannibals") from Montaigne, part of Racine's *Athalie*, various Psalms and fragments from the Song of Solomon, "Five Pieces out of Tasso's *Aminta*," and several fables of La Fontaine. What is more, Finch seldom translated whole works and she never translated long ones. Instead, she stuck with spare parts, bits and pieces, some of which she cut from larger works and some of which—the fables, for instance—are intrinsically atomistic. But it is precisely because of their fragmentary character that Finch's translations converge with those of other women to reveal what has been suppressed by a contemporary poetics of translation.

In the first place, neoclassical women were often drawn to texts that, either implicitly or explicitly, invoke written language's tendency to split, to dissolve into particles, and to reconvene only under duress and the condition that they might at any moment diverge again. Behn, for example, whipped out four-line verse renderings of all of Aesop's fables (already understood as ancient particles of significance) and arranged them alongside Latin and French transcriptions that made linguistic difference more visible than linguistic confluence. When she translated Fontenelle's *History of Oracles*, Behn was putting into English an account of how written signs supplant continuous voice, in part by breaking language down into small transferable units. Hutchinson's translation of Lucretius responds to a similar impulse, for *De rerum natura* posits a universe built out of the random collision of atoms, where "Bodies" themselves are "formd by chance" ("The Argument of the Fourth Book," l. 5, in Greer et al. 1988).

Like those of other women, then, Finch's fractured and fractional translations not only expose but also physically appropriate language's aleatory and reducible nature. And while translation forges continuities with the work of other women, it also reinterprets the myth of the confusion of languages at Babel, which neoclassical poets and grammatologists believed necessitated translation in the first place.[14] A self-consciously flawed or partial translation turns Babel from a catastrophe that good translation exists to repair into an active figure for disruptive forces still demonstrably at work in the behavior of letters.

Scattered through her preface to the folio manuscript that contains "The Goute and Spider," Finch's own prose comments on translation make just this point, and personalize it further. The preface itself reads like an apology. Strung together with quotations from literary authorities like Beaumont and Dryden, it casts Finch herself as an "Imperfect Peniten[t]" and her writing as transgressive, self-indulgent, a compulsive recreation of the fall: "I have writt, and expos'd my uncorrect Rimes, and immediately repented, and yett have writt again . . . till at last (like them) wearied with uncertainty, and irresolution, I rather chuse to be harden'd in an errour, then to be still at the trouble of endeavouring to over come itt" (Finch 1903:7). Finch's "(like them)" develops a half-covert analogy between the fallen (or falling) woman and "uncorrect Rimes." Both are tempted by the same desire for recognition that dooms the "Pleas'd Arachne" in "The Goute and Spider"; both are trapped in the same exhausting and "harden[ing]" ellipse that nevertheless consolidates somatic, mythic, and literary experience.

But the preface also looks for the cause of the transgressions it lists. And oddly enough it finds that women's "errour" is less certainly an innate fault than it is the fault *of* neoclassical translation, which in Finch's view has made the rules of literate conduct visible and now holds everyone accountable to them. After identifying neoclassical translation with conjugal authority (her husband, she tells us, "know[s] all the Rules"), Finch confesses that she has "written under the knowledge that Poetry has been of late so explain'd, and the laws of itt being putt into familiar languages, that even those of my sex (if they will be so presumptuous as to write) are very accountable for the transgressions against them. For what rule of Aristotle or Horace is there, that has not been given us by Rapin, Despreaux, D'Acier, my Lord Roscomon, etc.? What has Mr Dryden omitted, that may lay open the very misteries of this Art?" (9). Riddled with parentheses that may themselves be construed as performative signs of resistance and divagation, Finch's preface suggests that just because translations like those of Roscommon and Dryden have made discursive "rules" transparent, women's writing looks "imperfect and uncorrect"; confronted with examples that "omi[t]" nothing it is thus obliged to shrink from the public eye. Finch's own crumpled sentences recoil from the "lay[ing] open [of] the Misteries of this Art," and her

---

[14] For discussions of the myth of Babel in relation to neoclassical poetic practice and linguistic theory, see Cohen 1977; Allen 1949; and Derrida 1985.

admiring references to Roscommon and Dryden barely disguise a deeper ambivalence to their masterful translations and the linguistic assumptions that brought them into being.

When Finch comes to the subject of her own translations, we find frustration and internal division. In particular, Finch notes that her translations conspicuously lack one element she would rather like to have included—the erotic. "Keeping within those limmits which I have observ'd, I know not why itt should be more faulty, to treat of that passion, then of any other violent excursion, or transport of the mind." Yet while its erotic texture attracted her to Tasso's pastoral comedy *Aminta*, for example, "Love" remains a "more faulty subject" than any other, and this "wholly prevented me from putting [all of *Aminta*] into Engish verse, from the verbal translation I procured out of the Italian, after I had finish'd the first act extreamily to my satisfaction . . . but there being nothing mixt with it, of a serious morallity, or usefulnesse, I sacrafis'd the pleasure I took in itt, to the more sollid reasonings of my own mind; and hope by so doing to have made an attonement, to my gravest readers, for the two short pieces of that Pastoral, taken from the French, the Songs, and few lighter things, which yett remain in the following sheetts" (10). As translator, Finch splits between "sollid reasonings" and "pleasure," between intimate identification with an "original . . . as soft and full of beautys as ever anything of that nature was" and the external expectation that her work impart "a serious morallity, or usefulnesse." But it is also when she resists or rations the pleasures of translation that Finch's writing becomes most physically real to her; the task of translation itself can make it uniquely possible for the poet to embody her own splitting in the text. In an essay on the "arachnology" of women's writing, Nancy K. Miller suggests that women writers might weave their signatures into their work through "representations of writing itself" (1986a:275). Translation might reproduce this effect with specific and immediate reference to letters themselves, and it could thus bind the figural to the literal through performative references to the more linguistically and aesthetically self-conscious spaces in its original.

As it happens, the bits of Tasso's play that Finch did translate (out of a French translation, evidently) themselves center on "works of art in art." The third of the "Five Pieces out of the First Act," for example, introduces a magician who warns his interlocutor to avoid a particular town which "from our Plains this River do's divide." In that dividing and divided city live women who

>   subt'ly will thy solid Sense bereave,
>   And a false Gloss to every object give.

> Brass to thy Sight a polish'd Gold shall seem,
> And Glass thou as the Diamond shall Esteem.
> The very walls by Magick Art are wrought,
> And Repetition to all Speakers taught:
> Not such, as from our Ecchoes we obtain,
> Which only our last Words return again;
> But speech for Speech entirely there they give,
> And often add, beyond what they receive.
>
> (ll. 41–52)

Tasso's "soft enchantresses" are also translators who literally interfere with ideals of correspondence ("Ecchoes") and transparency ("Glass").[15] They thus bring out the vulnerability to addition and revision that attends not only "last Words"—normally the space of the moral—but also entire "Speech[es]." They weave walls of "false Gloss[es]" capable of dismantling their own originals; so it is only fitting that they seem to transform glass into diamond—and transparency into a cluster of self-ironizing refractions.

As they "abuse [visitors'] wond'ring Eyes / . . . And all they see with Imitation mock" (ll. 57,60), Tasso's enchantresses embody women's relationship to man-made signs. In the Italian *Aminta* they exist simply to warn against imitation's abusive, mocking, violent propensities. Reframed in a mosaic made up of vexed, discontinuous imitations of pieces of Finch's English *Aminta*, however, they necessarily turn the very writing that reproduces them back upon itself. In the end, Finch's own translation internalizes the implications of the imagery it at once adopts and resists. Finding its original inimitable as a whole, the translation breaks into the "Five Pieces" whose rocky genesis in the "sacrafis[e] of pleasure" Finch's manuscript preface records. But in the process it also discovers new angles of performative self-reference.

Similarly, when Finch decided to translate "Part" of Racine's girl's school tragedy *Athalie* (1687), she chose the moment when the play's eponymous heroine confronts her own ambition. Finch's "Athalia" recalls the time "when to the empty'd Throne I boldly rose, / Treating all interceptors as my Foes" (ll. 11–12). Her meteoric rise through all the possible barricades is interrupted by a vision of her mother, Jezebel, who invokes patriarchal authority to warn Athalia that "the *Hebrews* God . . . shall Thee . . . confound" (ll. 54–55) and that she is doomed to defeat.

---

[15] Finch's fascination with glass crystallizes in a short poem, "Glasse," which links glass not with ideals of transparency but rather with division and reversibility, as it metamorphoses into panes that "Light and Air . . . divide" (l. 2) and into "Flakes of solid Ice; / Which, silver'd o'er, redouble all in place" (ll. 5–6).

Appropriately, when Athalia tries to embrace her mother's "shade," she finds before her nothing but "a heap of Bones," and

> Flakes of mangled Flesh, that quiv'ring still
> Proclaim'd the Freshness of the suffer'd Ill;
> Distained with Blood the Pavement and the Wall,
> Appear'd as in that memorable Fall.
>
> (ll. 62–65)

Finch's Athalia lives in a world of phantoms, bloodstained impediments ("the Wall"), and material fragments ("Flakes of mangled Flesh") that are all partly, but never sufficiently, of her own making. Her efforts to enter the chain through which political power is transmitted identify her private phantasmagoria with Finch's own translation, linking both to the "memorable Fall" that Finch's folio preface treats as the constitutive myth in women's literate experience. Significantly, Finch published this "Part" of Racine's play in *Miscellany Poems*. Severed from its original setting—a French tragedy whose preface reveals Racine's anxious adherence to neoclassical unities and laws of probability—the "Part," through its own interruption, makes its relationship to its own textual environment transparent. Interactions between texts become the literal foundation of its own figures. Just as "The Goute and Spider" sank into conjugal submission and thus backed away from writing altogether, so the rhetorical gains here—the accession to powerful exemplarity—comes at the cost of the translation's own integrity. It breaks off with a grim observation by one of Athalia's courtiers: "Sure, Dreams like these are for Prevention given" (l. 67).

In fact, it is very often the female body that prevents Finch's translations from the ideals of correspondence they seem also to have internalized. The spider in "The Goute and Spider" digs her own grave because appetitite and art are inseparable: "The hungry Fiend does in close Ambush lurk / Untill some silly Insect shall repay / What from her Bowels she has spun that day" (ll. 14–16). The counter-assault also comes from a woman, the "Back stroke and fore" of whose "battering Engin" returns responsibility for disruption to a masculinized female body. When Athalia's mother dissolves into "Flakes of mangled Flesh," she likewise directs translation's truncation back to women's bodies and the threats they pose to the transmission of the very meanings that also define and constitute them. But while Finch's translations rehearse this effect over and over again in their own bodies, one of her most important poems about translation takes it as an explicit subject.

Finch never published her "Poem Occasion'd by the Sight of the 4th. Epist. Lib Epist. I of Horace," but she did include it in the folio manuscript, supplementing its lengthy title with an even longer subtitle: "Immitated and Inscrib'd to Richard Thornhill Esq. by Mr. Rowe, who had before sent heither, another translation from Horace." Finch's precise title at first tempts its reader to mistake her own poem for a translation, but the inscription that follows hastens to multiply the literary relations that come between Finch's poem and the one it promises to translate. Ultimately what occasions the poem is less the prospect of imitating Horace than that of illuminating its own distance from him as well as from the male homosocial network of sending and receiving that brought Horace to England in the first place. What is "Immitated and Inscrib'd" to the duellist Richard Thornhill is not even Finch's poem but its referent, Rowe's translation. The word "occasion'd" itself stems from the Latin *occidere* (also the root of *accident*), meaning "to fall," and Finch's title promises a poem motivated ("occasion'd") "by the Sight of" the very text that also pushes it away.

Significantly, Horace's epistle is about male friendship, and after her inscription has placed it in a modern cultural environment where men send things only to men, Finch's poem praises two recent translations of it:

> Twice in our Solitude has now appear'd
> Such verse as Rome throng'd with applauders heard,
> And twice, Her Horace been to us reviv'd
> As prais'd and polish'd as to them he liv'd.
> The Stuff and Workman's skill so nicely shown
> We think the Words as well as thoughts his own
> And joy to see that by relenting Fate
> (Which Speech confus'd) 'tis given thus to translate
> Whilst Babel's scatter'd streames unite again
> Beneath the conduct of th'industrious Pen.
>
> (ll. 1–10)

These first lines rehearse conventional ideals of translation as an open and manly affirmation of language's power to reinforce unity and analogy. The exemplary translations make their own rhetorical business so transparent ("The Stuff and Workman's skill so nicely shown") that "We think the words as well as Thoughts [Horace's] own." At the same time, however, Finch frames her praise in the perspective of the female reader, whose "Solitude" marks her separation from the male community. Nor does the poem shy away from the "scatter'd streames" that the exemplary translation presumably "unite[s]"; indeed, its own use of parenthesis makes both uncontainable "speech" and "confus[ion]" diverting forces within Finch's own language. The poem builds a syntactical frame

of displacement and distancing that contains and qualifies the cosy ho-
mologies that the proper "conduct of th'industrious Pen" presumably
institutes.

The result is very like satire. The first lines of the poem seem to celebrate a revival of Horace; in fact they lose him in a chain of revivals that
leave only empty analogies. Horace himself becomes a fictive personality
ultimately indistinguishable from the original man—"As prais'd and polish'd as to them he liv'd." While initially Finch seems to celebrate translation as a culture-constructing activity performed by talented male
contemporaries, the subtext of the opening lines actually establishes literary experience as a spurious system of substitutions that always threat-
ens to falsify and estrange reading experience exactly to the extent that
it makes translation seem authentic and, for that matter, simply possible.
Scattering, confusion, errant replication inevitably accompany "the conduct of th'industrious Pen"; when we "think the Words as well as
thoughts" of Rowe's translation Horace's "own," we are also reminded
that the words are *not* after all his own, and thus that the thoughts might
not be either.

The poem's middle lines swerve away from the opening rumina-
tion on translation to address the particular social situation behind
the translation at hand. It turns out that Rowe's current preoccupation
with "the softer Buisnesse of his heart" (l. 15) has taken him away
from the public, civic, masculine world of translation to the female one
of his lover's body. Thus what Rowe's translation ultimately occasions
for Finch is not a long meditation on the virtues and values of his
verse but rather a reflection on his work's relationship to an erotic life,
one spent "within the influence of Orania's face" (l. 126). Orania is
Finch's friend and Rowe's lover Frances Coell, and Finch encourages
Rowe to stay with her rather than return to "the Citty" (l. 118) and the
Vine coffeehouse that are both historically and poetically centers of
male literary society.

As it shifts away from literary relationships that are forged in communities of men, Finch's poem turns its attention from the image of
translation as a duplicitous and exclusive cultural project to a more interesting question about the relationship between the female body and
literary ambition, which is both troped and realized as the desire to produce good translations. Moreover, it is by using her own speculations
about the ties that might bind the female body to the task of the translator
that Finch herself becomes a critic—the author of her own reading—of
other texts. She allows herself to wonder, for example, how Thomas Otway's plays—*The Orphan, Venice Preserv'd*—might have been "plotted"
differently had Otway enjoyed a "State" as "bless'd" as the one Coell
and Rowe enjoy: "His Caracters," she decides, "had sure more perfet

been, / Not such as sullied in his Plays were shown, / One by another's guilt, one by her own" (ll. 34–36).

Ultimately, the middle section of Finch's poem about translation not only defends the devotion that keeps Rowe from participating in literate culture but also grants its own written characters the desired intimacy with Coell:

> Even I who to my Heart just bounds had sett
> And in my Friendship scorn'd to be coquette,
> Or seem indulgent to each new Addresse
> Which general Friends, in comon terms expresse
> Now (by so sweet a violence compell'd)
> The amplest room to kind Orania yield.
>
> (ll. 45–50)

As it makes itself an example of the process of persuasion, of deviation coaxed or (as the parenthesis makes visible) "by so sweet a violence compell'd," Finch's poem enters communion with Rowe's poem and with other literary texts. Orania's sweet violence ushers Finch's own writing into the textual universe it longs to inhabit. The "Poem Occasion'd" thus demonstrates its membership in a select group through its continuity with the very female body by which it is compelled, influenced, deformed. In turn, when women's bodies are included in writing, literature itself can acquire a greater fidelity to its referents—just as Otway's "Caracters had sure more perfet been." Translation becomes *more* reliable, not less so.

In Finch's poem, though, Rowe "return[s]" to male society. His return initiates the third and final section of the poem—a section that meshes the first part's linguistic play with the self-evidentiary speculation about the relationship between writing and the female body in the second. One might expect the mesh to be a smooth one, but it is in fact as "violent" as the compulsions attributed to Coell. For the analogies within which the poem is temporarily suspended are themselves inevitably crowded out by another and ultimately more imperious identification—between Finch as an author who inhabits a female body and the woman who in reality stays outside literate culture in spite (or perhaps because) of her capacity to transform it. Thus Finch's poem finally separates itself from the triumvirate at the Vine:

> Happy you three! Happy the Race of Men!
> Born to inform or to correct the Pen.
> To profitts pleasures freedom to command
> Whilst we beside you but as Cyphers stand

> T'increse your Numbers and to swell th'Account
> Of your delights which from our charms amount,
> And sadly are by this distinction taught,
> That since the Fall (by our seducement wrought)
> Ours is the greater losse, as ours the greater fault.
>
> (ll. 65–74)

Finch's poem ultimately resegregates the reproduction of literate culture (through translation) and the female body. More accurately, it finally admits the separation that has structured her poem throughout. It shifts, thus, to the inevitable calculus in which women figure only to the extent that they do not figure at all ("we beside you but as Cyphers stand"). At most, they are confined to biological reproduction ("t'increse your Numbers") and pleasure ("to swell th'Account / Of your Delights"). Although these metaphors invoke fertility, they also occasion exclusion and absence, reminding us of what is unassimilable and truly untranslatable. In its effort to fuse the material concerns that occasion it with the literary ones that it officially addresses, Finch's poem performs its own distance from the activity (translation) it has taken as its subject.

Nothing could mark this distance more emphatically than the poem's ultimate return to mythic history. Finch's last parenthesis—"(by our seducement wrought)"—both supplies an etiology for the symbolic arrangements the poem takes as its subject and obscures agency and cause, for it is not clear whether the fall already signaled in the poem's title ("Occasion'd") was "wrought" through Eve's "seducement" of Adam or through Eve's own seduction by the serpent. "Losse" and "fault" thus at once coalesce proportionally (both are "greater") and become indistinguishable, confused. At the same time, "distinction" reverses, as it is revealed to be not a natural truth but rather a rhetorical device. Its significance comes not from its inevitability but rather from its place in a habit of transmitting morals and messages through history. "Distinction" is ultimately exposed as a convention within translation. Its claims to authority are called into question, but the profits of that challenge can be reaped only at the risk of all intelligibility and law. In the end, Finch's poem stays inside the labyrinthine fictions of authority, resemblance, and transparency that hold translation, and indeed all linguistic activity, together and that render it intelligible.

Part III

Classical Transformations

12

On "The Journey"

EAVAN BOLAND

The Rock Island Line—a sound strange to me in October darkness. A sick baby, almost naked in a hospital crib. The beautiful, sinuous line of medication—crystal clear and amber—dripping from a plastic container into the baby's head.

Elements of form or fragments of a personal crisis? When I came to write "The Journey"—the poem drawn from these experiences—it seemed to me that the first had been disguised as the second.

I was in Iowa when our youngest daughter became ill with meningitis. She recovered wonderfully and quickly but the nights spent by her bedside left an indelible impression. At the human level, of course, there was a thankfulness for the child spared to us. But at a poetic level, there was a new edge and outline to questions I had already begun to ask.

The elements of form—those pressure changes in the immediate environment of the poem—are often not what goes into the finished piece at all. Rather they are those ghosts at the edges of the piece—the excluded, the barred, the banished particles of an experience whose relation with what is included is crucial to the authority of the completed poem.

When I came to write "The Journey" little enough of its origin remained. Not the sound of the train. Not even the plastic fascination of the tube in my baby's head. Nor the sounds and flickers of the hospital corridor and the sweet warmth of the October dusk when I walked out of the hospital. But it was these fragments which brought home to me that powerful experiences of mine ran the risk of remaining outside the craft I had learned and the tradition I inherited. The more I thought about it, the more it seemed necessary to me to subvert that relation between what is left out of the poem and what is included in it. As a young poet in Ireland, in a poetic climate dominated by the well-made poem and the masculine initiative, that relation had, in a very real sense, been prescribed for me.

I want to be clear about this. The subversion I am speaking about is historical as well as artistic. When I came to write "The Journey" I deliberately framed it in the elite dream convention. I deliberately prefaced it with the lines from Virgil that describe Aeneas's brusque encounter with dead infants on the shores of the underworld. I deliberately set out to subvert what I believed to be the orthodox relation between the poet and that convention. Where the convention prescribes that the poet is educated and enlightened by the dream, I wanted to make it clear that the dream of the death of children was a suffering beyond enlightenment and very nearly beyond expression.

In my early twenties, after I had resigned from teaching at Trinity College, I returned there to learn Greek. My early studies had been in Latin but Greek was an entirely different business. I learned to read it in an awkward and anxious way. I never learned—unlike with Latin—to write it or find my way around its verbal waywardness. But I took away from that year or so a powerful curiosity about Sappho: a woman poet born in an oral culture who died in a literate one. A woman who mobilized the formal, religious, and conventional elements of Ionic poetry into a visionary sexuality. A woman whose fragments of poetry about her daughter were so beautiful and memorable that my own mother would quote them to me when I was a child.

Who was she? What prejudices had she encountered and survived? How did her voice break through that high, dark, militaristic Hellenic moment? And what, finally, were the small human details about her that I, as a woman poet thousands of years later, could put my hand out to and touch, like a blind reading of a face?

The answers to all these questions remained unresolved. And then one spring night in the classical section of the library at Trinity I came across a note which an Alexandrian scholiast had written in a text about her: that she was small and dark and ill-favored, like the nightingale. I smiled out loud at my desk—if it were possible to do such a thing. Here at last was a mixture of love and backhanded flattery and irrelevant detail, such as literature has always thrived on. The remark stayed with me enough to become a reference in my poem "The Journey" where I refer to her as "the scholiast's nightingale."

I think I see in the work of many woman poets I admire today some element of subversion. Inevitably, as women and poets we have inherited an equilibrium between the poem and the experience that very often—as I found in the case of this particular poem—cannot be used unless it is subverted. I prefer to subvert the form from within: in other words, to take the formal elements, as in the dream convention, and wrench them into some relation with my own voice, my own feeling. Other women poets have made their statement an ironic rejection of the inherited forms. Both seem to me maneuvres toward a similar end: to radicalize and refresh that relation between what goes into the poem and what remains outside it. I have no doubt that this is one of the invisible, powerful currents of change in contemporary poetry.

The Journey

For Elizabeth Ryle
Immediately cries were heard. These were the loud wailing of infant souls weeping at the very entranceway; never had they had their share of life's sweetness for the dark day had stolen them from their mother's breasts and plunged them to a death before their time.
—Virgil, *The Aeneid*, Book 6

And then the dark fell and "there has never"
I said "been a poem to an antibiotic:
never a word to compare with the odes on
the flower of the raw sloe for fever

"or the devious Africa-seeking tern
or the protein treasures of the sea-bed.
Depend on it, somewhere a poet is wasting
his sweet uncluttered metres on the obvious

"emblem instead of the real thing.
Instead of sulpha we shall have hyssop dipped
in the wild blood of the unblemished lamb,
so every day the language gets less

"for the task and we are less with the language."
I finished speaking and the anger faded
and dark fell and the book beside me
lay open at the page Aphrodite

comforts Sappho in her love's duress.
The poplars shifted their music in the garden,
a child started in a dream,
my room was a mess—

the usual hardcovers, half-finished cups,
clothes piled up on an old chair—
and I was listening out but in my head was
a loosening and sweetening heaviness,

not sleep, but nearly sleep, not dreaming really
but as ready to believe and still
unfevered, calm and unsurprised
when she came and stood beside me

and I would have known her anywhere
and I would have gone with her anywhere
and she came wordlessly
and without a word I went with her

down down down without so much as
ever touching down but always, always
with a sense of mulch between us,
the way of stairs winding down to a river

and as we went on the light went on
failing and I looked sideways to be certain
it was she, misshapen, musical—
Sappho—the scholiast's nightingale

and down we went, again down
until we came to a sudden rest
beside a river in what seemed to be
an oppressive suburb of the dawn.

My eyes got slowly used to the bad light.
At first I saw shadows, only shadows.
Then I could make out women and children
and, in the way they were, the grace of love.

"Cholera, typhus, croup, diptheria,"
she said, "in those days they racketed
in every backstreet and alley of old Europe.
Behold the children of the plague."

Then to my horror I could see to each
nipple some had clipped a limpet shape—
suckling darknesses—while others had their arms
weighed down, making terrible pietàs.

She took my sleeve and said to me, "be careful.
Do not define these women by their work:
not as washerwomen trussed in dust and sweating,
muscling water into linen by the river's edge

"nor as court ladies brailled in silk
on wool and woven with an ivory unicorn
and hung, nor as laundresses tossing cotton,
brisking daylight with lavender and gossip.

"But these are women who went out like you
when dusk became a dark sweet with leaves,
recovering the day, stooping, picking up
teddy bears and rag dolls and tricycles and buckets—

"love's archaeology—and they too like you
stood boot deep in flowers once in summer
or saw winter come in with a single magpie
in a caul of haws, a solo harlequin."

I stood fixed. I could not reach or speak to them.
Between us was the melancholy river,
the dream water, the narcotic crossing
and they had passed over it, its cold persuasions.

I whispered, "let me be
let me at least be their witness," but she said
"what you have seen is beyond speech,
beyond song, only not beyond love;

"remember it, you will remember it"
and I heard her say but she was fading fast
as we emerged under the stars of heaven,
"there are not many of us; you are dear

"and stand beside me as my own daughter.
I have brought you here so you will know forever
the silences in which are our beginnings,
in which we have an origin like water,"

and the wind shifted and the window clasp
opened, banged and I woke up to find
the poetry books stacked higgledy piggledy,
my skirt spread out where I had laid it—

nothing was changed; nothing was more clear
but it was wet and the year was late.
The rain was grief in arrears; my children
slept the last dark out safely and I wept.

13

A Few Cranky Paragraphs
on Form And Content

MARILYN HACKER

I haven't written a sestina since 1986, and may never write another one. The lovely Provençal form I discovered through Auden and Pound in my teens has been so banalized as an (unmetered) exercise in creative writing workshops—whose products come across my desk in teetering stacks when I'm working as an editor—that I find myself disinclined to read, much less write, any more of them. Not long ago, at an International Feminist Bookfair, a crewcut, fresh-faced young woman came up to me to say she'd recognized me, and she loved my sestinas. I found myself wishing ungraciously that she'd said (instead, or also): I love the way you write about women's friendships, or convey a sense of urban movement, or mix credibly ordinary speech with imagery. Then I'd have known I'd met a reader, as well as a probable alumna of a creative writing workshop.

A few days before that, a poet much acclaimed for the stance of witness to contemporary history in her work, whose reading I'd been asked to introduce at a bookshop in Paris, said to me, "I've always liked your villanelles." And I felt she'd merely noticed my occasional use of a form she herself would consider clever but trivial; otherwise she had not found anything of substance in the poems on which to comment.

I'm not proud of my reaction to those well-meant remarks, a reaction which may only show how ill at ease I am when people talk to me about my work. But I've become impatient and uneasy about the fact that because I "use received forms," that is often all that's discussed about the work—oddly enough, by feminist critics and reviewers in particular. The dominance of so-called open forms in contemporary American (here meaning the United States) poetry, especially in the feminist provinces thereof, is so pronounced that use of another mode is cause for comment, taking sides, writing manifestoes. In a literary climate where metrics were part of everyone's prosodic vocabulary, the use of such forms wouldn't be remarked upon: the exceptionally brilliant, or maladroit, use of a schema or structure would be, instead. I'd like to see more of *that* in book reviews! Instead we still have debates about the "New Formalism" and its political ramifications, in which both sets of partisans seem to conveniently forget that poets as politically—and formally—diverse as Julia Alvarez, Gwendolyn Brooks, Rafael Campo, Hayden Carruth, Alfred Corn, Thom Gunn, Rachel Hadas, Carolyn Kizer, Derek Walcott, Marilyn Nelson Waniek, have frequently or consistently made use of formal/fixed metrical strategies in their work; that the usual suspects, in their thirties and forties, white, affluent, East Coast–based, and so forth, are only one part of a continuing tradition or conversation.

And yet, and yet—I choose to write metrically/formally: it's neither an imposition nor a philosophical/aesthetic conviction. I do it because it gives me pleasure; because (some have said) I do it well; because it's a challenge, and one I can meet. (I've never found myself to have a gift for extended figurative language, for example, could not prolong a metaphor to parallel the central movement of a poem, the way some writers whom I much admire do.) Most of all, I do it because it sometimes takes the poem to unexpected places, because language itself then becomes the contrapuntal force, establishes the subtext.

Of course every poem is formal: the writer's intention in setting it on the page as such, with (usually) line breaks rather than a right-hand margin, with white space, is that the reader recognize that it has a structure, that it is language somehow condensed, ordered, thought, and sculpted to do something beyond or besides conveying a fact, delivering a message. Which is not to say that every group of words or sentences arranged "like a poem" on a page has successfully undergone that transformation.

What makes a poem transcend wordplay, description, or rhetoric? What makes a poem? This kind of (privileged) question always makes me slightly queasy. Although making poems is one of the things I do, "poetry" is much less compelling to me as a subject about which to write, think, or act than, say, the homeless young black woman in army fatigues with a shaved head, and the homeless young white woman in jeans with long, unwashed, uncombed black hair, both begging on Broadway between 101st and 106th Streets, both of whom, in the same clothes, but bathed, laundered, shampooed, would be plausible Columbia University graduate students ten blocks uptown. Perhaps there's a more pertinent question that connects them to "poetry": what makes a poem relevant to the reader so that she or he does not turn the page impatiently, thinking "What's this got to do with me"—or "Tell me something I didn't know already!" Political relevance isn't enough. Last night I shut, in disappointment, a book of poems by a black British lesbian: poems which made necessary points, reclaiming street life and street talk, haranguing hypocritical white feminists and hypocritical black male activists, but the poems themselves were just as predictable as the white North Carolina academic's well-made sonnets about fishing with his twelve-year-old son, or the Jewish pacifist's free-verse sequence about visiting her grandmother in a nursing home. Poems about grandmothers in nursing homes, fishing trips, liberal hypocrisy, aren't a priori bad or good any more than are ones about unrequited love, the fear or the fascination of death, or devotion to a deity. It's not the predictable subjects that make so much contemporary "journeyman" poetry unremarkable, but the predictable language, structure, point of view, tone. (I make this remark as a once-and-future editor, under no illusion that there was any period in the recent or distant past when most of what was written *wasn't* predictable or mediocre.)

There's a place for mediocre fiction, as any commercial editor will affirm, if the subject is timely/original/in-the-news, something about which some group of people wants to read. Is there a place for mediocre poetry? Do we want there to be? (And who is "we"—me, Richard Wilbur, June Jordan, Miguel Algarín, Helen Vendler?) My first impulse is to say: no, there's not. Then I recall how much hot-headed, right-on, and mediocre feminist poetry it took to produce a climate where a woman poet isn't still Dr. Johnson's dancing dog (not that she does it well, but that she does it at all); how much African American verse rhetoric had to be written, read, and processed so that Yusef Komunyakaa, Rita Dove, Thylias Moss could free themselves of having to be representative or exemplary and can write—whatever and however they damn please! As an editor, I'm much more strongly inclined to work through drafts one, four, seven with a poet until we reach one I'm willing (eager) to publish if the poem deals with events, presents a point of view, not yet obvious: the point of view of an HIV-positive woman, a description of open-heart surgery, or a convincing rendering of a jam session. And I'd have the same inclination toward a not-yet-entirely successful poem in an intriguing/difficult/invented-but-rigorous form. The nursing home and fishing trip poems though—because they are so numerous—have got to be pretty exemplary on first reading.

Often enough, the formally ambitious poem is *also* the one where the point of view or narrative thrust is not merely "original" but compelling. I remember my excitement upon first reading the deceptively laconic, demotic syllabic quatrains of Hayden Carruth's *Asphalt Georgics*, or the rhetorically expansive, pyschologically and historically acute dramatic movements of Muriel Rukeyser's *One Life*. And I've experienced the same sensation of expanded possibilities reading new work by younger poets (an editorial privilege): Rafael Campo's sequence, "The Distant Moon," limning a first-year medical resident's tentative, erotically tinged interchange with an AIDS patient; Lynda Hull's long, pyrotechnical "Suite for Emily," juxtaposing delinquent girls in lurid, jeweled cityscapes with Dickinson's verbal rigors—which also happened to be the first AIDS elegy I'd read memorializing a woman.

(I didn't intend specifically to cite two AIDS-related poems, but the subject has imposed itself upon contemporary poets across generations. I remember, again, the two separate, gaunt, and obstreperous women panhandling on Broadway and realize that in mentioning them I also may be writing about AIDS.)

Formal ambition—as my examples may show—needn't mean invention from scratch, any more than breaking out of a metrical pattern which has come to seem overfamiliar implies plugging up one's ears to accentual-syllabic structures. Almost every contemporary American poet has read or heard quoted Ezra Pound's imperative, "Break the back of the iambic pentameter!"—including those student poets who have never composed ten lines of iambic pentameter in their lives. Hardly anyone recalls that in order to "break the back of the iambic pentameter," Pound, who *had* written reams of it, advised young poet Mary Barnard to "write Sapphics until they come out of your ears" (Barnard 1984:56). (Good advice: she became one of our finest translators of Sappho.) That is: compose metered verse stanzas in American English that were markedly *not* iambic—a different proposition than discarding fixed meter. And a difficult one: iambic pentameter is very "natural" to colloquial English. If you leave out the French and Latin words, you spin it out as easily as prose.

After I had written a kind of novel consisting of 200-odd sonnets interleaved with a couple of other, also iambic, forms, Pound's decades-old advice seemed particularly moot to me. I'd hovered around James Wright's "difficult, dazzling" hendacasyllabics, paid tribute to them in a slant-rhymed "Letter from the Alpes-Maritimes" (in *Assumptions*), and paid more attention to the rhythm's demands in "Elevens" (in *Going Back to the River*), a kind of response to Wright's lovely Sapphic/Horatian "Prayer to the Good Poet"—Horace—in *Two Citizens*. Somehow it took that gradual approach for me to finally attempt the "real" metric template: three lines of *trochee trochee dactyl trochee trochee* followed by a five-syllable *dactyl trochee* line called the adonic. This is about as close as you can come in English, where syllabic stress can be noted, but measures of syllable length are, at best, moot. "A Note Downriver" (in *Winter Numbers*) was the first entirely metrical poem I wrote in sapphics (James Merrill's elegies for David Kalstone in *The Inner Room* encouraged me).

It interests me that "distance"—in particular the distance and tension between the two cities, New York and Paris, in which I live, between my two languages/cultures, between a heritage of exile from a Europe which cast out its Jews and a coming-of-age coming back to it from the States mostly united in their rejection of feminists, anarchists, artists, and queers—is thematically important to me in just about all the poems in sapphic (and alcaic) stanzas which I've written (now about a dozen). It's as if dislocating my verbal/aural reveries—and I do sometimes *think* in a meter when I'm deeply engaged in writing it—into a noniambic meter, less natural to English, were a kind of "Invitation au Voyage," or one to examine the voyage my life has been for the last twenty-five years.

Alcaics, even more metrically intricate than sapphics, tempted me after reading for the tenth time Alfred Corn's graceful "Somerset Alcaics" from his book *The West Door*. (In general, those two Greek meters come to us Anglophones modulated by Latin poets' use of them; they are as Horatian as they are Attic.)

My own first presentable work in alcaics, the title poem of *Going Back to the River*, began (after days of practice sessions with the meter), as so many others have, where it describes itself, where I'm now sitting writing this page: at my worktable three floors up above the rue de Turenne, with the #96 bus belching at its stop just below, on the way to Belleville and the Porte des Lilas. Bus notwithstanding, the street is so narrow that the neighbors across the way and I live our lives more or less in view of each other; this decade, in what is one of the oldest neighborhoods in Paris, the spectre of what happened in this city, in this arrondissement, a mere fifty-odd years ago also lives nearby.

On 16 July 1942, almost thirteen thousand Jews, over four thousand of them children under sixteen, were summarily arrested by the *French* police. Single adults and childless couples were taken to a concentration camp at Drancy—before, and since, a banal suburb. The children and their parents, more than seven thousand people, were penned up for seven days without sanitation or first aid, starvation rations given them more brutally than they'd have been given to penned animals, in the Vélodrome d'Hiver, a sports stadium, before being sent to Drancy as well, and thence, with others, to Auschwitz. Except for those who escaped, or were rescued before deportation—a minimal number—not one of those 4,051 children returned.

The writer Primo Levi said, when asked why he didn't write about the Stalinist gulags as well as Auschwitz (of which he was a survivor), that he could only bear witness to what he had experienced: he knew no more about the gulags than did his interlocutor. (He said more than that:

he went on to elucidate the differences.) I don't think I could write a poem about the Vel d'Hiv (as it's referred to, even in historical accounts of the event). I know less about it than do my neighbors in their sixties, seventies, eighties, if they want to remember. But those events are still as present as the seventeenth-century plumbing, just as the fact of being a Jew is present in my consciousness, even without a fixed cultural or devotional meaning.

It has, in part, the meaning given to it by those events. In July 1942, I was a four-month fetus in my mother's womb, but in the Bronx, not in Paris. (Pregnant women were not exempted, nor were veterans.) Fifty-two years later, I know more about poet and anti-Semite Ezra Pound than about the twenty-seven children, my contemporaries, older sisters and brothers, who were arrested that day with their parents in just one antique tenement, 22 rue des Ecouffes—still standing, five minutes' leisurely walk from where I live.

Is this still about poetry? Poetry itself suffers when it's too pointedly "about poetry." ("Writing a Poem" as subject surfaced more often in those manuscript piles than did unrequited love or nursing homes.) It's difficult, though, for a poem not to be, on some level, about *language*, whether directly or indirectly, as a reflection of the conscious compression, shaping, intense attention-paying which the writer must do, whatever the *other* subject.

It would be comforting to align poetry with the forces of liberation. Those French police were ordered not to exchange "unnecessary conversation" with the French-speaking Jews they were to arrest (most of them were not yet naturalized citizens, or had been stripped by decree of citizenship awarded after 1928—except the children, citizens by virtue of having been born in France, who were arrested anyway)—official language for: don't talk to them. Exchanged words may lead to mutual recognition. But there was also the literate German officer army who wrote in his journal on 19 July about a stroll through Père Lachaise Cemetery: a lyrical meditation on the long-departed, not on what was happening to those who were—so briefly—still alive. And there was Pound, and there was Eliot, and there was, and is, every writer capable of brilliantly acknowledging the common humanity of Jews, of Africans or Arabs, of communists, Catholics, women, or queers.

Perhaps that's why I permit myself that impatience with readers and apprentice writers who only notice or comment on sestinas, sonnets, or sapphics. However modest and circumscribed are my attempts to bear witness, or, less ostentatiously, to say what I've seen for myself, I'd like to think that testimony can be perceived in its integrity, surface and ossature together. Which is the skin, which flesh, which skeleton—form, content—is impossible to discern: they're part of one body in motion.

A Note Downriver

Afternoon of hungover Sunday morning
earned by drinking wine on an empty stomach
after I met Tom for a bomb on Broadway:
done worse; known better.

I feel muggy-headed and convalescent,
barely push a pen across blue-lined paper,
scowl at envelopes with another country's
stamps, and your letter.

Hilltop house, a river to take you somewhere,
sandwiches at noon with a good companion:
summer's ghost flicked ash from the front porch railing,
looked up, and listened.

I would grouse and growl at you if you called me.
I have made you camomile tea and rye bread
toast, fixed us both orange juice laced with seltzer
similar mornings.

We'll most likely live in each other's houses
like I haunted yours last July, as long as
we hear rivers vacillate downstream. They say
"always"; say "never."

Chiliastic Sapphics

Sunday afternoon at the end of summer:
from the Place des Vosges come a busking harpist's
liquid notes to lap at the traffic noises
outside my window.

Car-horns honk: tail-end of a Jewish wedding's
automotive crocodile. Bridal party
at the head, they beep toward the *vingtième*, trailing
limp pink tulle streamers.

Flip in a cassette while I read the papers:
drought and famine, massacres. Cloistered sisters'
voices raise the Kyrie. A gay pastor
who was abducted

last week rated photographs and a headline.
This week, men in uniform: an invasion.
Refugees are interviewed crossing borders,
businessmen taken

hostage. An American in a golf cart
mobilizes teenagers to the oilfields.
Crowds in Jordan volunteer for the *jihad*'s
suicide squadrons.

Tanks and aircraft carriers take position
to wage war for Mecca and petrodollars.
Poison gas is brandished. (The Kurds were gassed, and
then, who protested?)

Death to Jews, to infidels, to invaders!
Kill the Arabs! We're going to blast the bastards
off the planet! Journalists feed the slogans
into computers.

They'll be heard tomorrow in every language
(even taking precedence over football).
Holy war or genocide: peace is everywhere untranslated.

Will she be in love with me when I'm fifty?
Will we still have names and our own diseases?
What's become of Pasteur Doucé? His lover
mourns, while reporters

flock toward war. The nuns who attain their limpid
a capella *O lumière joyeuse*
made their tape four years ago. They'd be singing
it now, at vespers.

At this moment, six o'clock sunlight blazes
roof and cornice opposite, where the neighbors,
just come home from holidays in the country,
throw open windows,

and the price of nectarines and tomatoes
by the kilo was what competing voices
cried in French and Arabic at the market
early this morning.

14

Genre Development and Gendered
Voices in Erinna and Nossis

KATHRYN GUTZWILLER

An epigrammatist of the Augustan age, surveying the history of Greek literature, constructed a canon of nine women poets, an earthly counterpart to the heavenly Muses (Antipater of Thessalonica, *AP* 9.26).[1] Yet the entire poetic production of these nine women, now surviving in tattered shreds or scanty selection, formed even in antiquity only a small percentage of the literature produced and disseminated in the Hellenic world. The genres in which women composed were severely restricted as well. Through the end of the fifth century the known literature authored by women consists primarily of lyric (Snyder 1989:40). In this as in so much else, the principal model was Sappho, who composed songs of love and longing in lyric meters to be performed in a private setting. The lyric poets who succeeded her in the fifth century—Myrtis and Corinna of Boeotia, Praxilla of Sicyon, and Telesilla of Argos—sometimes composed choral songs destined for public performance, but their topics tended to be local legends and their audiences were probably local as well (Snyder 1989:38–63).

The reason that women seem not to have composed in the genres of epic, elegy, and drama has to do not only with the often very public, sometimes even Panhellenic, setting for the performance of these genres but also with their traditional function in defining Greek patriarchal culture. The grand epics that memorialized the military achievements of mythical heroes, the elegies that conveyed the ethical standards of Greek culture to male citizens at symposia, the dramas that reinforced or in-

---

[1] I use the following abbreviations for editions of ancient works: *AP= Anthologia Palatina*, most accessible in the Loeb Classical Library edition of *The Greek Anthology* 1916–18; G-P = Gow and Page 1965; Pf. = Callimachus 1949–51; *PLF = Poetarum Lesbiorum fragmenta* 1955; *SH* = Lloyd-Jones and Parsons 1983.

terrogated civic values in democratic Athens were, through origin and custom, the province of male poets. Women, however, had their own traditions of oral song—including lament, love lyric, and lullaby—which must have been passed down from mother to daughter without the scrutiny of a male audience. The lyric compositions by women that found their way into the canon of Greek literature may well represent a distillation and extension of women's traditional repertoire (Skinner 1993:131). In this paper I focus on two women poets of a slightly later period— Erinna, who was writing, apparently, in the middle of the fourth century B.C.E., and Nossis, who lived in the first half of the third. The literature of this early Hellenistic period was strongly affected by a change in the standard mode of reception: in addition to oral performance, poetry was now commonly encountered through the reading of books (Bing 1988). Partly as a result of the shift from public performance to private reading, certain female poets seized the opportunity to remake genres traditionally associated with male activity as reflections of their own experiences as women.

Both Erinna and Nossis incorporate Sapphic themes and inspiration into verse that employs the meter, style, and diction of poetic forms traditionally composed by men. Erinna was even praised as the "equal of Homer" (*AP* 9.190.3) for composing, in epic meter, a lament of three hundred lines for her childhood friend Baucis; and Nossis, through the vehicle of the book collection, reworked the traditionally anonymous and separately situated form of epigram into a means of expressing a personal and woman-centered view of her own "Sapphic circle." Although neither woman is known as a major figure in the history of Western literature, I will argue that the generic renovations they accomplished had a lasting effect upon the course of Hellenistic poetry and the Latin literature derived from it. Yet their achievements have been rendered practically invisible, because they were taken up by male poets and incorporated into poetry that was written once again from a masculine perspective.

Erinna

Of Erinna's life almost nothing is known. Thought to have been a native of the small island of Telos, she is reported to have died unmarried at the age of nineteen. Yet innovative poets of the early third century were effusive in praise of her poetry, which they surely knew in the form of a written text. The fame of Erinna rested almost exclusively on her *Distaff*, a poem of three hundred epic hexameters on the death of her girlhood friend Baucis. An anonymous epigram proclaiming her excellence (*AP* 9.190) asserts that her *Distaff* was equal to Homer and that she surpassed Sappho in hexameters as much as Sappho surpassed her in lyric meters. This suggests that Erinna had two seemingly incompatible models for her work: the grand genre of epic and women's poetry, such as Sappho's tender reminiscences of love lost and friendship ended. I will argue that Erinna's achievement was to combine successfully these two models. In her *Distaff* she offered a new concept of epic by replacing the public narrator of Homeric poetry with a personalized narrating voice derived from lyric poetry composed by women.

Erinna was writing at a time when Greek poets were experiencing dissatisfaction with the composition of traditional epic. Choerilus of Samos, author of a *Persica*, complained that there were no untrodden paths in this genre (*SH* 317), while Antimachus of Colophon modified Homeric form in his *Thebaid* through erudition and preciosity of language. Erinna may have proved popular with Hellenistic poets because her *Distaff* pointed to a more successful way to revitalize Homeric epic. The competitive social system of Greek males had been the true object of the *Iliad* and *Odyssey*, as of so much other early Greek literature.[2] Women in epic were represented only in their roles of wife, mother, daughter, or lover—that is, in terms of their relationships with men. Male authors were concerned with female experience not so much in and of itself but only as it furthered or inhibited the male quest for honor and public recognition.[3] A female author, if she chose to compose in such traditionally masculine genres as epic, had to assert the value of her own experience as a woman within poetic forms that, through customary usage, denied the independent worth of that experience.[4] Erinna's three hundred lines could be judged "equal to Homer" because she created from within a subordinate form represented in Homeric epic—laments performed at funerals—an alternative world, the world of a woman's life as seen by a woman.

Until 1928 the *Distaff* was known only from ancient references, after that also from a fragmentary papyrus. I offer my own translation of the lacuna-filled text on the papyrus:

---

[2] For good descriptions of the value system of the ancient Greeks, see Adkins 1960 and Gouldner 1965. Adkins divides Greek values into two categories, competitive and cooperative, both of which are necessary for the smooth functioning of society. Although Adkins does not pay close attention to the gendering of these two categories, it is clear that competitive behavior is more highly valued for males, cooperative for females.

[3] Feminist scholars have been engaged, however, in the project of extracting women's own values and concerns from the relatively brief descriptions of their activities and representations of their speech in the Homeric epics; see Katz 1991, Felson-Rubin 1994, and Doherty 1995.

[4] For the success of Sappho in doing just that, see Rissman 1983; Winkler 1990.

... of a girl   3
... brides (or dolls)
... tortoise (or lyre)   5
... moon
... tortoise (or lyre)   7
....
... to shear   13
... wave (or sweet-apple)
[you leaped] with mad [feet] from [the horses].   15
Alas, I cried loudly ... tortoise (or lyre)
... the courtyard of the great hall ...
... these things, I lament you, wretched Baucis
these traces ... lie in my heart
still warm. ... embers already.   20
Of dolls ... in the chambers
brides (or dolls) ... Once at dawn
mother ... to the spinners
that one came to you ... sprinkled with salt.
the small ones ... Mormo brought fear   25
... and on her feet she stalks
... And she changed her appearance from ...
But when to the marriage bed [you came,] you forgot all that
which ... as a child ... having heard from mother,
dear Baucis. Aphrodite [brought you] forgetfulness.   30
Therefore lamenting you [in this way,] ... I leave aside.
For my feet ... are not allowed [to leave] the house,
nor to look upon [your body] with my eyes nor to lament
with unbound hair. ... Blushing restraint
tears about my [cheeks] ...   35
... before ...
nineteen ...
Erinna ... dear ...
looking upon the distaff ...
Know that ...   40
about ...
Thus restraint [to me] ...
maidenly ...
and looking ...
and hair ...   45
the gentle-speaking grey-haired women, who are the flowers of
     old age for mortals.
Therefore you, dear ...
Baucis, [I] lament ...

flame . . .
hearing a cry . . .   50
O Hymenaeus . . .
and touching much . . .
all of one, o Hymenaeus . . .
Alas, wretched Baucis . . .

(*Papiri greci e latini* 1090 = *SH* 401)

Although ancient sources had told us the poem's title, length, meter, and dialect,[5] the subject of the *Distaff* became known only with the discovery of the papyrus. It is now clear that two epitaphs for Baucis ascribed to Erinna continue the theme of her lament in the *Distaff* (*AP* 7.710, 7.712). It is also clear that Erinna's purported age at death—nineteen—derives from a reference in the poem (37) and that the title refers to her lonely spinning, perhaps also to the fateful unwinding of her life's thread (Levin 1962:200; A. Cameron and Cameron 1969:287–88). But it remains difficult to reconstruct the thought sequence in the lines preserved on the torn papyrus. According to a commonly accepted interpretation, the lines about the tortoise refer to a girl's game of tag.[6] Erinna recalls an occasion when Baucis, playing the role of Chelichelone (or "Tortitortoise," in translation), sat in the middle as children ran around her and exchanged a chant with her until she leaped up and tried to catch someone. But another interpretation, that the lines refer entirely to Baucis's wedding day, cannot be discounted (Michelazzo Magrini). What remains indisputable is that Erinna makes reference to her earlier life with Baucis—their dolls, the mother of one of them, the spinners in her household, the frightful bogey Mormo. One of the best indications of the poem's tone comes not from the papyrus but from a two-line fragment preserved elsewhere (*SH* 402): "An empty echo penetrates from here into Hades. There is silence among the dead and darkness falls upon their eyes." Erinna's poem is this echo, never to be heard by its most wished-for recipient.

The *Distaff* has been difficult to place within the literary tradition of laments. Its most recent editors describe it as a hexameter *thrēnos*, divided and connected by the complaints of the mourner (Lloyd-Jones and

---

[5] The *Suda* reports that Erinna wrote a poem of three hundred hexameter lines called the *Distaff* in a mixture of Doric and Aeolic dialects. The dialect mixture suggests that she has combined the vernacular Doric of her native Telos (the most likely of the homelands listed by the *Suda*) with Aeolic forms reminiscent of Sappho.

[6] This interpretation, based on Pollux 9.125, was first advanced by Bowra 1936:154–55. Bowra's theory has stimulated important intrepretive readings of the poem, such as that of Arthur 1980, who interprets the poem as a vicarious experience of all "the events in a woman's life" (64), and Pomeroy 1978, who points to the association of the tortoise with the lyre and loom.

Parsons 1983:189). But similar hexameter *thrēnoi*—Thyrsis's lament for Daphnis in Theocritus's first *Idyll*, Bion's *Lament for Adonis*, and the *Lament for Bion* falsely attributed to Moschus—are all later than Erinna and probably influenced by her (Bowra 1936:341). For the type of lament that Erinna is adapting to her own needs, we must look to earlier Greek literature, particularly to epic. Professional singers of *thrēnoi* are present at funerals in the *Iliad*. They are male bards, whose laments, though not recorded, probably consisted of generalized consolation (Alexiou 1974; Harvey 1955:168–72). But the Homeric *thrēnos* is punctuated by the mourning of women, apparently in the form of a refrainlike keening. From the group of women those closest to the deceased step forward to sing another kind of lament called a *goos*, which emphasizes the personal loss of the bereaved. Erinna's lament is more like these *gooi* than the *thrēnos* performed by male bards (Skinner 1982). Even the particle "to" (therefore), which sometimes introduces the close of the Homeric *goos* (*Iliad* 19.300, 24.773), appears in two of Erinna's refrainlike statements of grief for Baucis (31, 47).

But Erinna has not simply modeled her lament on these Homeric *gooi*, those of the Trojan women for Hector and that of Briseis for Patroclus. She has rather wrought a fundamental change in epic form by converting the Homeric representation of a woman's lament into a literary work in its entirety; that is, she has made a subordinate and subliterary form into the dominant and structuring form. I suggest that she accomplished this liberation of women's speech from its encasement in epic narrative through the inspiration of Sapphic song.[7] While laments for the death of a female companion are not found among the fragments of Sappho's poetry, there are poems concerning separation from a beloved friend, perhaps because of a marriage (94, 96 PLF). And as Erinna recalls the happy activities she shared with Baucis when they were children, so Sappho consoles her companion with memories of a joyful past, recounting for her the flowers, the perfume, even the lovemaking. While these similarities do not necessarily give evidence of a "recognized type" of song in which a woman lamented the departure of a companion (Rauk 1989:116), they do suggest that Erinna's modification of the *goos* represented in epic was effected under the influence of the personalized voice heard in women's poetry. This change had the result, of course, of eliminating the ventriloquization of the grieving woman by the epic narrator. The mourner now speaks for herself, not as the male narrator imagines her to speak.

---

[7] For Sapphic influence on Erinna, see Rauk 1989 and Cavallini 1991:129–30. For the taming of women's laments through appropriation into male genres, see Holst-Warhaft 1992.

All the Homeric women who sing *gooi* lament a hero, and they tend to emphasize their loss of protection through his death. Briseis grieves for Patroclus because he comforted her when she was captured, promising that Achilles would make her his wife (*Iliad* 19.287–300). Andromache laments her husband Hector as the defender of the city, without whom the women and children of Troy will be enslaved, herself included, and her son, if he survives, reduced to a life of misery (24.725–45; cf. 22.477–514). Even Helen laments Hector, because he protected her from the reproaches of her Trojan in-laws (24.762–75). One function of the *goos* in Homer, then, is to define the importance of the warrior to society by detailing the meaning his loss had for an individual woman. The grieving women are not themselves the focus of attention, but rather their laments make clear the value of the hero through a display of their dependence upon him. But Erinna, though writing in the tradition of the Homeric *goos*, mourns not a hero, or even a male relative, but a woman—and not even a kinswoman, merely a childhood friend, an age-mate, who had married and passed out of her circle of daily associates. Though the relationships established by Greek women with other females in the early years of their lives may have constituted the strongest emotional bonds they ever knew, affection such as Erinna felt for Baucis counted for nothing in the male-controlled value system of Greek society. This bond was in fact disruptive to woman's role as wife, keeper of the household, and bearer of children. As a result, societal structures tended to silence a woman's expression of affection for another woman, at least as a mode of public or published discourse. Of course, personal laments may have existed within the confines of the women's community, and it is testimony to the extraordinarily compelling nature of Sappho's poetry that her expressions of homoerotic longing were valued and preserved in the public at large. Erinna, who chose to mourn Baucis from within literary forms designed for other purposes, used her modification of those genres to complain about the restrictions they placed upon her.

In the early part of our fragment Erinna is reviewing the childhood experiences she shared with Baucis. Such sentiments may have been a standard component of *gooi*, and some of the Homeric singers mention happier times now ended because a loved one has died.[8] Yet the happiness of Erinna's youth was first brought to an end not by Baucis's death but by her wedding.[9] The inferential particle *to* in line 31 indicates that

[8] E.g., see Achilles's lament in the *Iliad* for Patroclus (19.315–18), Briseis's lament for Patroclus (19.295–99), and Helen's lament for Hector (24.767–72).

[9] According to one of the two epitaphs ascribed to Erinna, Baucis's wedding torches were used to light her funeral pyre (2.5–6 G-P = *AP* 7.712.5–6). In both drama and epitaph, the death of a girl before marriage was commonly treated as a wedding with Hades (Seaford 1987). For a girl's female relatives and friends from whom she was being parted, her mar-

the particular form Erinna's mourning takes is determined by the circumstance of Baucis's marriage. In early evaluations of the papyrus, scholars were puzzled by Erinna's claim that she could not attend Baucis's funeral, and some imagined that she was a priestess forbidden to look upon a corpse (Bowra 1936:334; Page 1941:489; Gow and Page 1965: 2.282). But it is more likely that her status as a *parthenos*, "unmarried woman," (cf. *partheniois*, "maidenly," 43) was the cause, either because she could not travel to Baucis's new homeland or because a single woman was not allowed to attend the funeral of one who was not a relative (West 1977:108–9; Arthur 1980:62). Erinna details the restrictions placed upon her mourning: she cannot leave her house, look upon the corpse, or sing the *goos* (*goasai*, 33) with loosened hair. Another standard sign of mourning, tearing the cheeks, is replaced here by the phrase "blushing restraint tears about my . . ." Erinna's conflation of the red marks of grief with the blush of shame is a sign of her poetic skill, full of significance.

Aidōs, "restraint" or "modesty," is the feeling that prevents a person from performing actions that would meet with the disapproval of others. It was a particularly important virtue for women, that which kept them from sexual relations with men other than their husbands. Since a Greek girl was normally married at a young age to a more mature man through arrangements made by her father, *aidōs* must often have been synonymous with the suppression of truly felt emotion or desire. When the Phaedra of Euripides' *Hippolytus* is physically ill from her suppressed love for her stepson, she gives a long speech (373–430) exploring the effects of *aidōs* on women and their reputations. A favorite topic of Hellenistic poets was the conflict in a woman between *aidōs* and *erōs*. The young Medea of Apollonius's *Argonautica* agonizes in a soliloquy (3.771–801) whether she should dismiss *aidōs* and court disgrace by aiding the handsome Jason. In Callimachus's *Aetia* a maiden who speaks to a courting youth lowers her eyes as her cheeks redden with "blushing modesty" (*aidoi . . . phoiniki*, fr. 80.10 Pf.). The last phrase, which appears also in later romantic poetry, seems an echo of Erinna (*[phoi]nikeos . . . aidōs*, 34). From the perspective of male poets *aidōs* is a desirable virtue for a woman, one that increases her attractiveness, though eventually to be overcome by a lover. For Erinna, however, *aidōs* is the internalization of restraints imposed upon her by society, restraints that control her ability to express her grief for the person she loved most in the world.

Martin West has suggested that a personified Aidos addresses Erinna in lines 37–41 (West 1977:109–11). The second *aidōs* in 42 does have a

<hr>

riage may have been conceived as a kind of death; for this theme in modern Greek laments, see Danforth 1982:75–77.

"resumptive air" in the manner of epic phrases that terminate direct speech, and it is attractive to think that the references to Erinna's name, age, and distaff come from the mouth of another, not the poet herself. But it is less likely that Aidos is here warning Erinna about approaching old age and her marriage prospects, as West assumes.[10] More probably, this personified Restraint reminds her of the behavior permitted a nineteen-year-old *parthenos*, namely, to remain at home gazing at her distaff. The address by Aidos thus assumes the conventional function of the *sphragis* or "seal," in which the poet is identified, sometimes with reference to a particular poetic posture (Kranz 1961). The lines bear close comparison with other passages in Greek literature in which inspiratory deities address poets, as the Muses appear to Hesiod (*Theogony* 22–35), Aphrodite answers the summons of Sappho (1 *PLF*), and Apollo warns Callimachus to write slender poetry (fr. 1.21–28 Pf.). I suggest that Aidos here functions as Erinna's Muse. The restraint that she feels as a maiden, isolated and confined to her distaff, forces her to compose this literary lament in place of performing an oral *goos* at Baucis's funeral. Her poetic achievement was thus a direct response to her limited opportunity to speak in a public setting.

But because of the advent of the book culture, Erinna's words became known as her person did not. She is perhaps the most celebrated of early Hellenistic poets in surviving Greek epigram. Asclepiades, who introduced erotic topics to epigram, praised her as "more influential than many others" despite the slightness of her poetic production (28 G-P = *AP* 7.11). Leonidas applies Erinna's own words chastizing Hades for his rape of Baucis to the fate that she herself suffered, to become the bride of Death (98 G-P = *AP* 7.13). Somewhat later her poetry was viewed, because of its brevity and fineness of style, as a direct forerunner of Callimachean poetics, which provided the dominating literary aesthetic of the Hellenistic era (*AP* 11.322). Yet despite this evidence from antiquity for her foundational importance in the development of new poetic sensibilities, modern scholars have made little progress in identifying her influence upon the major male poets of the day. I suggest that what Hellenistic poets found so compelling about the *Distaff* was its presentation of a personalized voice from within the traditionally objective form of epic. The success of Erinna's modification of epic was not simply that the subordinate form became the work in its entirety, but that the voice

[10] West's interpretation of the *Distaff* is based on his theory that the poem was composed by a male poet impersonating a girl named Erinna. He argues that a poem of such "exceptional ingenium" and "considerable ars" could not have been written by "a nineteen-year-old girl whose daylight hours had been spent at the loom and the spindle" (1977:117). For defense of Erinna as a sophisticated female poet, see Pomeroy 1978:17–21; Arthur 1980; and Skinner 1982.

of the character now became identical with the voice of the narrator. No longer was the perspective of a grieving woman determined by the anonymous narrator, whose perspective was essentially that of the male-dominated culture. Erinna spoke from within the traditional *goos* to complain about the restrictions society placed upon its use, and that was the source of the emotional power of her speech.

If we look in later poetry for successors to the *Distaff*, we find a host of speeches by troubled women, usually grieving for a lover. Prominent examples are Medea's lonely nighttime debate about whether she should betray her father and country to aid Jason in Apollonius's *Argonautica* and Simaetha's attempt to charm with magic her lost lover Delphis in Theocritus's *Idyll* 2. The most direct influence of the *Distaff*, as I have argued elsewhere, may be Callimachus's *Lock of Berenice*, in which a catasterized lock assumes the posture of a lost girlhood companion to grieve for its separation from the person of its beloved mistress Berenice (Gutzwiller 1992:375–76). Through Catullus's Latin translation of this poem (poem 66), which he composed because of his inability to express in his own poetic persona his grief for the death of his brother, the personalized voice of Erinna grieving for Baucis was transformed into the voice adapted by the male poets of Latin love elegy. It can be argued, then, that the female expression of love and longing that was traditionally discounted by male-controlled culture and restricted to the private sphere came, through Erinna's adaptation of oral lament to epic form, into the mainstream of Western literature. Yet through the conversion of the female voice to speak of male concerns, Erinna's own contribution was effaced, her poem lost, while the male poets influenced by her, like Callimachus and Catullus, gained fame for their poetic innovations.

Nossis

From the hand of Nossis, a native of Epizephyrian Locri in southern Italy, there survive twelve epigrams: eight dedicatory in form, seven of these concerning women. In contrast to Erinna, whose Sapphic inspiration must be surmised, Nossis directly avows herself a follower of Sappho—by reminiscences of her poetry in one programmatic epigram and by overt declaration of literary filiation in another poem. Yet in the past her orientation to other women either has not been discerned at all or else has been misunderstood. One theory from the end of the nineteenth century makes her a *hetaira*, or prostitute, because she celebrates dedications made in the temple of Aphrodite (Reitzenstein 1893:142; cf. Gow and Page 1965:2.436). Another group of scholars, who argue for a noble birth, explain her dominant interest in women through a disputed ancient theory that the Locrian aristocracy was based on matrilineal descent (Polybius 12.5.6).[11] Only recently, in several important studies, has Marilyn Skinner advanced the argument that Nossis's poetry is self-consciously woman-centered (Skinner 1989, 1991a, 1991b).[12] I will here extend Skinner's argument by turning the focus to genre, by examining how Nossis conveys her appreciation for women, for the fineness and delicacy of their accomplishments and beauty, through gendered changes in the traditional dedicatory epigram. My special concern will be to show that Nossis produced her unique perspective, that of a woman looking at other women, by forging her epigrams into a collection.

The first epigram collections were produced no earlier than the fourth century B.C.E., when editors began gathering inscriptional epigrams thought to have been written by famous poets, such as Simonides.[13] In the first half of the third century a number of epigrammatists seem to have published their own poetry books. Quite recently a hundred epigrams by Posidippus were discovered on a third-century papyrus (Bastianini and Gallazzi 1993), and considerable evidence suggests that other prominent epigrammatists of the day, such as Asclepiades, Leonidas, and Callimachus, issued their collected epigrams in published form.[14] I have argued elsewhere that the female poet Anyte, who in the early third century wrote tender epitaphs for animals and pastoral epigrams, was likely a forerunner in this business of publishing epigram collections (Gutzwiller 1993).[15] The invention of the poetry book was an essential step in the elevation of epigram from a minor inscriptional form to become perhaps the most characteristic literary mode of the Hellenistic era. While the composer of inscribed verse was traditionally anonymous, effaced by the convention of celebrating the dedicator or deceased, the reader of an epigram collection tends to attribute similarities of theme and connections suggested by arrangement to the controlling persona of a literary artist. The epigrammatists of the early third century, I propose, created collections that conveyed the sense of an authorial presence and

---

[11] For evidence that Nossis's name is aristocratic, see Cazzaniga 1972; and for a general analysis of Nossis's poetry taking account of what is known about the historical Locri, see Gigante 1974.

[12] See also Snyder 1989:77–84, who suggests, however, that it may be "only a curious coincidence that the epigrams of Nossis . . . seem to reflect a distinctly female world" (77); Furiani 1991.

[13] On the development of the epigram, see Reitzenstein 1893:104–92; Wilamowitz 1924: 1.119–51; West 1974:19–21; Hutchinson 1988:20–21. On the date of the Simonides collection, see Gow and Page 1965:2.516; Page 1981:119–23, 207–10.

[14] My book *Poetic Garlands: Hellenistic Epigrams in Context* (Berkeley: University of California Press, forthcoming) reconstructs the nature of these lost epigram books.

[15] On Anyte, see also Snyder 1989:67–77 and Barnard 1991.

so made it possible for the reader to deduce the poet's own literary, philosophical, or social perspective. By making evident their gender, female poets personalized the voice of the traditional epigrammatist, who was assumed despite his anonymity to be male.

Evidence that Nossis published her own epigram book derives from two poems in which she names herself and makes programmatic statements. The first of these is now generally accepted as the prooemium of her collection (Luck 1954:183; Skinner 1989, 1991a:91–93):

> Nothing is sweeter than love. Everything desirable
>   is second to it. I spit even honey from my mouth.
> Nossis says this: The one who has never been kissed by Aphrodite,
>   that woman does not know what sort of flowers roses are.
>
> <div align="right">(1 G-P= <i>AP</i> 5.170)</div>

Despite its apparent simplicity, this epigram offers a highly sophisticated and allusive statement of Nossis's poetic creed. In both language and structure, her quatrain evokes Hesiod's famous description of the poet's relationship with the Muses (Cavallini 1981): "Blest is the one whom the Muses love; sweet song flows from his mouth" (*Theogony* 96–97). Hesiod's "sweet song" becomes in a parallel passage "sweet dew upon the tongue" (*Theogony* 83), which, through the common association of dew with honey, stands as the direct antecedent of the "honey" that Nossis spits from her mouth. In her introductory manifesto, then, Nossis rejects the inspiration of Hesiodic epic, so proudly maintained by contemporary poets like Callimachus, in favor of a tradition of more personal, erotic verse. Nossis's substitution of Sappho for Hesiod as her primary archaic model is indicated by the Sapphic character of the prooemium: the replacement of the Muse by Aphrodite (cf. 1 *PLF*), the association of roses with poetic production (cf. "the roses from Pieria," 55.2–3 *PLF*), and the allusion in the first phrase to the famous priamel that opens Sappho 16 ("the most beautiful thing, . . . whatever one loves," 16.3–4 *PLF*). There seems little doubt that Nossis is here proclaiming Sapphic inspiration for her woman-centered poetry.[16]

Although other scholars have observed Nossis's gesturing toward her archaic models, it has not been noted that her quatrain alludes as well to her more immediate predecessor. The metaphor of honey in the mouth, which occurs elsewhere in Hellenistic poetry, depends not only upon the punning identification of *meli*, "honey," and *melos*, "song," but also upon the conventional representation of the poet as a bee. Yet Nos-

---

[16] See discussion of Nossis's debt to Sappho in Gigante 1974:25–27, 1981; Degani 1981: 49–52; Skinner 1989, 1991a; Furiani 1991:190–93.

sis's preference for *erōs* over *meli* cannot logically, in an introduction to a poetic collection, function as a simple rejection of poetry in favor of love. It seems likely that the contrast is rather that between the erotic poet and a nonerotic beelike poet, since already in Aristotle (*History of Animals* 553a18) we find mention of the chastity of bees. In fact, this nonerotic honey represents specifically the poetry of the maiden Erinna. In an admiring epigram Leonidas refers to her as a "maiden bee" (98.1–2 G-P = *AP* 7.13.1–2), and three later epigrams repeat the comparison of Erinna to a bee or of her poetry to honey (*AP* 2.110, 7.12.1, 9.190.1–2). This constellation of references to Erinna's beelike nature suggests that the symbol had a special aptness for the maiden poet, quite possibly because she had employed the image in her own *Distaff*. Nossis's concern to define herself as an erotic poet in contradistinction to Erinna arises from the immediate and profound influence that Erinna's poetry had upon her own. Herondas recognizes the temporal relationship between the two when he refers to a character named Nossis as Erinna's daughter (6.20).

Nossis follows in the footsteps of Erinna not only as a woman poet casting her gaze upon women but, more specifically, in composing four portrait poems that have as their direct model an epigram by Erinna celebrating the lifelike portrait of a certain Agatharchis:

> This painting comes from delicate hands. My good Prometheus,
>   there are humans who equal you in wisdom.
> If the one who so accurately painted this maiden had only
>   added a voice, it would have been you, Agatharchis, yourself.
>
> (3 G-P = AP 6.352)

Nossis apparently felt her originality to lie in her adaptation of Erinna's poetry to a different stage in women's lives: while Erinna, who supposedly died unmarried at nineteen, describes the portrait of the maiden Agatharchis and mourns the marriage of her girlhood friend Baucis in her *Distaff*, all of Nossis's female subjects, with the possible exception of Melinna in 8 G-P, are no longer *parthenoi*. This interpretation of the honey image as a reference to Erinna's poetry elucidates Nossis's proclamation in the second couplet of her prooemium. The one who is not kissed by Aphrodite is a maiden poet, like Erinna, and it is she who, though she culls flowers like a bee, does not know that roses are the best of blossoms. Roses, with their sensual and erotic associations, are here symbols of Nossis's own poetry or, what is much the same thing, symbols of the sensual, flowerlike women who form the subject matter of that poetry.

Although we cannot claim that Nossis was the first poet to issue a collection of her own poetry, her prologue poem is, to my knowledge, the earliest evidence for the collection conceived as a gathering of flowers. By the Middle Ages the "anthology" or "florilegium" had became a faded metaphor.[17] But not so for Nossis, who just may have invented it. Both Sappho (55.2–3 *PLF*) and Pindar (*Olympian* 6.105; cf. 9.27) had used the metaphor of song as flower, and the image of poet as bee had become explicit in Plato's *Ion* (534a). The extension of the metaphor to the collection came about when a woman poet sought to say what could not be said within the confines of conventional poetic language: that is, to state her place, as both follower and innovator, within the tradition of women's poetry. Although the dedicatory epigram had long been established as a concise, informational, unemotional form, Nossis could yet express her involvement with other women, the erotic excitement caused by their presence, by weaving a series of these short forms into a collection. The poet who was capable of composing poems that as a group delineate a woman's world was the one who understood "what sort of flowers roses are," the flowers beloved by Sappho and Aphrodite.

Another epigram, more directly expressing Nossis's poetic debt to Sappho, has long been viewed as the epilogue of her collection (Reitzenstein 1893:139; Wilamowitz 1924:1.135):

> If you, stranger, are sailing to Mitylene where dances are lovely
> in order to borrow the flower of Sappho's graces,
> Announce that a Locrian woman bore one dear to the Muses
> and to her. You should know that my name is Nossis. Now go.
>
> (11 G-P = *AP* 7.718)

Nossis's direct model for this poem was an epigram by Asclepiades in which a cenotaph asks the passerby to report to Euippus's father in Chios that his son has perished at sea so that only his name survives (31 G-P = *AP* 7.500). But Nossis's epilogue is a remarkable modification of epitaphic form to serve as a proclamation of her poetic lineage. As Euippus sends a message of his death to his father, so Nossis sends a message of her birth across both temporal and spatial seas to her poetic mother Sappho. Yet despite the conventions of the form, the message is addressed to a stranger who is not literally a passerby, but the reader of the collection. Nossis delivers to this unknown reader not just the "seal" of her name but, through a rhetorical slight of hand, a statement of her position within literary history. The type of reader who is summoned as Nossis's

---

[17] Gow and Page 1965:2.594 (see n. 2 for the history of the term *anthology*) attribute the invention of a garland of poetry, as a collection of various authors' works, to Meleager, whose *Garland* dates to about 100 B.C.E.

messenger is one who seeks inspiration from Sappho and is therefore an aspiring poet, most likely a woman poet. By insisting that this new poet speak Nossis's name when she sails to Mitylene, Nossis claims for herself the right to be acknowledged as the inheritor of Sappho's graces, as an intermediary between the mother poet and any future Sapphic composers. Ultimately, then, Nossis's epilogue is a plea for poetic immortality, for a place within the tradition of women's poetry.

Meleager, who anthologized Nossis's poetry about 100 B.C.E., highlights the erotic nature of her collection by claiming that Eros melted wax on her tablets (1.10 G-P = AP 4.1.10). It is not necessary to assume, as some have, that Meleager here refers to lost homoerotic epigrams later expunged from the anthology tradition.[18] Meleager's description of Nossis's collection seems in fact to be based directly on her prooemium, where the image of poet as bee is modified to accommodate erotic inspiration. The apparent contradiction between her programmatic claim that "nothing is sweeter than love" and the nature of her surviving epigrams may result from a continuing misunderstanding of female eroticism. Like Sappho before her, Nossis celebrates the beauty of individual women, the sensual appeal of objects prized in their world. The erotic excitement she claims as present in her collection arose not from any direct or indirect reference to sexual activity but merely from the casting of her gaze upon women as they go about the business of their private lives. There is no reason to assume, then, that the seven remarkably similar epigrams concerning dedications made by women or portraits painted of women were not to some degree exemplary of the whole collection. I here offer my own translation of these epigrams as a preliminary to considering how they may be read as a group:

> Esteemed Hera, you who often come from the sky
>   to look upon your fragrant Lacinian temple,
> Receive a linen robe that Theuphilis, Kleocha's daughter,
>   wove for you with her noble daughter Nossis.
>   (3 G-P = AP 6.265)

> Let us go to the temple and see Aphrodite's statue,
>   how it is intricately adorned with gold.
> Polyarchis set it up, enjoying the great wealth
>   she has from the beauty of her own body.
>   (4 G-P = AP 9.332)

---

[18] Gow and Page 1965:2.434; Skinner 1989:14–15. But in a later essay Skinner concludes that the position I posit here is "equally plausible" (1991a:94–95).

With joy, I think, Aphrodite has received this gift,
  a headband from the hair of Samytha.
For it is variegated and smells somehow of sweet nectar;
  With this she, too, anoints lovely Adonis.

                (5 G-P = AP 6.275)

Her portrait Callo dedicated in the house of fair-haired Aphrodite,
  having had her image painted, a perfect likeness.
How gently she stands! See how she blossoms with charm!
  Let her rejoice, for her life incurs no blame.

                (6 G-P = AP 9.605)

This portrait shows Thaumareta's form. How well it depicts
  the lively youthfulness of the gentle-eyed girl.
If your house-guarding puppy were to see you, she would wag her tail,
  thinking she looked upon the mistress of her mansion.

                (7 G-P = AP 9.604)

The essence of Melinna is depicted. Look at her gentle face.
  She seems to gaze at us tenderly.
How truly the daughter bears a perfect resemblance to her mother.
  It is good when children are like their parents.

                (8 G-P = AP 6.353)

From its beauty and bearing this image is recognizable
  even from afar as that of Sabaethis.
Observe! I think from here I see her wisdom and tenderness.
  Much joy to you, fortunate woman.

                (9 G-P = AP 6.354).

These seven poems bear an intriguing relationship one to another. Epigrams 4–6 are all dedications made in the temple of Aphrodite, linked by the repetition of the deity's name in the first line of each as they are differentiated by the variety of objects presented—a statue of the goddess, a headband, a portrait of the donor. Epigrams 7–9 also describe portraits of women. Although they are not specified as dedications, their resemblance to 6 suggests to the reader of the collection that these portraits, too, were presented to Aphrodite. Epigram 3, on a dedication to Hera made by Nossis and her mother, is the most distinctive of the poems. Skinner has argued that through the conventional association of weaving and poetry Nossis here pays "tribute to her mother as her earliest creative mentor" (Skinner 1991b:23). While the epigram may indeed contain a personal statement of this sort, its emphasis on the mother–

daughter relationship also links it to other poems. In 8 Melinna's portrait is praised because it shows forth her resemblance to her mother, while in the epilogue poem (11) Nossis identifies herself through reference to the "Locrian woman" who bore her. Such thematic links intertwining the poems suggest that the epigram book as a whole carries a meaning that could not be derived from any one poem read in isolation, either in inscribed form or in an anthology of works by various authors. Nossis's collection, it seems, delineated a society of Locrian women, bonded to one another through shared interests and values transmitted by women of the past.

Among the thematic links between poems are the descriptive terms for the objects dedicated: *bussinon* (3.3) for Hera's robe, probably designating its linen fabric, more certainly its costliness;[19] *chrusō daidaloen* (4.2) for Aphrodite's statue, referring perhaps to a patterned surface that is gilt; *daidaleos* (5.3) for the headband, too, now perhaps indicating embroidery. Delicacy of fabric, intricacy of design, and sweetness of scent serve to define a feminine aesthetic, standards of beauty held by the women known to Nossis and reflected in both their possessions and persons.[20] The sumptuousness of fine cloth is a proper gift for a noble family, proud to name three generations from grandmother to mother to daughter. The beauty of Aphrodite's golden statue mirrors the beauty of Polyarchis's own body from which came the means to purchase the gold. The multicolored headband has acquired its nectarous scent from the natural sweetness of Samytha herself, its former owner. The portraits all show forth a beauty that belongs both to the artistic object and to the woman it represents. The females mentioned in the epigrams, both human and divine, are linked as well by a set of shared qualities, in external appearance and in its internal reflection. Three of the portraits convey a woman's gentleness (*aganōs*, 6.3; *aganoblepharou*, 7.2; *aganon to prosōpon*, 8.1), a quality visible in the face or eyes. Likewise, Sabaethis's shapeliness and bearing seem external manifestations of her internal wisdom and tenderness. Tenderness appears also as a quality of Melinna. In fact, the echo of her name in the adjective describing her (*meilichiōs*, 8.2) may somehow explain why her very essence appears in the portrait from which she peers "tenderly." A similar kind of echo links Callo's visual "charm" (*charis*, 6.3) with the joy she is to feel in her portrait (*chairetō*, 6.4), as Sabaethis is to rejoice (*chairois*, 9.4) in her portrait and Aphrodite feels joy (*chairoisan*, 5.1) in the dedication of a headband. Callo's bloom-

[19] In Theocritus's *Idyll* 2.73 Simaetha dresses up in a chiton made of *bussos* to attend a festival; the term may designate linen, cotton, or silk, or perhaps even a color.
[20] For craft and elegance as elements of a general Hellenistic aesthetic, see B. Fowler 1989: 5–22; for the "feminization" of culture in the Hellenistic period, see Gutzwiller and Michelini 1991:72–75.

ing charm (*charis . . . anthei*, 6.3) echoes as well in the epilogue poem where Nossis claims inspiration from the "bloom of Sappho's graces" (*tan Sapphous charitōn anthos*, 11.2); this phrase, in turn, links Sappho's poetry with Nossis's own "blossoms" (*anthea*, 1.4) mentioned in the prooemium. The qualities of the women described in the epigrams, their visual charm and internal joy, are, then, the qualities of Nossis's own poetry, transmitted to her by a process of Sapphic inspiration.

This brings us to one of the most surprising and innovative aspects of Nossis's collection, her use of a dramatic narrator. The voice heard in the epigrams once they have been gathered into a poetry book, far from being the anonymous voice of traditional dedicatory style, now seems to emanate from a single personality, who guides us, as it were, on a tour of an art gallery. When in 4 G-P the narrating voice begins, "Let us go to the temple and see Aphrodite's statue," the participle *elthoisai* (4.1) shows that the speaker and addressees are all women. In the context of the collection it is natural to assume that the narrator is the epigram-matist herself. This "Nossis" who narrates thus assumes a double role: an internal dramatic narrator speaking to her Locrian friends on the site of the dedications and, at the same time, author and compiler speaking to us, her female implied readers, from some uncertain literary or imag-inative time and place. It is in the context of this dramatic narrator that we must consider another theme linking the epigrams on portraits, the lifelike nature of the depictions. Since realism had been a major criterion for aesthetic worth from at least the early fourth century, Nossis's em-phasis on verisimilitude is in part a compliment on the quality of the painting.[21] But when the epigrams are considered as a group, this realism takes on significance as the narrator's subjective impression of the paint-ings. I suggest that Nossis emphasizes the lifelike nature of the portraits in order to invite us to enter *her* world, to see *her* women through *her* eyes—to view Callo's gentle stance and blossoming charm, to observe Sabaethis's wisdom and gentleness, to imagine as she does Thaumareta's puppy fawning at the sight of her mistress's likeness. Each woman is spotlighted for a moment and the reader asked to visualize her, physi-cally and spiritually, as a type of woman worthy of adoration. But the true source of that adoration is the narrating voice, a projection of the epigrammatist, so that we come away from the collection not just with a sense of the women who belonged to Nossis's world but also with knowledge of the poet herself, a woman with a Sapphic attachment to other women.

The personalized authorial voice that speaks directly to the reader in

---

[21] On realism in the art of the fourth century and later, see Pollitt 1986:141–47. Zanker 1987 has studied the effects of a taste for pictorial realism in the poetry of the age.

Nossis's epigram book owes much to the tradition of women's poetry in which she consciously situates herself. She acknowledges most directly the influence of Sappho's lyrical voice and, more obliquely, if my interpretation of the prooemium is correct, that her manner owed something to Erinna, who developed a feminized voice of grief in the *Distaff* and apparently composed an epigram that stands as a direct model for Nossis's portrait poems. I see in Nossis's assertion of independence from Erinna—her preference for *erōs* over honey—not "anxiety of influence," which is Harold Bloom's term for a poet's rejection of his literary precursors in the manner of an Oedipal boy's longing to replace his father (Bloom 1973), but rather "anxiety of authorship," which is the alternative term coined by Sandra Gilbert and Susan Gubar to describe a woman author's "radical fear that she cannot create, that because she can never become a 'precursor' the act of writing will isolate or destroy her" (Gilbert and Gubar 1979a:49). For Nossis, the problem with Erinna was perhaps not so much Erinna herself as what male poets had made of her. She had in fact become the darling of contemporary male epigrammatists: Asclepiades and Leonidas wrote epigrams celebrating her, and Antiphanes later cited her as a favorite of Callimachus's pedantic followers (*AP* 11.322). But in becoming the acknowledged "precursor" of important Hellenistic male poets, Erinna had in fact been isolated and destroyed—kept a "child" (*pais*, Leon. 98.4 G-P) confined to her loom until Hades snatched her away as bride (Leon. 98.3 G-P; Asclep. 28.3–4 G-P). Asclepiades makes it clear that the charm of her poetry was its slightness, as befits a "nineteen-year-old maiden" (Asclep. 28.1–2 G-P). To become admired by male poets, Erinna had to die, and die before knowing the kiss of Aphrodite. But Nossis rejects this role of sacrificial maiden, offering as an alternative the Sapphic perspective of an adult woman speaking about women to a primary audience of women. As Skinner has pointed out, the historical result of Nossis's choice to define herself within a female subculture was denigration by some male authors and neglect by most others (Skinner 1991b:35–37).

The poetry book, arranged and published by the author, was one of the major innovations of the Hellenistic age. While Nossis's collection was likely not the first such book, the surviving selection of her epigrams suggests that she composed one of the most thematically coherent of these assemblages. By repetition of theme and similarity of form, by the use of a dramatic narrator who speaks across the boundaries of individual poems, Nossis creates a sense of an author's persona that was by rule of genre absent from the earlier tradition of dedicatory epigram. It is precisely this sense of a creative presence who shapes and selects the poems we are reading that characterizes the poetry books of later Latin literature. It should be acknowledged as well that Nossis likely produced the first "anthology," in the sense that she troped her epigrams as a gathering of flowers. By adapting Sappho's metaphorical equation of roses with poetry, Nossis textualized her own "Sapphic circle" as a garland of blossoms. Though Meleager's assumption of the flower metaphor for his *Garland* lies behind the later tradition of anthologies, whether collections of epigrams or other poetic types, Nossis's contribution has been neither acknowledged by the ancients nor observed by modern scholars. This effacement of her accomplishment is directly related to the persona she created, that of a female poet speaking to other women about the beauties and joys of the world they inhabit.

One of the clearest statements made in antiquity about the gendered nature of Greek literature is found in Euripides' *Medea*:

> To us Phoebus, leader of songs,
> has not given god-inspired poetry
> through knowledge of the lyre. Or else,
> I would have sung a song
> in answer to the male race. Length of time
> has as much to say about our lives as those of men.
>
> (424–30)

Euripides's female chorus attributes its inability to sing to a lack of inspiration from Phoebus Apollo. From a modern perspective I have characterized the problem differently, as the difficulty encountered by Greek women as they tried to compose in generic forms created to express male experience. Yet the poetry of Nossis and Erinna shows that at least with the advent of Hellenistic book culture, it became possible to adapt traditional literary types to accommodate the voices of women speaking about the subjects *they* chose, advancing the priorities *they* set. It has been a major premise of my essay that when women compose in genres encoded with the voices of male authors, these genres can undergo fundamental transformation. Erinna elevated to high literary status the previously subliterary form of the *goos*, which had found a place in earlier literature only when represented by a pseudo-objective narrating voice. By replacing the male narrator with her own voice of grief, she was able to expose the restrictions that had in the past been placed on this largely feminine form of expression. Nossis replaced the anonymous voice of traditional inscribed epigram with a personalized voice emanating from an individual who marks herself as female. By grouping epigrams describing portraits of women in a collection introduced and concluded by programmatic poems avowing Sapphic inspiration, she textualized through the book format both her own community of Locrian women and the historical literary community of female composers and readers, extending from Sappho to women reading Nossis today.

Both the epic lament of Erinna and the epigram collection of Nossis foreshadow major developments in Hellenistic and Roman poetry. It could be argued that once the male perspective of earlier literature had been made evident by the expression of an alternative female approach, the immanent movement of literature had to take both into account. The curious tone of much Hellenistic poetry composed by men and the "feminized" quality that some scholars have identified in certain forms of Latin poetry may be explainable in part by the strategies male poets developed to adapt this newly discovered female perspective to their own voices. I have tried to suggest the influence of Erinna's *Distaff* on the development of Greek and Latin love poetry and the importance of Nossis's epigram collection in the development of thematized poetry books by both Greek and Latin authors. But the careless transmission of the poetry written by these women as well as the eclipse of their contributions in the canonized versions of the history of Western literature support the statement of the chorus in Euripides' *Medea* about the difficulty women have had in patriarchal culture both speaking to be heard and writing to be read.

15
Sappho Shock

ANNE CARSON

A lyric poem is a highly concentrated action in which every letter and syllable counts. For example, consider Sappho's poem in which a single consonant rises up and obliterates the life of the poem's addressee:

> κατθάνοισα δὲ κείσῃ οὐδέ ποτα μναμοσύνα σέθεν
> ἔσσετ' οὐδὲ πόθα εἰς ὕστερον οὐ γὰρ πεδέχῃς βρόδων
> τὼν ἐκ Πιερίας, ἀλλ' ἀφάνης κἀν Ἀίδα δόμῳ
> φοιτάσῃς πεδ' ἀμαύρων νεκύων ἐκπεποταμένα.
>
> (fr. 55 L-P)[1]

Dead you will lie and not ever memory of you will
be nor desire into the aftertime. For you will have no share
in the roses of Pieria but invisible *too* in the house of Hades
you will go your way among the blotted dead—an exhalation.

It is a poem of resentment that, ancient editors tell us, was directed by Sappho at a woman of considerable wealth who had no interest in music, poetry, or knowledge (here symbolized by "the roses of Pieria"). It is a poem concerned to describe how the present affects the future but also to cause that effect imitatively. The text that lies before us renders some woman nameless to this day. When we look at the words we experience neither memory nor desire for her, we see an empty room through which she passed leaving no imprint. We see her invisibility. But at the same time we experience its cause. For we are her. The second-person singular

---

[1] I use the following editions of ancient works: for Sappho, *Poetarum lesbiorum fragmenta*, ed. D. L. Page (Oxford: Clarendon, 1955); for Aristotle's *Poetics*, Aristotle, *De arte poetica liber*, ed. Rudolf Kassel (Oxford: Clarendon, 1965).

verbs of the poem locate us within some woman by calling her "you." You transact your own invisibility by living in the present as if you were already dead—which, by the time you realize it, you are. The poem sets forth, in four verbs referring to the future, a somewhat unsurprising prediction: when you die you will be blotted out. But placed within these future references, like a trap of the kind called a "deadfall," is a much more surprising inference. Your trap is the small Greek word *kai*, a conjunction meaning "and," which appears in verse 3 abbreviated to a single *k* and conjoined by crasis to the preposition *en* following it: *kan*.

Now crasis is a metrical license permitting the compression of two open vowels into one long syllable for time-saving purposes. Crasis quickens the connective action of the conjunction *kai* and syncopates your posthumous nonentity upon its counterpart in present life. By the time you realize the retroactive force of this conjunction, you have already floated forward to verse 4 and to your darkening future, leaving behind you, lodged in a single kappa, the whole implication of your life without roses. In the *Poetics* Aristotle defines "conjunction" for us as follows: ἄρθρον δέ ἐστιν φωνὴ ἄσημος ἢ λόγου ἀρχὴν ἢ τέλος ἢ διορισμὸν δηλοῖ. οἷον τὸ ἀμφί καὶ τὸ περί καὶ τὰ ἄλλα (1457a6–8). A conjunction is a meaningless sound that makes clear the beginning, end, or definition of an utterance; so in fragment 55, Sappho has used the conjunctival action of *kai* to imitate an almost imperceptible causal connection between the beginning, end, and definition of some woman's meaningless life. She has used the syncopating action of crasis to speed up the meaninglessness and to introduce a lurch of hindsight into the reasoning process of her poem. You may think "reasoning process" is an inappropriate description of Sappho's fragment 55. But Aristotle tells us that "all the affect produced by words fall under the category of reasoning or *dianoia*" (ἔστι δε κατὰ τὴν διάνοιαν ταῦτα, ὅσα ὑπὸ τοῦ λόγου δεῖ παρασκευασθῆναι; 1456a36–37). The words of Sappho's poem move your mind through an action of reasoning that is, nonetheless, distinct from other types of *dianoia* in virtue of its thrill.

There is a classical Chinese proverb that says, "The closer you look at a word the more distantly it looks back at you." The thrill of lyric mimesis has something importantly to do with this collaboration of distance and closeness, whereby they approach, meet, and seem almost about to interchange, like a man shaking hands with himself in a mirror. Aristotle says the best mimetic actions are the ones that happen "contrary to expectation and through one another" (ἐπεὶ δὲ οὐ μόνον τελείας ἐστὶ πράξεως ἡ μίμησις ἀλλὰ καὶ φοβερῶν καὶ ἐλεεινῶν, ταῦτα δὲ γίνεται καὶ μάλιστα [καὶ μᾶλλον] ὅταν γένηται παρὰ τὴν δόξαν δι' ἄλληλα; 1452a1–4). One further example from Sappho may help us focus this observation.

φαίνεταί μοι κῆνος ἴσος θέοισιν
ἔμμεν' ὤνηρ, ὄττις ἐνάντιός τοι
ἰσδάνει καὶ πλάσιον ἆδυ φωνεί-
σας ὐπακούει

καὶ γελαίσας ἰμέροεν, τό μ' ἦ μὰν
καρδίαν ἐν στήθεσιν ἐπτόαισεν
ὠς γὰρ ἔς σ' ἴδω βρόχε', ὤς με φώναι-
σ' οὐδ ἔν ἔτ' εἴκει

ἀλλ' ἄκαν μὲν γλῶσσα [ἔαγε], λέπτον
δ' αὔτικα χρῶι πῦρ ὐπαδεδρόμηκεν,
ὀππάτεσσι δ' οὐδ' ἔν ὄρημμ', ἐπιρρόμ-
βεισι δ' ἄκουαι

κὰδ δέ μ' ἴδρως ψῦχρος ἔχει, τρόμος δὲ
παῖσαν ἄγρει, χλωροτέρα δὲ ποίας
ἔμμι, τεθνάκην δ' ὀλίγω 'πιδεύης
φαίνομ' ἔμ αὔτ[αι.

(fr. 31 L-P)

He seems to me equal to the gods that man
whoever he is who opposite you
sits and listens close
to your sweet speaking

and lovely laughing—oh it
puts the heart in my chest on wings
for when I look at you, a moment, then no speaking
is left in me

no: tongue breaks and thin
fire is racing under skin
and in eyes no sight and drumming
fills ears

and cold sweat holds me and shaking
grips me all, greener than grass
I am and dead—or almost
I seem to me.

It is a strangely theatrical poem, as brightly lit as a stage set and much concerned with the problem of seeming. It begins and ends with a form of the verb *phainesthai*, "to appear": *phainetai* (1), "he seems," *phainomai* (16), "I seem." Seeming is an activity that ordinarily posits a cast of two. The person who seems and the person to whom she seems. But on Sappho's stage the action is triangular, at least to begin with, for the opening stanza features three actors, "that man" and "you" and "me." And although Sappho immediately sets about reducing the cast to "you" and "me" in the second stanza and then "me" alone in the remaining verses, phenomena double and triple themselves insistently throughout the poem.

Duality is asserted in sound and syntax by verbal responsions like *phainetai ... phainomai* (1, 16); *emmen ... emmi* (2, 15); *phōneisas ... phōnaisa* (3, 7); *hōs ... hōs* (7); *hypakouei ... akouai* (4, 12). Sappho's catalogue of erotic reactions, on the other hand, is organized in sets of three. A triple psychological affect is three times recorded, each time in the same order—visual, oral/aural, tactile. So we find "he seems" (1); "he listens to your voice" (4); "my heart is on wings" (6); "I look" (7); "no speaking is in me ... tongue breaks" (7–9); "fire runs under my skin" (10); "no sight is in my eyes" (11); "drumming is in my ears" (11–12); "cold sweat holds me" (13). At the end of the catalogue, unity is reasserted by the protagonist; Sappho says, "shaking grips the whole me" (13–14). It is apparently a matter of some importance to her to gather the data of outer sense into one being. Aristotle agrees that an imitative poet should focus her imitation on one thing, not three:

ἐπεὶ γάρ ἐστι μιμητὴς ὁ ποιητὴς ὡσπερανεὶ ζωγράφος ἤ τις ἄλλος εἰκονοποιός, ἀνάγη μιμεῖσθαι τριῶν ὄντων τὸν ἀριθμὸν ἕν τι ἀεί, ἢ γὰρ οἷα ἦν ἢ ἔστιν, ἢ οἷά φασιν καὶ δοκεῖ, [ἢ] οἷα εἶναι δεῖ. (1460b8–11)

For a poet is an imitator like a painter or any image maker and it is necessary for him to imitate out of three things one at any given time: things as they are, things as they are said or seem to be, things as they ought to be.

Sappho proceeds in fragment 31 as if she has in mind these same three registers of discourse: the real, the apparent, the ideal. She disposes of ideality fairly early in the poem. "That man equal to the gods whoever he is" ceases to exist as soon as we do not care to know his name; the indefinite pronoun *ottis*, "whoever," obliterates him. The rest of the poem is a research through appearance to reality, beginning and ending (as we have already noted) with forms of the verb *phainesthai* and framing a revelation at the core. The action of the poem is in a true sense spectacular. We see the modes of perception reduced to dysfunction one by one; we see the objects of outer sense disappear, and on the brightly lit stage at the center of her being we see Sappho recognize herself: *emmi,* "I am," she asserts at verse 15.

"Seeing" or "spectacle" or *opsis* is the "most ravishing" aspect of dramatic mimesis, according to Aristotle (ἡ δὲ ὄψις ψυχαγωγικὸν, 1450b16–17). He applies to visual spectacle the adjective *psychagōgikon,* which means something like "it kidnaps your soul." So too is Sappho's soul kidnapped by the spectacle of her own mimesis, or so it seems. "I am greener than grass," she says at verse 15, predicating of her own being an attribute observable only from outside her own body. The experience Sappho describes is one well known to Greek aesthetic theory and commended by Aristotle. It is the condition called *ekstasis,* "standing outside oneself," widely regarded as characteristic of madmen, geniuses, or lovers and ascribed particularly to poets by Aristotle at *Poetics* 1455a32–34: διὸ εὐφυοῦς ἡ ποιητική ἐστιν ἢ μανικοῦ· τούτων γὰρ οἱ μὲν εὔπλαστοι οἱ δὲ ἐκστατικοί εἰσιν (Thus the art of poetry belongs either to geniuses or madmen. For of those the former are good plastic, the latter able to stand out of themselves). It is nonetheless noteworthy that Sappho's *ekstasis* does not clear the stage at the center of her being. On the contrary, as she stands outside her own body looking in, a mysterious figure seems to be coming into focus there. "To have died—or almost, I seem to myself," she says (16), implying at least two and possibly three actors engaged in this final episode of the action. There is Sappho the subject, Sappho the object, and perhaps also Sappho the word that separates subject and object by naming them. But this third presence remains problematic. The problem of the third actor is a real and controversial one for the history of the Greek theater, which Aristotle treats in the opening chapter of *Poetics* (1449a). Yet it must be admitted that Sappho leaves it unclear, at the end of fragment 31, just how many people she imagines herself to be.

Sappho Fragment 31
(from the unfinished sequence *TV Men*)

> TV makes things disappear. Oddly the word comes from Latin *videre*
> "to see."   Longinus *de Sublimitate* 5.3

Sappho is smearing on her makeup at 5 AM in the woods by the TV studio.
He She Me You Thou disappears

Now resembling a Beijing concubine Sappho makes her way onto the set.
Laugh Breathe Look Speak Is disappears

The lighting men are setting up huge white paper moons here and there on
the grass.
Tongue Flesh Fire Eyes Sound disappears

Behind these, a lamp humming with a thousand broken wasps.
Cold Shaking Green Little Death disappears

Places everyone, calls the director.
Nearness When Down In I disappears

Toes to the line please, says the assistant camera man.
But All And Must To disappears

Action!
Disappear disappears

Sappho stares into the camera and begins, *Since I am a poor man-*
Cut

16

Sappho Doubled: Michael Field

YOPIE PRINS

In 1889 a volume of Sapphic lyrics called *Long Ago* was published in London by Katherine Bradley (1846–1914) and Edith Cooper (1862–1913), aunt and niece, who lived together as a married couple and wrote together as "Michael Field." Preferring to keep their authorial identities and the duality of their authorship unknown, they had published several lyrical dramas in the previous decade under this pseudonym. *Long Ago* was Michael Field's first collection of poetry—seven more were to follow, along with numerous plays—and it raises important questions about Bradley and Cooper's claim to authorship, as well as about the relationship between lyric subjectivity and sexual identity in Victorian poetry. How shall we read these poems written by two women writing as a man writing as Sappho? Hailed by *The Academy* as "one of the most exquisite lyrical productions of the latter half of the nineteenth century" (18 June, 1889, 389), *Long Ago* seems to reproduce Victorian ideas about the lyric as a genre, but the collaboration of Bradley and Cooper also complicates generic assumptions about the lyric as the solitary utterance of a single speaker. Their volume of Sapphic imitations, inspired by the Greek fragments of Sappho, proves to be a complex performance of the Sapphic signature: simultaneously single and double, masculine and feminine, Michael Field's Sappho is a name that opens itself to multiple readings.

In Victorian England, Sappho was increasingly invoked as the original and exemplary lyric poet and indeed the very embodiment of lyric poetry—as in Swinburne's vision of Sappho "singing till the whole world sings," in his controversial but influential poem "Anactoria" (1866). At the end of this dramatic monologue written in the voice of Sappho, all the world becomes "metaphors of me." Sappho is metaphorized as well in *Studies of the Greek Poets* (1873), where John Addington Symonds singles out Sappho "of all the poets of the world" as "the one whose every word has a peculiar and unmistakable perfume, a seal of absolute perfection and illimitable grace." Although Sappho's words survive only in fragmentary form, Symonds reads these "dazzling fragments" as the essence of Sapphic song, "the ultimate and finished forms of passionate utterance" (129–30). Placed at the origin of the lyric tradition and read as originary voice, Sappho thus becomes the figure for voice upon which lyric reading is predicated. And yet the more Sappho is idealized—as transcendent voice, as the perfection of song, as pure essence or "perfume" of lyric poetry—the more her poetry materializes as fragmented text. Alongside the tendency to idealize Sappho in Victorian poetics, Victorian philology develops a textual approach to the Sapphic fragments that demonstrates the mutual implication of idealist and materialist reading. Not only does the literal fragmentation of Sappho's texts lead to the figurative reconstitution of Sappho's voice, but the reverse is also true: toward the end of the century there is increasing emphasis on the reconstruction of Sappho herself as fragment. In 1885, for example, a medical doctor and amateur classicist named Henry Thornton Wharton published *Sappho: Memoir, Text, Selected Renderings, and a Literal Translation*; these "renderings" of Sappho imply her "rending" into fragments as well, in a compilation of Greek texts alongside multiple English translations that proved to be the most popular British edition for several decades.

Long Ago emerges out of this general Victorian interest in Sappho, and the influence of Wharton in particular. The Greek epigraphs to the Sapphic lyrics of Michael Field are drawn from Wharton's text, and the endnote acknowledges his edition as "a work which will be found of the highest value by those who desire to obtain a vivid impression of the personality, the influence, and the environment of the poet" (1889). Yet what emerges from Wharton's edition of Sappho is less "the personality . . . of the poet" than a composite image made up of many Sapphos, in a multiauthored text that allows signatures to multiply under her name. This multiplication of different versions inspires Michael Field to publish their own Sapphic poems, which are, in turn, eagerly reincorporated as "felicitous paraphrases" by Wharton in subsequent editions of his book, as yet another contribution to the name of Sappho (Preface to 3d ed.,1895: vi). The poetic doubling of Sappho by Michael Field differs from Wharton's scholarly project, however, in redefining lyric authorship by means of a collaboration that destabilizes the Sapphic signature more radically than do the "selected renderings" collected by Wharton. Instead of reclaiming Sappho's identity or proclaiming identity with Sappho, the collaborative writing of Michael Field uses the figure of Sappho to reconfigure the assumption of voice in lyric poetry.

Of course there is nothing new about two writers collaborating, as

Walter Besant observes in 1892 in *The New Review*. His article "On Literary Collaboration" nevertheless reflects a renewed interest in and an increasing trend toward dual authorship in the last decade of the nineteenth century, particularly (according to Besant) in the writing of drama and fiction. He compares such collaborations to "the partnership of marriage" (207), uniting two in one, and insists that "true literary partnerships" achieve a unified voice: "We must hear—or think we hear—one voice" (205). Collaborative writing reaches its limit, however, on occasions "when there is need of profound meditation, of solemn self-interrogation, or of lofty imagination" (203)—the conventional occasion of lyric, that is, in an allusion to John Stuart Mill's famous definition of poetry as "the natural fruit of solitude and meditation," or "feeling confessing itself to itself, in moments of solitude" (Mill 1976:13,12). The genre of lyric is commonly understood, at least in its late nineteenth-century definition, as the written representation of an utterance not addressed to another person but spoken in private, a voice not heard but "overheard" by the reader. Besant therefore excludes lyric poetry from experiments in collaboration, because lyrics depend on the fiction of "one voice" more fundamentally than do other genres. "To touch the deeper things one must be alone," Besant writes, and again, "One must, alone, speak to the alone" (1892:203).

What then of Sappho, the "original" lyric poet, doubled by dual authorship? If lyric as a genre assumes a single speaker, then Michael-Field-as-Sappho simultaneously exploits and explodes that generic assumption. On one hand, Katherine Bradley and Edith Cooper seem to unify their voices into one as Michael Field; the first product of their collaboration under this name, the drama *Callirrhoë*, was hailed by critics in 1884 as "the ring of a new voice which is likely to be heard far and wide" (Sturgeon 1922:27). Michael Field's readers heard—or thought they heard—one voice, according to Besant's ideal, and Bradley and Cooper themselves also idealized their literary partnership by analogy to marriage. In a letter of introduction to Robert Browning, who was to become their friend, Cooper writes: "This happy union of two in work and aspiration is sheltered and expressed by 'Michael Field.' Please regard him as the author."[1] What emerges between Katherine and Edith— between their respective nicknames "Michael" and "Field"—is a "him" authorized by the existing institutions of authorship, a voice that may be read in the masculine singular as "the author."

[1] Field 1933:3. Hereafter selections from the journals of Michael Field published in *Works and Days* are cited as *WD* by page number. Quotations from the Michael Field journals in manuscript at the British Library (Add. Mss. 46776–804) are cited by manuscript number and date. I am grateful to the British Library for permission to quote from Michael Field's unpublished journals of 1868-1914 ("Works and Days").

On the other hand, they describe their happy union of two not as wedlock in any conventional sense, but surpassing what Victorians considered to be the ideal marriage of the Brownings. After a visit with Robert Browning, Bradley reflects in her journal: "Those two poets, man and wife, wrote alone; each wrote, but did not bless or quicken one another at their work; *we are closer married*" (*WD* 16). In the contrast between two poets who "wrote alone" and two who write together, heterosexual marriage is dismissed as an inadequate metaphor for literary partnership; the *"closer"* marriage of Bradley and Cooper makes writing for, with, and through "one another" the central metaphor for a relationship they never quite call lesbian. Nevertheless they turn to Sappho, whom they certainly understand to be Lesbian in more than the proper sense of the name, in order to develop a model of lyric authorship in which voice is the effect of an eroticized textual mediation between the two of them rather than the representation of an unmediated solitary utterance.

Bradley and Cooper therefore manipulate the conventions of authorship in ways that cross-couple gender and genre, and it is significant that this cross-coupling happens through Greek. Recognizing the erotic subtext of their poetry, Robert Browning called them his "two dear Greek women," and particularly admired the "Sapphics" in *Long Ago*. After reading the poems in draft he "prophesied they would make their mark," but added that Michael Field might have to "wait fifty years" (*WD* 20). The implication here is not only that *Long Ago* is long ahead of its time but also that the very structure of the Sapphic signature—"their mark"—requires the mediation of reading: it will be left to the reader of the future to decipher this sign. This is what I propose to do in the following pages: to read Michael Field's Sappho as an exploration of lesbian writing that is not predicated on the assumption of sexual identity or lyric voice, but nevertheless puts those terms into play. Elizabeth Meese describes such an approach—and performs it rhetorically—in her essay "Theorizing Lesbian: Writing—A Love Letter." The colon in this title marks a break between sexuality and textuality, yet anticipates the implication of each in the other and points to the space in between as "a metaphorical field" or "a scene of transposition" (1990:75).

I use the colon in the title of my essay to similar effect, allowing Sappho and Michael Field to be read in relation to each other but without being identified with each other; what happens in the break between the two names is transposition rather than identification. In reading Sappho: Michael Field, with the implicit assumption of a colon that makes these terms simultaneously continuous and discontinuous, we enter a textual space where the crossing (out, over, through) of sexual identities can be performed. I will consider briefly why Bradley and Cooper turn to Greek to create that textual space, and then trace in more detail how the figure of voice in their imitations of Sappho is displaced by a process of eroticized intertextual exchange, or—to use their term—"interlacing." Thus the tracery of *Long Ago* is less the proclamation of a proper name— Katherine Bradley, Edith Cooper, Michael Field, Sappho, or Lesbian— than it is the circumscription of a metaphorical field of writing in which the Sapphic signature is already in play as its own suggestive and seductive figure.

Sly Scholars

Long Ago first appeared in a limited edition of one hundred copies, bound in vellum and printed in two colors: the English poems in black letters, and Greek epigraphs in orange-gold. Copy No. 2 was posted to Robert Browning, fondly called "the reverend elder," with a Greek inscription after his name: ἐκ θεοῦ δ' ἀνὴρ σοφαῖς ἀνθεῖ ἐσαεὶ πραπίδεσσιν (46777, 23 May 1889). This compliment to Browning as "a man forever eminent in wise understanding from god" declares an alliance based on the command of ancient Greek, the cultural property of a privileged masculine elite. Like Browning, who had been publishing translations from Greek in the previous decade, Bradley and Cooper make a claim to classical scholarship in *Long Ago*. The bilingualism of their volume places Michael Field within an elite circle of poets who turn to Greek literature to redefine the language of English poetry, and Michael Field's assumption of poetic authority draws on the cultural prestige of Victorian Hellenism. Bradley and Cooper were pleased to hear, then, that Browning had lent *Long Ago* to a young man "to teach him the uses of Greek learning!" (*WD* 30–31). What Greek learning signifies, in this context, is more than linguistic: it marks a distinct though unspoken set of assumptions about sexuality as well as class and gender.

By imitating Sappho's Greek fragments, Michael Field enters into a domain often coded as masculine, and, by the end of the nineteenth century, increasingly homosexual. Recent criticism on Victorian Hellenism has explored, from various perspectives, the formation of British culture, politics, and aesthetics by analogy to ancient Greece. Richard Jenkyns (1980) and Frank Turner (1981) survey both radical and conservative tendencies in classical scholarship of the period, influencing a wide range of cultural practices, and this line of argument is developed by Linda Dowling (1994), who demonstrates how an aestheticized reading of classical Greek culture in Victorian Oxford opens a space for the discourse of homosexuality to emerge. Richard Dellamora also describes "the hermeneutic space known as 'thinking Greek'" with reference to the practice of pederasty in the history of the Dorians (1994:54); he notes that Sappho was invoked as model for the Greek genius, defined by *male* pederasty (50). The philhellenism of Michael Field is derived, at least in part, from this discourse of homosexual desire and reflects, as Martha Vicinus points out, "Michael Field's fascination with the tropes of male homosexuality" (1994:103).

Bradley and Cooper tended to affiliate with homosexual couples, such as the artists Charles Ricketts and Robert Shannon, who also considered themselves married. After meeting Ricketts, Cooper observes in her journal that "he is an ardent lover of Shannon . . . loving him as my Love loves me" (46781, 1893). A subsequent journal entry describes Ricketts's interest in the art and poetry of the Romanians because they are "a people with Sapphic passion" who celebrate same-sex marriages (46787, 1898). Here Bradley and Cooper simultaneously adopt and adapt the homosexual discourse surrounding them: the "Romanians" are lesbianized in terms of "Sapphic passion." While drawing on the established associations between Hellenism and homosexuality, Bradley and Cooper therefore imply a lesbian eroticism distinct from the troping of homosexual desire. They imagine an ancient Greek world inhabited not only by the pupils of Socrates but also by young women. Cooper describes a Greek ceramic figure she saw at an art exhibit: "Two young women sit in gossiping ease on a wayside sarcophagus—their knees are crossed under the chitons—one of the talkers has her hand on her hips, the breath of conversation hurries through their mouths—Every gesture tells of intercourse & emotion. . . . These bits of domestic art give me a sense of the grace of intimate Greek life" (46777, 13 June 1889). The intimacy of this vision resonates with Browning's description of Bradley and Cooper as "two dear Greek women," a couple whose every gesture tells of "intercourse & emotion" but without telling exactly how much. In this way Bradley and Cooper open Victorian Hellenism to the possibility of a lesbian reading that allows for the circulation of Greek eros among women as well as men.

Yet the lesbian implications of "Greek learning"—or "thinking Greek"—remain largely unexplored in current work on Victorian Hellenism. Critics have described the role of classical scholarship in the cultural construction of masculine identities and homoerotic desire, but without acknowledging the emergence of a Hellenizing discourse of lesbianism. Often denied access to formal education in Greek and Latin, Victorian women had a different relationship to classical discourses than their male counterparts. By the end of the century, however, the women's colleges at Oxford and Cambridge had created a place for students to pursue classical languages, and scholars like Jane Ellen Harrison at Newnham College were revolutionizing classical studies. Katherine

Bradley herself had learned classical languages as a student at Newnham College, and later she initiated her niece Edith Cooper into the study of Latin and Greek as well. Together they read the *Greek Anthology*, and Wharton's 1885 edition of Sappho appealed in particular to Bradley and Cooper, who depended on the English translations of the primary texts, along with the secondary notes offered by Wharton, in order to assimilate Sappho's Greek.

While Bradley and Cooper create a scholarly context for their reading of the Sapphic fragments, they also remain aware of themselves as women who must resort to the popularized pseudo-scholarship of "Dr." Wharton, another amateur classicist. Excluded from the masculine domain of classical scholarship, Bradley comments balefully on "one sentence of Mr. Pater's which I would not say I could never forgive, because I recognised its justice; but from which I suffered, and which was hard to bear—that in which he speaks of the scholarly conscience as male" (*WD* 137). And later, again, she expresses a sense of inadequacy in her Greek learning: "I demonstrate that women cannot have the scholarly conscience" (*WD* 192). As Michael Field, however, Bradley and Cooper are able to claim the masculine authority of classical scholarship and use it transgressively, for their own purposes. This is the implication of a private journal entry, eagerly anticipating the publication of *Long Ago* to announce their public entry into the literary establishment: "Every day we are expecting the first copy of *Long Ago* (a specimen copy). Tiny marsh violets have been sent to Edith——they are like Violets that have put aside their loving, & made sly little scholars of themselves, mystic & 'beguiling'—tricky & fanciful—rather than luring and recluse" (46777, 9 May 1889). As they await a specimen copy of their book Bradley and Cooper receive flowers—another kind of specimen—that prompt an association between their poems and the violets that have made "sly little scholars" of themselves: their Sapphic lyrics are also beguiling, tricky, and fanciful in their assimilation of Sappho's fragments, seeming to "put aside their loving" yet still making good use of the Greek tongue. Indeed, in writing *Long Ago*, Bradley and Cooper themselves seem to have become "sly little scholars," who might teach the uses of Greek learning not only to young men but to young women as well. Their version of Victorian Hellenism, while mediated by a set of homosexual conventions, nevertheless implies the entry of Michael Field into lesbian writing as another "field" yet to be defined.

Bradley and Cooper therefore prove to be important figures for the historical recovery of lesbian writing, as is now evident in the resurgence of critical interest in Michael Field.[2] Angela Leighton (1992) devotes a

---

[2] In addition to Leighton and White, work on Michael Field includes Locard 1979; Mor-

chapter to Michael Field in her book on Victorian women poets, and Chris White (1992, 1996) reads the Sapphic lyrics in conjunction with the largely unpublished journals of Bradley and Cooper, in order to reclaim a nineteenth-century discourse of lesbianism that manifests sexual desire between women. Contrary to Lillian Faderman's vision (1981) of nineteenth-century friendships between women as romantic rather than erotic, White critiques this orthodoxy of lesbian history and its implication in a lesbian feminism that does not recognize the particularity of lesbian sexualities. It is important to trace the emergence of a lesbian discourse in Victorian England, particularly by the end of the century when the figure of Sappho is increasingly lesbianized: she is invoked by decadent poets, sexologists, and classical scholars as "historical" evidence for the practice of lesbian sexuality at the moment of, and in response to, the regulatory heterosexual construction of male homosexuality. More often than not, however, the fin de siècle construction of lesbianism serves as specular symmetrical opposite to the category of the homosexual: Sappho "the lesbian" is an emanation of a discourse that is variously heterosexual and homosexual but primarily masculine. Bradley and Cooper therefore turn to Sappho as a highly overdetermined trope, within a long tradition of Sapphic imitations.[3] It is precisely this proliferation of imitations, at a time when many Victorian poets are writing in the name of Sappho, that creates the possibility of lesbian imitation without presuming lesbian identity. Thus Bradley and Cooper are able to appropriate Sappho as a name simultaneously proper and improper, their own and not their own.

The Double Signature

Embossed in gold on the cover of *Long Ago* is the figure of an archaic Greek woman—a smiling profile, with hair looped in intricate involutions around the ear, and her neck twined with a budding garland, or perhaps it is a string of beads wrapped twice around the throat (fig. 3).[4]

---

iarty 1986; Koestenbaum 1989; Vicinus 1994; Prins 1995; Laird 1995; Vanita 1996; Reynolds 1996; and essays in Armstrong and Blain 1997; see also selections from the poetry of Michael Field in Leighton and Reynolds 1995.

[3] Surveys of Sappho's reception and the traditions of Sapphic imitation include Robinson 1923; Rudiger 1933; Saake 1972; Gubar 1984; Lipking 1988; DeJean 1989; Prins 1997; for recent classical scholarship on Sappho, see also duBois 1995; Williamson 1995; Greene 1997a, 1997b. For current work focusing more specifically on the figure of Sappho in nineteenth-century England, see S. Brown 1994; Peterson 1994; Reynolds 1996; Vanita 1996; and my own, *Victorian Sappho* (Princeton: Princeton University Press, forthcoming).

[4] Inspired by a Greek black-figured calpis from about 500 B.C.E. (the earliest inscribed representation of Sappho), the profile on the cover of *Long Ago* is identified in Michael

LONG AGO

MICHAEL FIELD

Figure 3. Profile of Sappho on the cover of Michael Field's *Long Ago* (1889).

The five buds, or beads, on the necklace combine into an ornamental pattern that is repeated in five Greek letters below the profile: Φ Σ A Θ O [*sic*].⁵ That graphic repetition of five tiny circles on a string and five curlicued letters in a row, spelling out the name of Sappho, connects the face and the name and indeed gives face *to* the name, as if the letters outside the figure were already prefigured within it, internalized to make that figure legible and allowing it to be read, emblematically, as signature. But whose signature? Suspended in midair, the letters maintain an ambiguous relation to the face: are they issuing from the mouth or traveling to the ear? Is the figure of "Sappho" speaking or listening, naming herself or being named? While the mouth is closed, the ear is an open receptacle marked by a pattern of concentric circles, emphasizing the ear's receptivity to a name that is the written representation of a spoken utterance no longer her own, though it might once have been, "long ago."

To identify the figure as Sappho, we therefore read her as destination rather than origin of the name, following the long and involuted trajec-

---

Field's endnote as follows: "The archaic head of Sappho reproduced on the cover of this volume is taken from a nearly contemporary vase, inscribed with her name, which is now in Paris, the property of Prince Czartorysky (De Witte, *Antiquitées conservées a l'Hôtel Lambert*, pl. 3)" (1889).

⁵ The archaic spelling of Sappho's name is erratic. Here the name begins with a phi and a sigma (these two letters are equivalent to the digraph psi), followed by alpha, theta (probably substituting for phi), and omikron (the old Attic version of omega).

tory of its reception, the prolongation of which is already announced in the title, LONG AGO (printed over the figure), and further prolonged by another signature (printed below): MICHAEL FIELD. How shall we interpret this name in relation to Φ Σ A Θ O ? Has the Greek been translated into English by Michael Field, or is Michael Field a translation of Sappho? The gold letters in English typeface are another attempt to give face to Sappho, ascribing a name to the figure by inscribing it within that figure, making it readable by the same logic that produces Sappho's signature— that is to say, readable only as the effect of a repetition or doubling. Here again, the name designates not a point of origin but the structure of naming itself, of deriving a name, of the name as derivation. Who is the "original" author of the lyrics in this volume? The double signature beneath its title leaves us wondering—perhaps Sappho, perhaps Michael Field, perhaps both—and this ambiguous doubling is duplicated in the pseudonym of Katherine Bradley and Edith Cooper, who sign their nicknames "Michael" and "Field" together as one: Michael Field, a doubled signature that doubles Sappho, one double signature inside another.

Michael Field's self-doubling through the figure of Sappho is also evident in a miniature portrait of Edith Cooper, designed by their friend Charles Ricketts (fig. 4). Like Sappho on the front cover of *Long Ago*, Cooper is depicted in profile with her hair loosely gathered in a knot and a ribbon tied around her neck. The visual repetition is further emphasized by the placement of the initials MF below the chin (with M joined to F), exactly where the name of Sappho appears in relation to the Greek profile. As English letters take the place of the Sapphic signature in Greek, this figure opens itself to yet another double reading: Edith Cooper is named by two letters simultaneously divided and joined in a single line, "M" and "F" both masculine and feminine, both singular and plural, two letters that do not quite spell out "ME" yet allow the figure to be identified as the "I" of Michael Field. Ingeniously, the portrait reiterates the complex structure of the signature on the cover of *Long Ago*, simultaneously giving face to a name and name to a face, but only through the inscription of a self-doubling.

We might read the Sapphic signature of Bradley and Cooper as example of the female autograph, inscribing a split subject rather than asserting the identity of the proper name; this logic has been elaborated in debates within feminist criticism around the status and signature of the signature in women's writing (Stanton 1984). At the same time, Michael Field's signature as Sappho also points to the subversion of linguistic propriety that Lee Edelman associates with homographesis, where "homo" serves as signifier of self-contradictory sameness and "graphesis" points to the inscription of inscription itself as difference

Figure 4. The initials of Michael Field (joined together and finely etched to the right of the profile) are visible in the original portrait of Edith Cooper. The portrait is part of a jeweled pendant designed by Charles Ricketts. Reproduced by courtesy of the Fitzwilliam Museum, Cambridge.

(Edelman 1994:xix). The ambiguous ownership of the Sapphic signature—belonging to Bradley and Cooper, or to Michael Field?—suggests a continual exchange between autograph and homograph, both produced by an act of writing that defers identity and signifying (albeit in different ways) the impossibility of a single, self-authorizing, self-present feminine subject. Thus, when Bradley writes that she and her niece "make up a single individual, doubly stronger than each alone, i.e. Edith and I make a *veritable Michael*" (WD 6), her insistence on the singularity of their authorship coincides with the moment of its doubling and thus allows Michael to emerge as a third term that produces the interplay between identities, an "I" that can shift to "we" and "you" and "he" and "she" and "they" (or "the Michaels," as Ricketts called them). The name is "*veritable*" not because it verifies authorial identity but because it enables the structure of their writing together.

The ambiguous authorship of Michael Field was, in fact, an open secret. Bradley writes to Browning: "It is said that the *Athenaeum* was taught by you to use the feminine pronoun. Again, someone named André Raffalovich, whose earnest young praise gave me genuine pleasure, now writes in ruffled distress; he 'thought he was writing to a boy—a young man . . . he has learnt on the best authority it is not so.' I am writing to him to assure him that the best authority is my work" (*WD* 6). What authorizes Michael Field is the work itself, and that proves to be "the best authority," especially when the question about authorship, be it masculine or feminine, singular or plural, implicitly opposes and subordinates the second term to the first, to the detriment of writers like Bradley and Cooper. "It cannot be too frequently repeated," Bradley and Cooper warn in a letter to Vernon Lee, "that belief in the unity of M.F. is absolutely necessary, alike for the advance of his glory & his attaining of his favor. He is in literature *one*. Where the secret of his chance dualism is not known, the wise & kind preserve it & even public reference to him should be masculine. But need scarcely warn Vernon Lee on this point?"[6] Violet Paget, who wrote under the name Vernon Lee and also lived with a woman companion, might understand the need to preserve a secret, even when it is already known.

Nevertheless by the time *Long Ago* appeared, its reviewers referred knowingly to Michael Field as "she," and in a letter praising the Sapphic lyrics as "a voice of one heart" George Meredith also knows "it is an addressing-of-two when one writes to Michael Field" (*WD* 67). Bradley's concern is not simply the devaluation of "lady authorship" or "dual authorship," however. By appealing to "the unity of M.F." she holds open the possibility of reading Michael Field within the context of homosexual writing—two women playing the part of "a young man" in circles where Sappho would be recognized as a trope for homoerotic desire. For contemporaries like Raffalovich and Vernon Lee, "the unity of M.F." is a signature that also signifies the merging of masculine and feminine in the third sex, exemplifying the theory that homosexuality unites a female soul in a male body or vice versa.

"Michael Field" is therefore more than merely a pseudonym to disguise the "true" identities of Bradley and Cooper, as Chris White points

---

[6] Michael Field to Vernon Lee, 20 January 1890, in the Vernon Lee Collection at the Miller Library of Colby College. I am grateful to Christa Zorn-Belde for bringing this letter to my attention.

out: "The name contains a compelling contradiction: they both deploy the authority of male authorship and yet react against such camouflage. Michael Field is not a disguise. Nor is it a pretence at being a man" (1992:40). By looking at various constructions of sexual identity embedded in their poetry, White concludes that the development of a "joint poetic persona" allows Bradley and Cooper to play out different ways of understanding a lesbian relationship. But the hypothesis of a persona, because it still assumes a speaker with an implicitly identifiable sexual identity, does not fully address the complexity of the Sapphic lyrics in *Long Ago*. Rather than personifying a speaker, even a "contradictory" one, these lyrics repeatedly call into question the figure of voice upon which lyric reading is predicated. The Preface to *Long Ago* invokes Sappho as "the one woman who has dared to speak unfalteringly of the fearful mastery of love," and although White interprets this invocation as Michael Field's claim to Sapphic voice, it significantly ends in repetition with a Greek quotation: "again and again the dumb prayer has risen from my heart—σὺ δ' αὔτα σύμμαχος ἔσσο." The Greek phrase "you be my ally" comes from the famous Ode to Aphrodite (Sappho frag. 1) and allows Michael Field to conflate Sappho's appeal to the goddess with their own appeal to Sappho. This reenactment of Sappho's prayer may suggest an alliance or merging of voices, but only in an ancient language that is no longer spoken.

Indeed, the presentation of Greek script alongside English typeface throughout the volume leaves us hovering between languages, in a textual bilingualism to be read rather than voiced; each poem begins with a fragmentary Sapphic epigraph, to emphasize the loss of a speaking voice and its fragmentation into text. Even the epigraph that introduces the entire volume is disconnected from a speaking "I": Ἠράμαν μὲν ἔγω σέθεν, Ἄτθι, πάλαι πότα is only partially translated on the back of the title page, as "A great while since, a long, long time ago." The translation leaves out "I loved you, Atthis," a first-person address to a second person, thus distancing the utterance from its source and marking the absence of a speaker for, and in, this text. Throughout *Long Ago*, the relation between epigraph and poem is structured by a similar gap, disarticulating a single "I" who desires "you" and tracing a more erratic trajectory of desire: not a movement from one fixed point to another, from origin to destination, but a reversible relation that is textually mediated.

What emerges from this performative space between Sappho's Greek and Michael Field's English is a poetic practice that does not assume identity with the original Sappho, nor assume her voice; instead, it emphasizes a belated and secondary relationship to Sappho in order to perform the intertextuality of its own writing. The lyrics in *Long Ago* are self-consciously nonoriginal, the textual copy of a voice not their own, the doubling of Sappho's signature rather than the reclamation of her song. Bradley and Cooper in fact associate their Sapphic imitations with the cuckoo, as a model for themselves as Sapphic imitators. When *Long Ago* first appeared in print, their journal gives thanks to God "for this accomplishing" and records a verse dedicated "To a cuckoo, heard early in the morning." Here the cuckoo's "iterating Voice" is the copy of "other song" heard only as echo:

> I hear thine iterating Voice in flight,
> While in the hedgerow other song is furled:
> To rise like thee! To take my range of light,
> And spread unravished echoes through the world!
>
> (46777, 23 May 1889)

A similar echoic figure structures the opening invocation in *Long Ago*, where a "maiden choir" of muses is recalled from the past to come "hither now," leaving "sweet haunts of summer sound"—the echoing realm of long ago—in order to enter the present moment of reading. The next poem in the volume returns us to the past, however, to establish a contrast between women who sang "in their time" and the loss of Sapphic song in the present. The Greek epigraph is translated into the first line of each stanza:

> Αὐτὰρ ὁραῖαι στεφανηπλόκευν

> They plaited garlands in their time;
> They knew the joy of youth's sweet prime,
>   Quick breath and rapture;
> Theirs was the violet-weaving bliss,
> And theirs the white, wreathed brow to kiss,
>   Kiss, and recapture.

> They plaited garlands, even these;
> They learnt Love's golden mysteries
>   Of young Apollo;
> The lyre unloosed their souls; they lay
> Under the trembling leaves at play,
>   Bright dreams to follow.

> They plaited garlands—heavenly twine!
> They crowned the cup, they drank the wine
>   Of youth's deep pleasure.
> Now, lingering for the lyreless god—

> Oh yet, once in their time, they trod
> A choric measure.

The first word in the Greek epigraph (Αὐτὰρ, "but") emphasizes the gap between "their time" and "now," so that "Oh yet" in the final stanza also implies "but no more." In the passing of time whatever "they" knew is lost, and whoever "they" were is unknown. How is the inspiration of those women, their "quick breath and rapture," to survive in the "lyreless" present? Transposing the measure "they trod" to the rhythm of its own metrical feet, this poem suggests that their song and dance might continue in the choreography of writing.

Thus Michael Field creates a textual space for the doubling and division of voices, in order to "kiss, kiss, and recapture" another kind of choral song. Preferring a chorus of voices to a single "I," this poem pluralizes and textualizes lyric voice by analogy to how "they plaited garlands," a phrase repeated at the beginning of each stanza and translated from the Greek ὀραῖαι στεφανηπλόκευν. Here the verb στεφανηπλόκευν serves as figure for the plaiting, weaving, wreathing, and "heavenly twine" of words themselves, allowing the garlands to accumulate reference, especially in stanza 2: "even these" refers back to the women garlanded by the songs of their time, while also presenting the words on this page garlanded into a poem and anticipating the garlanding of all the poems within the pages (or "under the trembling leaves") of this book. The poem is therefore structured by a textual figure that is, itself, derived from the text of a Greek epigraph and interwoven with English. Sappho's fragment generates the rhetorical structure of this poem and introduces recurrent figures for such interweaving and intertwining of texts throughout *Long Ago*.

Poem 6, for example, translates the "sweet-voiced girl" of its epigraph (Πάρθενον ἀδύφωνον) into Erinna, a poet included among "we who have laurel in our hair" and given "immortal bloom" by one of the muses:

> Soon as my girl's sweet voice she caught
> Thither Euterpe sped,
> And, singing too, a garland wrought,
> To crown Erinna's head.

In this simultaneous reciprocation and transformation of her song, Erinna's voice is "caught" and "wrought" into a garland. Gorgo with "the strings of tender garlands twine / About her tender neck" receives similar praise in poem 8, and poem 13 urges Dica to put garlands in her hair to please the immortals and be immortalized herself:

> They love the crowned and fragrant head
> But turn their face away
> From those who come ungarlanded,
> For none delight as they
> In piercing, languorous, spicy scent,
> And thousand hues in lustre blent:
> Such sacrifice, O Dica, bring!
> Thy garland is a beauteous thing.

Just as the plaiting of garlands was transferred from the verb στεφα-νηπλόκευν to the intricate texture of poem 1, the Greek epigraph to poem 13 is woven into the English text, as it elaborates a contrast between Σὺ δε στέφανοις and ἀστεφανώτοισι, between "thy garland" and "those who come ungarlanded." Dica's garland, with its "thousand hues in lustre blent," likewise suggests the blending of Greek and English into the garland of this poem; ungarlanded, her voice could not live on as text.

The garlanding of Erinna, Gorgo, and Dica enables their names to live on in the garland of Sappho's poetry and refers back to Sappho as she appears on the cover of *Long Ago*. Here, with her poems refigured as a garland around the head, and the letters of her name prefigured in the garland around the neck, Sappho becomes a figure for the textuality of her writing. Even Sappho's hair, gathered in a knot, is a textual figure. In "A Knot of Hair," written by Michael Field around the time of *Long Ago* (though not in response to any particular Sapphic fragment), a woman who wears her hair always in "the same deep coil about the neck" seems both infinitely readable and ultimately unreadable, because of the many threads twisting and turning, mazelike, into a knot: "But there it twined / When first I knew her, / And learned with passion to pursue her." In the Ricketts portrait, Cooper's hair is also gathered into a knot at the nape of her neck; perhaps Bradley addressed this poem to Cooper as one of many love lyrics written for her.

But the similarities in Cooper's portrait, Sappho's profile, and this poem also suggest a deeper logic at work. The unnamed woman, invoked as "O first of women who hast laid / Magnetic glory on a braid," inspires a kind of musing that is like reading:

> The happy lot
> Be mine to follow
> These threads through lovely curve and hollow,
> And muse a life-time how they got
> Into that wild, mysterious knot.

The poem, with its weaving lineation, leads us into a process of following "these threads" in the text and discovering them to be inextricably intertwined, like the texture of the hair. The woman is in fact a text to be read, brought to life by a reading that seems to originate within her (as "the first of women") yet also implicates the reader—a reader who will not disentangle but rather "follow" the tangle of "that wild, mysterious knot." What emerges from this textual entanglement is the structure of a double signature, the woman as repetition and doubling of the reader's own "musing," producing—as one possible reading—the name of Sappho.

"We cross and interlace"

Bradley and Cooper's entanglement in the figure of Sappho's signature, like the plaiting of garlands in Michael Field's Sapphic lyrics, demonstrates the textual mediation necessary for the construction of voice—if we may still call it that—in their own writing. "We cross and interlace," they avow in a letter to Havelock Ellis, who might comprehend their collaboration in terms of an eroticized textual exchange between each other: "As to our work, let no man think he can put asunder what God has joined. . . . The work is perfect mosaic: we cross and interlace like a company of dancing summer flies; if one begins a character, his companion seizes and possesses it; if one conceives a scene or situation, the other corrects, completes, or murderously cuts away" (Sturgeon 1922:47). Crossing from one to the other, simultaneously completing and cutting away, Bradley and Cooper prefer to think of their work as a "perfect mosaic" of textual fragments rather than a living voice: it is the product of writing and reading and rewriting, taking possession of each other's words yet also losing track of who owns what. The writing is "like mosaic-work—the mingled, various product of our two brains" and not to be "disentangled," according to Cooper (WD 3). Sturgeon's biography of Michael Field adds: "The collaboration was so close, so completely were the poets at one in the imaginative effort, that frequently they could not themselves decide (except by reference to the handwriting on the original sheet of manuscript) who had composed a given passage" (63). Their plays and poems are therefore "composed" not by analogy to song but in the literal sense of being pieced together, placing bits of text next to each other and allowing them to interlace. The composition of Sapphic poems is particularly suited to this process, since Sappho's lyrics are themselves fragments for piecing together in English—and of course Wharton's edition of Sappho contributes even more pieces to the mosaic. Composing poems for *Long Ago*, Bradley and Cooper enact the very

premise of their collaboration, the mutual implication of each in the writing of the other and the eroticizing of that textual entanglement by turning it into an infinitely desirable feminine figure.

I would not conclude as Sturgeon does, however, that they are "at
one" in a "union so complete, that one may search diligently, and search
in vain, for any sign in the work both wrought that this is the creation
of two minds and not one" (1922:62), nor do I wish to pursue the biographical reading of nineteenth-century romantic friendships proposed
by Faderman, who argues that Bradley and Cooper achieved "perfect,
absolute equality" in their relationship (1981:213). To the contrary, the
intertextuality of their relationship, the very possibility of crossing and
interlacing, depends on difference between the two, and it is this asym-
metrical doubleness produced by writing together that allows their work
to be "joined" and them to be "*closer married.*" My reading of their relationship, in other words, emerges from the rhetorical structures operating within their poetry, particularly the figure of chiasmus or
cross-coupling. Here I depart from Angela Leighton, who discovers "a
new language of desire" in the Sapphic poems of Michael Field (1992:
209) and concludes that "Sappho has finally been recuperated for women
as a model of poetry and of love together" (237). Indeed, the language
of desire developed by Michael Field works against the recuperation of
Sappho as unified lyric subject or lesbian identity, insofar as it depends
on rhetorical doubling.

The poems in *Long Ago* that are inspired by Sappho's epithalamia demonstrate how various kinds of sexuality may be constituted through such
textual doubling. These wedding poems, dedicated to Hymen, simultaneously repeat and exceed the binary opposition on which heterosexual
marriage depends. For instance, poem 42, introduced by the epigraph
Χαίροισα νύμφα, χαιρέτω δ' ὁ γάμβρος (the bride rejoicing, let the bridegroom rejoice), expands this self-doubling fragment into eight stanzas
that focus primarily on the bride. In the first stanza, she predominates:

> She comes, and youthful voices
>   On Hymen praise confer;
> She comes, and she rejoices,
>   Rejoice with her,
> O bridegroom! Let her see
>   Thy brave felicity.

The groom's appeareance is deferred until line 5; meanwhile, "She
comes" is doubled in lines 1 and 3, and within line 3 "she" is doubled
again in "she comes, and she rejoices," and even the pairing of verbs in
"she rejoices / rejoice with her" places her before and after a "him" who

is never quite present. In fact, although the poem is written in the form of a second-person address to the groom, he exists only to be invoked, and the very structure of invocation renders him absent. The apostrophe "O bridegroom" affirms this absence, and when the apostrophe is repeated in the final stanza it renders him silent as well:

> She comes, thy hope fulfilling;
>   O happy bridegroom, see,
> How gracious and how willing
>   She comes to thee.
> Rejoice! Oh be not dumb!
> Rejoice, for she is come!

The bride comes "thy hope fulfilling," yet when she arrives at the end of the poem it is the groom who must respond to her. Here the Victorian ideology of marriage—as a complementary relationship between husband and wife, with her defined only in relation to him—is reversed: he is defined only in relation to her, while she is a self-doubled pair that exists both within and beyond their pairing.

The figure of Hymen is therefore deployed by Michael Field as a rhetorical chiasmus, or cross-coupling, that reverses the subordination of feminine to masculine in the union of marriage and inverts heterosexual difference between two by articulating an already self-differing structure within one. This rhetorical doubling is emphasized in the invocation to the god of marriage in poem 55, where the Greek epigraph Ὕμεν' Ὑμήναον (altered from Ἔσπετ' Ὑμήναον, "Sing Hymenaeus," as the fragment appears in Wharton 1898/1974:144) is translated into "O Hymen Hymenaeus"—the name generates its own repetition, but with a difference, allowing simultaneous union and division. When poem 55 concludes, "Thou linkest in a living joy / This virgin and this noble boy," the Hymen linking "virgin" and "boy" is also the hymen that separates the virgin from the boy. The contradictory logic of Hymen—a link that joins and separates—works throughout this volume of Sapphic lyrics, in which celebrations of marriage coincide with the celebration of maidenhood.

Thus in poem 47, another wedding song, the bride about to be joined with the groom is also kept separate, "undescried" and "inviolate":

> She has been kept for thee, I know not how;
>   As, undescried,
> A blushing apple on the topmost bough,
>   Heaven kept thy bride

> A fragrant, rare, inviolate thing
> For season of thy cherishing.

The girl is like an apple to be picked by the groom, an image that recalls Sappho's fragment about the apple beyond the reach of apple pickers, forever "on the topmost bough." That famous fragment is translated into prose in Wharton's edition: "As the sweet-apple blushes on the end of the bough, the very end of the bough, which the gatherers overlooked, nay overlooked not but could not reach . . ." (1898/1974:132). The very syntax of the protracted subordinate clause makes the apple more and more distant ("on the end . . . the very end . . . overlooked, nay . . . could not reach"), and likewise the comparison between apple and bride is never completed; as Anne Carson concludes from her reading of this Greek fragment, "If there is a bride, she stays inaccessible. It is her inaccessibility that is present" (1986:27).

Michael Field's poem likewise suspends the girl in the moment of Hymen, in a state of in-between-ness that is neither the presence nor the absence of the hymen, and cannot be described in either/or terms: "I know not how." The girl eludes description, as the Greek epigraph to this poem emphasizes: Οὐ γὰρ ἦν ἐτέρα πάϊς, ὦ γάμβρε, τοιαύτα, "For there was no other girl, O bridegroom, like her," in Wharton's translation (1898/1974:144). The Greek fragment is translated into the present tense, however, in the final stanza of poem 47, keeping the girl perpetually suspended in the present moment of being about to be married:

> There is none like her, like thy girl, thine own,
>   And, bridegroom, see!
> Honouring Hera of the silver throne,
>   She turns to thee.
> Sappho, with solitary eyes, afar
> Will watch the rising of eve's fairest star.

Here again, instead of fixing the bride's identity in relation to the groom, marriage produces rhetorical doubling. Even as she "turns to thee" to become "thy girl, thine own," the poem also turns her into "eve's fairest star," not only far from "solitary" Sappho but separated from the groom as well, and still beyond reach.

By presenting Hymen as a rhetorical operation that simultaneously joins and separates, *Long Ago* opens a space for mediation, a way to cross binary oppositions and articulate what is between and beyond. This crossing is most strikingly performed in poem 52, in which the Greek prophet Tiresias crosses from the male sex into the female, to learn "the mystic rapture of the bride." What he discovers, in comparing masculine and feminine experience of marriage, is greater "receptivity of soul:"

> When womanhood was round him thrown
> He trembled at the quickening change,
> He trembled at his vision's range,
> His finer sense for bliss and dole,
> His receptivity of soul;
> But when love came, and, loving back,
> He learnt the pleasure men must lack.

Here Tiresias becomes an interchangeably doubled self: both masculine and feminine, self-divided yet coupled together. His "quickening change"—the ability to cross between sexual identities and be receptive to the split—also suggests the possibility of being *"closer married,"* as Bradley and Cooper describe themselves. They were fascinated with the figure of Tiresias, not only in this poem but in a journal entry that describes an idyllic portrait of a girl "yielding" to a shepherd. Quoting from the Tiresias poem, Cooper writes: "It is one of those works of art that 'reveal / What woman in herself must feel.' The diverse sexual frankness of enjoyment in giving (or rather taking) & receiving is clear as in Michael's *Tiresias*" (46780, 25 April 1892). This vision of Tiresias, simultaneously active and passive, defines the erotic interchangeability within Michael Field's Sapphic lyrics, as well as the textual exchange that makes the writing of these lyrics possible.

Read this way, Tiresias embodies the contradictions of a poem written by two women (Bradley and Cooper) writing as a man (Michael Field) writing as a woman (Sappho) who writes about a man (Tiresias) who was once a woman. It is significant that the Greek epigraph to the Tiresias poem is also quoted in the preface to *Long Ago*, as introduction to the contradictory authorship of the entire volume. The preface is written in the first-person singular of Michael Field:

When, more than a year ago, I wrote to a literary friend of my attempt to express in English the passionate pleasure Dr. Wharton's book had brought to me, he replied: "That is a delightfully audacious thought—the extension of Sappho's fragments into lyrics. I can scarcely conceive anything more audacious." In simple truth all worship that is not idolatry must be audacious; for it involves the blissful apprehension of an ideal; it means in the very phrase of Sappho—

"Ἔγων δ' ἐμαύτᾳ τοῦτο σύνοιδα.

"And this I feel in myself" is Wharton's translation of the Greek phrase from Sappho (1898/1979:80), asserting the language of personal experience yet also pointing to self-division: the doubling of "I" (the masculine or feminine pronoun ἐγώ) and "myself" (the feminine pronoun ἐμαύτᾳ), to produce "this" (the neuter demonstrative τοῦτο), as a knowledge that is neither masculine nor feminine but both simultaneously. Such cross-gendering anticipates the scenario of the Tiresias poem, but it also describes the multiple identifications and transgressions of gender involved throughout Michael Field's reading of Sappho—a "passionate pleasure" that is "delightfully audacious" because of its transgressive possibilities. The imitation of Sappho's fragments—or what is here called "the blissful apprehension of an ideal"—depends on this proliferation of selves: whatever Sappho knew "herself" Michael Field must assume "himself," and this assumption of a woman's ἐγώ by a man is implicitly doubled by the assumption of a man's ἐγώ by two women. So whose ἐγώ is it?

Not surprisingly, contemporary reviewers of *Long Ago* singled out Tiresias to pose questions about the authorship of the volume as a whole. In *The Academy* Tiresias is praised as "a myth in this poet's hands, serving to illustrate, in singularly penetrative fashion, the bi-sexual make of the poet" (18 June 1889, 388). This review substitutes bisexuality for dual authorship in order to avoid speaking of Michael Field in the plural, but the unspoken question is nearly audible: is Michael Field one sex, two sexes, or, perhaps, the third sex? A more censorious review in *The Spectator* considered the penetration of Tiresias by Michael Field "rude and coarse," however, if not altogether unspeakable: "It remains among the ἄρρητα: and we wish that it had not found expression by a writer for whose power we entertain, as we have more than once avowed, a profound respect" (27 July 1889, 119). Through Tiresias, whose story is to be spoken only in Greek, Michael Field has introduced "the ἄρρητα" (literally, "unspeakable things") into the English language.

Insofar as *Long Ago* finds expression for such things, it is precisely because of the ambiguity that surrounds Michael Field as the "speaker" of these Sapphic lyrics. Through the Greek fragments of Sappho, Bradley and Cooper enter a space for the interplay between sexuality and textuality, allowing various sexualities to emerge and finding new ways to engender the lyric as a genre. Their doubling of Sappho, I have suggested, takes many different forms: lyric voice is doubled by means of an eroticized textual exchange that is figured within their poems as interweaving; the self-doubling figure of Hymen enacts the rhetorical reversal and inversion of gender differences; and Tiresias embodies an interchangeably doubled self. This continual interchange defines the closer marriage of Bradley and Cooper, who invoke a traditional Victorian ideology of marriage even while they rework its fixed opposition of masculine and feminine. Indeed their skepticism about "the modern sacrament of Matrimony" is expressed in a letter that recounts the wedding of Havelock Ellis: "It is revolting. 'Free love, free field,' is sacreder," they proclaim (WD 193). What would it mean to celebrate, instead, "Free love, free field"? By imitating Sappho, Bradley and Cooper allow Michael Field to inhabit a metaphorical field of lesbian writing, freely crossing between genders without crossing them out altogether. In this reconfiguration of both gender and genre, we discover the multiple effects of their Sapphic signature: as the event and eventuation of a name, a signature from long ago doubled in Long Ago.

17

Sappho's Gymnasium

OLGA BROUMAS AND T BEGLEY

We began collaborating in 1983 when the American, new to Provincetown from Classical Greek studies at Yale, asked the Greek to read a passage of Aeschylus into a tape recorder for her pleasure and understanding. The latter was amusingly quelled by the contrast between T's Erasmian pronunciation of Greek vowels and Olga's modern Greek, as taught in the Greek gymnasium and later lyceum, but pleasure remained in cadence and embodied emotion. "The wind of life hits you before its material body, as the aroma of a woman before her actual presence. What remains is the embrace, and love"; Odysseas Elytis. Syntax swooped and leaned. Congas, saxophone, piano stood by.

Soon we began improvising in their syntax, and others we were to invent or be invented by over the years, including sculpture (in schistolith, metal, and epoxy) video, photography, installation, and performance art. Syntax, the choreography of interval, dimension, tempo, and mood was and is our primary medium, happily fertilized by snatches of Indonesian, Latin, German, the Romance languages, Old English, pentatonics, twelve-tone and Mixolydian scales, the microtonals of Asia, African drum complexities abstracted in rock, chance, and divinized operations

We have a poet's passion for this smattering of knowledges, eroticized by suggested punctualities or ellipses, verbs in a variable middle voice, nouns followed by their adjectives (imagine the object, then color it), time divided into units other than Western certitudes. A tense for faith? A tense for dream and trance? A semiotics of generosity? We practice meditation in many forms. Who speaks? Metis, Outis. But, who speaks? A voice of pluracination, heard partially, as always, gracing one of us with particulars, the other with the hallucinated breath of verbally unintelligible but musically incontrovertible dictions. That was one time, which recurs. Another is certitude of the field it requires us to serve—eros: gracious, philoxenous, augmenting, lubricant, remorseless faith.

We dwell, like most, in the lugubrious, cacophonous chaos of the imperial globe absorbed in its Babel complex. We don't have to sing about it. "We wouldn't assist the hand that struck us, we wouldn't eat garbage," says Plousia L. of the rules conscience imposed on her and her campmates for their survival during and after the Second World War. "That which disempowers you is unfit for your song"; Odysseas Elytis. The lyric refuses its raptor. Sappho's legacy to her daughter Kleis, her *gymnasium*, is "Tears unbecome the house of poets." This translation honors her lithe tongue, if not the exact plurality of her meaning. The word for "tears" is *thrēn'*, a contraction of *thrēnoi* (as in threnody), which is onomatopoetic and doesn't immediately imply words (why ode is needed in threnody). It is the sonoric and somatic act of lamentations. For "unbecome" she uses *ou Themis*, not Themis, the female god of Justice and ethics.

In Sappho's time the primary gods were female, *from your mouth to god's ear* an umbilical whose native wealth and dignity we never tire of guessing. Performance as the origin and culmination of text. What occurs in the simple swap is pleasure. Pleasure is infant, it too saves nothing. I mean the now that would have us undergo a surgery wherein "all light" is the only possible and desirable transplant. "Few know the emotional superlative is formed of light, not force"; Sappho's island-mate through millennia, Odysseas Elytis. My skin is the volunteer cipher of your emotion. I need a wafer, equal in body and propulsion, that develops an entirely immaculate congregation of the tongue so that we might address you in words your love shapes.

Who speaks? The first draft of *Sappho's Gymnasium* consumed six reams of an intensely orange paper we had found for pennies. It stands a ragged tower in the towel closet, robe-colored, Buddhist. Collaboration is compassion. Erasure of "ego" and "muse."

Proem to Sappho's Gymnasium

Sappho's Gymnasium:
οὐ γὰρ θέμις ᾿εν μοισοπόλων οἰκίαι θρῆνον ἔμμεν'.
Tears unbecome the house of poets.

    Gymn: nude, trained, exposed, athletic, flexible, practice.
    Gymnasteon: imperative: tears unbecoming.

    Incest animal
    you stop to give me a ride

    grace is rendering
    my old self unchanged

    oppressing witness by innocence
    birdsong in fist undressing

Ink where to care, founder of joy: ancestral, historical, female, only.

———

    "I threw my whole self into psychagogia. I danced,
I sang, I was in plays. I made up my mind and so did
a lot of the youngest girls. I was 16. You tried to give
something, a sweet note, to cheer the rest of the camp.
We paid in beatings and solitary. We never put the
banner down. Released from solitary, start singing,
then solitary again. In and out. Solitary and singing."
Plousia L., Ikaria, Chios, Trikeri, Makronisos island
camps, 1947–52; Janet Hart, *Women in the Greek
Resistance.*

Psychagogia: soul rearing.

———

    ". . . in unequal battle the whole human comes
awake. Also the poet. The idea of a book held me as
icons hold others. I saw it and turned its pages. The
poems I had not written and would have wanted to
write filled its pages with their external shape. I had

but to 'fill it' as you fill a row of empty glasses and,
immediately, what power, what freedom, what disdain
toward bombs and death it gave me."

"That which disempowers you is unfit for your
song."
—*The second great Lesbian, Odysseas Elytis*

———

"I write because I do not trust anyone to say these
things for me." —*Adrienne Rich*

> *Trust so broad we cash chromosomes*
> *praising floor carried into fields a synonym of life*
> *I shall be all with her and protect her*
> *from any harm and shall defend her in the midst*
> *of peace*

> *Call inexplicable ex spirit mental*

Narrative comforts you skim it.
    "Any completed utterance runs the risk of being
ideological." Roland Barthes
Gymnosophist imperative: antonym clutter.

Grief under anger, doxa interrupts praise;
constant grief: just depression.
    Narrative: doxa: thought police: recorded
grammar.

Aphrodytian celebrants: therapaenidae: from
ther:heat-summer-harvest and *poio*:god-poet-creator.

> *Pupil only to you*
> *fleece of dew.*

———

> "There was never a time
> when you were not walking toward me
> from under great trees
>   —

"Late I came
to the joy of this
whatever I have is yours

—

"Yours is the radiance
you say is mine since you met me
pearl of heaven

—

"We stand in line
taking up
one space

—

"We tell each other of a language
and it breathes
between us

—

"Some of what
you say to me I forget
but I remember you saying it in the dark

—

"Always I want
you to say
more

—

"Each of us is one
side of the rain
we only have one shadow"
—*The second great Psapphian, W. S. Merwin*

Sappho's Gymnasium

~

Outside memory worship never dies

That wish to embrace the great poplar

I woke and my bed was gleaming

Trees fill my heart

Torn mist doves I will love

Light struts cannot be broken

Make praise populations will last

~

"I have a young girl good as blossoming gold
her ephemeral face I have formed of a key
dearer than skylark homelands" *

A full twelve hours like a toiler like Lorca
archaic to bone we parse lark grove

dutyfree dove seapitched Eleni
nectar your carafe seafounder

Preumbilical eros preclassical brain

~

Blueprint I have hearing over knife
prime workshop these forests verbed by breezes

Horizon helicoptera
Lesbian your cups

Hermaphrodyte phototaxis

~

*Quoted stanza intuited from Sapphic fragment.

Limblooser sweetbitter's scale holds the hem
kitesilk the mind at your ankles

Tides and grape-heaver grammar owl
more soft than agapanthi erotopythons

~

Her face could still last tone of swaying habit
as if by accident the sea
exactly.

~

Godparent beaker
thirst glued to drink
unbulimic fresh water

Spasm my brakes
downhill oaks
eros wind

Beacon praise
hourless night
poet-taken

~

Pansappho unscalp unfleece unscalpel
        unskin of flowers our kin

~

Lesmonia, Lemonanthis, Lesaromas, Lesvaia

~

Bird is drunk inside me
remembering the smell
at your door

You are the guest
heart traces

Out loud you fill
that doesn't exist

~

Justice missed hyperventilates poet
Buddha vowel in Mohammet child dared cross
far from mother olive groves father almonds
lyric sap of maple far from Lesvos

~

The soul has a knee
just risen just rinses

Laurel to air I speak your lips
lantern in the abyss

I am what astonishment can bear
tongue I owe you

Pupil only to you
fleece of dew

~

Owl to her narrow hipped tunic bread to her athlete sleep

Small iconostasis clay girls
recombine danger and Homer

~

Dearest on the unrolled robe
young wife with peace in her hair

In the dark before the candle
where the archetypes take our unconscious to build
this work is forever

~

Wanderer gathers dusk in mountains
to its end the wind the stream
only riverbank hurry me

Only poetry

Part IV

Biblical Transformations

18

Entering the Tents

ALICIA OSTRIKER

I am and am not a Jew. To the rest of the world the Jew is marginal. But to Judaism I am marginal. Am woman, unclean. Am Eve. Or worse, am Lilith. Am illiterate. It is said: Whoever teaches his daughter Torah, teaches her obscenity. It is said: The voice of woman leads to lewdness. I am afraid to write: but it seems obvious, doesn't it. Everyone is afraid. Do what you fear. *I don't know if it says that in some text, but women have to run on these hobbled legs, have to pray and sing with our throttled voices. We have to do it sometime. We have to enter the tents/texts, invade the sanctuary, uncover the father's nakedness. We have to do it, believe it or not, because we love him. It won't kill him. He won't kill us.*

I define myself as a child of exile, diasporic, dispersed. A child of the Enlightenment, squeezed from knowledge's apple. Bubbled from the pulp of science, art, literature, philosophy. Two centuries distilled, a swallow of that hard cider. My speck of a planet is composed of stone, largely covered with water, in a universe limitless and still expanding. Do not ask me to worship a tribal idol. Do not expect me to forget, either, that the people of the Book are my people, and their God my God.

Do I contradict myself? My case is (something like) that of the poet Emily Dickinson, who worshiped and did not worship the Father, or the poet H.D., who worshiped Isis and Aphrodite along with Jesus, or the poet Anne Sexton, who asked Is it true? Is it true? and imagined that she was Christ and imagined that she was Mary, and believed that God eats beautiful women. My case is (something like) that of the poet William Blake, who declared, "Everything that lives is holy" and "All deities reside in the human breast." But it is also like that of Franz Kafka: "What do I have in common with Jews? I have hardly anything in common with myself."

Or Baruch Spinoza, lens grinder of tolerant Amsterdam, two steps away from the Spanish Inquisition, into whose focus the divinity of Nature enters, or those later heretics Marx, Trotsky, Rosa Luxemburg, Emma Goldman, believers in humanity, wrestling to fuse the light of justice from Sinai with the light of pure reason from Europe.

Or it is (something) like that of Solomon, who builds the Temple and cries out on its accomplishment: "Behold, the heaven of heavens cannot contain thee; how much less this house which I have builded." Or that of the rabbis who declare that the Holy One, Blessed be He, intends each of the meanings that He has made us capable of discovering. Behind every speculation the plea of King David, whose soul pants after God as the hart pants after the water brook. Or the call of the Shulamite who rises, and goes about the city in the streets, and in the broad ways seeks him whom her soul loveth. Reader, my case is like yours, perhaps. Perhaps yours is like mine. A case of (some kind of) love.

A Meditation in Seven Days

i

> Hear O Israel
> the Lord our God
> the Lord is One
> —Deuteronomy 6:4

If your mother is a Jew, you are a Jew
—Here is the unpredictable

Residue, but of what archaic power
Why the chain of this nation matrilineal

When the Holy One, the One
Who creates heaven and earth from formless void

Is utterly, violently masculine, with his chosen
Fathers and judges, his kings

And priests in their ritual linen, their gold and blue,
And purple and scarlet, his prophets clothed only

In a ragged vision of righteousness, angry
Voices promising a destructive fire

And even in exile, his rabbis with their flaming eyes
The small boys sent to the house of study

To sit on the benches
To recite, with their soft lips, a sacred language

To become the vessels of memory,
Of learning, of prayer,

Across the vast lands of the earth, kissing
His Book, though martyred, though twisted

Into starving rags, in
The village mud, or in wealth and grandeur

Kissing his Book, and the words of the Lord
Became fire on their lips

—What were they all but men in the image
Of God, where is their mother

*

The lines of another story, inscribed
And reinscribed like an endless chain

A proud old woman, her face desert-bitten
Has named her son: laughter

Laughter for bodily pleasure, laughter for old age triumph
Hagar the rival stumbles away

In the hot sand, along with her son Ishmael
They nearly die of thirst, God pities them

But among us each son and daughter
Is the child of Sarah, whom God made to laugh

*

Sarah, legitimate wife
Woman of power

My mother is a Jew, I am a Jew
Does it teach me enough

In the taste of every truth a sweeter truth
In the bowels of every injustice an older injustice

In memory
A tangle of sandy footprints

ii

> Whoever teaches his daughter Torah,
> teaches her obscenity.
> —Rabbi Eleazer

If a woman is a Jew
Of what is she the vessel

If she is unclean in her sex, if she is
Created to be a defilement and a temptation

A snake with breasts like a female
A succubus, a flying vagina

So that the singing of God
The secret of God

The name winged in the hues of the rainbow
Is withheld from her, so that she is the unschooled

Property of her father, then of her husband
And if no man beside her husband

May lawfully touch her hand
Or gaze at her almond eyes, if when the dancers

Ecstatically dance, it is not with her,
Of what is she the vessel

If a curtain divides her prayer
From a man's prayer—

iii

> *We shall burn incense to the queen of heaven, and shall pour her libations*
> *as we used to do, we, our fathers, our kings and our princes, in the cities*
> *of Judah and in the streets of Jerusalem. For then we had plenty of food*
> *and we were all well and saw no evil.*
>
> —Jeremiah 44:17

Solomon's foreign wives, and the Canaanite daughters
Who with Ishtar mourned the death of Tammuz

Who *on the high places, under every green tree, and alongside*
The altars set fig boughs, images of Ashtoreth

Who offered incense to the queen of heaven
And sang in a corner of the temple, passing from hand to hand

In token of joy the fruited branch, body
Of the goddess their mothers loved

Who made cakes bearing her features
And their husbands knew

The Lady of Snakes
The Lady of Lilies

She who makes prosper the house
Who promulgates goodness, without whom is famine

Cursed by the furious prophet, scattered screaming
Burned alive according to law, for witchcraft

Stoned to death by her brothers, perhaps by men
She has nakedly loved, for the free act of love

In her city square
Her eyes finally downcast

Her head shaved
Is she too the vessel of memory

iv

> *. . . for out of Zion shall go forth the law, and the word of the Lord from Jerusalem. And he shall judge among the nations, and shall rebuke many people: and they shall beat their swords into plowshares, and their spears into pruninghooks: nation shall not lift up sword against nation, neither shall they learn war any more.*
>
> —Isaiah 2:3–4

Here is another story: the ark burned,
The marble pillars buried, the remnant scattered

A thousand years, two thousand years
In every patch of the globe, the gentle remnant

Of whom our rabbis boast: *Compassionate sons
Of compassionate fathers*

In love not with the Law, but with the kindness
They claim to be the whole of the Torah

Torn from a whole cloth
From the hills of Judea

That ran with sweetness, and from the streams
That were jewels, yearning for wholeness, next

Year in Jerusalem, surely, there would be
Milk and honey, they could see

The thing plainly, an ideal society
Of workers, the wise, the holy hill flowing

Finally with righteousness—
Here they are, in the photographs of the 1880s,

The young women, with their serious eyes
Their lace collars and cameo brooches

Are the partners of these serious young men
Who stand shaven, who have combed their hair smoothly

They are writing pamphlets together, which describe
In many little stitches the word *shalom*

They have climbed out of the gloomy villages
They have kissed the rigid parents good-bye

Soon they will be a light to the nations
They will make the desert bloom, they are going to form

The plough and pruninghook Isaiah promised
After tears of fire, of blood, of mud

Of the sword and shame
Eighty generations

Here in their eyes the light of justice from Sinai
And the light of pure reason from Europe

v

> *I intend to convict God for murder, for he is destroying his people and the*
> *Law he gave them from Mount Sinai. I have irrefutable proof in my hands.*
> —Elie Wiesel, *The Gates of the Forest*

> *And Esau said unto his father, Hast thou but one blessing, my father?*
> *bless me, even me also, O my father. And Esau lifted up his voice, and*
> *wept.*
> —Genesis 27:38

Does the unanswered prayer
Corrode the tissue of heaven

Doesn't it rust the wings
Of the heavenly host, shouldn't it

Untune their music, doesn't it become
Acid splashed in the face of the king

Smoke, and the charred bone bits suspended in it
Sifting inevitably upward

Spoiling paradise
Spoiling even the dream of paradise

vi

Come my friend, come my friend
Let us go to meet the bride
            —Sabbath Song

And in between she would work and clean and cook. But the food, the food:
salmon croquettes, clam cakes, casseroles, cream puffs, sweet and sour
meatballs, and then, through the years, as you and your sister left and money
was looser, escalating in gourmet finesse, spinach crepes, sole almadine, soufflés
and vichyssoise and chiffon pie. O the visits were filled with food.
            —Melanie Kaye/Kantrowitz

Not speculation, nothing remote
No words addressed to an atomic father

Not the wisdom of the wise
Nor a promise, and not the trap of hereafter

Here, now, through the misted kitchen windows
Since dawn the dusk is falling

Everywhere in the neighborhood
Women have rushed to the butcher, the grocer

With a violet sky she prepares the bread, she plucks
And cooks the chicken, grates the stinging horseradish

These are her fingers, her sinewy back as she scrubs
The house, her hands slap the children and clean them

Dusk approaches, wind moans
Food ready, it is around her hands

The family faces gather, the homeless
She has gathered like sheep, it is her veiny hands

That light the candles, so that suddenly
Our human grief illuminated, we're a circle

Practical and magical, it's
Strong wine and food time coming, and from outside time

From the jewelled throne
Of a house behind history

She beckons the bride, the radiant
Sabbath, the lady we share with God

Our mother's palms like branches lifted in prayer
Lead our rejoicing voices, our small chorus

Our clapping hands in the here and now
In a world that is never over

And never enough

vii

> For lo, the winter is past; the rain is over and gone; The flowers appear on
> the earth; the time of the singing of birds is come . . .
> —Song of Solomon 2:11–12

What can I possess
But the history that possesses me

With whom must I wrestle
But myself

And as to the father, what is his trouble
That leaves him so exhausted and powerless

Why is he asleep, his gigantic
Limbs pulseless, dispersed over the sky

White, unnerved
No more roar

He who yesterday threatened murder, yanking
At his old uniform, waving his dress sword

He's broken every glass in the house, the drunkard
He's snapped the sticks of furniture, howling

And crying, liquor spilled everywhere
He's staggered to the floor, and lies there

In filth, three timid children prod him
While screwing their faces up from the stink

That emanates from his mouth—
He has beaten them black and blue

But they still love him, for
What other father have they, what other king—

He begins to snore, he is dreaming again
How outside the door a barefoot woman is knocking

Snakes slide downhill in the forest
Preparing to peel themselves in rebirth, wriggling

Fiddlehead ferns uncurl, a square of blue sky
Flings its veil, pale mushrooms

Raise their noses after the downpour
A breeze rustles through her yellow dress

Don't come back, he whispers in his sleep
Like a man who endures a nightmare

And in my sleep, in my twentieth century bed
It's that whisper I hear, *go away,*

Don't touch, so that I ask
Of what I am the vessel

Fearful, I see my hand is on the latch
I am the woman, and about to enter

19

In Her Own Images:
Lucille Clifton and the Bible

AKASHA (GLORIA) HULL

The Bible has functioned as a sourcebook for Lucille Clifton throughout her illustrious, twenty-five-year poetic career. In three cycles of poems written between 1972 and 1991, she directly treats many of its major
characters and events. On one level, her use of this biblical material is—
in every sense of the word—faithful; yet, in fundamental and crucial
ways, she is startlingly heterodox. Perhaps the simplest way to describe
her transformative mode is to say that she (1) Africanizes, (2) feminizes,
(3) sexualizes, and (4) mysticizes the original text. Thus she rewrites it
in her own image as a black and cosmically spiritual woman. The poetic
genre through which she mediates her vision is the personal, free verse
lyric but here, too, she negotiates a mutually illuminating relationship
between the traditional and the new, the ordinary and the extraordinary.
Invariably lowercased, brief, and deceptively simple in form, style, and
diction, her poems ultimately authorize themselves as complexly crafted
pieces redolent with both mystical-spiritual and sociopolitical consciousness.

As important context, it should be mentioned that Lucille Clifton is
one of an impressive number of contemporary African American women
writers whose spiritual consciousness is providing both content and modality for their work. They are writing about supranatural experiences
and phenomena, and also utilizing what Toni Morrison has called "ways
of knowing beyond the five senses" to access their material. Morrison
herself has spiced her novels with flying Africans, ghosts, supernatural

The initial draft of this essay was written with the support of a 1991 postdoctoral fellowship from the American Association of University Women. I wish to acknowledge this
funding and express my sincere appreciation.

All of the unreferenced quotations of Clifton are taken from an interview I conducted
with her in May 1991. I am deeply indebted to her for this cooperation.

birth, rootworking, and so forth. She has also spoken in propria persona about her connection through her grandmother and father to the world of dreams and spirits (Strouse 1981). Alice Walker has said that the characters of *The Color Purple* (1982) visited her to have her transmit their story (A. Walker 1983); and in a later book, *The Temple of My Familiar* (1989), she deals undramatically with such matters as karmic union, reincarnation, and the physical materialization of energy.

Adopting science fiction, Octavia Butler deploys shape-shifters and an array of telephatic powers, as in *Mind of My Mind* (1977) and *Wild Seed* (1980), two of her earlier works. Another poet, Dolores Kendrick, prefaces her 1989 volume with these words:

> I thank these women
> for coming, and I thank
> the good God who sent them.

> The Women of Plums

Toni Cade Bambara's novel *The Salt Eaters* (1980) is a brilliant compendium of ancient, black, and New Age spiritual wisdoms. Paule Marshall's heroine in *Praisesong for the Widow* (1983) undergoes a psychic rebirth that catapults her into ancestral visions and Yoruba gods. This list could be extended to further enforce the point that spirituality is a vital current for black women writers—just as it increasingly is for United States society and the whole of pre-twenty-first-century civilization. This special dimension of their work seems to account significantly for their current popularity, for the way unprecedented masses of readers are attracted to their writings.

Fitting generally into this movement, Lucille Clifton is yet unique in her unclouded self-revelation and the meshing of personal autobiography with her art. Spiritually endowed, she practices her gifts in both her life and her poetry. Clifton hears voices, automatically writes, reads palms, senses realities, and speaks normally unknowable truths. She and her family—which she has described as "spiritual and even perhaps mystical" (Clifton 1983)[1]—learned over time to "incorporate the nonvisible" into their everyday cosmology. How she does so makes her spirituality a force that could be described with the following adjectives: black, natural, rooted, unpretentious, practical, quietly powerful, good-

---

[1] Lucille Clifton's more recent volume *The Book of Light* (1993) adds a fourth set of texts to this category. The final section of the book is a sequence titled "brothers," "a conversation in eight poems between an aged Lucifer and God, though only Lucifer is heard" (69).

natured, good-humored, ethically and politically edged, humanly respectful, lovingly shared, transformative.

Clifton's way of functioning in this area breaks down the boundaries between this world and the "other" world. Likewise, her spirituality-driven poetry transgresses categories of form, genre, and artistic convention. One very striking example of this is her poem "the light that came to lucille clifton" (from *two-headed woman*, 1980). Immediately, the use of her own, real name is arresting. In earlier poems, she had incorporated fanciful references to "lucy girl," but she had never instated herself with this degree of fullness, formality, and solemnity. Thus, with a dramatic move that upsets modesty and convention, the reader is invited to see the person behind the persona, the lady behind the mask.

Poetically working Clifton's actual experience, "the light that came" recounts a pivotal time when "a shift of knowing" makes possible the breakthrough to higher levels of awareness and personal power.

> it was the summer
> she understood that she had not understood
> and was not mistress even
> of her own off eye. then
> the man escaped throwing away his tie and
> the children grew legs and started walking and
> she could see the peril of an
> unexamined life.
>
> (Clifton 1987a:209)

Among this series of concrete details is Clifton's allusion to her half-blind eye, whose functions she cannot control. This image inversely resonates with her finally being able to see that she needs to scrutinize her own autonomous be-ing more closely. However, she closes her eyes, "afraid to look for her / authenticity."

> but the light insists on itself in the world;
> a voice from the nondead past started talking,
> she closed her ears and it spelled out in her hand
> "you might as well answer the door, my child,
> the truth is furiously knocking."
>
> (209)

Thus the poem ends, with reference to an automatic writing experience and active resignation/acceptance.

In addition to incorporating her full name, this poem presents the oddness of Clifton referring to herself in the third person within a work that otherwise fits into the "I" frame of confessional or autobiographical verse. This disassociative effect is heightened by the way she linguistically distances obviously intimate elements: "the man" is her husband, "the children" her own six maturing ones (whose just-growing legs strike an almost surreal chord). These features tip the ambiance of the poem toward madness—which is reflected in its initially de-ranged lines. Yet this craziness is effectively contravened by a simultaneous, convincing lucidity.

For an epiphanic poem, "the light that came to lucille clifton" is strangely low-key; as a rendition of mystical experience, it is singularly nonelevated. Seemingly, Clifton is conveying through her form and style what she believes: that the extraordinary is really quite ordinary, nothing to get overly excited about, and available to us all. Cumulatively, this is a highly original poem. It is followed by a remarkable final sequence through which Clifton testifies to having seen the light and heard the voices of another world. Despite being called mad, she holds onto the truth of her experience and authoritatively declares in the last lyric:

> in populated air
> our ancestors continue.
> i have seen them.
> i have heard
> their shimmering voices
> singing.
>
> (221)

From this point on, spiritual-mystical themes and materials become an even more prominent feature of her work.

Situated against this background of expressed—and expressive—spirituality, Lucille Clifton's handling of the Bible effects a perhaps contradictory-seeming union of Christian subject matter and her own brand of spirituality, which is certainly not traditionally religious but rather mystical in the broadest sense of the word. Having defined herself as "someone who is aware of mystery," Clifton illuminates on multiple levels the even more marvelous mysteries that lie behind received Mystery.

Moreover, her treatment of the Bible places her among contemporary women poets who, like herself, are engaged in what the critic Alicia Ostriker terms "revisionist mythmaking"—the poets' appropriation "for altered ends" of "a figure or story previously accepted and defined by a culture," including historic and quasi-historical figures, folktales, legends, and Scripture (1986:212–13). Ostriker notes that these poets no longer hide behind the characters to make their socially seditious points but openly "deviate from or explicitly challenge the meanings attributed to mythic figures and tales." She sums up the revisionist mythmaking of this poetry thus:

> These poems generically assume the high literary status that myth confers and that women writers have often been denied because they write "personally" or "confessionally." But in them the old stories are changed, changed utterly, by female knowledge of female experience, so that they can no longer stand as foundations of collective male fantasy or as the pillars sustaining phallocentric "high" culture. Instead, they are corrections; they are representations of what women find divine and demonic in themselves; they are retrieved images of what women have collectively and historically suffered; in some cases they are instructions for survival. (Ostriker 1986:215)

Ostriker's emphasis on the legitimacy gained through employing respected cultural myths and the ultimate feminization of this material is a particularly helpful context for understanding Clifton's work.

Another necessary context is Clifton's own African American religious background. Her mother belonged to the Sanctified church, and her father was Baptist. She grew up in the Baptist church of her father, no doubt absorbing the Bible along with its interpretations and embellishments in Sunday school and sermons. Though she does not believe it "as a literal book," she herself has read the text from cover to cover. Clifton says that she finds it interesting but really does not know why she uses it so extensively in her writing: "It just interests me. The figures there interest me." One might also surmise that the Bible has possibly influenced her literary style. Both it and her poems possess a terse but affluent concreteness, an elliptical fullness.

As an African American woman, Clifton effortlessly balances a respectful—and even, one could say, affectionate—use of the Bible with her other nonorthodox attitudes, ideas, and beliefs. As is true for many of her counterparts (especially of her generation), she feels no need to rail against God and Christianity. It would be highly unusual to find someone like her expressing angry, negative sentiments about this religious code. It is too African American, too much who we are—our culture, blood, survival; the faith of our fathers and grandmothers. Not surprisingly, while Clifton relentlessly lowercases absolutely everything else, she always capitalizes "God" and his pronouns. Furthermore, as a truly spiritual person, Clifton would know that (1) fundamentally, all spiritual systems are essentially the same, and (2) they all (can) work for whoever sincerely believes and faithfully practices them.

Clifton's equipoise of contrasting doctrines can also be framed as an agile juxtaposition of folk and religious beliefs. Dianne Johnson uses this dyad in her helpful discussion of Clifton's books for children. She notes that even though, after 1947, (mostly) white writers of black children's books tended to eliminate superstition, while continuing to portray black people as religious, Clifton "sees no reason to avoid the 'superstitious' merely because it may evoke images of the 'primitive' or to deny the overlay of the superstitious with the religious." Her perpetuation of these "superstitious" images can, in fact, be "viewed as an acceptance of a world view rather than as a resignation to stereotypes" (Johnson 1990: 86–87). This notion of seeing what Clifton does as considered ontology is absolutely correct. As both her life and her work demonstrate, she accepts phenomena usually dubbed superstition as valid reality and does so from a deep rootedness in her cultural identity as an African American woman.

Johnson illustrates Clifton's syncretism of the folk and the religious with a discussion of her children's book *The Lucky Stone* (1979). This stone—originating as a talisman that helped save the life of a slave girl Mandy and subsequently handed down to generations of her successors—is now, after Emancipation, in the possession of Mandy's daughter, Vashti. One Sunday when the weather is "strange and threatnin'," Vashti attends a special and very spirited church service. The last to ascend the platform to testify, Vashti does so with her mother's stone worn in a pouch around her neck. The pouch string breaks, "hurling the stone to the ground"—and just as she jumps down to retrieve it, a mighty bolt of lightning strikes the platform, destroying it with fire. In the story, Vashti's descendant, Tee, who is being told this tale by her great grandmother, whispers, "That stone was sure lucky for her." The "Grandmama" replies with a smile, "That's cause it's a lucky stone" (Johnson 1990:88). Johnson comments on the meaning of this passage:

> [T]here is little or no differentiation between the "religious" and the "superstitious" as commonly understood in everyday English. Recognizing this, the passage is both remarkable and unremarkable for the same reason—for the Black worshippers on this stormy afternoon, Vashti's shiny black stone is a savior just as God himself is a deliverer. Belief in God's power is at the base of the events taking place. Yet the power of the stone is an inextricable element too. Both are part of the acknowledged order of things. In this version of the event, in fact, it is the stone that is finally hailed as the protector. (88)

Born of African cosmology and of experiences in America that often made no "sense," this ability to live well and happily with apparent contradiction is a notable feature of African American culture. It is certainly relevant for Clifton's overall spirituality and for her handling of the Bible and Christianity in her work.

These biblical poems occur in three primary places: (1) the "some je-sus" sixteen-piece final section of *good news about the earth* (1972), (2) the eight-poem sequence about Mary in *two-headed woman* (1980), and (3) the "Tree of Life" section in *quilting* (1991), which consists of ten poems revolving around Lucifer, the fallen angel. One of the most immediately striking features of all these selections is Clifton's ability to see the or-dinary in the extraordinary, to bring heaven "down" to earth and make "men" of gods (the hierarchical metaphors are inappropriate). This is a critical ingredient of her uniqueness and success. The intermingling of ordinary and extraordinary—whether she begins with one side or the other—is a characteristic feature of her consciousness and is reflected in her style. She reports that a friend of hers expresses the same idea by saying that she, Clifton, tries to find "the human in the mythology and the mythology in the human."

A single work from *Next* (1987), "my dream about God," illustrates Clifton's manipulation of these two dimensions. The beginning stanzas of the poem read:

> He is wearing my grandfather's hat.
> He is taller than my last uncle.
> when He sits to listen
> He leans forward tilting the chair
>
> where His chin cups in my father's hand.
> it is swollen and hard from creation.
> His fingers drum on His knee
> dads stern tattoo.
>
>   (Clifton 1987b:41)

Here, God becomes anthropomorphic, family, familiar, complete with the appurtenances and mannerisms of the poet's male relatives, down to his work-hardened hands. This poem is reminiscent of Gwendolyn Brooks's "the preacher: ruminates behind the sermon" from her first collection, *A Street in Bronzeville* (1945). Brooks's work begins with the arresting lines: "I think it must be lonely to be God. / Nobody loves a master." It goes on to picture a Jehovah who strides importantly through his halls, but who has no one to take his arm, tweak his ear, or buy him a coke or beer. Perhaps, the poet wonders, "He tires of looking down. . . . Perhaps sometimes He tires of being great / In solitude. Without a hand to hold" (Brooks 1963:8). Not so with Clifton's God. He is a companionable father who, in the poem, "leans forward" and "strains to hear" his good daughter's wishes. Clifton has taken this basic conceit one step further, from the problem of Divine isolation to a solution which releases Him from His misery. Everyone is happier.

Her anthropomorphic strategies in this poem appear on a larger, amplified scale in the "some jesus" sequence. These are brief (as usual), first-person monologues, which read like soliloquies rather than like traditional dramatic monologues that assume a listener and an active context. The biblical characters—who obviously do interest Clifton—are projected as ordinary folk. They are demythologized, debunked, leveled through homely imagery and contextualizations. Cain "plants tears" in the desert every morning that his brother Abel, whom he has slain, does not rise up (1972). And Job comes to the rags of his suffering "like a good baby / to breakfast." Perhaps the most heterodox (for some readers) of Clifton's strategems is that she further "levels" these biblical figures by making them racially black. This is apparent throughout in their language, for they speak an African American folk dialect of "be's," third-person subject–verb "disagreements," and colorful metaphor.

In addition, as if this were not enough to make her point, Clifton either clearly Africanizes history and historical context or slyly suggests their Afrocentric possibilities. Moses becomes "an old man / leaving slavery," which is literally and biblically true and also redolent of black United States history. Solomon blesses blackness in all its forms, from "the black skin of the woman" (the dark lover in his Song of Solomon or Songs) to the "black / night turning around her." On Palm Sunday, the people lay turnips for Christ's mule to walk on and wave beets and collard greens in the air (an especially humorous visualization). John the Baptist, the forerunner of Jesus Christ, announces:

> somebody coming in blackness
> like a star
> and the world be a great bush
> on his head
> . . . .
> i'm just only a baptist preacher
> somebody bigger than me coming
> in blackness like a star
>
> (98)

The "great bush" calls to mind God inaugurating Moses' mission by speaking to him from the burning bush, while it simultaneously—and almost as a pun—becomes a head of natural black hair, also called a "bush." After a reference like this and locutions such as "he be calling the people brother," it is almost impossible not to make John a *black* "baptist preacher."

Another arresting poem in this category is "jonah":

> what i remember
> is green
> in the trees
> and the leaves
> and the smell of mango
> and yams
> and if i had a drum
> i would send to the brothers
> —Be care full of the ocean—
>
> (97)

Speaking from the belly of the whale that swallowed him, Jonah waxes nostalgic about the sights, smells, and tastes of his tropical home. The crowning touch, however, is his yearning for one of the famed talking drums with which to warn his kin about the dangers of the ocean, a trope that spells enslavement and the Middle Passage—in addition to its accurate Bible reference.

Even in their biblical guises, many of the figures about which Clifton writes exhibit ordinary human traits—and this is probably what attracted her to them in the first place. (Limning these traits is certainly one way that Baptist preachers make their sermons interesting and effective for their congregations.) Jonah himself, for instance, runs away from responsibility, sleeps during a crisis, gets angry, inflexibly holds a grudge, and sulks (see his story in the Book of Jonah). Clifton picks up on human cues like these and refracts them in her own image. The result is sometimes surprising, sometimes humorous, and always impressive. Her working in this way fits into the anthropomorphizing tendencies of African American folktales, where characters from the Bible and even God himself are similarly "raced" and humanized. Another, earlier woman writer, Zora Neale Hurston, displays this approach in her highly original folklore collection, *Mules and Men* (1935). Finally, it must be said that transforming biblical figures into plain black folks is a move that simultaneously levels and elevates. It brings the Bible's inhabitants down to earth, while it imparts to black people some of the status of universal heroes and heroines.

Clifton treads even further into heterodox territory when she adds sexual overtones to the human characteristics that these biblical personages exhibit. Often this is ambiguously referenced and ripples as a delicate undercurrent, but for almost any perceptive reader, it is there. Attend to her poem "mary":

> this kiss
> as soft as cotton
>
> over my breasts
> all shiny bright
>
> something is in this night
> oh Lord have mercy on me
>
> i feel a garden
> in my mouth
>
> between my legs
> i see a tree
>
> (1972:99)

This poem recounts Mary, the virgin betrothed to Joseph, being "gotten with child" by the Holy Spirit. However, it adds flesh and body to traditional projections of this event, corporealizing and even eroticizing what is usually treated as a strictly nonphysical and ethereal phenomenon. In the incoherence of their grammatical structure and the vague wonder of their words, the first two "couplets" indicate a mating experience. After this, a series of short, definite sentences follow, even though fear and awe are still present—especially in the plea to God for mercy. The final two "couplets" show Mary as a visionary who sees through this present happening to its ultimate result.

The garden in her mouth is Gethsemane, the place where Christ prayed shortly before the Last Supper, and the tree is certainly representative of his subsequent Crucifixion. The sexual language—"between my legs"—and the phallic symbolism of the tree placed there circle back to the kiss and the breasts at the beginning of the poem. Given the Africanization that marks most of the poems in this series, one gives weight to the cotton in her initial simile (the picking of which assured black people's continued status as slaves to a Southern economy) and thinks about trees as the site of black men's hanging (like Christ on the cross, a comparison sometimes made for dramatic effect).

"mary" is an excellent example of how much dense matter Clifton can encapsulate in a very brief poem through her unerringly chosen diction and images. Christ's life is here, from his inception to his death, and Mary herself—as well as the supernatural event that sanctified her—have been given indelible body *and* race. Clifton's tour de force becomes all the more amazing when we compare it with the scant bit that the Bible tells. During the annunciation, Mary asks Gabriel, the angel who breaks the news, "How shall this be, seeing I know not a man?" He answers: "The Holy Ghost shall come upon thee, and the power of the Highest shall overshadow thee" (Luke 1:34–35). That is all. Clifton's poetic imagination supplies the rest. Finally, because Mary's is simultaneously a visionary and an erotic experience, the poem unites mysticism and sexuality, a combination that through the ages has been linked intuitively by thinkers both visionary and erotic.

This poem is Clifton's most overt and sustained treatment of sex and sexuality among the group. It is followed by "joseph," set at a later time when Christ is a "boy." Almost as baffled as Mary, Joseph notes that "something about this boy / has spelled my tongue." Even when his fingers "tremble" in love on Mary, his "mouth cries only / Jesus Jesus Jesus" (1972:100) Perhaps Clifton is thinking—almost as a sly joke—of the tendency of many people to call Jesus Christ's name during the rigorous pleasure of making love and thus is facilitating our identification with the poem in this personal way. Repetition and agitated rhythmn are the techniques by which she also suggests sexuality in a third poem, "holy night," from the Marian cycle in *two-headed woman*. Mary is again the speaker. She concludes her troubled words to her husband with, "joseph, i shine, oh joseph, oh / illuminated night"(1980:189).

It is safe to say that Clifton "fleshes out" these biblical figures, making them more interesting and independent, and imparting to them a subjectivity greater than the object/ive status they tend to have in received religious discourse. She probes their minds, their psychologies, their personalities. As she does when she herself is the subject of a poem, she invites us to see the person behind the persona, the human behind the myth. In addition to her treatment of them on this level, Clifton further shows these characters as human beings who are being "worked," handled, used by a magic and mystery they can scarce understand. Seeing them thus enhances the mystery, but it also evokes our empathetic sympathy for the characters. All of this contributes to the success of Clifton's poems that specifically focus on Mary.

In "some jesus," Eve appeared in the first poem with Adam, and included there was the one poem that has been discussed about Mary. The remainder of the figures were male. This markedly contrasts with the religious sequence in *two-headed woman*, where all eight poems are devoted to Mary. Biblical tradition remains a kind of background, but these works are even less literally tied to the Bible. Twice in Luke, we are told that Mary "ponders" things "in her heart." Beyond this, there is silence about her thoughts. This is the kind of intriguing lacuna that Clifton's imagination fills, the kind of gaps that summon speculation and creation. In the Bible, Mary questions and then favorably responds to Gabriel. During an ensuing conversation with her cousin Elizabeth, John the Baptist's mother, about the miraculous births coming to both of them, Mary "magnifies" the Lord in ten rapturous verses (which, given the terse economy of the Bible, almost amounts to chattering). Otherwise, she is objectified in brief mentions or altogether absent from the text. Clifton constructs a very different picture.

First, she makes Mary important enough to have been the subject of an astrologer's predictions at her birth, a move paralleling all of the signs and prophecies that surround the imminence of the holy male figures. In "one-liners" as cryptic as predictions are wont to be, the astrologer accurately foresees her future. "Old men will follow" her, calling "mother mother," her "womb will blossom then die," "at a certain place" she will see something that will "break her eye" (1980:196). In phrases like these, her entire sad career as the mother of Jesus is foretold.

The second poem in the cycle continues to make her more worthy than incidental by addressing her parentage and early years: "anna speaks of the childhood of mary her daughter." Interestingly, the apocryphal gospels portray Anna's own birth of Mary as a miraculous occurrence. The Lord had "shut up" her womb, but she nevertheless gave birth to Mary after "her husband had fasted and prayed for 40 days and 40 nights in the wilderness" (Wigoder et al. 1986:662). Perhaps the scribes who established the canonical form of the Bible left out this account since such a proliferation of holy births adjacent to Jesus' might have vitiated the force of his own. In Clifton's poem, Anna narrates her recurring dream, also prescient, about Mary being "washed in light" and looking up on a hill with her "face all long tears." Her response is:

> and shall i give her up
> to dreaming then? i fight this thing.
> all day we scrubbing   scrubbing.
>   (197)

Her question is that of a loving, protective mother, but she has no choice or power in the matter. Her woman's work—even in its repetitive, fierce insistence—does not stay the divine plan.

Mary herself dreams of being hailed by "winged women," whom she joins. And, after her Son's birth, she reminisces in a song about her days as a "maiden" in her mother's house. While the cosmic events in which she played a leading role were evolving, she was "watching" her mother, "smiling an ordinary smile." Mary, Anna, and the astrologer all speak a form of Caribbean dialect. He says "she womb will blossom," a grammatical usage that is still current in Jamaica among other places. Ignoring standard rules of agreement, omitting auxiliary verbs, and employing the nominal for the objective possessive, Mary says "women was saying," "i afraid," and "i hands keep moving." In this way, Clifton implies a comparison between the early Christians and present-day Rastafarians. As she glosses them, they were/are both "small, somewhat despised" sects with "who knows what promise."

The Caribbean dialect is thickest in the last poem in Mary's voice, appropriately entitled "island mary":

> after the all been done and i
> one old creature carried on
> another creature's back, i wonder
> could i have fought these thing?
> surrounded by no son of mine save
> old men calling mother like in the tale
> the astrologer tell, i wonder
> could i have walk away when voices
> singing in my sleep? i one old woman.
> always i seem to worrying now for
> another young girl asleep
> in the plain evening.
> what song around her ear?
> what star still choosing?
>
> (202)

Aged, looking back, Mary summarizes her life as a "creature" of fate, wondering—in an echo of her mother—if she could have "fought." What concerns her now is the possibility that some other young girl will have to undergo a similar existence. Her worry sounds like an ultimate commentary on the action, a final choric glossing of all that has gone before.

This Marian cycle concludes with a poem that projects her into perpetuity, where she is prayed to and prayed for as the "holy woman split by sanctified seed," the "sister woman shook by the / awe full affection of the saints." Apparently, neither Mary herself or the women (presumably) who pray for her forever see her lot as an enviable one. In *Just a Sister Away: A Womanist Vision of Women's Relationships in the Bible*, black Christian feminist Renita J. Weems gives a similar, though dualistic, judgment of Mary's fate: "To be chosen by God is a humbling experience. To be used by God is an awesome experience. To be blessed by God is a joyous experience ... most of the time" (1988:113; her ellipsis). And she calls Mary and her older cousin Elizabeth two women "trying to grapple with the hand of God in their lives, sharing with each other the blessedness and the burdensomeness of being blessed" (122).

The similarly skeptical, if not totally critical, attitude toward being singled out for divine attention that Clifton suggests in these poems about Mary is extended even further in three later works about Leda, who was "taken" by Zeus in the form of a swan (Clifton 1993:59–61). She is a woman from a different milieu than Mary's but their stories are comparable. These Leda poems lend a harsher glare to the sentiments prefigured in the earlier Marian pieces. At the outset, in images that suggest Mary's situation, Leda declares that "sometimes / it all goes badly":

> the inn is strewn with feathers,
> the old husband suspicious
> and the fur between her thighs
> is the only shining thing.
>
> (60)

Continuing to speak bitterness in the second poem, she denounces the "pyrotechnics" of these "stars spinning into phalluses / of light" and tells them that if they "want what a man wants," then next time they should "come as a man / or don't come." Whatever Clifton may have been thinking when she devised these initial images, they bitingly mimic contemporary rock supercelebrities bursting onto a stage of fireworks for a one-show-only performance. Leda's ultimate judgment is that "there is nothing luminous" about her experience:

> they took my children.
> i lived alone in the backside
> of the village.
> my mother moved to another town.
> my father would follow me,
> when i came to the well,
> his thick lips slavering.
> and at night my dreams were full
> of the cursing of me fucking god
> fucking me.
>
> (59)

A ruined woman, regarded as a freak sexual object by even her own father, Leda is both the cursed and the cursing one. Using diction that never shows up elsewhere in Clifton's work, these last two lines are particularly scathing.

Clifton is aware that she has written many poems about Mary, and she says it is not "lost on her" that she currently teaches at St. Mary's College in St. Mary's City, Maryland—another coincidence that she thinks is "most interesting." Clifton reports that once, when she was listening to a speaker at the college lecture about Mary and the chosen women, she found herself thinking, "I bet some of these chosen women were quite annoyed." She admits that this "must be something that I think, and I don't know why." Whether she knows why or not, many of her women readers—be they feminists or not—will be able to comprehend her sentiment.

In sum, Clifton's work on Mary fills in the Bible's silences and invents a whole, new womanly mythology for her. Mary herself is centered and given an individuated, female primacy that in some ways reflects yet ultimately transcends her traditional status as Jesus Christ's mother. Implicit in Clifton's revision is a critique of patriarchal privilege, whether it emanates from heaven with God the Father or from his earthly sons who inscribe the story in *their* image. That she is able to accomplish her ends attests to her spiritual ability to shed her limiting ego and compassionately to project herself into other beings and consciousnesses. So doing, she rewrites the old myths into startling new scripts.

Certainly, Clifton's original treatment of her Christian material—from her dialect and Africanization to her bold characterization of Mary—exemplifies the strategy of "defamiliarization" that Ostriker finds in contemporary women poets. Defamiliarization draws "attention to the discrepancies between traditional concepts and the conscious mental and emotional activity of female re-vision," accentuating its argument "to make clear that there *is* an argument, that an act of theft is occurring." Colloquialism, for instance, "not only modernizes what is ancient, making us see the contemporary relevance of the past. It also reduces the verbal glow that we are trained to associate with mythic material. . . . With women poets we look at or into, but not up at, sacred things; we unlearn submission (Ostriker 1986:236).

Lucille Clifton began brooding on the figure of Lucifer with her sixth book of poetry, *quilting* (1991). Having already completed the initial manuscript, she wrote poems about the fallen angel which she "liked very much" and added them under the internal title of "Tree of Life" (continuing her pattern of naming each section with a traditional quilt design). She explains: "I think I was struck with the idea of Lucifer being the Light-Bringer, and Lucille meaning 'light.' " Originally, she was supposed to have been named Georgia after her two grandmothers. But when her father saw her "so pretty," he wished to name her after her mother, Thelma, who asked him to provide a second name. This became Lucille—after his sister and his grandmother Lucy, the "first Black woman legally hanged in the state of Virginia" (Clifton 1987a:240). Something about the Lucifer-Lucille-Light conjunction came together and she began to write these poems: "Who knows where these things come from? I swear I don't."

Clifton admits, further, that she "has a thing" with light because "there is a light. It's so hard to talk about." However, when pressed to explain, she offers the following brief story. Once she asked her supernatural source, "What is God?" and was told that "God is Love is Light is God." She continues: "I don't say God particularly because it's too externally defined, so I talk about the universe, but for me the universe is sort of like Light, big L. And I believe that there is a Light, whatever that means—and it is like that, it is like the making clear what has not been clear, being able to see what has not been seen. I just feel an instinctive trust in that. Now *why* I have no idea. That's something else again."

Her poetry reveals a preoccupation with the concept and depiction of light/Light long before she began her work on Lucifer. It first appears in *an ordinary woman* (1974) in a poem titled "roots." There, light is synonymous with the survival "craziness," "wildness," "whatever" which is "the life thing" in African American people that "will not let us die" (1974:12). A few poems later, she recounts the geneology of her own name, declaring proudly at the end: "mine already is / an afrikan name." Her next book, *two-headed woman* (1980), contains the already-mentioned magnificent sequence of poems that describe her encounters with the light of her ancestral spirits. Writing about Clifton in *The Southern Review*, Hank Lazer believes that these poems establish her "lineage as one based on light": "We know that that light is a history, a narrative refiguring of an otherwise often ahistorical image of inward illumination. The strength of Clifton's mysticism is that it is grounded in history and in a familial mother tongue" (Lazer 1989:765). Proceeding from historical family to spirit ancestry, Clifton achieves the "inward illumination" of mystics, a transcendent sense of the "God-Spirit-Universe" complex that she images as light/Light—which is not at odds with its genesis in her concrete circumstances. Her use of the term—and her consciousness—is large enough to encompass all of these resonances.

The real conundrum, though, is how—after being told that "God is Light"—Clifton maintains her designation of Light as "personification" for "Transcendent Being," but still attaches it to Lucifer, who is God's opposite, or, at the least, is certainly not God. She responds to this puzzlement by asking, "If God is God—is there a 'not God'?"—which means that if God is everything, "He" is also Lucifer, who can then be seen as (part of) God, and hence as Light. Clearly, the ground has shifted to the philosophical-mystical-occult understanding that the separative sense of God transcendent and distinct which underlies habitual, linear thinking must give way to the knowledge of God as also immanent in the whole of his creation.

Clifton grounds her depiction of Lucifer in Christian interpretation and in other—for example, Gnostic—traditions. The actual biblical basis for the mass of material about him is slight. The most extended reference occurs when the Old Testament prophet Isaiah decries the ruler of Babylon as "Lucifer": "How art thou fallen from heaven, O Lucifer, son of the morning! *how* art thou cut down to the ground, which didst weaken the nations! For thou hast said in thine heart, I will ascend into heaven, I will exalt my throne above the stars of God: . . . I will ascend above the heights of the clouds; I will be like the Most High. Yet thou shalt be brought down to hell, to the sides of the pit" (Isaiah 14:12–15). In the New Testament book of Luke, Jesus says to his faithful, "I beheld Satan as lightning fall from heaven" (Luke 10:18). These references—together with two others in Revelation and Ezekiel—lay the foundation for the "doctrine that the Devil was a great archangel who rebelled against God from pride" (Cavendish 1983:1662).

Lucifer's name, meaning "light-bearer" or "light-bringer," was the Latin name of the Morning Star (the planet Venus). In *The Woman's Encyclopedia of Myths and Secrets*, Barbara Walker finds that seventh-century Canaanite pagan scriptures included a dirge for the fallen Morning Star (which she quotes) whose words are so similar to those in Isaiah that she concludes: "Centuries later, a Jewish scribe copied this Canaanite scripture into the Bible and pretended it was written by Isaiah" (B. Walker 1983:551). She notes, too, that the "pit" was "the same as Helel, or Asherah, the god's own Mother-bride; and his descent as a lightning-serpent into her Pit represented fertilization of the abyss by masculine fire from heaven": "In short, the Light-bringer challenged the supreme solar god by seeking the favors of the Mother. This divine rivalry explains the so-called sin of Lucifer, *hubris*, which church fathers translated 'pride'—but its real meaning was 'sexual passion.' " Tellingly, during the Christian era, Lucifer "continued to be linked with both lust and lightning" (552).

Sexual passion is certainly the splendid and agitated center of Clifton's "tree of life" poems (Clifton 1991). Beginning her virtuoso changes on light, she writes a story of creation based on sex/sexuality—not simply as the forbidden something which Eve and Adam discovered when they opened their eyes with apple-knowledge, but as the motive power for events even before God spoke the world into being with his fiat, "Let there be light." An angelic narrator reporting from heaven remembers that at Lucifer's birth, when he "broke" as a flash of light "from the littlest finger / of God," the seraphim (the highest order of angels) knew that the "shimmer" and "flush" of him was "too much for / one small heaven." When he eventually falls from the kingdom, leaving it "all shadow" and the cherubim singing kaddish, "light breaks / where no light was before" as God, "the solitary brother," rises and points a wooden stick toward the garden (of Eden). Thus, Lucifer's fall and the creation of the world are synonymous. The angelic voice—speaking from a "less radiant / less sure" heaven—calls Lucifer "beautiful" and asks in trepidation, "oh lucifer / what have you done" (1991:40). Clearly, something frightfully awesome has occurred.

Whatever it is has to be inquired about in whispers (in the poem, "whispered to lucifer"), like gossip, secrets, and sex (which often travel together):

>   oh son of the morning
>   was it the woman
>   enticed you to leave us
>
>   was it to touch her
>   featherless arm
>   was it to curl your belly
>
>   around her
>   that you fell laughing
>   your grace all ashard
>   (73)

This image of a laughing, licentious Lucifer falling, splintered and askew with abandon, is magnificent. Subsequent poems reveal that yes, indeed, it is the love of sex, or sexual love—with all of its origins and generations—which has motivated (perhaps unconsciously) the mighty upheaval in heaven. Lucifer comes to understand that his has been a divine mission, despite any and all appearances to the contrary. "Thy servant lord," he—courtly—calls himself, "bearer of lightning / and of lust." In an image that is triply copulation, fertilization, and birth (and that suggests the Gnostic premysteries), he describes his descent as a "thrust between the / legs of the earth / into this garden" (82).

Moreover, he links God with all of his doings, implicating Him in this other, sexual work of creation and simultaneously giving it sanction: "phallus and father / doing holy work." The oppositions between God's mission and Satan's, between the holy and the profane, are thus totally obliterated. Lucifer concludes his soliloquy of understanding with a rhapsodic smacking of the lips:

oh sweet delight
oh eden

if the angels
hear of this

there will be no peace
in heaven
(75)

His own "rebellion" has been justified. What he fell for is "sweet" enough to entice to earth another heaven full of angels (were they also to be "enlightened").

With Lucifer in the garden, it is, in Eve's words, "wild country": "brothers and sisters coupling / claw and wing / groping one another." Adam, whom she calls a "slow," "clay two-foot" (making him sound like a mentally dense, prehistoric male animal), needs her help to join the action. While she plots to "whisper into his mouth / our names" as he sleeps, he himself is struggling to "roar" erotic desire, sensing his own desperate "hunger to tunnel back / inside" her, to "reconnect the rib and clay / and to be whole again." Eve already has the words, knows the language. Satan has slid into her dreams and infected her with a hunger for her "own lush self" which has given her the necessary knowledge. Autoerotic images inspire her, becoming the basis of her quest for further pleasure. Her dreams are of

apple
apple snug as my breast
in the palm of my hand
apple sleek apple sweet
and bright in my mouth
(74)

In Clifton's story, Eve leads the human fall from grace, just as she does in the Biblical tale. However, here, her revised role is a splendid one (just like Lucifer's). "Clay and morning star"—that is, Adam and Satan—follow her "bright back" out of the garden.

One poem in particular seems to support a reading of this series as Clifton's general exploration of the meaning and consequences of sexual knowledge or passion. Having given sexuality a cosmic and titanic setting, then brought it down to primeval earth, she further universalizes it in a piece that has no fixed voice or temporal situation (again, as she often does, permitting us a place of entry into the events and conversation, a way to try to connect ourselves and our lives to what she has placed before us). Titled "the garden of delight," it metaphorizes the various meanings of sex for different types of people:

>   for some
>   it is stone
>   bare smooth
>   as a buttock
>   rounding
>   into the crevasse
>   of the world
>
>   for some
>   it is extravagant
>   water   mouths wide
>   washing together
>   forever   for some
>   it is fire
>   for some air
>
>   and for some
>   certain only of the syllables
>   it is the element they
>   search their lives for
>
>   eden
>
>   for them
>   it is a test

(76)

Using the four basic alchemical and astrological elements, she posits four possibilities, from the grounded and fleshy earth to fire and air. Her fifth possibility is a wordless empyrean, a sibilant search that tries the seeker for all of his or her life. The nature of the test is left unspecified. It could be celibacy, or promiscuity, or finding the right use(s) of eros, or whatever. The challenge for Eve, and Adam, was initially restraint—and viewed from this angle, they surely failed. However, looked at again in light of Clifton's perspective, their test could just as well have been the courage to embrace: and at this they succeeded, with the aid of Lucifer, whose mission, we must remember, was—"despite" its results—preordained ("thy servant lord . . . doing holy work").

Ultimately, Clifton seems to be saying that sexuality is life, or the way of and to life—or that wrestling with it determines what life is about. Literally, sexual connection is the means by which life is propagated and continues. Perhaps it was or is this fundamental connection between the two which explains the "Freudian slip" that resulted in the "tree of life" quilt pattern from which Clifton titled this sequence of poems. Traditionally, there are two patterns with this name, one that is made up solely of trees and another that has a serpent coiled around the tree. Clifton reports that this latter "seemed right" to her. What is interesting here is that the biblical tree of knowledge has somehow been confused with the tree of life. In Genesis chapter 2, God commands Adam not to eat "of the tree of the knowledge of good and evil"; and it is this tree, in the middle of the garden of Eden, from which Eve is led to pluck the fruit by the serpent.

This tree is not the tree of life, for after the Lord has discovered their actions, He reasons: "Behold, the man is become as one of us, to know good and evil: and now, lest he put forth his hand, and take also of the tree of life, and eat, and live for ever," he and his partner must be driven from the garden (Genesis 3:22–24). The question is, why have these two trees—with their attendant meanings and symbolism—been conflated? Perhaps it is because of the instinctive linkage of sexuality, life, and immortality through one's "generations" made by human minds, including quiltmakers and Clifton, who certainly must know about the two distinct trees in the garden. Additionally, there is the parallel understanding which links knowledge and life, the belief being that without consciousness of "good and evil" (that is, struggle and morality), there can be no life. These are the real stakes that Clifton's human-centered poems highlight—not the old tale of obedience and transgression.

With little apparent effort, Lucille Clifton succeeds at transforming the Bible from a patriarchal to an Afrocentric, feminist, sexual, and broadly mystical text. The poetry that effects this metamorphosis is itself a kind of magic, deceptively simple but capable of producing shivers in any reader who is drawn to marvelous manifestations of the spiritual. Her favored form is the subjective, free-verse lyric, which she employs with the deliberate and open personalization that is characteristic of many contemporary women poets. She also removes the "high," "poetic" elitism from this quintessential genre, making it widely accessible, flexible, and oral. However, no matter how seemingly simple or even colloquial any poem of hers may be, it always authorizes itself as fine poetry, deftly bearing a craft that does not ever permit it to be mistaken for prosaic utterance.

Although Clifton encodes herself as female and, more than that, feminist through the content of her work (valorizing goddesses, heroines, and woman power; glorifying menstruation, menopause, motherhood, and the womb; probing the sexual abuse of young girls; etc.), she does not appear to think of her style in gendered terms except in one poem. "when i stand around among poets" contrasts the poets' "long white heads," the "great bulge" in their pants, and their "certainties" about their authorial identities and work, with the speaker's own embarrassed confession:

> i don't know how to do
> what i do in the way
> that i do it, it happens
> despite me and i pretend
>
> to deserve it,
>
> but i don't know how to do it,
> only sometimes when
> something is singing
> i listen and so far
>
> i hear.
>
> (Clifton 1991:79)

Her situation is not generalized to other women poets, but the poem does set up a dichotomy between abstract masculine rationality and feminine intuitiveness that appears in other of her works, notably the title selection of this *quilting* volume. However, the major difference expressed has to do with the modality of creative production. "When I stand around" suggests a connection between Clifton's spirituality and her poetics that is made explicit by some of her remarks.

Early in her career, she learned to respond when "something that was not alive, someone in spirit, wished to catch [her] attention." The electrical tingle in her arm would always result in her writing "something of value, even if it was just a little thing." Clifton theorizes the creative process in this way: "You get something and then you try to help it become what IT seems to want to be, not what you want it to be. . . . If you get a feel (and feeling seems to me to be first) for what this is trying to be, then you try to help it to do that. Not what you want it to be. Not what you think it ought to be. Not what you want your friends to think you think it ought to be. But what it seems to want to be." For her, it is a process that has more to do with feeling than external analysis: "That's why, if you can take simple words and feel them as well as know them and imbue them with real power, that works." Even poets "don't exactly know" where poems come from, but Clifton agreed that what she termed "living art" probably emanates from the realm of spirit. And, perhaps, poetry transmits from that realm better, "gets closer than prose because it has so little room to be full of crap. I think just the terseness [and urgency] of the language helps poetry, although there are many other ways."

Clearly, the openness to extraordinary vision that characterizes Clifton's life in general and the content of her poetry also helps determine her attitude toward genre and her style, making her reliant on intuitively perceived and not prescribed form. Clifton will not call herself a mystic or a mystical poet. Yet she defines language in a way that echoes the mystic's attempt to capture the noumenal world: "Language is translation of that which is beyond language. Language is a trying to express that which probably is not really expressible." Here, the epigraph that she uses for one of her poems in *The Book of Light* where Lucifer talks to God is apropos. It is a line from Carolyn Forché: "the silence of God is God." In all of her poetry about what Hurston synthesized as "God, Man, and the Devil" in one of her *Mules and Men* subtitles, Clifton confronts the classic paradox of the spiritual poet—having to render the ineffable in language, to distill what is beyond language into words. That she brings it down to earth helps, but the challenge remains.

In practice, Clifton's powerfully evocative, spare, and profoundly simple poems approximate the fleeting clarity and intensity of transcendent moments when "God-Love-Light" is apprehended. This same spiritual acuity directed toward the material realm accounts for the abundant, incisive truths about social and political realities that interpenetrate her biblical and spiritual matter, further developing the dialectic of multiple worlds that lies at the heart of her work. Without extravagance, we might say of Clifton creating what she writes about Eve:

> as she walked past
> . . . .
>
> into the unborn world
> chaos fell away
> before her like a cloud
> and everywhere seemed light
>
> seemed glorious
> seemed very eden.
>   (Clifton 1991:49)

the woman's mourning song:
a poetics of lamentation

BELL HOOKS

When we were very small children, each taking our turn to recite Scripture from the Bible before eating, we would often repeat the verse that states simply: "Jesus wept." Early on we learned that lamentation was essential to any experience of spiritual ecstasy. According to the biblical book of John, Jesus weeps when he arrives and finds his good friend Lazarus dead. Before he brings him back to life, he cleanses his own spirit by weeping.

Knowing grief and expressing sorrow are central to the process of self-actualization. In my childhood, I was deeply moved by the Bible's focus on the primacy of lamentation. At that time I did not think of it any way as a particularly female experience. Indeed, it was in the church of my youth that I first saw men weep with intense passion and abandonment. And it was there that I learned that grieving was necessary for the healing of the wounded spirit.

Just as I am drawn to spiritual teachings and religious experience because of the mystical dimensions of faith, I have been most deeply moved throughout my life by poetry that speaks to grief and loss. I first found a poetics of lamentation in biblical writing and then later in the writing of poets. Certainly my poetry has been deeply influenced from girlhood to the present day by the work of Emily Dickinson, particularly her works that speak directly to grief and loss. All over the world, women play a central role in public expressions of mourning. Even so, much of the poetry of lamentation considered "great" and memorable has been written by men. Within global patriarchal cultures women's lamentations, like our public grief, often receive little notice. Yet certainly in the poetry of women cross-culturally we see expressed that lamentation often brings solace, that it is central to personal and communal healing.

Tibetan Buddhism teaches that the only way out of suffering is through it. To experience anguish, to process it through lamentation, is the way the soul nurtures its growth. Since death is that common experience globally that is an agreed-upon time for mourning, it is the space where diverse cultural traditions meet. While there may be vastly different ways of dying, mourning has its common signs. These marks of mourning are clear to the onlooker even if we do not share the same language, culture, or destiny.

Living as we do in the West in cultures that still wish to contain and confine mourning, it is not surprising that so many poets, including myself, look to the traditions of lamentations in non-Western experiences to create a cultural fusion, to name our solidarity. Shared suffering is still one of the passions that bind us together. Hence, the necessity for a poetics of lamentation, for poems that speak our grief. Women poets in the West continue to deepen our creative process by working with grief and loss to speak sorrow against the culture of repression that would have us confine, silence, and bury pain.

The academic study of poetry has yet to study women's emphasis in our writing on lamentation. It would be impossible to do that without looking at the impact of domination, particularly patriarchy, on women's psyche. Poetry has been the one place outside the realm of the spiritual where grief and loss can speak itself. In this sense it has been that genre of creative writing that allows for subversion by creating a cultural space for speaking against the taboo. Poetry as a genre has always embraced the reality of death and dying, the place of lament. Even though I work with many other genres, poetry remains that location where lamentation can be evoked without shame. My poetry grows out of the grounding in sorrow and grief that arise when we confront death and dying.

Understanding how to balance the knowledge of our dying and how to use this knowing to live fully while also cultivating patience represents for me the height of spiritual enlightenment. Often, I have meditated on that biblical passage that reminds us, "They that wait on the Lord, shall renew their strength; they shall mount up with wings as eagles; they shall run, and not be weary; and they shall walk and not faint" (Isaiah 40:31). When the choir at Virginia Baptist Church sang this as a song at Sunday service, it had a refrain that pleaded "teach us, Lord, teach us how to wait." It was that refrain that let me know patience could be learned. My life has been about learning how to wait. I am waiting even now, waiting for answers—for directions.

The poems that follow speak about death. As a young girl I was fascinated by death. In the racially segregated world of our childhood, there was only one tiny hospital black people could enter. When folks were known to be near dying they stayed home. It was hard then not to know death. It was present and familiar. At times it was dreadful and at other times it was sweet (like Sister Ray passing during afternoon sleep, just like that, without sound or words, all quiet like). I wanted even then to stare death down, to gaze upon it unafraid, to know death intimately, love it even. When I left home it was not long before I realized that black folks had our own special way of dealing with dying, that those slaves who tenderly sang "come down, death, right easy" had laid the foundation for us to reflect on and know death in a unique way. It was this comfortableness with dying that lead the poet James Weldon Johnson in his funeral sermon to call death "a welcome friend."

These poems inspired by meditation on death and dying draw from diverse traditions, African American folk experience, Native American culture, and Sufi mystical teachings that speak about death as that dying away from the world that enables one to live in the world more fully. I speak also about death in war, political killing, about the dying away of loved ones, about the pain and ecstasy of death. Together they are poems of lamentation. They are meant to ease sorrow. They are an invitation, a preparation, a call.

poem for the first life

in the first life
i was uncertain
i was a snake with eyes closed
with no hands
i was only one body
slow moving in the dark

alone in my heart
digging a house of dirt and stone
a temple to all unknowing
there to worship
there to sing
there to pray
there to wait the end
all things fall into

turning your face away

sweet daughters of jerusalem
remember your sisters
dark and comely
braiding their hair
into thick tapestries
mapping world history
in each movement
traces of the love
you did not share
threaded red and weary
piercing memory
wets our flesh
with abandonment
the shaved heads of bondage
the shared secret of captivity
and the death they take us to
public and unmourned betrayal

alcheringa

dream time
time without time
never never land
in the face of our mother
a great black bear
closing in winter
the crops under the snow weep
i go about the house
sad all the time
for at the grave of our dead brother
whose face we never saw
a voice spoke to us
embraced us with knowledge
of who we were
before we became ourselves in this life
we heard of an endless land
world without boundaries
a space open enough for peace
we returned to our habits lonely
unsure of how to go about
the daily meditations

the body inside the soul

i am listening for your footsteps death
i am waiting here
with my young hammer
here with my little knife
i shall pound your fingers
as you open the door
i shall grind them like corn
i shall make bread
i shall sing a praise song
a song my mother taught me
the earth it is round
there is no edge
there is no way to fall off

the woman's mourning song

i cry
i cry high
this mourning song
my heart rises
sun in hand
to make the bread
i rise
my heavy work hand
needs
the voice of many singers
alone
the warmth of many ovens comfort
the warrior in me returns
to slay sorrow
to make the bread
to sing the mourning song
i cry high
i cry high
i cry
the mourning song
go away death
go from love's house
go make your empty bed

21

"Where Are We Moored?":
Adrienne Rich, Women's Mourning,
and the Limits of Lament

When it comes to claiming received poetic genres, even to subversive ends, Adrienne Rich's position has been notably wary. While she acknowledges the aesthetic and ideological power that others have derived from recovering or appropriating traditional kinds of verse, her own task has been to make a cleansing assault on various entrenched forms and their attendant tropes, reminding us "that there is another story to be told" (Keller 1994:261, Rich 1971/1979:33-49). Indeed, as Charles Altieri observes in a 1984 essay, much of her poetry can be understood as emanating from an aesthetic generated in response to the absence of usable models (1984/1993:353). But this is a poet for whom "change" is an operative condition of being, a poet for whom the "road" serves as a dominant image, a way of representing a commitment to an ongoing interrogation of the terms of belonging. This commitment burns more fiercely than any programmatic resistance to form; and so, after twenty years devoted to scrutinizing the "damage done" in the name of tradition, Rich returns to the infamous "wreck"—this time, to find the "treasures that prevail" ("Diving into the Wreck," in Rich 1993a:53).

I want to clarify, at the outset of this discussion, that Rich does not seek to assume the cloak of neoformalism, even in the name of aesthetic reformation. For such a move runs the risk of being construed as alignment with an ahistorical aesthetic—a position counter to Rich's steadfast belief that poetry must not "escape history " (1993b:xiv). Indeed history, our moment in history, is what compels her to invoke the archaic as a way of recovering a conviction in poetry as a socially restorative force: choosing to "sieve up old, sunken words, heave them, dripping with

I thank Vince Cheng, Tamara Eskenazi, Rachel Adler, Yopie Prins, and Bill Cutter for reading and commenting on this chapter at various stages.

silt," turning them over, and bringing them into "the air of the present" (1993b:xiv–xv). At a moment when our vocabulary for social justice is severely compromised, Rich invokes the ancient to defamiliarize and hence renew such faded terms as "democracy" and "citizen." As I will argue, her investment in such politically fraught words is part of a sustained effort to mourn America, a nation lost to itself, and to heal its wounds by reanimating an ancient, more nebulous version of nation as *natio*—community, or condition of belonging.

This project as it is played out in the 1991 volume, *An Atlas of the Difficult World*, leads Rich to renew an old quarrel with poetic enactments of mourning. As Jahan Ramazani, among others, has observed, Rich is deeply ambivalent about the elegy, poetry's dominant form for grieving (1994:311). She is particularly uneasy about the elegy's proclivity for melancholia, a fruitful condition of what Ramazani calls "ambivalent and protracted grief," as the locus of inspired artistry and genius (28). "A Woman Dead in Her Forties" is perhaps Rich's best-known expression of generic discontent, as the speaker first confronts the form's potential inadequacy, feeling "half-afraid" to write for one who didn't "read it much"—and then gropes for an alternative: ". . . from here on I want, " she writes, "more crazy mourning, more howl, more keening" (1984:255). With this wail she seems to seek not only a suitable way of grieving a beloved friend but also a remedy for the silences that characterized their relationship, filled with jokes and "mute" loyalties. That is, the speaker works to exchange melancholia for mourning, which according to Juliana Schiesari is "a cultural practice that in the West has been the privileged province of women" (1992:61). As Schiesari understands it, melancholia, the more revered of the two conditions, tends to dwell, indeed capitalize, on loss as requisite to one's aesthetic, intellectual, even moral development. Mourning, on the other hand, has been typically regarded as a more prosaic process during which, in the course of grieving, the subject disassociates from the loss ("gets over it"). In Schiesari's revisionary analysis, however, the work of mourning entails a refiguring of one's relation to the loss rather than an unequivocal emptying out of the affect. The loss is neither cherished nor denied (in the summoning up of some compensatory totem), nor is it repressed. Instead it becomes the grounds upon which a psychically and socially redemptive response to loss is formulated. During the Italian Renaissance, for example, women writers took loss as an occasion for *collective* mourning—thus restoring what had been denied them through a long history advocating the suppression of *public* mourning by women (Schiesari 1992:166–69).

Rich's own claim for an alternate expression of loss, which features mourning as a communal enterprise, acquires a generic specificity when read in the context of cultural anthropological studies devoted to the lament. Beginning perhaps with Margaret Alexiou's landmark study, *The Ritual Lament in Greek Tradition* (1974), the form has garnered extensive attention as a gendered discourse. Throughout antiquity, in both Greek and Middle Eastern culture, the lament as a standard feature of ritual life belonged largely to the women who gathered to lead the community in the rites of grief. But with the fifth century dicta of Solon, "forbidding everything disorderly and excessive in women's festivals, processions and funeral rites," the lament becomes increasingly a severely marginalized kind of speech (Holst-Warhaft 1992:114; see also Alexiou 1974: 14–16). Later, during the fourteenth century, the lament again emerges as the focus of a gendered conflict; in a letter to the lord of Padua, Petrarch advocates strong legislation against women's public mourning, deeming it a custom "contrary to any decent and honorable behavior" (Schiesari 1992:162). Over time the lament goes virtually underground. Once a central feature of communal life, it is displaced by governing social orders and seems to become an oppositional discourse. Studies of contemporary Greek lament, focusing on the current ritual practices of an ever-dwindling rural population, note how the form comes to serve as a means of lodging social dissent; the death of a beloved becomes an occasion to protest the more generalized injuries of war, or the dehumanizing consequences of medical technology (Caraveli 1986:182–83). These songs are particularly striking in that they are not isolated expressions; instead, as Anna Caraveli has argued, they are part of an alternative social order, constructed out of an adversarial relation to dominant institutions such as those of church and state (1986:177).

The prospect of a countertradition, however embattled, in which loss is figured as the grounds of community, provides a strong frame for understanding the status of mourning in some of Rich's later work. As previously noted, Rich begins her quarrel with poetic mourning in 1974 with "A Woman Dead in Her Forties." In that poem she questions the conventions of poetic mourning largely from the perspective of gender, reading its formal constraints as part of a larger social tendency to perpetuate a divisive silence between women. But nine years later, when she again resists the elegiac position, the principal ideological frame is that of ethnicity rather than gender. Writing to Alfred Conrad, her former husband who committed suicide in 1970, she explains her long silence: "But, you, I've had a sense of protecting your existence, not using it merely as a theme for poetry or tragic musings." Noting how living writers "are terrible projectionists," she then protests "the way they use the dead" (1983:xxii). Rather than capitalizing on death as an aesthetic opportunity, Rich seeks to speak to the profound lack, the ache of cultural estrangement from which Alfred Conrad suffered: "There must be those among whom we can sit down and weep" (xxii). Echoing the Hebrew psalmist who sings by the rivers of Babylon ("there we sat down, and there we wept, when we remembered Zion"), Rich makes a claim for lament as a redemptive discursive practice—a way of recuperating a viable configuration of community. For, as in the Classical tradition, the Hebrew lament has (as I will show) long been associated with the feminine, and would thus seem to offer Rich a way of affiliating as a Jew, without necessarily compromising her feminist identity. That is, when Rich turns to the lament, in the 1991 volume *An Atlas of the Difficult World*, she lays claim to the form as a woman *and* as a Jew. The project thus extends the concerns first expressed in the 1982 essay "Split at the Root: An Essay on Jewish Identity," as Rich renews her efforts to reconcile those aspects of herself that she experiences to be at odds with one another (in 1986:100–23).

The link between feminism and Judaism, however, is not altogether benign, inasmuch as it returns us to what has emerged as a vexed issue for some of Rich's readers—the poet's insistence on retaining a relation to paternal authority (see, for example, Erkkila 1992). In *Sources*, the volume most conspicuously devoted to questions of Jewish identity, Rich trades in a prior account of her father, "as the face of patriarchy," for a more hospitable one—having seen male "power and arrogance" as his "true watermark" without noticing "beneath it the suffering of the Jew" (1983:15). This refiguring of the father is central to understanding the dynamics at play in Rich's most sustained efforts to make use of distinctly Jewish discursive forms. For it suggests the degree to which the authority informing Rich's claim to lament is not only that of a feminine tradition of public mourning but also that of the paternal kind, as mediated by way of the culturally entrenched image of the Jew as the feminized other.

In Hebrew discursive practice, the paternal lineage of the lament is a complex sociocultural phenomenon. Generally speaking, in biblical culture, as in the Classical tradition, women are typically cast in the role of professional mourners (as is also the case in many other cultures, including Japanese and Irish).[1] In Jeremiah, songs of communal loss are a maternal legacy: "and teach your daughters wailing, and one another lamentation" (9:19). When the world splits open, when history fails, the feminine is made audible. This rhetorical tradition notwithstanding,

---

[1] Though there is no single text documenting extensive cultural interaction between Greece and the Middle East in the early periods, there is plenty of textual evidence to support the cross-cultural argument I have in mind. For example, the Mishnaic injunctions legislating against women's mourning rituals (*Mo'ed Qatan* 28b) (200 C.E.) are roughly contemporary with Plutarch's dismissive remarks about women's mourning, indicative of the rhetoric used to suppress lament (Holst-Warhaft 1992:26).

there is no documentation in Hebrew letters of those mourning songs that women sang in their own voices.[2] Indeed, in the Talmudic tractate *Mo'ed Qatan* (28b), it is specified that women's public mourning is to be restricted, in a manner comparable to Solon's injunctions, and later to those of Petrarch. What we do have is the Book of Lamentations, the most sustained biblical example of a national lament, where, trading on the form's gendered history, the poet appropriates a female persona, singing *as if* a woman. This history of appropriation, which constitutes the first part of this discussion, provides a generic frame for my subsequent analysis of Rich's efforts to marshall into service a form ostensibly available to her by virtue of ethnicity and of gender; in short, I am less interested in taxonomizing Rich's poem than in seeking terms that will help address how the text participates in the construction of a social poetics.[3]

As it turns out, these generic excavations lead to a discovery of the limits of a form co-opted by the Judeo-Western tradition. "An Atlas of the Difficult World" bears witness to bell hooks's observation (as it appears in essay 20, above) that to speak of lamentation means necessarily to examine the impact of "domination, particularly patriarchy," on the history of women's writing. Reading Rich's work within this sort of rhetorical context not only helps explain specific textual problems engendered by the poem, it also renders suspect an unqualified claim for lament as a "woman's genre." Finally, the wrestling with lament that her poem occasions leads to a recognition that runs counter to current trends in Jewish cultural theory. For insofar as Jewishness, a patriarchal construct, is thoroughly implicated in the dominant history of Western civilization, it cannot simply be represented as a "minority discourse"[4]—but must itself be interrogated.

... Pollution Clings to Her Skirts

In an essay provocatively entitled "Women as Creators of Biblical Genres," S. D. Goitein argues that in the Bible women sang laments on oc-

---

[2] Emanuel Feldman (1977) notes that without exception laments sung by professional female mourners are in Aramaic, the lingua franca; nearly all other laments (sung presumably by men) are in Hebrew, the sacred tongue. Furthermore, there are no records of women's laments being sung for specific individuals whose names are preserved. Instead, women's laments are notably generalized and formulaic in structure.

[3] The "long poem" may also be an operative category. For a fuller discussion of the genre, see Susan Stanford Friedman's discussion in chapter 1 of this volume.

[4] Daniel Boyarin's (1994) efforts to recast the Jew as the "colonized" instead of the "colonizer" are a strong example of the trend I have in mind. Peter Erickson similarly notes Rich's refusal to invoke Jewishness as a way of mitigating her "whiteness" (1995:104).

casions of communal, as well as personal, loss (1988:25). This is the aesthetic milieu in which the poet of the Book of Lamentations (586 B.C.E.) locates his own poetic production.[5] Composed in response to the fall of Jerusalem at the hands of the Neo-Babylonian King Nebuchadnezzer, Lamentations records a nation's struggle to know itself in the wake of a profound severing of its relation to God—the divine principle that confers meaning upon the social order. And in this poem, catastrophe is extravagantly gendered. Not only is the feminine subject to appropriation, she *is* the object of exploitation, as the poet represents the feminine body as the site of social disrepair. In this way, Lamentations provides yet another textual example of the culturally ubiquitous trope of nation-as-woman, ever vulnerable to foreign invasion (A. Parker et al. 1992:6). This double marking of gender suggests that women are cast as the ideal speakers of loss and rupture, for that is the condition which they embody—a proposition that potentially troubles the status of lament (as a feminine genre) as evidence of women's public authority, since that authority is undermined by a pre-scribed condition of essentialized brokenness.

Lamentations opens with a cluster of images figuring Jerusalem as an abandoned woman; she is likened variously to a slave, a fallen princess, and a widow, an *almanah*—a term, as Alan Mintz points out, that "designates not so much a woman who has lost her husband as the social status of a woman who has no legal protector and who may thus be abused with impunity" (1984:24). Focusing on the structures of meaning in the Hebrew Bible, Elaine Scarry identifies a crucial division between God as voiced and humanity as embodied: "to have a body is to be creatable, . . . and woundable. To have no body, to have only a voice, is to be none of these things; it is to be the wounder but not oneself woundable" (1985:206). The distinction is central to Lamentations, where Israel is represented, especially in the first chapters, as virtually all body, broken and disabled. Suffering in a state of extreme powerlessness, precisely because he is estranged from God, upon whose presence voice depends, the poet of Israel despairs of his ability to speak adequately of the crisis: "What can I compare or liken to you, O Fair Jerusalem? What can I match with you to console you?" (2:13).

What should be stressed here is that the body in question belongs to the unruly female. From the metaphoric likening of Israel to the boundless sea, ruined beyond repair (2:13), to the ritually specific image of

[5] The authorship of Lamentations, traditionally attributed to Jeremiah, is the subject of extensive debate. No one seems to dispute, however, the gender of the poet (or the poem's editor) as male (Hillers 1972:xix–xxii).The translation quoted throughout is that of the Jewish Publication Society (Lamentations 1969).

Israel as a menstruant, Lamentations depends upon the abject feminine to register maximum pain and distress (1:9):

> Her pollution clings to her skirts.
> She gave no thought to her future;
> She has sunk appallingly,
> With none to comfort her.[6]

The image of the *niddah*, the ritually impure menstruating woman, helps us understand how the poem at once seeks to represent the dissolution of national boundaries and to remind its members of the rules that once bound it together. Building on the work of cultural theorists Michel Foucault and Mary Douglas, Howard Eilberg-Schwartz argues that Hebraic laws governing bodily fluids index how the culture establishes and controls communal boundaries (1990:177–94). Purity laws, particularly those legislating the body, redress anxieties about the security of communal boundaries. Both menstrual blood and seminal discharge have the power to contaminate, but the former is a more powerful pollutant and thus is subject to a more lengthy purification process. On the basis of this distinction, Eilberg-Schwartz concludes that issues of contamination are bound up with those of social control: fluids such as menses and the blood of birth are highly contaminating because they are "passively released"—they cannot be regulated (187). This inquiry into the semiotics of purity laws makes apparent the extent to which Israelite social order depends upon stable associations between gender and control: "Males are disciplined and orderly, females disorderly and out of control" (188).

The gendered code of Lamentations informs another of its dominant images, that of the demonic or cannibalistic mother. In the construction of nation, which is typically fashioned as a "passionate brotherhood," the Mother, a trope of idealized femininity, is often invoked to mediate and secure what is essentially a male-male alliance (A. Parker et al. 1992: 6). Lamentations, an account of a nation in utter disrepair, is replete with images of maternal abuse, beginning with chapter 2, where Jerusalem weeps as children die in her streets for want of food: "their life runs out at their mothers' bosoms" (2:12). The image of the helpless mother is subsequently replaced by a more gruesome incarnation, the cannibalistic mother: "Alas, women eat their own fruit, / Their new-born babes!" (2: 20) The political significance of the devouring mother becomes more pronounced in the fourth chapter: "They [the women] became vampires to

---

[6] The word *tumah* is rendered in the Jewish Publication Society's translation as "uncleanness," but this word does not fully capture the stigma of the identification. I offer "pollution," another viable translation, as a stronger alternative.

them [their children]" (4:10).[7] There is more at stake here than a stock reference to famine. As a symbol of national invasion, the vampire mother is an agent of racial impurity, importing "outsider" blood into the group by way of exogamy (Stevenson 1988:140); that is, internal, as much as external forces, put the community's integrity at risk.

Lamentations does not seek solely to represent a violated body politic; it also serves a therapeutic function, as the poet works to imaginatively restore social order and to repair the link between God and Israel (Mintz 1984:40). This compensatory function informs the poem's status as one of the most elaborately formal books of the Hebrew Bible. Two chapters of twenty-two verses each flank, on either side, a chapter of sixty-six verses; three of these five chapters comprise alphabetical acrostics; the third chapter is a triple acrostic, hence its sixty-six verses. The textual body is thus as whole and coherent as the national one is broken and disordered. In keeping with the poem's social codes, the voice that calls this order into being is marked as masculine. In an extraordinarily nuanced reading, Alan Mintz (1984:39–40) attributes the success of Lamentations, as a poem of mourning and of restoration, to its capacity to represent collective grief as if experienced by a strongly individuated "I." What he doesn't mention, however, is that according to the discursive codes of Lamentations, collective, undifferentiated identity is marked as feminine, while individual subjectivity belongs to the masculine. The crucial maneuver begins in chapter 3, where the poet drops the feminine persona and speaks as a masculine presence: *"ani ha gever"*—"I am the *man* who has known affliction" (3:1; emphasis mine). (One should note here that the Hebrew word *gever* is gender-specific and cannot be translated neutrally as "person.") Therefore, according to the poem's discursive codes, the woman can both represent and articulate loss, but she cannot fix what has been broken—for that is her own essential condition. In the sociology of this text, only the male has recuperative agency; only the male can speak as an individuated subject, with the authority to bestow order.

"Here is a map of our country"

Writing in response to the Gulf War crisis, a moment which requires that she question her conviction in "nation" as a way of configuring community, Rich longs to convey what she knows to be true: that poetry can be a powerful, socially constitutive force (1993b:xiv). Such are the circumstances informing her long poem, "An Atlas of the Difficult

[7] My gloss depends here on Robert Gordis's translation of the verse (1967:57).

World"—circumstances not unlike those represented in Lamentations. In both texts, the experience is one of a world split open. I do not mean to suggest that the biblical text is explicitly referenced or invoked. Rather, it is part of an intertextual cultural matrix that is absorbed and transformed in Rich's poem. Lament as a generic category, as well as the specific instance of Lamentations, provides a context in which to make an account of the full scope of the poet's project—of its courage and its shortcomings.

The interpretive value of such conceptual grounding can be demonstrated by briefly turning to an early review by Helen Vendler, who is mostly critical of the poem's tendency to oversimplify social ills. The essay is uncanny in its frequent invocation of the term "lament" (in the most general sense of the word) to name the poet's position. Indeed, at one point Vendler likens Rich to a "good mother" for whom "lament" is the only rhetorical recourse (1991:51). This identification touches upon the important question of the poem's place in a discursive tradition, but Vendler quickly moves on to another set of complaints. The most glaring instance of the interpretive possibilities lost for want of a fuller generic analysis occurs when Vendler writes, "For all of their [Rich's poems'] epic wish to generalize to the social whole, they are both limited by, and enhanced by, their essentially first-person lyric status" (53). Where Vendler sees opposition, Rich envisions the complementary. After all, to combine the individual and the collective, the public and the personal, has long been understood as one of Rich's signature concerns (Altieri 1984/1993:349). In "Atlas" this concern acquires generic specificity when read against Lamentations, where communal ruin is represented as a matter of individual anguish.

As in Lamentations, Rich's poem represents a world where social connections are severely fractured. Conditions of belonging are immediately at issue as "Atlas" opens with a bleak account of what passes for community in America at the end of the millennium. Beginning with migrants picking strawberries in chemical-dusted fields, working "in close communion," the speaker then turns to the bored, disenfranchised housewives who buy the berries, and for whom it all "feels like nothing" (1991:3). In exhuming "communion," an instance of Rich's commitment to "siev[ing] up old, sunken words," she foregrounds the profound absence of those transformative rituals that once bound us together in spiritual fellowship. Neither religion nor poetry serves to compensate; in the next sequence she indicts contemporary poetic practice with a caricature of the sentimental poet with his "tears" and "frugal beard" (4). In the absence of self-irony on Rich's part (since the pitiful would-be poet is conspicuously male), the question quickly becomes: are we looking at a poem that is long on pathos, but short on ethos?

Rich's poetry frequently quarrels with the past, even as it marks a longing for usable aesthetic models (Altieri 1984/1993:353). Indeed, this struggle to find models may be among her most sustaining poetic legacies. The problem comes sharply into focus in "Atlas" where, after a difficult recounting of a woman's death at the hands of her husband (a chilling incarnation of the abject feminine upon which "nations" are founded), Rich confesses that she doesn't want to know "wreckage, dreck and waste, but these *are* the materials" (1991:4; emphasis mine). Subsequently, in section VI she returns to this terrible recognition that the cultural materials typically used to represent national crises include that of the woman's broken body. Here Rich chronicles the true story of two lesbians, victims of a hate crime, relaying how the man "tracked" the two women, killing one while the other dragged herself back to town; even as Rich resists the details, she recognizes that "these are the materials" (14). Unable to deny these ubiquitous images, she uses them to a different end, challenging their powerful metaphoric function. In Lamentations, the violated woman is the site and sign of national disaster; in "Atlas," the literal narratives of actual female abuse serve as condemnation of the nation itself.

Rich turns then from the biblical/patriarchal carnage to another model, with lines that bring Wallace Stevens ("The Man on the Dump") to mind—with the "slow lift" of the moon "over wreckage, dreck and waste" while "wild treefrogs" call (4). Like Stevens's Man on the Dump, who "beats and beats for that which one believes" (1978:202). Rich conducts what Terrence Des Pres describes as a "bardic practice" (1988:xvii). Yet while Stevens, at least in Des Pres's account, is known for his capacity to bless, Rich chooses to curse paratactically: "Here is the map of our country" and "here is the Sea of Indifference, glazed of salt." Pointing out that we dare not drink from its waters, she reminds her readers that this is the desert "where missiles are like corms" and that "This is the breadbasket of foreclosed farms" (1991:6).

She refuses, however, to claim the part of the anonymous, disembodied prophet of Lamentations, for this moral allegory is grounded in no authority other than her own—as she indicates with an admission that is at once admirable and illustrative of the poem's dilemma, conceding that instead of the map she had promised, she offers "a mural" (6). For Rich, the mural, as a prospective prototype for public, collective expression, fulfills a generic function comparable to that of lament. Yet even the mural is not wholly available; for by her own account, her aesthetic practice depends upon a fruitful tension between the "lyric" conditions of solitude and private intuition and the conditions of those more recognizably public "political" modes (1993b:43–53).

In view of Rich's desire to write a poem of national mourning and of healing, the public demands on "Atlas" are enormous—demands that are, in light of the problematic status of discursive authority, hard to fulfill. In search of a remedy, Rich turns from those allegorized states of spiritual disrepair to a highly specific moment of personal brokenness. While the "Everyman" of Lamentations can speaks fully *as* the people because the conditions of belonging are known to him, Rich's only recourse is to carefully display those personal credentials that perhaps entitle her to speak on behalf of others. Such is the ideological premise of the poem's third section, where she returns to Vermont to a house filled with broken, mismatched, profoundly unusable objects and memories of her failed marriage. Alluding to the sources of her own fractured sense of community and of self, Rich recalls the couple's pitiful efforts at self-revelation as mediated through poetry: while she brings to the table Auden's "In Sickness and in Health," a Christian meditation on Eros and Agape, her husband responds with Karl Shapiro's *Poems of the Jew*—a collection notable for its portrayal of the Jew as the emasculated, alienated outsider. This staged theological debate suggests that Shapiro's disclosures can't quite measure up to Auden's certainty and compassion; biblical patriarchy may give way to the Jew as feminized Other, a prominent trope of the late-nineteenth- and early-twentieth-century Western imagination, but the preoccupation with masculine identity continues to dominate. Such recollections seem to leave Rich with a profound sense of betrayal, as the terms of connection continue to evade her. Watching a spider spin a solitary home amid the dusty remains, and perceiving perhaps an alternative to her own efforts to reconstitute a place of collective belonging, she darkly observes that "labor" doesn't always yield "sweetness" (1991:10). Even the "winds" of poesy turn toxic, suggestive of "warm pneumonia" and the "death of innocence" (9).

In contrast to Lamentations, whose shape reflects an almost willful desire to render order out of chaos, "Atlas" has an episodic, open-ended structure. With each new section, one gets the impression that Rich is seeking yet another way into her "difficult" subject. Sections IV–V, for example, feature the now-recovered image of the map, as the poet takes us on another tour of national disasters, including Appomattox, Wounded Knee, Los Alamos, and Selma (12). This time she takes Muriel Rukeyser as her guide, citing lines from Rukeyser's *Book of the Dead*, another poem that may be profitably read under the sign of lament: *"There are roads to take . . . when you think of your country"* (13). The allusion is especially apt; elsewhere Rich celebrates Rukeyser as a poet who was able to write as a "sexual woman and as a Jew—unapologetically" (1993b:100), identifying for us again a rift that afflicts Rich's own poetic practice. Fundamental questions thus come into focus: what are the terms requisite to a woman mourning her country, her community? what versions of collective identity are available to her? For the knotty possibility that national identity may be at odds with other versions of oneself is at the heart of Rich's exhaustive inquiry into the meaning of citizenship. A "patriot," she reasons, is not a missile or weapon; a patriot, rather, "is one who wrestles" for "the soul of her country" just as she would "for her own being" (1991:23). She concludes by asking questions central to the remaking of lament: "Where are we moored? / Where are the bindings? / What behooves us?" (23) What are the historical, cultural, or religious and, above all, ethical conditions under which it can be said that we constitute a nation, a community?

"A race of perfect Mothers—is what is needed"

Throughout this discussion I have been reading "Atlas" in the context of Hebraic lament, as a way of addressing what drives Rich and what inhibits her efforts to speak to her country at a moment of political and spiritual disrepair. To establish the extent to which nationalism, as a patriarchal ideology, eludes her, I will invoke a more proximate text that traverses some of the same interpretive territory—Whitman's political essay, *Democratic Vistas*. When asked to write about Whitman in the winter of 1991, the same time during which Rich was presumably composing her would-be lament, Alicia Ostriker responded: "I write this essay during the first weeks of a war, the Gulf War.... My primary emotions since it began are gloom, fear, disgust with the stupidity of my species.... It would seem more appropriate to read Ecclesiastes or the Lamentations of Jeremiah than the cheerful Walt Whitman" (1992:229). *Democratic Vistas*, one of Whitman's darkest achievements, is the only text she deems sufficiently pessimistic. What Ostriker neglects to mention, however, is that Whitman's dominant metaphor for a nation that has lost its way is yet another version of the diseased body politic: "—everywhere the youth puny, impudent, foppish, prematurely ripe—everywhere an abnormal libidousness, unhealthy forms." Symptomatic of this dismal state of affairs is a diminished capacity for fruitful reproduction: "The capacity for good motherhood deceasing, or deceas'd." The diagnosis, which brings to mind those ineffectual mothers of Lamentations, is followed by a prescription: "I say a new founded literature, not merely to copy and reflect existing surfaces,—but a literature underlying life, ... and as perhaps the most precious of its results, achieving the entire redemption of woman [and] ... thus insuring to the States a strong and sweet Female Race, a race of perfect Mothers—is what is needed" (W. Whitman 1892/1964:372). Ecstatically placing the Mother at the center of his account of a more "perfect union," Whitman's vision, like that of biblical society, trades upon an account of nation as a homosocial alliance. As Jonathan Goldberg has put it, under the sign of the "ancient mother, women are translated into a trope of ideal femininity, a fantasmatic female that se-cures male-male arrangements and all male history" (1992:63).

In Rich's poem, such paradigmatic images, informed by a fear of the unboundaried feminine, are thoroughly rejected. She virtually buries the trope of the perfect mother with a gothic account of a family fractured beyond repair. A child is "swept under" by the sea into which the mother walks, unnoticing of her loss; the father stands with his back to the sea while an elaborate picnic remains uneaten, soon to be "exca-vated" by scurrying sandcrabs, dune-rats, and ants (1991:18). Unable to transform the "materials" or to otherwise render them usable, Rich puts the helpless mother of Lamentations in the starkest light possible, being sure to include in *her* family portrait an equally inadequate father.

Taking such sequences as a case in point, this analysis has focused largely on how Rich's poem constitutes a critique of long-standing struc-tures of national, social and religious unity. But it remains to be asked: what does she offer in the way of a countervision? Upon what ground does she stand as she seeks, Atlas-like, to hold up this "difficult world"? My answer begins with "Dedications," the poem's final section, where in a particularly self-absorbed version of a Whitmanesque catalogue Rich envisions a constituency of readers, as part of an alternative *natio*: "I know you are reading this poem," whether reading "late, before leaving your office" after the rush hour, or "in a bookstore far from the ocean" (25). Seeking to transform pathos into ethos, Rich works to envision a community, based on an ethical system of relation other than those pre-viously asserted in the name of God or the state. The invocation acquires a certain conceptual specificity, as well as moral complexity, when read in the context of Emmanuel Levinas's account of "responsibility for the Other" as "the primal and fundamental structure of subjectivity" (1985: 95). In *Ethics and Infinity* he explains: "I understand responsibility as responsibility for the Other, thus as responsibility for what is not my deed, or for what does not even matter to me; or which precisely does matter to me, is met by me as face"—the "face" meaning the fully vul-nerable presence of the Other (95–97). In a face-to-face encounter, the "I" is bound to the Other with the formulation "here I am"—an enunciation that in Rich's poem takes the form of "I know you are reading . . ." For purposes of reading Rich, what should be stressed about Levinas's ac-count of responsibility is that it is essentially an aysmmetrical relation. The Other, who for Levinas is best figured in the biblical category of "the orphan, the widow, the stranger," must be perceived as wholly other, independent of the "I." It is in the representation of the Other that Rich's figuring of relation becomes problematic; as Vendler puts it, in many instances "Rich's 'children,' whose fate she laments, whose unjust treatment she protests against, seem mostly versions of her present or past self" (1991:51). In "Dedications," for example, the "you" who bounds "up the stairs" toward "a new kind of love" may be read as an early incarnation of the poet who was married before claiming a lesbian identity; and the "you" who waits "for the newscast from the *intifada*" may be either a displaced Palestinian or an American or Israeli sympathizer (who is perhaps also Jewish), who sits immobilized by pity and guilt. In short, most of these "Others" can be read to some extent as projections of herself—an instructive dilemma, since the poem points up the problematics of determining who or what constitutes one's community. Seeking to write a "song of the times," Rich is obliged to negotiate a relation to Whitman, both to acknowledge a debt and to address his limits. In later essays such as "The Genesis of 'Yom Kippur 1984' " and "Beginners," she writes with enormous insight of Whitman's failure to represent difference and its attendant discontinuities (1993a:252–57; 1993b:90–101). But poetically, she is culpable in some of the same ways. While she works hard to avoid Whitman's invasiveness, she nonetheless ends up duplicating his tendency to make universal sameness the grounds for sympathetic identification.

Praise to Life

In "Notes towards a Politics of Location" (1984), Rich repudiates Virginia Woolf's anationalist claim as she writes: "As a woman I have a country; as a woman I cannot divest myself of that country merely by condemning its government or by saying three times 'As a woman my country is the whole world' " (in 1986:212). These good intentions notwithstanding, the poetics of nationalism are difficult to disentangle from the patriarchal ideology that engenders them—as the encounter with the limits of lament found in "Atlas" makes apparent. But Rich's inquiry into the possibilities of communally constitutive poetics does not end with "Atlas," nor does she fully abandon the prospect of speaking to her nation.[8] Instead she continues to seek out other modes of figuring connection. "Dedications," for example, announces a model of relation that finds its full expression in another poem from the same volume, "Tattered Kaddish," which commemorates the twentieth anniversary of the death of Alfred Conrad, her former husband and the "other Jew" in her life, who died by suicide (1983:xvii). Here the lyric (the "I–You" dyad)

---

[8] Questions of nation continue to be at issue in Rich's 1995 volume, *Dark Fields of the Republic.*

gives way to the liturgical (the unspecified collective), as Rich turns again to an ancient form as a way of transforming the personal into the collective. Eight years earlier, in *Sources,* she grieved Conrad's unmitigated isolation as a wound beyond any remedy she might offer (25). With this poem, however, she does considerably more than sympathize. Perceiving him as an Other, in Levinas's sense of the term, who suffers from a particular kind of lack, Rich is able to act responsibly *as a poet.* To envision a condition of wholeness, predicated on the knowledge of the necessary brokenness of things, and to confer the blessing of community, she practices the work of poetry. And in the process of putting this long-suffering ghost to rest, Rich is able to reclaim mourning as a socially constitutive act. For this expression of loss serves as the site of an alternative configuration of community.[9]

The generic frame to which poem refers is, of course, the kaddish—one of the oldest prayers in Hebrew liturgy. Best known as a mourner's prayer, the kaddish foregrounds and enacts the need to represent loss as a communal experience. Counter perhaps to contemporary intuition and practice, the kaddish does not subscribe to the notion of grief as a private state of affairs. Precisely at the moment when one might be inclined to withdraw, to weep in solitude, one is obligated to publicly affirm a communal alliance. For one is required to recite kaddish in the company of a minyan—a prayer quorum. Indeed, the prayer itself is structured as a kind of call and response: the introductory paragraph is said by the mourner, who is then answered by the congregation.

In her "tattered" reworking of this ancient prayer, Rich extends the project begun in "An Atlas of the Difficult World," announcing an end to the structured denial of the privilege of mourning for women in patriarchal society. For among other transgressions, Rich represents the speaker as feminine—a violation of the Orthodox practice forbidding women to publicly lead prayers or to be included in a minyan. Identifying the speaker as the "reaper of the wild apple field," Rich indicates, in an accompanying note, that she means to invoke the Kabbalistic figure of *Malkut.* This wisdom figure, a source of "secrets and new meanings of Torah," is known also as *Shekhinah,* the feminine designation of the Godhead whose name means "dwelling." That is, her presence connotes both belonging and displacement: she is the divine principle which calls community into being, and she is that aspect of God who dwells with her people (Israel) in exile. To summon the Shekhinah is to envision a

---

[9] I would have liked to cite "Tattered Kaddish" in its entirety, for my discussion assumes and depends on familiarity with the text of this short poem. Unfortunately, Adrienne Rich denied my request for permission to do so. Therefore, I suggest readers turn to p. 45 of *An Atlas of the Difficult World* (1991), where "Tattered Kaddish" may be found.

community whose boundaries are subject to perpetual renegotiation. Finally, one must note that the Shekhinah, who has multiple incarnations, goes by many other names, including "Matrona" and "Mother Rachel" (Fine 1984:310). Importing into her text a prospective account of feminine religious and social authority, Rich speaks vividly to Kaja Silverman's theoretical account of what it might mean to imagine a counterdiscourse where the mother is not given up as a lost object but is rediscovered *through* mourning as an object of love (see Schiesari 1992:77)—and, I would add, as an agent of community.

"Tattered Kaddish" is a strong example of how a secularized text may at once evacuate and intensify the sacred narrative it takes as its precursor. To put it another way, poetic power is to be derived through rendering a religious form defamiliar (by transplanting it into a secular venue). For God is conspicuously absent from Rich's "prayer." Indeed the text functions both inside and outside the dictates of Jewish law and practice, with several important transgressions. Not only does it protest the genre's traditional injunctions against feminine speakers, it insists that a victim of suicide be treated no differently from any other person mourned; for this "tattered kaddish" is to be spoken for "all suicides." According to rabbinic practice, the suicide must be mourned an entire year, instead of the eleven months deemed appropriate for everyone else; but in Rich's prayer-poem, the suicide is subject to the conventional rather than the exceptional.

There is more at stake here than legal quibbling, indifference, or even heresy, for with "Tattered Kaddish" Rich seeks to call into being an alternative version of community. One remarkable consequence of this effort is that she intuitively recovers one of the earliest liturgical functions of kaddish. Before it became central to the synagogue service as a mourner's prayer the kaddish, as a doxology, served in mystical circles as a mind-expanding mantra—a transformative kind of speech (Hoffman 1979:60). With the poem's repeated invocation "Praise to Life," Rich's poetics of mourning exploits the socially constitutive possibilities of praise, going beyond grief to summon forth a community grounded in the recognition of brokenness and of finitude (the very sorts of recognitions that made lament the subject of repression)—a community achieved through the determined refiguring of the necessary fragility and power of feminine accounts of belonging.

Lamentations, as a prototype of national mourning, takes an equivocal stand when it comes to conditions of rupture and restoration. On the one hand, its preoccupation with textual symmetry suggests a compensatory impulse. On the other hand, the poem itself ends not in consolation but in a dark complaint: "For truly you [God] have rejected us / Bitterly raged against us" (5:22). The discomfort engendered by such a declaration is ultimately deemed intolerable by the institutions to which the poem is attached; hence, when the poem is recited as part of the synagogue service, it has become customary to smooth out or defang the text's own jagged edges by repeating the penultimate verse as a conclusion: "Take us back, O Lord, to Yourself, / And let us come back; / Renew our days as of old" (5:21). With "Tattered Kaddish" Rich speaks to this discomfort, insisting that institutions, whether they be religious or political, be able to accommodate pain and unmitigated loss. Writing of the contemporary liturgical use of psalms, Walter Brueggemann (1986) argues that the lament as an expression of social injustice is requisite to reconstitution, which is accomplished through praise. This account of the complementary nature of the relation between lament and praise poems speaks powerfully to the conditions informing Rich's own beautifully complete utterance. For the integrity with which it extends to us the possibility of passages of wholeness and belonging is earned by the recognition of brokenness as a normative condition of being, from which none of us is exempt. Further, by virtue of its transgressive moves, the poem occupies the kind of adversarial relation to governing institutions once fulfilled by women's lament. Even as it bears witness to those losses which are irrecoverable, it insists that we must maintain the right and capacity to comfort one another. And so, structured as a communal utterance, "Tattered Kaddish" recovers the possibility of mourning as the site of a feminine collective enterprise. Within this discursive space such formidable concepts as nation, ethnicity, gender, and genre—and their connections—can be scrutinized, in an ethical interrogation of our individual and communal moorings.[10]

---

[10] Gail Holst-Warhaft (1992) concludes, in her study of Greek lament, that the genre may have run its course. But then, as Fredric Jameson (1981) notes, genres never really die; they just get transformed.

22

Wrestling the Angel of Inscription

ELEANOR WILNER

In the midst of that criminally insane slaughter of young men that the history books call World War I (the West has always confused itself with the world), a group of women from countries then at war and so officially defined as "enemies," a definition outlined in blood, gathered at The Hague in Holland and founded WILPF, the Women's International League for Peace and Freedom. This is what strikes me as the most significant kind of gender dislocation of genre—the type of fiction in this case being something called Nation, its borders defied and crossed by women who were calling the game in the name of something conjured in its absence: peace and freedom. Or perhaps those things did exist somewhere in the lives of the women who came there, perhaps that experience brought them to this meeting, along with a sleepless sense of the real, of what was out there in those trenches.

There is behind this World War I meeting a sanity so radical as to seem in an insane world a last resort; and behind it, too, was a belief in possibility and in friendship, a freedom of thought preserved in those denied ascendance to the power seats of the public world. For here were some, though they were thought impressionable (for wasn't it the nature of women to be like wet cement, ready to harden around the first footprint?), who were, in fact, remarkably unimpressed by the ideas which had both tradition and armies to uphold them. Class privilege does not adequately explain what gave these women the nerve and fidelity to act as "traitors" in wartime, transcending the borders which just then had become greasy ditches filled with the bodies and broken lives of the young. For so the lines on the maps get drawn, and afterward become the excuse for guarding them.

The next war is always in part about the last one, so that "our honored dead will not have died in vain." And how to end an infinite regress of violence summoned and excused by the old plot, the one with crosses row on row on row? Coming together in defiance of the borders of that plot, the WILPF story suggests another paradigm, but different in kind from narrative as we have known it, and by which we have known ourselves. This story is not shaped by its end, for its end is not foretold, nor is its effect measurable. Act engenders act, and who can say where it leads, except away from cul-de-sac. "To dwell in possibility." We are taught in school that line of Santayana's: "Those who don't know history are condemned to repeat it." But perhaps the opposite is at least as true— it is precisely the history we know that we are condemned to repeat.

Let me pause for what may seem like a digression. Years ago I was reading Melville criticism when I came across, for the first time, the concept of the Shekhinah. I have never been able to find again that source, but the figure has worked on me ever since. Apparently Melville, in his study of comparative religions, had come across this notion of Immanence, an indwelling (*shakhan*: Hebrew verb for "dwell," root of Shekhinah) and merciful side of the biblical divinity, what suffers with us. This figure dwells in *Moby-Dick*, in "the measureless sobbing that stole out of the center of the serenity around" when the cruel stepmother world becomes, for a moment, motherly, and Ahab, just once, weeps and almost relents, almost calls off his mad revenge (Melville 1851/1961:132). This compassionate female side of the Divine, residing in the world rather than presiding over it, makes the world itself sacred. Banished from the canonical writings, though she turns up in various gnostic and apocryphal sources, the Shekhinah is, as Melville perceived her, the missing aspect of Ahab's terrible Puritan God. It is the Shekhinah whose mundane avatar appears at the end of the novel in the form of *Rachel*, the ship whose mourning captain has lost his son and which picks up Ishmael, the orphan of history.

These two kinds of "dwellings," to my mind, are inextricably linked— the indwelling mercy of the Shekhinah that suffers with and sorrows for us, and the "dwelling in possibility" of those who step out of the determinism of the old story with its comforting promises and its flattering teleology. In fact, though I was delighted to find an ancient source figure for it in the Middle Eastern tradition, still it is hard not to think of compassion as something that entered the world when God—as conceived by the Bible—was sleeping, or slipped up.

Which already suggests the integral relation of mercy and disobedience. To wit, the story of Abraham and Isaac, the Akedah or Binding of Isaac. For this is the tale of obedience to an unthinkable command, so dreadful a command that an angel is required to play Kent to God's Lear. This troubling story is one of the founding fictions on which Western history has modeled itself, which has its cosmic parallel in the New

Testament when a father, this time God himself, completes the story of the Akedah and sacrifices his "only begotten son," who becomes the salvational figure for the universalizing of the Chosen Culture. As its many commentators and apologists over the centuries, such as Kierke-gaard, have understood, this story is the keystone in the arch.

Who could pull the keystone from such an arch? Perhaps only the progenitress—Sarah, the mother of this founder's story line—the wife of Abraham and mother of Isaac. As soon as you make her the moral agent of the action, rather than merely the receptacle of a blessing, everything changes. Perhaps that is why, in the poem "Sarah's Choice," when Sarah considers her position, she experiences an understandable anxiety: "per-haps she was afraid the firmament would shudder and give way"—that old solid arch of sky that the ancestors believed was what sheltered us. Emily Dickinson's "Everlasting Roof—The Gambrels of the Sky" (1955: poem 657), her eternal structure of possibility which made Death so se-ductive, was being shaken by earthquake, the tremors set going by a plot-changing question: what if God had asked not Abraham but Sarah to sacrifice Isaac? A year or so before I addressed this question in the poem, I asked it on an exam (not as a test, but as a matter of curiosity to keep myself interested) of Japanese university students in Tokyo. Only one said that Sarah would have been too afraid to disobey. All the rest answered the same way—women and men. As one student put it, "She would have said no. She was his mother."

You will remember the judgment of Solomon, where the true mother is revealed because she will give up the child rather than see it hurt. But Abraham, putative father of this "chosen" line, is living a different ethic; he has a sense of ownership so complete that it includes his sense of the right to sacrifice the life of his son in obedience to a God who, we know from the stories, would not hesitate to do the same with his own peo-ple—to make a point. This absent, bodiless divinity, as Elaine Scarry points out, can only prove his presence and power by injury to our bod-ies—as nations argue that the "Justice" of their cause is proven by the body count of their enemies (1985). So goodbye, Sodom, a nice town, people just trying to get by on the desert's edge. Or Guernica, London, Dresden, Hiroshima, Baghdad.

"For me there was no silence before armies." That is how Susan Howe opens her book *The Europe of Trusts* (1990); she too was born in 1937, the year when the bombing of Guernica opened nearly a decade of the terror bombing of cities, the time of our mutual growing up when the horror of such mass extinction was to become routine. Given the advanced state of our technology and the barbaric state of our humanity, the old stories began to seem deadly in a new or at least more immediate way. It became easier to understand what it meant to look up and see death raining from the sky; to see from the vantage of Isaac, coming of age, bound to the rock, looking up into your father's knife. Wilfred Owen had seen it that way, a poet-soldier killed in the war that brought those women to The Hague.

A poem is like a life—we can act as if we know where it's going, but if it is to be a poem, it goes its own way. Once Sarah had been called up, once she had been set free from the story and its determinism, she became none of those things that women have traditionally been considered to be—neither submissive to the will of others (including mine), nor a victim, nor even a heroine. She became a lonely moral agent, stuck in the middle of the desert night, her confused teenage son tossing, sleepless, in the tent—sensing but not knowing that he had been drafted. She had been awakened, shaken into thought by being ordered to act and by realizing that a command is really a question, an opportunity to choose. There is little exhilaration in this freedom, and much silence. American rhetoric has always acted as if freedom were an end in itself, as if it had substance, rather than being what it is: merely a space in which to take action.

And it was then that Sarah surprised me, for really I knew nothing of her except what was apparent to everyone—that she would say "No." What she did then was to explain the meaning of her choice, which she understood to preclude the notion of being "chosen." But in addition to her disputation on how Election leads to determinism and a monstrous deformation of morality, she decided upon an action: to leave the tents of Abraham and seek out the very pair she had herself cast out, Hagar and Ishmael, to encounter the woman turned Other, the brother turned Enemy—for Ishmael, according to the prophet Mohammed, was to father the Arab line, which would eventuate in Islam. She acknowledges her complicity in this transformation of kin into enemy when she had played out her role, jealous of her prerogatives as a mother and "first wife."

This decision of Sarah's to set out after Hagar and Ishmael was entirely unpremeditated, for I was not the author of this transpersonal figure, but rather her auditor, her transcriber. The dislocation of the original story had indeed freed our protagonist, given her a separate skin (the woman wrapping herself "in a thick dark cloak against the desert's enmity" serves as the sign both of autonomy and of the necessity for the protective disguises of art). And what she chose to do with her freedom was to cross another border in the direction of reconciliation.

This changed the story for me in a way I hadn't expected. For to simply refuse to sacrifice her son could be seen as yet another self-interested action, even if one that seems far saner and more just than Abraham's. But to set out as she does after Hagar, to offer her son the choice to accompany her, to be willing to leave without him should he choose to remain, is to be a moral agent willing to risk herself and to offer her son, instead of the certainty of a self-flattering but deadly determinism, the same unsettling path she had herself chosen. This new story was not imposed from above but seemed to shape itself from within, as if the process by which it was made were emblematic of the story it was both undoing and rewriting.

In that doubleness lies the struggle at the heart of this kind of poetics. The angel that this poetics must wrestle is the angel of inscription. Its fixity in letters (and thus in the literal) is the danger of the written word, unlike the oral story that changes as it passes from teller to teller. The question, which Abraham's failure keeps always before us, is how to be an iconoclast without casting fresh icons to replace the old ones. For Abraham began his career as a smasher of idols, a promising start. So here are consciously anti-iconic figures, who, though finding themselves in writing, are like the cursive of a stick in the sand and seem to smile at the sight of their tracks being swallowed up by the desert wind, or of the sea closing their wake behind them like a healing wound. For they are able to continue moving right out of the frame of the fiction, their passage having opened the future in a new direction. As if aware of the paradox of its own statement, this movement has within it an antiscriptural impulse that is part of its propulsion: what spurs its motion also helps efface its track—the spirit has shifted and become a following wind, moving once again on the face of the waters.

For the poetic genre being made doubtful here has a monumental status—it is Scripture, what is by cultural definition canonical—not canonical as literature but as Revelation. Most if not all of the earlier commentators on Scripture assumed that they must somehow come to terms with the story as it is written, rather than, as some of us find ourselves doing, changing those terms radically. For what people wrote, others can amend. Even as it is childish to think we can do without authority, it is equally childish to demand that authority be absolute. To reconstitute authority with uncertainty built-in means to change the figures who embody that authority even as we find more fluid forms to carry it. To make the spirit dwell in forms that gave light millennia ago is like imprisoning a genie in a brass lamp—it makes the spirit furious and vengeful. To allow the spirit of our own age to dwell in figures that carry communal memory, thus permitting both continuity and the change it requires, it is necessary to let those figures move in their own way, as Sarah does—refusing to end the story, asserting her "I don't know" regarding the outcome of her intention. Her last statement is radically anti-teleological, and, as she angrily mimes the sound of that old Great Amen, she reminds us of the price of a beautiful finality: "it is written   what will happen   if you stay."

Winners write history, so goes the saying. If we understand the word "winners" differently, we write our own. Sarah gets clear away in this poem, we see her preparing for a journey. We don't know what Isaac will do—for that would predispose choice. Nor do we know what happens next, for we can never know that. And not knowing becomes a blessing, an opening of the stone valves of determinism. The Western way has been to march forward under the teleological banner that may serve to console and sustain the oppressed but has principally functioned to justify the amassing and abuse of power—a Higher Purpose, a Second Coming, Progress, the End of History, the coming of the Kingdom—a great drama in which God is the Director and we are the Actors whom the spotlight of history follows, leaving the real bodies in the necessary shadow of all that Glory. A compelling story, and one that has entranced people for centuries—often the vanquished as well as the conquerors.

For many many centuries, humanists and critics and radicals have been analyzing and deconstructing the Bible. And the Bible has survived, as have the beliefs it encodes. It is such a satisfying story. It seems to me that the only way to rid ourselves of a compelling story is to tell a better one, by which I mean a story more suited to our own century and situation, one that takes cognizance of a changed reality, and of all the consequences we have seen of playing out the old one. A new version that radically alters the meaning and shape of the old one is perhaps a way out of the bloody passes of the old Mountains of Meaning, with their sublime peaks and ice bridges over the abyss of time into which so many lives have fallen. Perhaps our gender makes it easier to see another way across, trying to come down to where we can breathe.

The world, as Muriel Rukeyser said somewhere, is not made of atoms; it is made of stories. The narrative is a shaping force of meanings, no doubt, and as such a dangerous instrument. But it remains the most powerful instrument we have, the fire with which we must fight fire. And it is only necessary to remember how it was as a child when you fell asleep before the story was over, and it led you into your own dream, a world in which stories were endless, where someone was out there, moving across the desert, maybe with her own child beside her, on the way to encounter her sister, and to tell another story, then, about that, the two of them around the same fire.

Sarah's Choice

A little late rain   *The testing*
the desert in the beauty of its winter   *of Sarah*
bloom, the cactus ablaze
with yellow flowers that glow
even at night in the reflected light
of moon and the shattered crystal of sand
when time was so new
that God still walked
among the tents, leaving no prints
in the sand, but a brand burned into
the heart—on such a night
it must have been, although
it is not written in the Book
how God spoke to Sarah
what he demanded of her
how many questions came of it
how a certain faith was
fractured, as a stone is split
by its own fault, a climate of extremes
and one last drastic change
in the temperature.

"Go!" said the Voice. "Take your son,
your only son, whom you love,
take him to the mountain, bind him
and make of him a burnt offering."
Now Isaac was the son of Sarah's age,
a gift, so she thought, from God. And how
could he ask her even to imagine such a thing—
to take the knife
of the butcher and thrust it
into such a trusting heart, then
light the pyre on which tomorrow burns.
What fear could be more holy
than the fear of *that?*

"Go!" said the Voice, Authority's own.
And Sarah rose to her feet, stepped out
of the tent of Abraham to stand between
the desert and the distant sky, holding its stars
like tears it was too cold to shed.

Perhaps she was afraid the firmament
would shudder and give way, crushing her
like a line of ants who, watching
the ants ahead marching safe under the arch,
are suddenly crushed by the heel
they never suspected. For Sarah,
with her desert-dwelling mind, could
see the grander scale in which the heel
might simply be the underside of some Divine
intention. On such a scale, what is
a human son? So there she stood, absurd
in the cosmic scene, an old woman bent
as a question mark, a mote in the eye
of God. And then it was that Sarah spoke
in a soft voice, a speech
the canon does not record.

"No," said Sarah to the Voice.   *The*
"I will not be chosen. Nor shall my son—   *teachings*
if I can help it. You have promised Abraham,   *of Sarah*
through this boy, a great nation. So either
this sacrifice is sham, or else it is a sin.
Shame," she said, for such is the presumption
of mothers, "for thinking me a fool,
for asking such a thing. You must have known
I would choose Isaac. What use have I
for History—an arrow already bent
when it is fired from the bow?"

Saying that, Sarah went into the tent
and found her restless son awake, as if
he'd grown aware of the narrow bed in which he lay.
And Sarah spoke out of the silence
she had herself created, or that had been there
all along. "Tomorrow you will be
a man. Tonight, then, I must tell you
the little that I know. You can be chosen
or you can choose. Not both.

The voice of the prophet grows shrill.
He will read even defeat as a sign
of distinction, until pain itself
becomes holy. In that day, how shall we tell

the victims from the saints,
the torturers from the agents of God?"

"But mother," said Isaac, "if we were not God's
chosen people, what then should we be? I am afraid
of being nothing." And Sarah laughed.

Then she reached out her hand. "Isaac,   *The*
I am going now, before Abraham awakes, before   *unbinding*
the sun, to find Hagar the Egyptian and her son   *of Isaac*
whom I cast out, drunk on pride,
God's promises, the seed of Abraham
in my own late-blooming loins."

"But Ishmael," said Isaac, "how should I greet him?"
"As you greet yourself," she said, "when you bend
over the well to draw water and see your image,
not knowing it reversed. You must know your brother
now, or you will see your own face looking back
the day you're at each other's throats."

She wrapped herself in a thick dark cloak
against the desert's enmity, and tying up
her stylus, bowl, some dates, a gourd
for water—she swung her bundle on her back,
reached out once more toward Isaac.

"It's time," she said. "Choose now."

"But what will happen if we go?" the boy
Isaac asked. "I don't know," Sarah said.
"But it is written   what will happen   if you stay."

23

Otherhow (and permission to continue)

RACHEL BLAU DUPLESSIS

Possession of many of the elements that make poetry into poetry somehow depends on positioning women? Poetry gendered in a different way
than fiction is? Sometimes it is possible to think so (Vickers 1982). Love,
Beauty, Nature, Seasonal Change, Beauty Raked by Time, Mediating Vision or Muse, the pastoral, the carpe diem motif, the satire—all these
prime themes and genres from the history of poetry seem to have swirls
of gender ideas and gender narrative blended like the marbleized end-
papers of old books. It's so beautiful, so oily with color, who could want
to pick it apart?

> Knowing when to begin and end is knowing what to say between
> poems being part
>
> of the poem.
>
> Helping them write a report, they need
> silvery sky dusk lilac stars stars starry
> bibelots rosy as a local coral
> flouncing the poem is that the answer?
>
> small folding arrangements?

Further, the centrality of the lyric voice (few characters in a poem little
dialogue) means that one point of view is privileged. And the speaking
subject is most often male.

> 'my female side' proudly
> 'my anima'

Overexposed post
card of the 50's sans one bitty cloud to darken
azure at the pectoral monument.
By implication or odd window, houses'
estranged effect
boasting seedy pleasure withered or perspicacity
deranged; what circle, what perimeter

to draw around such interlinear spannings.

If, in a bourgeois novel, the truth lies

in between, what "in"

is in "the bourgeois poem":

Now in the modern period, that lyric voice is ruptured, and poems can feature a controlled social array, as do novels. They may be "polyphonic," as novels. Even the masculine subject can be refused, interestingly, curiously, awkwardly, by a male poet, as by fiat or assertion— Tiresias in Eliot's notes to *The Waste Land*. And women writers speaking in a female, or a neutral-yet-gendered voice are not necessarily confessional of their lives, though still they may be "confessing" their throwing themselves wildly against, careening into conventions of representation. Into the terrible inadmissable congruence of poetry and gender. So all in all, even with exceptions, the institution of gendered poetry and the male-gendered poetic voice are imbedded in the history of poetry.

As a woman writing, my language space, my cultural space is active with a concatenation of constructs—prior poems, prior poetics—a lot of which implicate women. But not often as speaker. As ideal. As sought. As a mediator toward others' speech. As object. As means. As a thing partially cannibalized. Neutralized.

"Avant-garde" or experimental poets cannot simply discount this past; they must consciously address the social and formal imbeddings of gender. Nothing changes by changing the structures or sequences only. Narrative "realist" poets, including feminists, cannot simply discount this past; they must consciously address the formal and social imbeddings of gender. Nothing changes by changing the content only.

A woman, while always a real, if muted or compromised, or bold and unheard, or admired but forgotten (etc.), speaker in her own work is most often a cultural artifact in any of the traditions of meaning on which she draws.

Poems Today

Many poems look too much alike. They sometimes act and sound alike. They repeat. They repeat the relations and they repeat the exclusions. They repeat the satisfactions. Many a poem says the same kinds of things: these things are, or are called, poems. This is a tautology that protects nostalgias, sentimentalities, implicitly moralized short stories, domesticated mystery, and shallow transcendence. Protections may sometimes extend to banal fragmentation and shocking diction. Moreover, the iconicity of the text (the lyric icon on the page) seems deeply related to the beauty, inviolability, self-containment, and iconicity of the Female Figure as object that the text denominates.

Alexei Kruchenykh (translated by Marjorie Perloff): "before us, the following things were demanded of language: clarity, purity, propriety, sonority, pleasure (sweetness for the ear), forceful expression (rounded, picturesque, tasty)," which, the Russian futurists noted, represented, in critical language, the grounding of poetry on Woman: "as a matter of fact: fair, pure (oh of course!), virtuous (hm! hm!), pleasant sounding, tender (exactly!), finally—tasty, picturesque, round . . . (who's there? come in!)" (Perloff 1986:125).

How, then, to disturb these long-imbedded pleasures? How, then, to invest in the possibilities of a critical language that ruptures deep (constitutive?) assumptions of poetry as a genre? "What language" (asks Philippe Sollers) "would escape this insidious, incessant language which always seems to be there before we think of it?" (1981:61)

Language and Gender

Writer? Becoming one on whom language plays and through whom language exacts poetic convention, etymology, terrible puns, vernacular turns, ugly gobbets, professional jargon, mindless babble, baby syllables, dialect renderings, nursery rhymes, old pop music, precious adjectives and dubious adjectives, connectives, newspaper information, disinformation, conjunctions, pronouns playing with the social space evoked ("he" "she" "it" "we" "they"), 'little" words like *as* or *with*, like *the*.

"by" whom, beside whom and made by whom it may course or occur, declaring the destruction of uncontested rhetoric (but never the destruction of rhetoric).

Writer? A position to activate elements of language to join so that its activities enjoin the reader, you (to hear a sound to know a space that "never" was before).

> Comb the hairy
> language a vernac
> vert knack of saying what
> no one esp.
> desires
> hearing—how much it's the same.

But always prior inscriptions. Incessant marking. A writing whose condition is over writing. Want "in fact" a description of our language situation? Neither language use nor language acquisition are gender neutral, but are "imbued with our sex-inflected cultural values" (Nelly Furman cited by Kolodny 1985:148). Talking. Eliding. Agreeing. Questioning. Completing. Insisting. Leaving no space for others to speak. A woman's silence is a "social silence." It is created by the praxis of "protecting others' speech" (Kaplan 1986:79). How to depict the kinds and quantities of social silence at the core of works. Banality. Pause. "Utterance . . . is constructed between [at least] two socially organized persons" even in the absence of an actual addressee. Thus social status, hierarchical status, gender status all matter: "there is no such thing as an abstract addressee, a man unto himself, so to speak" (Bakhtin 1973: 85).

Foregrounded, this statement suggests the multifarious gender allusions or gender situations that can be called up just by language and its shifting, its tones, the social resonances of idiom, of the colloquial. The dialogic creation of meaning, the subtle capacities for cueing, status, power, and the interconnection of social and verbal realms are facts that have barely been self-consciously accounted for in the understanding of poetry.

> Still one could refind
> a taste for old beauty.
> Spillways of leaping
> abyss to azure
> extend thin ness ness ness
> that rusts rustle rond soft spectacle.

If language is "overpopulated with the intentions of others," it is teeming with, inter alia, gender ideas (Bakhtin 1981:294). I mean, I'm not talking of the signifier/signified, but of palimpsests of (saturations of) signifying. "Each word *tastes* of the context and contexts in which it has lived its socially charged life" (Bakhtin 1981:293). If each word has lived a socially charged life, each word has a "narrative" or two which it brings with it. What are the tactics that can either reaffirm the narrative(s) the word is telling or can try to break into by distorting or deforming, opening the storied words?

If literary language itself as the reasonably smooth formation of meaning cannot account for the sheer brutality of voicelessness, and if "giving voice to the voiceless"—what I used to say I was doing, an early feminist formulation—begins to sound both patronizing and unconscionable, then poetry has to be allowed to depoeticize itself and enact a rejection of the cultural character of its own idiom.

Depoeticize: reject normal claims of beauty. Smoothness. Finish. Fitness. Decoration. Moving sentiment. Uplift.

Want the poetry of shifters, a pronominal poetry, where discourses shift, times shift, tones shift, nothing is exclusive or uniform, the "whole" is susceptible to stretchings and displacements, the text marks itself, and there is no decorum. Anything can be said. Want the poetry of a raggedy, hewn, and situational character, with one criterion: that it has caused pleasure in the making. Pleasure in the writing and intransigence in the space for doing writing, and that is it. My only interest: in making objects that give me pleasures; they may also be interesting enough to sustain and renew whatever regard, look, or reflection is by chance cast upon them. That is it. Period.

Thinking about language in my poetry, I imagine a line below which is inarticulate speech, aphasia, stammer and above which is at least moderate, habitual fluency, certainly grammaticalness, and the potential for apt, witty images—perceptive, telling, and therefore guaranteed "poetic." That is, readable (reasonable) within intentions we assume. Since "Medusa" (finished in 1979) and again since "Crowbar" (finished 1983) my poetry wanders, vagrant, seeking to cross and recross that line: mistaking singular for plural, proposing stressed, exposed moments of genuine ungrammaticalness, neologisms, nonstandard dialect, and nonnormative forms. I struggle to break into the sentences that of course I am capable of writing smoothly. I want to distance. To rupture. Why? In part because of the gender contexts in which these words have lived, of which they taste.

Rupturing Iconization—Text as Object

Because of the way canonical texts are culturally used, especially by literary criticism, as objects, as if final or fixed, with no sense of historical movement (no sense of the way texts are continually reused and transformed, remade in social conjecture with readers), I wanted to invent works that would protest or resist this process, not protect it.

(No more poems, no more lyrics. Do I find I cannot sustain the lyric; it is no

longer. Propose somehow a work, the work, a work, the work, a work otherhow of enormous dailiness and crossing. All the "tickets" and the writing. Poems "like" essays: situated, breathless, passionate, multiple, critical. A work of entering into the social force of language, the daily work done everywhere with language, the little flyer fallen to the ground, the corner of a comic, a murder, burning cars, the pouring of realization like a squall green amber squall rain; kiss Schwitters and begin)

Iconization seemed to be considerably abetted by text as one-way street—ending in one place, repressing its drafts or choices, discounting in the poem events not-this-poem. The invitation to read once in one direction, start to finish, top to bottom, beginning to end seemed to symbolize iconization.

(One way to disturb the "one-way street" of the poem is to make a text run, like a musical piece, *da capo al fine* in a recursive structure that, by virtue of repeating the middle, drew attention to ongoingness, and impeded closure.)

A second way, in an homage to Emily Dickinson, could draw upon her rhetorical strategy of indicating variants, to keep the poem open, perhaps; to indicate the enormous changes of meaning, even in a narrow compass, that could be achieved by a minute (in some cases) alteration of a word. I'd like to think that the variant words, lines, and, more rarely, stanzas which she invented constituted her protest against the iconization of a text, against ending as statement, climax, moral thought. Against the stasis of poetry.

In "Crowbar" (1983), the whole argument comes to a poised end in the doubling of two words: *hungry* and *angry*, which grasp towards the odd *-ngry* ending they hold in common. *Hungry* meant complicit with the psychic cultural construction of beautiful, seductive, and seduced women; *angry* meant critical of the same. The simultaneous overvoicing of the penultimate word in a very long poem means that ambivalence marks the end as it had the beginning. Explanation generates its own self-questioning.

In a twenty-eight-section work called "Writing" (1984–85), I put words on the margin, try to break into the lyric center with many simultaneous writings occupying the same page space. I overwrite, or interleave typeset lines of writing with my own handwriting, not trying to obliterate, or to neutralize but to—to what? To erode some attitude toward reading and writing. I wanted simultaneous presence without authority. Wanted to make meanings that undid hierarchies of decidability. I wanted no right/correct sequences of feeling emblematic in right/correct sequences of reading, in order to state there is no center, just parallels: "everything is happening on the side." The desire to create something that is not a complete argument, or a poem with a climax, but where there are ends and beginnings all over the work. A working work. This is explicitly contrasted with lyric poetry and with novels.[1]

I was also rejecting that singular voice which "controls tone." The lyric voice. Controls tone? It hears the itch of, is in the center of languages. Voices are everywhere—the bureaucratic, the banal, the heightened, the friendly, the deadpan, the dreamy. Saturated with the multivocal, who can think of controlling tone? It is enough to collect them in one spot, and call that spot a poem.

[. . .]

It would be appropriate to interrupt "Otherhow" as originally published with the following remarks prepared for *Dwelling in Possibility*.

The acting out of my resistance to poetry-as-usual, to the lyric with its problematic of the female, and to the whole of Poetry as a contestable site came in the works called *Drafts*.

The Drafts are a series of interdependent, related long poems on which I have been working since 1986. The first two Drafts, and the deeply related poem "Writing," were published in *Tabula Rosa* (1987). In 1986, I had a stunned realization that I was indeed embarked on a long poem, recognizing that the first two titles ("Draft 1: It" and "Draft 2: She") could quickly be summed up as—there's a lot of "it" out there and "she" will have to deal with it. So from 1986 to 1991, I produced fourteen of these works. The book *Drafts 3-14* appeared in November 1991; a third book called *Drafts 15-XXX, The Fold* was prepared for publication in 1996. Drafts have become, in the ten years that I have, to date, devoted to them, a large-scale project with no end in sight; indeed, I have barely gotten to the middle.

There are many provocations and untamed feelings involved when one begins a long poem (an endless poem, one might postulate). Among them are Pound and Williams, Creeley, my special love for *Spring & All*, a beautiful notebook—a gift from Kathleen Fraser—and writing from George Oppen, a poet who has been terrifically important to my sense of poetry and to the intransigent ethics with which a poetic career might be conducted. (I was, at that time, working on the edition of Oppen's letters.) But the key event that tipped me into my poem was my reading of Beverly Dahlen's work *A Reading*, whose scope, passion, and design struck me with pleasure and desire. Later I wrote about Dahlen's text, and noted her "heuristic establishment of form by the reading of those words she has 'happened' to write" (1990:118).

---

[1] "Crowbar" and "Writing"—two long poems—appear in DuPlessis, 1987. The Emily Dickinson poem "Oil" appears in DuPlessis 1980 and 1987. "The 'History of Poetry'" is one of two sections of that second book.

Tracking the intricate meanings of one's own accidents (of thought, of autobiography, of historical moment, of memory, of fatedness), a practice also related to H.D.'s in *Tribute to Freud* and to Robert Duncan's essays in *The H.D. Book*, gives rise to a midrash-like quality of continuous linkages of interpretation, where the production and productivity of meanings is continuous. And one wants a series of shifting weights and balances on the page; one wants to be engaged in the momentary designation of flicker. These Drafts, then, are poems challenged by, moved by, the plethora, the extent, the intricacy of the sites that seem to be at stake in their composition.

In form Drafts are closest to collage, with an ethos of accumulation, clarity of the excerpt, preservation of edges, and juxtaposition. I have a strong sense of seriality and use serial procedures of all kinds as ways of achieving a narrative of thought without the pleasant blandishments of story. In this work story as such has only local claims and is never continuous. At the same time, the works (each individually finished, but deeply linked) seem symphonic, declaring a vast performance space in which interesting sounds occur, develop, and reverberate.

Structurally, the works are linked by subtle forms of repetition, presenting the reader with sets and bits of recollections from one Draft to another, creating the evanescent sensation of déjà vu, as if the poems constituted the space of memory. In addition, after the first nineteen poems, and presumably after each subsequent group of nineteen, a fold is created. This means that each new work will correspond in some sensuous, formal, intellectual, or allusive way to the specific former draft(s) exactly nineteen before. This tactic creates a regular, though widely spaced, recurrence among the poems, and a chained or meshed linkage whose periodicity is both predictable and suggestive. The strategy of "the fold," layering and reconsidering materials, does something very interesting to my conception of the work. First, it's my way of "solving" the insoluble problem of the long poem—essentially the question what holds it all together. And, although no genre is the master mode in a poem in which genre is continually at issue, the description of layering and reconsidering, of allowing the work to create a texture of multiple and matted glosses, does connect the work to the genre called "midrash."

Drafts could in fact be described as heterogeneric, making allusive loops around and through concepts of genre which the poems both appropriate and disturb, genres such as elegy, autobiography, meditation, and midrash. Correspondingly, in texture they are heteroglossic—open to a range of voices, tones, verbal ploys, social codes, and rhetorics. These long poems are, almost programmatically, neither narrative nor lyric, although they have both narrative and lyric elements. As much as I resist lyric or narrative, or make critiques of their normalizing and naturalizing of gender, of causality, of trajectory, of telos, of memory—my resistance is porous. It is riddled by holes through which leak these discourses and their histories of use. My resistance itself is contained within a complex cultural netting in which the very histories of these genre(s) are constructed by the materials I would (claim to) resist. Drafts are the sites of these struggles, the site of my wariness.

In all the Drafts, there is an attempt simply to ignore the lyric and the issues of beauty, unity, finish, and female positions within these ideas, and instead to articulate the claims and questions of Otherness, not as a binary to something else but rather as a seam opening inside existence. I made up the word "otherhow" for this proposal to indicate a space, a practice, a further distance implicit within method. There have appeared, as the work goes on, a number of allusions to elements of Jewish tradition. It's a creolized mix: certain holidays and customs, certain compelling biblical stories like Jacob and the angel, some words in Yiddish, a pervasive and incurable nomadism and sense of the exilic, a number of humble shadows of the Holocaust. Can this be summarized? The poem is inflected with a peculiar (and of course resistant) "Jewishness" because it is about text and textuality? about debris? about "anguage"—a cross between language and anguish, and maybe anger?

In short, "one might postulate another kind of textual space through which and onto which a plethora of 'polygynous' practices teem."

Writing—Marginalities?

"Also, there were notes, comments, scribbled over and across and on the margins of the original text, in red pencil. These, hard to decipher, were in themselves a different story or, at least, made of the original a different story" (Lessing 1958/1970:269).

"What would be a word, not the word 'marginal' to describe this?" (asked Jeanne Lance). "Marginal is a word which asks for, demands, homage to center."

Not "otherness" in a binary system, but "otherhow" as the multiple possibilities of a praxis.

Even "margins" decisively written are another text. The margins must multiply. Woolf kept her first diary in the white quads between the printed lines of a book. Where did I read that? Midrash makes annotation keep perpetual dialogue, conflicting interpretations put next to each other. Did I read that? So write crossings, contradictions, the field of situations, the fields of "placelessness" and mobility. " 'Do what you can' " (Baker 1984:202).[2]

Write through the page, unframed, a text that plays its affiliations. Strange croppings. Social densities of reference brought to the surface. A writing through the page from edge to edge. Evacuate the margins! A writing over the edge.

A writing over the edge! That's it. Satisfying one's sense of the excessive, indecorous, intense, crazed and desirous. She's over the edge! And the writing drives off the page, a variagated channel between me and you.

Being $\begin{Bmatrix} \text{a woman} \\ \text{a writer} \end{Bmatrix}$ is a $\begin{Bmatrix} \text{political} \\ \text{poetical} \end{Bmatrix}$ act.

[. . .]

What Writes?

pigs as fingers, toes
hat tassel a "powder puff" tickle
tummy
doh doh doh doh

as transformation d——g d——g d——g.
long cadences ending maybe in yougurt.

pulling upon those wide winging blank labia
dat? dat?

Wandering stars and little mercies, space
so empty, notched each moment.

---

[2] Houston Baker's conclusion (1984:202):

> Fixity is a function of power. Those who maintain place, who decide what takes place and dictate what has taken place, are power brokers of the traditional. The "placeless," by contrast, are translators of the nontraditional. . . . Their appropriate sign is a crossing sign at the junction.
>
> The crossing sign is the antithesis of a place marker. It signifies, always, change, motion, transience, process. To adept adherents of wandering, a crossing sign is equivalent to a challenge thrown out in brash, sassy tones by a locomotive blowing by: "Do what you can," it demands. "Do what you can—right here—on this place-less-place, this spotless-spot."

When I read that, it seemed completely apposite to "Otherhow."

Tufted white nut rising who or which is
"I" is "yo" the parade feather tit
mouse, did she see her first real bird?

Made from hearing the deep insides of language, language inside the
language; made from pick-scabbing the odd natural wounds of language
outside, unspecial dump of language everywhere here.

"Paradoxically the only way to position oneself outside of
that hegemonic discourse is to displace oneself within it—to
refuse the question as formulated, or to answer deviously
(though in its words), even to quote (but against the
grain)" (De Lauretis 1984:7).
my father said my mother never had any talent
how to acknowledge alterity the marginality and speak from
its
historically, personally wounding presence without
so that she never did anything; implied, that they had discussed
it
come to the conclusion, some people just have it some don't.
how to acknowledge anonymous (ourselves) but compel the
structures and tones, the social ocean of language to babble
burble, to speak
real talent, he said, would have found a way, this
conversation does not go on too long, shifts to "blacks"
of course.

The sung-half song.

If poems are posies what is this?
To whom?
And who am I, then, if it matters?

I am a GEN $\begin{cases} \text{der} \\ \text{re} \end{cases}$ made by the writing, I am a GEN $\begin{cases} \text{re} \\ \text{der} \end{cases}$
read in the writing.

Jan. 1985/June 1985/Aug. 1985/June
1989/addendum 1995
a poetics gives permission to
continue.

Draft 6: Midrush

Works
thru the dead   to circle

the living flood-

flung expectations   lit wreathes,
and came to meet the cowering   wassail
pairs   doors and houses
in a tarred ark.   edged in blinking.

                No one
                could give particulars
                enough
                play, enough force
                for what
                claims

circles pustules, chick-thick   circle garden overlooked
baby pox, MD sez boring   dying deeper down flat
disease with flex enough to   even, from the com-
twang a sour lyre   promises
"of days";   "of green";

                pairing the letters
                  underneath
                siting   citing
                the writing under wrting.

        When the living began
        to "labor" (as S. wrote,
        rushed "to die"

        10 years work
        10 years walk
        foot fell into lemony simples
        my heart at once in glee and grey
        Bar David's star and Marry holly pricks
        a day, all day, alway
        had, has had had
        unseasonable rip-tides
        and easily washed away

the flexing thorns and toss amid which we;
shattered the nest to scree,
whereupon whatever thrifty
pots and bits, little
stuff, special mug,
had to be set rite, had to be
set. Assume it. To paddle
dog-wise
in a covenant of breaking—
I tell you!
Like always working against time.

Some flatten the paper
for next year.
Ark opened, the paired
zoo aired and marched.
The colors had been beautiful.
And we have gained more objects
whose provenance is tombs: lavish
pristine colors of the acrid lock.

Swirling marks and snags
low tidy times settle
clays the pull sedentary.
Yet who will doubt the evidence
silted thru the claim-ragged dirt?

I labor because it was never
spoken and too much, or don't know
much. Or how.

Wraithes of poets, Oppen and oddly
Zukofsky
renew their open engagement with me
wreathing smoke-veils
my eyescreen tearing their insistent
opaque   startled
writing was speaking here was

saying words but,
befit a shady station,
sear swallowed up within the
mouths speaking
and all the words
dizzy with tears
passed again away.

"Where are they now
          dead people?"

"Nowhere."
               "but where
ARE they?"

Human shards   marked
markers   ash   the foiled
feathers of an eaten bird
maintain at the boundaries
of sense and tact
their dun features,
move
mostly much as did in life,
and away, blown
into the incomparable.

What emptiness
they cup for me
from floods
wherein they home?

"Death is the moment
when

what

has been given
away

must be reclaimed."

A clin-
ical rationalist

once dead
tempered his endless explanatory head
in wilds and wells of Hebrew prayer.

Walk thru the living
say the dead
our rustling voices
strain
more westerly words

BLOWN

when we have no more   back hosta pods
fluency   flat black, glossy
cannot, as it turns   seeds
out   layered in the leafy mast,
form either fully   letter bits, the scattered
intelligible wonder or grief tabernacle

It is they that speak
silt
we weep
silt
the flood-bound
written over and under with their
muddy marks

of writing under the writing.

Some epyllion—
pastoral, reclusive, elegiac, flooded
shards drifted up "forever"
thru the clay.
Always another little something—
a broken saucer flower fleck
unremarkable wedge, except its timing
working itself loose in the rain
thru the mum patch
and impatience
some glittery sharp a-flat the wet wide shade.

The house was built on a dump.

Or midrash—
overlaying stories so
that calling out the ark, it's
Noah hails and harks
new name and number
for
what stinking fur and tuckered feather-fobs
did clamber forth
disoriented. Cramped. Half-dead.

Two names, four names
everything
paired
with words in secret twin
the dry the flooded
remark the same
thing the done
the continual

or unpaired, odd markèd dabs,
but somehow matched
together in their claims

walk thru the dead
to tell the living.

Dressed as a hunter
a robin
hood in a tunic-top
of mother-lavish velvet
she talks swords,
greenling
"what are swords FOR?"
"for cutting people
like I cut the meat;
to try to hurt."

Rousing myself
to a cultural foray
attend, in Merz-y dote,
a chittering sonata.
Amid the *Europäische*
no sense glissades
repeats
this unmistakable refrain:
"rat-ta-tat-tat
bébé."

I will never survive
all this   narrowing skeptical
at straight arrow and oppositional
both. Where is my place?
The name is no,
is name twin, double yolk,

no too? Is no plus no
a raggy margined yes?
Is no plus no a triangle
wedge of scribbled clay
worked thru claim-slid mud?
How even is with odd.

I get so homeless
mid-race, mill-race, mis-chance,
mezzo "cambio,"
it's lucky I've a house
grounded in this camouflaged locale.

I'm just trying to make
whatever rushed
arrangements
I can and can't
even hear
long distance

because nearer louder
"mommy don't go mommy don't go"
while I have to

work at understanding even
nominally
crossing out and re-
writing odd scraps
in the little ticket square, of days.

December 1987–January 1988

The citation "Death is the moment..." from Annette B. Weiner, "Stability in Banana Leaves: Colonization and Women in Kiriwina, Trobriand Islands," in *Women and Colonization: Anthropological Perspectives*, ed. Mona Etienne and Eleanor Leacock (New York: Praeger, 1980), 287. "Rat-ta-tat-tat bébé" from Kurt Schwitters, UR-SONATA, 1923.

Works Cited

Addison, Joseph. 1711/1965. *The Spectator*. Ed. Donald F. Bond. 5 vols. Oxford: Oxford University Press.

Adkins, A. W. H. 1960. *Merit and Responsibility: A Study in Greek Values*. Oxford: Oxford University Press.

Alexiou, Margaret. 1974. *The Ritual Lament in Greek Tradition*. Cambridge: Cambridge University Press.

Allen, Don Cameron. 1949. "Some Theories of the Growth and Origin of Language in Milton's Age." *Philological Quarterly* 28:5–16.

Altieri, Charles. 1984/1993. "Self-Reflection as Action: The Recent Work of Adrienne Rich." In *Adrienne Rich's Poetry and Prose: Poems, Prose Reviews, and Criticism*, 342–56. New York: Norton.

Aristotle. 1965. *De arte poetica liber*. Ed. Rudolf Kassel. Oxford: Clarendon.

Armstrong, Isobel, and Virginia Blain, eds. 1997. *Women's Poetry, Late Romantic to Late Victorian: Gender and Genre, 1830–1900*. London: Macmillan.

Arthur, Marylin. 1980. "The Tortoise and the Mirror: Erinna *PSI* 1090." *Classical World* 74:53–65.

Averill, James H. 1980. *Wordsworth and the Poetry of Human Suffering*. Ithaca: Cornell University Press.

Baker, Houston. 1984. *Blues, Ideology, and Afro-American Literature*. Chicago: University of Chicago Press.

Bakhtin, M. M. 1981. *The Dialogic Imagination: Four Essays by M. M. Bakhtin*. Trans. Caryl Emerson and Michael Holquist. Ed. Michael Holquist. Austin: University of Texas Press.

Barbera, Jack. 1985. "The Relevance of Stevie Smith's Drawings." *Journal of Modern Literature* 12:221–36.

Barbera, Jack, and William McBrien. 1985. *Stevie: A Biography of Stevie Smith*. New York: Oxford University Press.

Barnard, Mary. 1984. *Assault on Mount Helicon*. Berkeley: University of California Press.

Barnard, Sylvia. 1991. "Anyte: Poet of Children and Animals." In *Rose di Pieria*, ed. Francesco de Martino, 163–76. Bari: Levante.

Barthes, Roland. 1953/1968. *Writing Degree Zero*. Trans. Annette Lavers and Colin Smith. New York: Hill & Wang.

Bastianini, Guido, and Claudio Gallazzi. 1993. "Il poeta ritrovato." *Rivista Ca' de Sass* 121:28–39.

Beebee, Thomas O. 1994. *The Ideology of Genre: A Comparative Study of Generic Instability*. University Park: Pennsylvania State University Press.

Behn, Aphra. 1688. Translator's Preface to *A Discovery of New Worlds*, by Bernard de Fontenelle. London.

Beilin, Elaine. 1987. *Redeeming Eve*. Princeton: Princeton University Press.

Benet, William Rose. 1965. *The Reader's Encyclopedia*. New York: Thomas Y. Crowell.

Benfey, Christopher. 1984. *Emily Dickinson and the Problem of Others*. Amherst: University of Massachusetts Press.

Benjamin, Walter. 1969. *Illuminations*. Trans. Harry Zohn. New York: Schocken.

Bennett, Paula. 1990. *Emily Dickinson: Woman Poet*. Iowa City: University of Iowa Press.

Berg, Temma, Anna Shannon Elfenbein, Jeanne Larsen, and Elisa Kay Sparks, eds. 1989. *Engendering the Word: Feminist Essays in Psychosexual Poetics*. Urbana: University of Illinois Press.

Bergin, Osborn. 1896. "Caoineadh Airt Uí Laoghaire." *Irisleabhar na Gaedhilge/The Gaelic Journal* 7:18–23.

Bernstein, Michael André. 1980. *The Tale of the Tribe: Ezra Pound and the Modern Verse Epic*. Princeton: Princeton University Press.

Besant, Walter. 1892. "On Literary Collaboration." *The New Review* 6:200–209.

Bing, Peter. 1988. *The Well-Read Muse: Present and Past in Callimachus and the Hellenistic Poets*. Göttingen: Vandenhoeck & Ruprecht.

Bingham, Millicent Todd. 1945. *Ancestors' Brocades: The Literary Debut of Emily Dickinson*. New York: Harper.

Bloom, Harold. 1973. *The Anxiety of Influence: A Theory of Poetry*. New York: Oxford University Press.

Bono, Barbara. 1986. "Mixed Gender, Mixed Genre in Shakespeare's *As You Like It*." In *Renaissance Genres: Essays on Theory, History, and Interpretation*, ed. Barbara Kiefer Lewalski, 189–212. Cambridge: Harvard University Press.

Boswell, James. 1964–1971. *Life of Johnson: Together with Journal of a Tour to the Hebrides and Johnson's Diary of a Journey into North Wales*. Ed. George Birkbeck Hill. Rev. L. F. Powell. 6 vols. Oxford: Clarendon.

Bourke, Angela. 1988a. "The Irish Traditional Lament and the Grieving Process." *Women's Studies International Forum* 11.4:287–91.

———. 1988b. *Working and Weeping: Women's Oral Poetry in Irish and Scottish Gaelic*. Women's Studies Working Papers no.7. Dublin: University College Dublin Women's Studies Forum.

———. 1993. "More in Anger Than in Sorrow: Irish Women's Lament Poetry." In *Feminist Messages: Coding in Women's Folk Culture*, ed. Joan Nelson Radner, 160–82. Urbana: University of Illinois Press.

———. 1995. "Reading a Woman's Death: Colonial Text and Oral Tradition in Nineteenth-Century Ireland." *Feminist Studies* 21.3:553–86.

Bowra, C. M. 1936. "Erinna's Lament for Baucis." In *Greek Poetry and Life*, 325–42. Oxford: Oxford University Press.

Boyarin, Daniel. 1994. *A Radical Jew: Paul and the Politics of Jewish Identity*. Berkeley: University of California Press.

Broe, Mary Lynn, and Angela Ingram, eds. 1989. *Women's Writing in Exile*. Chapel Hill: University of North Carolina Press.

Bromwich, Rachel. 1948a. "The Keen for Art O'Leary, Its Background, and Its Place in the Tradition of Gaelic Keening." *Éigse* 5:236–52.

——. 1948b. "The Continuity of the Gaelic Tradition in Eighteenth-Century Ireland." *Yorkshire Celtic Studies: The Yorkshire Society for Celtic Studies, Transactions* 4:2–28.

Brooks, Gwendolyn. 1963. *Selected Poems*. New York: Harper & Row.

——. 1967. *Blacks*. Chicago: Third World Press.

——. 1968. *In the Mecca*. New York: Harper & Row.

Brown, Rosellen. 1977. *Cora Fry*. New York: Norton.

Brown, Susan. 1994. "A Victorian Sappho: Agency, Identity, and the Politics of Poetics." *English Studies in Canada* 20.2:205–25.

Browning, Elizabeth Barrett. 1857/1979. *Aurora Leigh: A Poem*. Chicago: Academy Chicago.

——. 1864. *Aurora Leigh: A Poem*. New York: J. Miller.

——. 1974. *The Poetical Works*. Boston: Houghton Mifflin.

Brueggemann, Walter. 1986. "The Costly Loss of Lament." *Journal for the Study of the Old Testament* 36:57–71.

Buchan, David. 1972. *The Ballad and the Folk*. London: Routledge & Kegan Paul.

Buckler, William E. 1973. *The Major Victorian Poets: Tennyson, Browning, Arnold*. Boston: Houghton Mifflin.

Bundez, Julia. 1984. *From the Gardens of Flora Baum*. Middletown, Mass.: Wesleyan University Press.

Burke, Carolyn. 1980. "Mina Loy." In *Dictionary of Literary Biography*, vol.4, *American Writers in Paris, 1920–1939*, ed. Karen Lane Rood, 259–60. Detroit: Gale Research.

——. 1985a. "The New Poetry and the New Woman: Mina Loy." In *Coming to Light: American Woman Poets in the Twentieth Century*, ed. Diane Middlebrook and Marilyn Yalom, 37–57. Ann Arbor: University of Michigan Press.

——. 1985b. "Supposed Persons: Modernist Poetry and the Female Subject." *Feminist Studies* 11:131–40.

——. 1987. "Getting Spliced: Modernism and Sexual Difference." *American Quarterly* 39:98–121.

——. 1990. "Mina Loy." In *The Gender of Modernism: A Critical Anthology*, ed. Bonnie Kime Scott, 230–38. Bloomington: Indiana University Press.

Butler, Judith. 1991. "Imitation and Gender Insubordination." In *Inside/Out: Lesbian Theories, Gay Theories*, ed. Diana Fuss, 13–31. New York: Routledge.

——. 1993. *Bodies That Matter: On the Discursive Limits of "Sex."* New York: Routledge.

Cadava, Eduardo, Peter Connor, and Jean-Luc Nancy, eds. 1991. *Who Comes after the Subject?* New York: Routledge.

Callimachus. 1949–51. *Callimachus*. Ed. Rudolf Pfeiffer. 2 vols. Oxford: Oxford University Press.

Cameron, Averil, and Alan Cameron. 1969. "Erinna's *Distaff*." *Classical Quarterly* 19:285–88.

Cameron, Deborah. 1985. *Feminism and Linguistic Theory*. London: Macmillan.

Caraveli, Anna. 1986. "The Bitter Wounding: The Lament as Social Protest in Rural Greece." In *Gender and Power in Rural Greece*, ed. Jill Dubisch, 169–94. Princeton: Princeton University Press.

Carson, Anne. 1986. *Eros the Bittersweet*. Princeton: Princeton University Press.

Case, Sue-Ellen, ed. 1990. *Performing Feminisms: Feminist Critical Theory and Theatre*. Baltimore: Johns Hopkins University Press.

Castle, Terry. 1993. *The Apparitional Lesbian: Female Homosexuality and Modern Culture*. New York: Columbia University Press.

Cavallini, Eleonora. 1981. "Noss. A. P. V 170." *Sileno* 7:179–83.

——. 1991. "Due poetesse greche." In *Rose di Pieria*, ed. Francesco de Martino, 97–135. Bari: Levante.

Cavendish, Richard, ed. 1983. *Man, Myth, and Magic: The Illustrated Encyclopedia of Mythology, Religion, and the Unknown*. New York: Marshall Cavendish.

Cazzaniga, Ignazio. 1972. "Nosside, nome aristocratico per la poetessa de Locri?" *Annali della Scuola Normale Superiore di Pisa* 2:173–76.

Cha, Theresa Hak Kyung. 1982. *DICTEE*. New York: Tanam.

Chaves, Anna Caraveli. 1980. "Bridge between Worlds: The Greek Women's Lament as Communicative Event." *Journal of American Folklore* 93:129–57.

Christensen, Jerome. 1980. "Wordsworth's Misery, Coleridge's Woe: Reading 'The Thorn.' " *Papers on Language and Literature* 16:268–86.

Christian, Barbara T. 1987. *From the Inside Out: Afro-American Women's Literary Tradition and the State*. Center for Humanistic Studies Occasional Paper no.19. Minneapolis: University of Minnesota Press.

Cixous, Hélène. 1974/1980. "The Laugh of the Medusa." In *New French Feminisms: An Anthology*, ed. Elaine Marks and Isabelle de Courtivron, 245–64. Amherst: University of Massachusetts Press.

Clifton, Lucille. 1974. *An Ordinary Woman*. New York: Random House.

——. 1976/1987. *Generations: A Memoir*. In Clifton 1987a:223–77.

——. 1979. *The Lucky Stone*. New York: Delacorte.

——. 1980. *Two-Headed Woman*. Amherst: University of Massachusetts Press.

——. 1983. "A Simple Language." In *Black Women Writers (1950–1980): A Critical Evaluation*, ed. Mari Evans, 137–38. Garden City, N.Y.: Anchor/Doubleday.

——. 1987a. *Good Woman: Poems and a Memoir, 1969–1980*. Brockport, N.Y.: BOA Editions.

——. 1987b. *Next: New Poems*. Brockport, N.Y.: BOA Editions.

——. 1991. *Quilting: Poems, 1987–1990*. Brockport, N.Y.: BOA Editions.

——. 1993. *The Book of Light*. Port Townsend, Wash.: Copper Canyon Press.

Cohen, Murray. 1977. *Sensible Words: Linguistic Practice in England, 1640–1785*. Baltimore: Johns Hopkins University Press.

Conover, Roger L. 1982. Introduction to Loy 1982.

Cottle, Joseph. 1837. *Early Recollections: Chiefly Relating to Samuel Taylor Coleridge*. 2 vols. London: Longman.

Croft, Herbert. 1780. *Love and Madness. A story too true. In a series of letters between parties, whose names would perhaps be mentioned, were they less known, or less lamented*. London: G. Kingsley.

Croker, Thomas Crofton. 1824/1969. *Researches in the South of Ireland*. Shannon: Irish University Press.

Cullen, L[ouis] M. 1993. "The Contemporary and Later Politics of Caoineadh Airt Uí Laoghaire." *Eighteenth-Century Ireland: Iris an dá Chultúr* 8:7–38.

Culler, Jonathan. 1975. *Structuralist Poetics: Structuralism, Linguistics, and the Study of Literature*. Ithaca: Cornell University Press.

——. 1981. *The Pursuit of Signs: Semiotics, Literature, Deconstruction*. Ithaca: Cornell University Press.

——. 1988. "The Modern Lyric: Generic Continuity and Critical Practice." In *The Comparative Perspective on Literature*, ed. Clayton Koelb and Susan Noakes, 284–99. Ithaca: Cornell University Press.

Curtis, L. P., Jr. 1968. *Anglo-Saxons and Celts: A Study of Anti-Irish Prejudice in Victorian England*. Bridgeport, Conn.: Conference on British Studies.

——. 1971. *Apes and Angels: The Irishman in Victorian Caricature*. Washington, D.C.: Smithsonian Institution Press.

Daly, Mary. 1978. *Gyn/Ecology: The Metaethics of Radical Feminism*. Boston: Benson.

Danforth, Loring. 1982. *The Death Rituals of Rural Greece*. Princeton: Princeton University Press.

Deane, Seamus. 1986. *A Short History of Irish Literature*. Notre Dame, Ind.: University of Notre Dame Press.

Degani, Enzo. 1981. "Nosside." *Giornale filologico ferrarese* 4:43–52.

DeJean, Joan. 1988. *Fictions of Sappho, 1546–1937*. Chicago: University of Chicago Press.

DeKoven, Marianne. 1983. *A Different Language: Gertrude Stein's Experimental Writing*. Madison: University of Wisconsin Press.

De Lauretis, Teresa. 1984. *Alice Doesn't: Feminism, Semiotics, Cinema*. Bloomington: Indiana University Press.

Dellamora, Richard. 1994. "Dorianism." In *Apocalyptic Overtures: Sexual Politics and the Sense of an Ending*, 43–64. New Brunswick, N.J.: Rutgers University Press.

De Man, Paul. 1984. *The Rhetoric of Romanticism*. New York: Columbia University Press.

Dembo, L. S. 1965. *Conceptions of Reality in Modern American Poetry*. Berkeley: University of California Press.

Derricotte, Toi. 1983. *Natural Birth*. Trumansburg, N.Y.: Crossing Press.

Derrida, Jacques. 1976. *Of Grammatology*. Trans. Gayatri Chakravorty Spivak. Baltimore: Johns Hopkins University Press.

——. 1980. "The Law of Genre." *Critical Inquiry* 7:55–79.

——. 1985. "Des Tours de Babel." In *Difference in Translation*, trans. Joseph F. Graham, 165–248. Ithaca: Cornell University Press.

Des Pres, Terrence. 1988. *Praises and Dispraises: Poetry and Politics, the Twentieth Century*. New York: Viking.

Dickinson, Emily. 1890. *Poems by Emily Dickinson*. Ed. Mabel Loomis Todd and T. W. Higginson. Boston: Roberts Brothers.

——. 1955. *The Poems of Emily Dickinson*. Ed. Thomas H. Johnson. Cambridge: Belknap Press of Harvard University Press.

——. 1958. *The Letters of Emily Dickinson*. Ed. Thomas H. Johnson and Theodora Ward. Cambridge: Belknap Press of Harvard University Press.

——. 1981. *The Manuscript Books of Emily Dickinson*. Ed. R. W. Franklin. Cambridge: Belknap Press of Harvard University Press.

——. 1986. *The Master Letters of Emily Dickinson*. Ed. R. W. Franklin. Amherst: Amherst College Press.

Dillon, Wentworth, Earl of Roscommon. 1684. *Essay on Translated Verse*. London.

DiPrima, Diane. 1978. *Loba*. Berkeley: Wingbow Press.

Doherty, Lillian E. 1995. *Siren Songs: Gender, Audiences, and Narrators in the "Odyssey."* Ann Arbor: University of Michigan Press.

Dostoevsky, Fyodor. 1968. *Great Short Works of Fyodor Dostoyevsky*. New York: Harper & Row.

Doubiago, Sharon. 1982. *Hard Country*. Minneapolis: West End Press.

Dove, Rita. 1986. *Thomas and Beulah*. Pittsburgh: Carnegie-Mellon University Press.

Dowling, Linda. 1994. *Hellenism and Homosexuality in Victorian Oxford*. Ithaca: Cornell University Press.

Dryden, John. 1685. *Sylvae; or, The Second Part of Poetical Miscellanies*. London.

——. 1700/1958. *Fables, Ancient and Modern: Poems of John Dryden*. Ed. James Kinsley. 4 vols. Oxford: Clarendon.

DuBois, Page. 1995. *Sappho Is Burning*. Chicago: University of Chicago Press.

Dubrow, Heather. 1982. *Genre*. London: Methuen.

DuPlessis, Rachel Blau. 1980. *Wells*. New York: Montemora.

——. 1985. *Writing beyond the Ending: Narrative Strategies of Twentieth-Century Women Writers*. Bloomington: Indiana University Press.

——. 1987. *Tabula Rosa*. Elmwood, Conn.: Potes & Poets Press.

——. 1990. *The Pink Guitar: Writing as Feminist Practice*. New York: Routledge.

——. 1991. *Drafts 3–14*. Elmwood, Conn.: Potes & Poets Press.

——. 1992. " 'Seismic Orgasm': Sexual Intercourse, Gender Narratives, and Lyric Ideologies in Mina Loy." In *Studies in Historical Change*, ed. Ralph Cohen, 264–91. Charlottesville: University Press of Virginia.

——. 1997. *Drafts 15–XXX: The Fold*. Elmwood, Conn.: Potes & Poets Press.

Eaton, Sara. 1990. "Beatrice-Joanna and the Rhetoric of Love in *The Changeling*." In Case 1990:237–48.

Edelman, Lee. 1994. *Homographesis: Essays in Gay Literary and Cultural Theory*. New York: Routledge.

Eilberg-Schwartz, Howard. 1990. *The Savage in Judaism: An Anthropology of Israelite Religion and Ancient Judaism*. Bloomington: Indiana University Press.

Eliot, George. 1868/1899. *The Spanish Gypsy*. In *Poems*, 1.1–245, 2.1–54. London: Hawarden Press.

Eliot, T. S. 1975. *Selected Prose of T. S. Eliot*. Ed. Frank Kermode. New York: Harcourt Brace Jovanovich.

Erickson, Peter. 1995. "Singing America: From Walt Whitman to Adrienne Rich." *Kenyon Review* 18 (Winter): 103–19.

Erkkila, Betsy. 1992. *The Wicked Sisters: Women Poets, Literary History, and Discord*. New York: Oxford University Press.

Faderman, Lillian. 1981. *Surpassing the Love of Men: Romantic Friendship and Love between Women from the Renaissance to the Present*. New York: Morrow.

Feld, Steven. 1982. *Sound and Sentiment: Birds, Weeping, Poetics, and Song in Kaluli Expression*. Philadelphia: University of Pennsylvania Press.

Feldman, Emanuel. 1977. *Biblical and Post-Biblical Defilement and Mourning: Law as Theology*. New York: Yeshiva University Press.

Felson-Rubin, Nancy. 1994. *Regarding Penelope: From Character to Poetics*. Princeton: Princeton University Press.

Ferguson, Frances. 1977. *Wordsworth: Language as Counter-Spirit*. New Haven: Yale University Press.

Ferguson, Margaret, Maureen Quilligan, and Nancy J. Vickers, eds. 1986. *Rewriting the Renaissance: The Discourses of Sexual Difference in Early Modern Europe*. Chicago: University of Chicago Press.

Field, Michael. 1889. *Long Ago*. London: Bell.

——. 1933. *Works and Days: From the Journal of Michael Field*. Ed. T. and D. C. Sturge Moore. London: John Murray.

Fienberg, Nona. 1991. "Mary Wroth and the Invention of Female Poetic Subjectivity." In Miller and Waller 1991:175–90.

Finch, Anne. 1903. *Poems of Anne, Countess of Winchilsea*. Ed. Myra Reynolds. Chicago: Univerisity of Chicago Press.

Fine, Lawrence. 1984. "Kabbalistic Texts." In *Back to the Sources: Reading the Classic Jewish Texts*, ed. Barry W. Holtz, 305–59. New York: Summit Books.

Fineman, Joel. 1986. *Shakespeare's Perjured Eye: The Invention of Poetic Subjectivity in the Sonnets*. Berkeley: University of California Press.

Finke, Laurie A. 1990. "Painting Women: Images of Femininity in Jacobean Tragedy." In Case 1990:223–36.

Finnegan, Ruth. 1970. *Oral Literature in Africa*. Oxford: Oxford University Press.

Forster, Leonard. 1969. *The Icy Fire: Five Studies in European Petrarchism*. Cambridge: Cambridge University Press.

Foster, R. F. 1993. *Paddy and Mr. Punch: Connections in Irish an.. English History*. London: Allen Lane/Penguin.

Fowler, Alastair. 1982. *Kinds of Literature: An Introduction to the Theory of Genres and Modes*. Cambridge: Harvard University Press.

Fowler, Barbara H. 1989. *The Hellenistic Aesthetic*. Madison: University of Wisconsin Press.

Freccero, John. 1986. "The Fig Tree and the Laurel: Petrarch's Poetics." In *Literary Theory/Renaissance Texts*, ed. Patricia Parker and David Quint, 20–32. Baltimore: Johns Hopkins University Press.

Fried, Michael. 1987. *Realism, Writing, and Disfiguration: On Thomas Eakins and Stephen Crane*. Chicago: University of Chicago Press.

Friedman, Susan Stanford. 1986. "Gender and Genre Anxiety: Elizabeth Barrett Browning and H.D. as Epic Poets." *Tulsa Studies in Women's Literature* 5:203–28.

——. 1987. "Modernism of the 'Scattered Remnant': Race and Pc'itics in H.D.'s Development." In *Feminist Issues in Literary Scholarship*, ed. Shari Benstock, 208–32. Bloomington: Indiana University Press.

——. 1990. "When a 'Long' Poem is a 'Big' Poem: Self-Authorizing Strategies in Women's Twentieth-Century 'Long Poems.' " *LIT* 2:9–25.

——. 1994. "Craving Stories: Narrative and Lyric in Contemporary Theory and Women's Long Poems." In Keller and Miller 1994:15–42.

Froula, Christine. 1983. "When Eve Reads Milton: Undoing the Canonical Economy." *Critical Inquiry* 10:321–47.

Furiani, Patrizia L. 1991. "Intimità e socialità in Nosside di Locri." In *Rose di Pieria*, ed. Francesco de Martino, 177–95. Bari: Levante.

Gallop, Jane. 1992. *Around 1981: Academic Feminist Literary Theory*. New York: Routledge.

Garth, Samuel. 1717. Preface to *Ovid's Metamorphoses in Fifteen Books, Translated by the Most Eminent Hands*. London.

Gascoigne, George. 1910. *The Complete Works of George Gascoigne*. Ed. John W. Cunliffe. Vol.1. Cambridge University Press.

Gerhart, Mary. 1992. *Genre Choices, Gender Questions*. Norman: University of Oklahoma Press.

Gigante, Marcello. 1974. "Nosside." *Parola del passato* 29:22–39.

——. 1981. "Il manifesto poetico di Nosside." In *Letterature comparate: Problemi e metodo*, 1.243–45. Bologna: Patron.

Gilbert, Sandra M., and Susan Gubar. 1979a. *The Madwoman in the Attic: The Woman Writer and the Nineteenth-Century Literary Imagination*. New Haven: Yale University Press.

——, eds. 1979b. *Shakespeare's Sisters: Feminist Essays on Women Poets*. Bloomington: Indiana University Press.

——, eds. 1985. *The Norton Anthology of Literature by Women*. New York: Norton.

——. 1989. " 'She Meant What I Said': Lesbian Double Talk." In *No Man's Land: The Place of the Woman Writer in the Twentieth Century*, 2.215–57. New Haven: Yale University Press.

Glancy, Diane. 1991. *Lone Dog's Winter Court*. Albuquerque: West End Press.

Glazener, Nancy. 1989. "Dialogic Subversion: Bakhtin, the Novel, and Gertrude Stein." In *Bakhtin and Cultural Theory*, ed. Ken Hirschkop and David Shepherd, 109–29. Manchester: Manchester University Press.

Goitein, S. D. 1988. "Women as Creators of Biblical Genres." *Prooftexts* 8.1:1–33.

Goldberg, Brian. 1996. "Romantic Professionalism in 1800: Robert Southey, Herbert Croft, and the Letters and Legacy of Thomas Chatterton." *ELH* 63:681–706.

Goldberg, Jonathan. 1992. " 'Bradford's Ancient Members' and 'A Case of Buggery amongst Them.' " In Parker et al. 1992:60–76.

Gordis, Robert. 1967. "A Commentary on the Text of Lamentations." In *The Seventy-fifth Anniversary Volume of the Jewish Quarterly Review*, ed. Abraham Neuman and Solomon Zeitlin, 267–286. Philadelphia.

Gouldner, Alvin W. 1965. *Enter Plato: Classical Greece and the Origins of Social Theory*. New York: Basic Books.

Gow, A. S. F., and D. L. Page, eds. 1965. *The Greek Anthology: Hellenistic Epigrams*. 2 vols. Cambridge: Cambridge University Press.

Grahn, Judy. 1978. *The Work of a Common Woman: The Collected Poetry, 1964–1977*. Trumansburg, N.Y.: Crossing Press.

——. 1982. *The Queen of Wands*. Trumansburg, N.Y.: Crossing Press.

——. 1983. Introduction to Pat Parker 1983:17.

——. 1985. *The Highest Apple: Sappho and the Lesbian Poetic Tradition*. San Francisco: Spinsters Ink.

——. 1987. *The Queen of Swords*. Boston: Beacon.

Gray, John M. 1889. Review of *Long Ago. The Academy*, 18 June, 388–89.

Greek Anthology, The. 1916–18. Trans. W. R. Paton. 5 vols. Loeb Classical Library. Cambridge: Harvard University Press.

Greenblatt, Stephen. 1982. *The Power of Forms in the English Renaissance*. Norman, Okla.: Pilgrim Press.

Greene, Ellen, ed. 1997a. *Reading Sappho: Contemporary Approaches*. Berkeley: University of California Press.

——, ed. 1997b. *Re-reading Sappho: Reception and Transmission*. Berkeley: University of California Press.

Greer, Germaine, Susan Hastings, Jeslyn Medoff, and Melinda Sansone, eds. 1988. *Kissing the Rod: An Anthology of Seventeenth-Century Women's Writing*. New York: Farrar Straus Giroux.

Gubar, Susan. 1984. "Sapphistries." *Signs* 10:43–62.

Gutzwiller, Kathryn J. 1992. "Callimachus' *Lock of Berenice*: Fantasy, Romance, and Propaganda." *American Journal of Philology* 113:359–85.

——. 1993. "Anyte's Epigram Book." *SyllectaClassica* 4:71–89.

Gutzwiller, Kathryn J., and Ann N. Michelini. 1991. "Women and Other Strangers." In *(En)Gendering Knowledge*, ed. Joan E. Hartman and Ellen Messer-Davidow, 66–84. Knoxville: University of Tennessee Press.

Hacker, Marilyn. 1986. *Love, Death, and the Changing of the Seasons*. New York: Norton.

Hannay, Margaret P. 1990. *Philip's Phoenix: Mary Sidney, Countess of Pembroke*. New York: Oxford University Press.

——. 1991. " 'Your Vertuous and Learned Aunt': The Countess of Pembroke as a Mentor to Mary Wroth." In Miller and Waller 1991:16–34.

Harding, Sandra. 1986. *The Science Question in Feminism*. Ithaca: Cornell University Press.

Harper, Frances Watkins. 1869. *Moses: A Story of the Nile*. Philadelphia: Merrihew.

Harvey, A. E. 1955. "The Classification of Greek Lyric Poetry." *Classical Quarterly* 5:157–80.

Haselkorn, Anne M., and Betty S. Travitsky. 1990. *The Renaissance Englishwoman in Print: Counterbalancing the Canon*. Amherst: University of Massachusetts Press.

Heilbrun, Carolyn. 1989. *Writing a Woman's Life*. New York: Norton.

Henderson, Diana E. 1995. *Passion Made Public: Elizabethan Lyric, Gender, and Performance*. Urbana: University of Illinois Press.

Hendricks, Margo, and Patricia Parker. 1994. *Women, "Race," and Writing in the Early Modern Period*. New York: Routledge.

Herford, C. H., Percy Simpson, and Evelyn Simpson, eds. 1947. *Ben Jonson*. Vol.8. Oxford: Clarendon.

Hernadi, Paul. 1972. *Beyond Genre: New Directions in Literary Classification*. Ithaca: Cornell University Press.

H.D. (Hilda Doolittle). 1944–46/1973. *Trilogy*. New York: New Directions.

——. 1961/1974. *Helen in Egypt*. New York: New Directions.

——. 1972. *Hermetic Definition*. New York: New Directions.

——. 1982a. *The Gift* [abridged]. New York: New Directions.

——. 1982b. *Vale Ave*. Ed. James Laughlin. New Directions in Prose and Poetry 44. New York: New Directions.

——. 1983. *Collected Poems, 1912–1944*. Ed. Louis L. Martz. New York: New Directions.

Higginson, Thomas Wentworth. 1882. *Atlantic Essays*. Boston: Lee & Shepard.

——. 1890. Preface to Dickinson 1890, iii–vi.

——. 1900. *Women and the Alphabet: A Series of Essays*. Boston: Houghton Mifflin.

Hillers, Delbert R. 1972. *The Anchor Bible: Lamentations*. New York: Doubleday.

Hinnant, Charles B. 1994. *The Poetry of Anne Finch*. Newark: University of Delaware Press.

Hirsh, Elizabeth. 1989. "Modernism Revised: Formalism and the Feminine (Irigaray, H.D., Barnes)." Ann Arbor: UMI, Dissertation Information Service.

Hoffman, Lawrence A. 1979. *The Canonization of the Synagogue Service*. Notre Dame, Ind.: University of Notre Dame Press.

Holmes, Charles S., Edwin Fussell, and Ray Frazer, eds. 1957. *The Major Critics: The Development of English Literary Criticism*. New York: Knopf.

Holst-Warhaft, Gail. 1992. *Dangerous Voices: Women's Laments and Greek Literature*. New York: Routledge.

Homans, Margaret. 1980. *Women Writers and Poetic Identity: Dorothy Wordsworth, Emily Brontë, and Emily Dickinson*. Princeton: Princeton University Press.

——. 1983. " 'Oh, Vision of Language!': Dickinson's Poems of Love and Death." In Juhasz 1983:114–33.

——. 1985. " 'Syllables of Velvet': Dickinson, Rossetti, and the Rhetorics of Sexuality." *Feminist Studies* 11:569–93.

——. 1986. *Bearing the Word: Language and Female Experience in Nineteenth-Century Women's Writing*. Chicago: University of Chicago Press.

Honko, Lauri. 1974. "Balto-Finnic Lament Poetry." *Studia Fennica* 17:9–61.

Howe, Susan. 1982. *Pythagorean Silence*. New York: Montemora.

——. 1983. *Defenestration of Prague*. New York: Kultur Foundation.

——. 1985. *My Emily Dickinson*. Berkeley: North Atlantic Books.

——. 1990a. *The Europe of Trusts*. Los Angeles: Sun & Moon Press.

——. 1990b. *Singularities*. Middletown, Mass.: Wesleyan University Press.

——. 1993. *The Nonconformist's Memorial*. New York: New Directions.

Hughes, Langston. 1951. *Montage of a Dream Deferred*. New York: Henry Holt.

Huk, Romana. 1993. "Eccentric Concentrism: Traditional Poetic Forms and Refracted Discourse in Stevie Smith's Poetry." *Contemporary Literature* 34:240–65.

Hutchinson, G. O. 1988. *Hellenistic Poetry*. Oxford: Oxford University Press.

Irigaray, Luce. 1985a. *Speculum of the Other Woman*. Trans. Gillian C. Gill. Ithaca: Cornell University Press.

——. 1985b. *This Sex Which Is Not One*. Trans. Catherine Porter. Ithaca: Cornell University Press.

Jackson, William. 1818. *The New and Complete Newgate Calendar; or, Malefactor's Universal Register. A new edition, with very great additions*. 8 vols. London.

Jacobs, Carol. 1975. "The Monstrosity of Translation." *Modern Language Notes* 90: 755–66.

Jacobus, Mary. 1976. *Tradition and Experiment in Wordsworth's "Lyrical Ballads" (1798)*. Oxford: Clarendon.

Jameson, Fredric. 1981. *The Political Unconscious: Narrative as a Socially Symbolic Act*. Ithaca: Cornell University Press.

Jardine, Lisa. 1983. *Still Harping on Daughters: Women and Drama in the Age of Shakespeare*. Totowa, N.J.: Barnes & Noble.

Jenkyns, Richard. 1980. *The Victorians and Ancient Greece*. Cambridge: Harvard University Press.

Johnson, Dianne. 1990. *Telling Tales: The Pedagogy and Promise of African-American Literature for Youth*. Westport, Conn.: Greenwood.

Jones, Ann Rosalind. 1990. *The Currency of Eros: Women's Love Lyric in Europe, 1540–1620*. Bloomington: Indiana University Press.

Jones, Ann Rosalind, and Peter Stallybrass. 1984. "The Politics of *Astrophil and Stella*." *SEL* 24.1:53–68.

Joplin, Patricia Kleindienst. 1984. "The Voice of the Shuttle Is Ours." *Stanford Literary Review* 1:25–53.

Juhasz, Suzanne, ed. 1983. *Feminist Critics Read Emily Dickinson*. Bloomington: Indiana University Press.

Kamboureli, Smaro. 1991. *On the Edge of Genre: The Contemporary Long Poem*. Toronto: University of Toronto Press.

Kaplan, Cora. 1986. *Sea Changes: Culture and Feminism*. London: Verso.

Katz, Marylin A. 1991. *Penelope's Renown*. Princeton: Princeton University Press.

Kaufman, Shirley. 1984. *Claims: A Poem*. New York: Sheep Meadow Press.

Keller, Lynn. 1987. "Poems Containing History: Problems of Definition of the Long Poem." Paper delivered at the meetings of the Modern Language Association, 27–30 December, San Francisco.

——. 1992. " 'To remember / our dis-membered parts': Sharon Doubiago and the Complementary Woman's Epic." *American Literary History* 4:305–28.

——. 1993. "The Twentieth-Century Long Poem." In *Columbia History of American Poetry*, ed. Jay Parini, 534–63. New York: Columbia University Press.

——. 1994. "Measured Feet 'in Gender-Bender Shoes': The Politics of Form in Marilyn Hacker's *Love, Death, and the Changing of the Seasons*." In Keller and Miller 1994:260–86.

——. N.d. "Forms of Expansion: Recent Women's Long Poems." Work in progress.

Keller, Lynn, and Cristanne Miller, eds. 1994. *Feminist Measures: Soundings in Poetry and Theory*. Ann Arbor: University of Michigan Press.

Kendrick, Delores. 1989. *The Women of Plums: Poems in the Voices of Slave Women*. New York: Morrow.

Kennelly, Brendan, ed. 1970. *The Penguin Book of Irish Verse*. Harmondsworth: Penguin.

Klepfisz, Irene. 1982. *Keeper of Accounts*. Watertown, Mass.: Persephone Press.

Koestenbaum, Wayne. 1989. *Double Talk: The Erotics of Male Literary Collaboration*. New York: Routledge.

Kolodny, Annette. 1985. "Dancing through the Minefield: Some Observations on the Theory, Practice, and Politics of Feminist Literary Criticism." In Showalter 1985b:144–67.

Kouidis, Virginia. 1980. *Mina Loy: American Modernist Poet*. Baton Rouge: Louisiana State University Press.

Kranz, W. 1961. "SPHRAGIS: Ichform und Namensiegel als Eingangs- und Schlußmotiv antiker Dichtung." *Rheinisches Museum* 104:3–46, 97–124.

Kristeva, Julia. 1980. *Desire in Language: A Semiotic Approach to Literature and Art*. Trans. Leon S. Roudiez. New York: Columbia University Press.

Kroll, Richard. 1991. *The Material Word: Literate Culture in the Restoration and Early Eighteenth Century*. Baltimore: Johns Hopkins University Press.

La Fontaine, Jean de. 1668–92/1967. *Fables choisies*. Paris: Garnier Flammarion.

Laird, Holly. 1995. "Contradictory Legacies: Michael Field and Feminist Restoration." *Victorian Poetry* 33.1:111–28.

Lamentations. 1969. In *The Five Megilloth and Jonah: A New Translation*. Philadelphia: Jewish Publication Society.

Laplanche, Jean. 1976. *Life and Death in Psychoanalysis*. Trans. Jeffrey Mehlman. Baltimore: Johns Hopkins University Press.

Laqueur, Thomas. 1989. "Bodies, Details, and the Humanitarian Narrative." In *The New Cultural History*, ed. Lynn Hunt, 187–204. Berkeley: University of California Press.

Lawrence, Karen. 1980. *The Inanna Poems*. Edmonton, Alta.: Longspoon Press.

Lazer, Hank. 1989. "Blackness Blessed: The Writings of Lucille Clifton." *Southern Review* 25.3:760–72.

Leach, Maria, ed. 1949. *Standard Dictionary of Folklore, Mythology, and Legend*. 2 vols. New York: Funk & Wagnalls.

Leighton, Angela. 1992. *Victorian Women Poets: Writing against the Heart*. Charlottesville: University Press of Virginia.

——, ed. 1996. *Victorian Women Poets: A Critical Reader*. Cambridge, Mass.: Blackwell.

Leighton, Angela, and Margaret Reynolds, eds. 1995. *Victorian Women Poets: An Anthology*. Cambridge, Mass.: Blackwell.

Lessing, Doris. 1958/1970. *Landlocked*. New York: New American Library.

Levertov, Denise. 1971. *To Stay Alive*. New York: New Directions.

Levi, Peter. 1984. *The Lamentation of the Dead*. London: Anvil Press Poetry.

Levin, Donald N. 1962. "Quaestiones Erinneanae." *Harvard Studies in Classical Philology* 66:193–204.

Levinas, Emmanuel. 1985. *Ethics and Infinity*. Trans. Richard Cohen. Pittsburgh: Duquesne University Press.

Lewalski, Barbara Kiefer. 1993. *Writing Women in Jacobean England*. Cambridge: Harvard University Press.

Li, Victor P. H. 1986. "The Vanity of Length: The Long Poem as Problem in Pound's *Cantos* and Williams' *Paterson*." *Genre* 19:3–20.

Lipking, Lawrence. 1988. *Abandoned Women and Poetic Tradition*. Chicago: University of Chicago Press.

Lloyd-Jones, Hugh, and Peter Parsons, eds. 1983. *Supplementum Hellenisticum*. Berlin: Walter de Gruyter.

Locard, Henri. 1979. "Works and Days: The Journals of 'Michael Field.'" *Journal of the Eighteen Nineties Society* 10:1–9.

Loeffelholz, Mary. 1991. *Dickinson and the Boundaries of Feminist Theory*. Urbana: University of Illinois Press.

Lord, Albert B. 1960. *The Singer of Tales*. Cambridge: Harvard University Press.

Lorde, Audre. 1984. "Uses of the Erotic: The Erotic as Power." In *Sister Outsider: Essays and Speeches*, 53–59. Trumansburg, N.Y.: Crossing Press.

Loy, Mina. 1982. *The Last Lunar Baedeker*. Ed. Roger L. Conover. Highlands, N.C.: Jargon Society.

Luck, G. 1954. "Die Dichterinnen der griechischen Anthologie." *Museum Helveticum* 11:170–87.

Mandel, Charlotte. 1988. *The Life of Mary—A Poem-Novella*. Upper Montclair, N.J.: Saturday Press.

——. 1991. *The Marriages of Jacob: A Poem-Novella*. Marblehead, Mass.: Micah.

Maresca, Thomas. 1979. *Epic to Novel*. Columbus: Ohio State University Press.

Marlatt, Daphne. 1984. *Touch to My Tongue*. Edmonton, Alta: Longspoon Press.

Marlatt, Daphne, and Betsy Warland. 1988. *Double Negative*. Charlottetown, P. E.I.: Gynergy Books.

Masten, Jeffrey. " 'Shall I turn blabb?': Circulation, Gender, and Subjectivity in Mary Wroth's Sonnets." In Miller and Waller 1981:67–87.

May, Stephen W. 1992. "The Countess of Oxford's Sonnets: A Caveat." *English Language Notes* 29.3:9–19.

Mayer, Bernadette. 1982. *Midwinter Day*. Berkeley: Turtle Mountain Press.

Mayo, Robert. 1954. "The Contemporaneity of the *Lyrical Ballads*." *PMLA* 69:486–522.

McCoy, Richard C. 1979. *Sir Philip Sidney: Rebellion in Arcadia*. New Brunswick, N.J.: Rutgers University Press.

McGovern, Barbara. 1992. *Anne Finch and Her Poetry: A Critical Biography*. Athens: University of Georgia Press.

McNeil, Helen. 1986. *Emily Dickinson*. New York: Virago/Pantheon Pioneers.

Meese, Elizabeth. 1990. "Theorizing Lesbian: Writing--A Love Letter." In *Lesbian Texts and Contexts: Radical Revisions*, ed. Karla Jay and Joanne Glasgow, 70–87. New York: New York University Press.

Melville, Herman. 1851/1961. *Moby-Dick*. New York: New American Library.

Memmi, Albert. 1965. *The Colonizer and the Colonized*. Boston: Beacon.

Michaels, Walter Benn. 1987. *The Gold Standard and the Logic of Naturalism: American Literature at the Turn of the Century*. Berkeley: University of California Press.

Michelazzo Magrini, M. 1975. "Una nuova linea interpretativa della *Conocchia* di Erinna." *Prometheus* 1:225–36.

Middlebrook, Diane, and Marilyn Yalom, eds. 1985. *Coming to Light: American Women Poets in the Twentieth Century*. Ann Arbor: University of Michigan Press.

Mill, John Stuart. 1976. *Essays on Poetry*. Ed. F. Parvin Sharpless. Columbia: University of South Carolina Press.

Millard, Elaine. 1989. "Frames of References: The Reception of, and Response to, Three Women Poets." In *Literary Theory and Poetry: Extending the Canon*, ed. David Murray. London: Batsford.

Millay, Edna St. Vincent. 1931. *Fatal Interview: Sonnets*. New York: Harper.

Miller, James E., Jr. 1979. *The American Quest for a Supreme Fiction: Whitman's Legacy in the Personal Epic*. Chicago: University of Chicago Press.

Miller, Nancy K. 1986a. "Arachnologies: The Woman, the Text, and the Critic." In Nancy Miller 1986b:270–95.

——, ed. 1986b. *The Poetics of Gender*. New York: Columbia University Press.

Miller, Naomi. 1996. *Changing the Subject: Mary Wroth and the Figurations of Gender in Early Modern England*. Lexington: University Press of Kentucky.

Miller, Naomi, and Gary Waller, eds. 1991. *Reading Mary Wroth: Representing Alternatives in Early Modern England*. Nashville: University of Tennessee Press.

Milton, John. 1667/1975. *Paradise Lost*. Ed. Scott Elledge. New York: Norton.

Mintz, Alan. 1984. *Hurban: Response to Catastrophe in Hebrew Literature*. New York: Columbia University Press.

Monroe, Jonathan. 1987. *A Poverty of Objects: The Prose Poem and the Politics of Genre*. Ithaca: Cornell University Press.

Montefiore, Jan. 1987. *Feminism and Poetry: Language, Experience, Identity in Women's Poetry*. New York: Pandora Press.

Montrose, Louis. 1977. "Celebration and Insinuation: Sir Philip Sidney and the Motives of Elizabethan Courtship." *Renaissance Drama* 8:3–35.

Moody, Ellen. 1989. "Six Elegaic Poems, Possibly by Anne Cecil de Vere, Countess of Oxford." *English Literary Renaissance* 19.2:152–70.

Moraga, Cherríe, and Gloria Anzaldúa, eds. 1981. *This Bridge Called My Back: Writings by Radical Women of Color*. New York: Kitchen Table/Women of Color Press.

Morgan, Robin. 1976. *Lady of the Beasts*. New York: Random House.

Moriarty, David J. 1986. " 'Michael Field' (Edith Cooper and Katherine Bradley) and Their Male Critics." In *Nineteenth-Century Women Writers of the English-Speaking World*, ed. Rhoda B. Nathan, 121–42. New York: Greenwood.

Morris, Timothy. 1995. *Becoming Canonical in American Poetry*. Urbana: University of Illinois Press.

Neely, Carol Thomas. 1988. "Constructing the Subject: Feminist Practice and the New Renaissance Discourses." *Engish Literary Renaissance* 18.1:5–18.

Ní Chuilleanáin, Eiléan. 1985. *Irish Women: Image and Achievement*. Dublin: Arlen House.

Nussbaum, Felicity A. 1989. *The Autobiographical Subject*. Baltimore: Johns Hopkins University Press.

Ó Coileáin, Seán. 1988. "The Irish Lament: An Oral Genre." *Studia Hibernica* 24: 97–117.

Ó Concheanainn, Tomás. 1978. *Nuadhuanaire, Cuid III*. Dublin: Dublin Institute for Advanced Studies.

O'Connell, Mrs. Morgan John. 1892/1977. *The Last Colonel of the Irish Brigade*. Cork: Tower Books.

Ó Foghludha, Ristéard, ed. 1936. *Caoineadh Seámus Mhic Choitir* [The lament for Sir James Cotter]. *Irish Press*, 27 April, 4.

Ó hAilin, Tomás. 1971. "Caointe agus Caointeori" [Laments and lamenters]. *Feasta*, January, 7–11; February, 5–9.

Ó Madagáin, Brendán, ed. 1978. *Gnéithe den Caointeoireacht* [Aspects of the lament]. Dublin: An Clóchomhar.

——. 1982. "Irish Vocal Music of Lament and Syllabic Poetry." In *The Celtic Consciousness*, ed. Robert O'Driscoll, 311–31. New York: George Braziller.

Ó Muirithe, Diarmuid. 1978. "Tuairiscí na dTaistealaithe." In Ó Madagáin 1978: 20–29.

Ó Murchadha, Gearóid, and Caitlín Ní Bhuachalla, eds. 1939. "Caoineadh Dhiarmada whic Eoghain Mhic Cárthaigh" [The lament for Diarmaid McCarthy]. *Éigse* 1:22–28.

Ong, Walter, 1982. *Orality and Literacy: The Technologizing of the Word*. London: Methuen.

Ostriker, Alicia Suskin. 1971. *Once More out of Darkness*. New York: Horizon Press.

——. 1980. *The Mother/Child Papers*. Santa Monica, Calif.: Momentum Press.

——. 1986. *Stealing the Language: The Emergence of Women's Poetry in America*. Boston: Beacon.

——. 1992. "Loving Walt Whitman and the Problem of America." In *The Continuing Presence of Walt Whitman: The Life after the Life*, ed. Robert K. Martin, 217–31. Iowa City: University of Iowa Press.

Ó Tuama, Seán. 1961. *Caoineadh Airt Uí Laoghaire* [The lament for Art O'Leary]. Dublin: An Clóchomhar.

——. 1987. "The Lament for Art O'Leary and the Popular Keening Tradition." In *Mythe et folklore celtiques et leurs expressions littéraires en Irlands*, ed. R. Alluin and B. Escarbelet. Lille: Université de Lille. Reprinted in Seán Ó Tuama, *Repossessions: Selected Essays on the Irish Literary Heritage*, 78–100. Cork: Cork University Press, 1995.

Page, D. L. 1941. *Greek Literary Papyri*. Vol.1. Cambridge: Harvard University Press.

——. 1981. *Further Greek Epigrams*. Cambridge: Cambridge University Press.

Parker, Andrew, Mary Russo, Doris Sommer, and Patricia Yaeger, eds. 1992. *Nationalisms and Sexualities*. New York: Routledge.

Parker, Pat. 1983. *Movement in Black: The Collected Poetry, 1961–1978*. Trumansburg, N.Y.: Crossing Press.

Parker, Patricia. 1987. *Literary Fat Ladies: Rhetoric, Gender, Property*. New York: Methuen.

Parrish, Stephen M. 1957. " 'The Thorn': Wordsworth's Dramatic Monologue." *ELH* 24:153–63.

Partington, Wilfred, ed. 1930. *The Private Letter-Books of Sir Walter Scott*. New York: Frederick Stokes.

Partridge, Angela. 1980. "Wild Men and Wailing Women." *Éigse* 18:25–37.

——. 1983. *Caoineadh na dTrí Muire: Téama na Páise i bhFilíocht Bhéil na Gaeilge* [The lament of the three Marys: The Crucifixion in Irish oral poetry]. Dublin: An Clóchomhar.

Peirce, Charles Saunders. 1982. *Writings of Charles Saunders Peirce: A Chronological Edition*. Ed. Max H. Fisch. Bloomington: Indiana University Press.

Perloff, Marjorie. 1986. *The Futurist Moment: Avant-Garde, Avant Guerre, and the Language of Rupture*. Chicago: University of Chicago Press.

Peterson, Linda. 1994. "Sappho and the Making of Tennysonian Lyric." *ELH* 61: 121–37

Phillippy, Patricia. 1989. "Gaspara Stampa's Rime: Replication and Retraction." *Philological Quarterly* 68.1:1–23.

Pinch, Adela. 1988. "Female Chatter: Meter, Masochism, and the *Lyrical Ballads*." *ELH* 55:835–52.

Plath, Sylvia. 1981. *The Collected Poems*. Ed. Ted Hughes. New York: Harper & Row.

Poetarum lesbiorum fragmenta. 1955. Ed. Edgar Lobel and Denys Page. Oxford: Clarendon.

Pollak, Vivian R. 1984. *Dickinson: The Anxiety of Gender*. Ithaca: Cornell University Press.

Pollitt, J. J. 1986. *Art in the Hellenistic Age*. Cambridge: Cambridge University Press.

Pomeroy, Sarah B. 1978. "Supplementary Notes on Erinna." *Zeitschrift für Papyrologie und Epigraphik* 32:17–22.

Pottle, Frederick H. 1965. *Boswell's Literary Career: An Illustrated Biography*. Oxford: Clarendon.

Pound, Ezra. 1910/1968. *Spirit of Romance*. New York: New Directions.

——. 1954/1975. *Literary Essays*. Ed. T. S. Eliot. New York: New Directions.

Powell, J. V. 1933. *New Chapters in the History of Greek Literature*. London: Oxford University Press.

Preminger, Alex, ed. 1974. *Princeton Encyclopedia of Poetry and Poetics*. Princeton: Princeton University Press.

Prins, Yopie. 1995. "A Metaphorical Field: Katherine Bradley and Edith Cooper." *Victorian Poetry* 33.1:129–48.

——. 1997. "Sappho's Afterlife in Translation." In Greene 1997b:36–67.

Prior, Mary, ed. 1985. *Women in English Society, 1500–1800*. New York: Methuen.

Pumphrey, Martin. 1991. "Play, Fantasy, and Strange Laughter: Stevie Smith's Uncomfortable Poetry." In *In Search of Stevie Smith*, ed. Sanford Sternlicht, 97–113. Syracuse: Syracuse University Press.

Quilligan, Maureen. 1990. "The Constant Subject: Instability and Authority in Wroth's *Urania* Poems." In *Soliciting Interpretation: Literary Theory and Seventeenth-Century English Poetry*, ed. Elizabeth D. Harvey and Katharine Eisaman Maus, 307–35. Chicago: University of Chicago Press.

Ramazani, Jahan. 1994. *Poetry of Mourning: The Modern Elegy from Hardy to Heaney*. Chicago: University of Chicago Press.

Rauk, John. 1989. "Erinna's *Distaff* and Sappho Fr. 94." *Greek, Roman, and Byzantine Studies* 30:101–16.

Reed, Joseph W., and Frederick Pottle, eds. 1977. *Boswell: Laird of Auchinlock, 1779–1782*. New York: McGraw-Hill.

Reitzenstein, Richard. 1893. *Epigramm und Skolion*. Giessen: J. Ricker'sche Buchhandlung.

Reynolds, Margaret. 1996. " 'I Lived for Art, I Lived for Love': The Woman Poet Sings Sappho's Last Song." In Leighton and Reynolds 1996:277–306.

Rich, Adrienne. 1971/1979. "When We Dead Awaken: Writing as Re-vision." In *On Lies, Secrets, and Silence*, 33–50. New York: Norton.

——. 1973. *Diving into the Wreck: Poems, 1971–1972*. New York: Norton.

——. 1978. "Twenty-one Love Poems." In *The Dream of a Common Language*, 25–38. New York: Norton.

——. 1983. *Sources*. Woodside: Hyeck Press.

——. 1984. *The Fact of a Doorframe: Poems Selected and New, 1950–1984*. New York: Norton.

——. 1986. *Blood, Bread, and Poetry: Selected Prose, 1979–1985*. New York: Norton.

——. 1991. *An Atlas of the Difficult World*. New York: Norton.

——. 1993a. *Adrienne Rich's Poetry and Prose: Poems, Prose Reviews, and Criticism*. New York: Norton.

——. 1993b. *What Is Found There: Notes on Poetry and Politics*. New York: Norton.

Riddell, Joseph N. 1978. "A Somewhat Polemical Introduction: The Elliptical Poem." *Genre* 11:459–77.

Rissman, Leah. 1983. *Love as War: Homeric Allusion in the Poetry of Sappho*. Königstein: Anton Ham.

Roberts, Josephine, ed. 1983. *The Poems of Lady Mary Wroth*. Baton Rouge: Louisiana State University Press.

Robinson, David M. 1923. *Sappho and Her Influence*. Boston: Marshall Jones.

Rogers, Katharine M. 1979. Introduction to *Selected Poems of Anne Finch, Countess of Winchilsea*. New York: Frederick Ungar.

Rollins, Hyder E., and Herschel Baker, eds. 1954. *The Renaissance in England*. Lexington, Mass.: D. C. Heath.

Rose, Mary Beth, ed. 1986. *Women in the Middle Ages and the Renaissance: Literary and Historical Perspectives*. Syracuse: Syracuse University Press.

Rosenthal, M. L., and Sally M. Gall. 1981. "The Modern Sequence and Its Precursors." *Contemporary Literature* 22:308–25.

——. 1983. *The Modern Poetic Sequence: The Genesis of Modern Poetry*. New York: Oxford University Press.

Rosmarin, Adena. 1985. *The Power of Genre*. Minneapolis: University of Minnesota Press.

Rudiger, H. 1933. *Sappho, ihr Ruf und Ruhm bei der Nachwelt*. Leipzig: Dieterich.

Saake, Helmut. 1972. *Sapphostudien*. Munich: Schöningh.

Salvaggio, Ruth. 1988. *Enlightened Absence: Neoclassical Configurations of the Feminine*. Urbana: University of Illinois Press.

Sanchez-Eppler, Karen. 1993. *Touching Liberty: Abolition, Feminism, and the Politics of the Body*. Berkeley: University of California Press.

Sankovitch, Tilde. 1986. "Inventing Authority of Origin: *The Difficult Enterprise*." In Rose 1986:227–43.

Sayre, Henry. 1990. "Performance." In *Critical Terms for Literary Study*, ed. Frank Lentricchia and Thomas McLaughlin, 91–104. Chicago: University of Chicago Press.

Scarry, Elaine. 1985. *The Body in Pain: The Making and Unmaking of the World*. New York: Oxford University Press.

Schaum, Melita. 1986. " 'Moon-flowers out of Muck': Mina Loy and the Female Autobiographical Epic." *Massachusetts Studies in English* 10:254–76.

Schenck, Celeste M. 1986. "Feminism and Deconstruction: Re-constructing the Elegy." *Tulsa Studies in Women's Literature* 5:13–28.

——. 1987. "Songs (from) the Bride: Feminism, Psychoanalysis, Genre." *Literature and Psychology* 23:109–19.

——. 1988. "All of a Piece: Women's Poetry and Autobiography." In *Life/Lines: Theorizing Women's Autobiography*, ed. Bella Brodzki and Celeste Schenck, 281–305. Ithaca: Cornell University Press.

——. 1989. "Exiled by Genre: Modernism, Canonicity, and the Politics of Exclusion." In Broe and Ingram 1989:225–50.

Schiesari, Juliana. 1992. *The Gendering of Melancholia: Feminism, Psychoanalysis*, *and the Symbolics of Loss in Renaissance Literature*. Ithaca: Cornell University Press.

Scott, Bonnie Kime, ed. 1990. *The Gender of Modernism: A Critical Anthology*. Bloomington: Indiana University Press.

Seaford, R. 1987. "The Tragic Wedding." *Journal of Hellenistic Studies* 107:106–30.

Sedgwick, Eve Kosofsky. 1992. "Gender Criticism." In *Redrawing the Boundaries: The Transformation of English and American Literary Studies*, ed. Stephen Greenblatt and Giles Gunn, 271–302. New York: Modern Language Association of America.

Seremetakis, Nadia. 1987. "Women and Death: Cultural Power and Ritual Process in Inner Mani." *Canadian Women Studies/Les Cahiers de la Femme* 8.2:108–10.

Sexton, Anne. 1971. *Transformations*. Boston: Houghton Mifflin.

Shakinovsky, Lynn J. 1990. "Hidden Listeners: Dialogism in the Poetry of Emily Dickinson." *Discours Social/Social Discourse*, nos. 1–2 (Spring/Summer): 199–215.

Shange, Ntozake. 1976. *For colored girls who have considered suicide/when the rainbow is enuf*. New York: Bantam.

Sheats, Paul. 1973. *The Making of Wordsworth's Poetry, 1785–1798*. Cambridge: Harvard University Press.

Shelley, Percy Bysshe. 1987. "A Defence of Poetry." In *Romantic Critical Essays*, ed. David Bromwich, 212–43. Cambridge: Cambridge University Press.

Showalter, Elaine. 1985a. "Feminist Criticism in the Wilderness." In Showalter 1985b:243–70.

———, ed. 1985b. *The New Feminist Criticism: Essays on Women, Literature, and Theory*. New York: Pantheon.

———, ed. 1989. *Speaking of Gender*. New York: Routledge.

Shurr, William H. 1983. *The Marriage of Emily Dickinson*. Lexington: University of Kentucky Press.

Sidney, Sir Philip. 1595/1970. *An Apology for Poetry*. Ed. Forrest G. Robinson. Indianapolis: Bobbs-Merrill.

Silberman, Lauren. 1986. "Singing Unsung Heroines: Androgynous Discourse in Book 3 of the *Faerie Queene*." In Ferguson et al. 1986:259–71, 383–86.

Siskin, Clifford. 1988. *The Historicity of Romantic Discourse*. New York: Oxford University Press.

Skinner, Marilyn B. 1982. "Briseis, the Trojan Women, and Erinna." *Classical World* 75:265–69.

———. 1989. "Sapphic Nossis." *Arethusa* 22:5–18.

———. 1991a. "Aphrodite Garlanded: Eros and Poetic Creativity in Sappho and Nossis." In *Rose di Pieria*, ed. Francesco de Martino, 77–96. Bari: Levante.

———. 1991b. "Nossis *Thelyglossos*: The Private Text and the Public Book." In *Women's History and Ancient History*, ed. Sarah B. Pomeroy, 20–47. Chapel Hill: University of North Carolina Press.

———. 1993. "Women and Language in Archaic Greece, or, Why Is Sappho a Woman?" In *Feminist Theory and the Classics*, ed. Nancy Sorkin Rabinowitz and Amy Richlin, 125–44. New York: Routledge.

Smith, G. G., ed. 1904. *Elizabethan Critical Essays*. 2 vols. Oxford: Clarendon.

Smith, Martha Nell. 1992. *Rowing in Eden: Rereading Emily Dickinson*. Austin: University of Texas Press.

Smith, Stevie. 1936. *Novel on Yellow Paper*. London: Jonathan Cape.

———. 1979. *The Holiday*. London: Virago.

———. 1981. *Me Again: Collected Writings of Stevie Smith Illustrated by Herself*. Ed. Jack Barbera and William McBrien. New York: Farrar Straus Giroux.

———. 1983. *The Collected Poems of Stevie Smith*. Ed. James MacGibbon. New York: New Directions.

Snyder, Jane McIntosh. 1989. *The Woman and the Lyre: Women Writers in Classical Greece and Rome*. Carbondale: Southern Illinois University Press.

Sollers, Philippe. 1981. "The Novel and the Experience of Limits." In *Surfiction: Fiction Now and Tomorrow*, ed. Raymond Federman, 59–74. Chicago: Swallow Press.

Spalding, Frances. 1989. *Stevie Smith: A Biography*. New York: Norton.

Spivak, Kathleen. 1974. *The Jane Poems*. New York: Doubleday.

Stanton, Domna, ed. 1984. *The Female Autograph*. New York: New York Literary Forum.

Staten, Henry. 1995. *Eros in Mourning: Homer to Lacan*. Baltimore: Johns Hopkins University Press.

Stein, Gertrude. 1914/1962. *Tender Buttons*. In *The Selected Writings of Gertrude Stein*, ed. Carl Van Vechten, 459–510. New York: Vintage.

———. 1927/1980. "Patriarchal Poetry." In *The Yale Gertrude Stein*, ed. Richard Kostelanetz, 106–46. New Haven: Yale University Press.

———. 1956. *Stanzas in Meditation, and Other Poems, 1929–1933*. New Haven: Yale University Press.

Stephen, Leslie. 1890. "Herbert Croft." In *Dictionary of National Biography*, 13.107–10. New York: Macmillan.

Stephen, Leslie, and Sidney Lee. 1890. "James Hackman." In *Dictionary of National Biography*, 23.422–23. New York: Macmillan.

Sternlicht, Sanford. 1990. *Stevie Smith*. Boston: Twayne.

Stevens, Wallace. 1978. *The Collected Poems of Wallace Stevens*. New York: Knopf.

Stevenson, John Allen. 1988. "A Vampire in the Mirror: The Sexuality of Dracula." *PMLA* 103 (March): 139–49.

Strouse, Jean. 1981. "Toni Morrison's Black Magic." *Newsweek*, 30 March, 52–57.

Sturgeon, Mary. 1922. *Michael Field*. New York: Macmillan.

Sylvester, Richard S., ed. 1974. *English Seventeenth-Century Verse*. Vol.2. New York: Norton.

Symonds, John Addington. 1873. *Studies of the Greek Poets*. Vol.1. London: Smith, Elder.

Synge, John Millington. 1911. *The Aran Islands*. Boston: John W. Luce.

Thomson, Clive. 1989. "Mikhail Bakhtin and Contemporary Anglo-American Feminist Theory." *Critical Studies: A Journal of Critical Theory, Literature and Culture* 1.2:141–61.

Tighe, Mary. 1805/1978. *Psyche, or The Legend of Love*. New York: Garland.

Tiwary, K. M. 1978. "Tuneful Weeping: A Mode of Communication." *Frontiers: A Journal of Women's Studies* 3.3:24–27.

Travitsky, Betty, ed. 1989. *The Paradise of Women: Writings by Englishwomen of the Renaissance*. New York: Columbia University Press.

Turner, Frank M. 1981. *The Greek Heritage in Victorian Britain*. New Haven: Yale University Press.

Vanita, Ruth. 1996. *Sappho and the Virgin Mary*. New York: Columbia University Press.

Vendler, Helen. 1991. "Mapping the Air." *New York Review of Books*, 21 November, 50–56.

Vicinus, Martha. 1994. "The Adolescent Boy: Fin de Siècle Femme Fatale?" *Journal of the History of Sexuality* 5.1:90–114.

Vickers, Nancy. 1982. "Diana Described: Scattered Women and Scattered Rhyme." In *Writing and Sexual Difference*, ed. Elizabeth Abel, 95–109. Chicago: University of Chicago Press.

——.1985. " 'The blazon of sweet beauty's best': Shakespeare's *Lucrece*." In *Shakespeare and the Question of Theory*, ed. Patricia Parker and Geoffrey Hartman, 95–115. New York: Methuen.

Voloshinov, V. N. [M. M. Bakhtin]. 1973. *Marxism and the Philosophy of Language*. Trans. Ladislav Matejka and I. R. Titunik. New York: Seminar Press.

Walker, Alice. 1983. "Writing *The Color Purple*." In *In Search of Our Mothers' Gardens*, 355–600. San Diego: Harcourt Brace Jovanovich.

Walker, Barbara. 1983. *The Woman's Encyclopedia of Myths and Secrets*. San Francisco: Harper & Row.

Wall, Wendy. 1993. *The Imprint of Gender: Authorship and Publication in the English Renaissance*. Ithaca: Cornell University Press.

Waller, Gary. 1979. *Mary Sidney, Countess of Pembroke: A Critical Study of Her Writings and Literary Milieu*. Salzburg: Universität Salzburg.

——. 1986. *English Poetry of the Sixteenth Century*. New York: Longman.

——. 1991. "Mary Wroth and the Sidney Family Romance: Gender Construction in Early Modern England." In Miller and Waller 1991:35–63.

Warland, Betsy. 1987. *Serpent (W)rite (A Reader's Gloss)*. Toronto: Coach House Press.

——. 1990. *Proper Deafinitions: Collected Theorograms*. Vancouver: Press Gang.

Weems, Renita J. 1988. *Just a Sister Away: A Womanist Vision of Women's Relationships in the Bible*. San Diego: Lura Media.

Weinstein, Norman. 1970. *Gertrude Stein and the Literature of the Modern Consciousness*. New York: Frederick Ungar.

Weisbuch, Robert. 1972. *Emily Dickinson's Poetry*. Chicago: University of Chicago Press.

West, Martin L. 1974. *Studies in Greek Elegy and Iambus*. Berlin: Walter de Gruyter.

——. 1977. "Erinna." *Zeitschrift für Papyrologie und Epigraphik* 25:95–119.

Wharton, Henry Thornton. 1885, 1895, 1898/1974. *Sappho: Memoir, Text, Selected Renderings, and a Literal Translation*. London: David Stott. 1895: 3d ed. London: John Lane. 1898/1974: reprint of 4th ed. Amsterdam: Liberac.

White, Chris. 1992. " 'Poets and lovers evermore': The Poetry and Journals of Michael Field." In *Sexual Sameness: Textual Differences in Lesbian and Gay Writing*, ed. Joseph Bristow, 26–43. London: Routledge.

——. 1996. "The Tiresian Poet: Michael Field." In Leighton and Reynolds 1996: 148–61.

Whitman, Ruth. 1977. *Tamsen Donner: A Woman's Journey*. Cambridge, Mass.: Alice James Books.

Whitman, Walt. 1892/1964. *Democratic Vistas*. In *Prose Works, 1892*, ed. Floyd Sto-
vall, 2.361–426. New York: New York University Press.

Widoger, Geoffrey, et al., eds. 1986. *Illustrated Dictionary and Concordance of the
Bible*. New York: Macmillan.

Wilamowitz-Moellendorff, Ulrich von. 1924. *Hellenistische Dichtung in der Zeit des
Kallimachos*. 2 vols. Berlin: Weidmannsche Buchhandlung.

Williamson, Margaret. 1995. *Sappho's Immortal Daughters*. Cambridge: Harvard
University Press.

Wills, Clair. 1989. "Upsetting the Public: Carnival, Hysteria, and Women's Texts."
In *Bakhtin and Cultural Theory*, ed. Ken Hirschkop and David Shepherd, 130–
51. Manchester: Manchester University Press.

Wilson, Katharina M., ed. 1987. *Women Writers of the Renaissance and Reformation*.
Athens: University of Georgia Press.

Winkler, John J. 1990. "Double Consciousness in Sappho's Lyrics." In *The Constraints of Desire*, 162–87. New York: Routledge.

Winters, Yvor. 1967. *Forms of Discovery: Critical and Historical Essays on the Forms
of the Short Poem in English*. [Denver]: Alan Swallow.

Wolff, Janet. 1990. *Feminine Sentences: Essays on Women and Culture*. Cambridge:
Polity.

Wolfson, Susan J. 1994. "*Lyrical Ballads* and the Language of (Men) Feeling:
Wordsworth Writing Women's Voices." In *Men Writing the Feminine: Literature,
Theory, and the Question of Genders*, ed. Thais E. Morgan, 29–57. Albany: State
University of New York Press.

Woolf, Virginia. 1929. *A Room of One's Own*. New York: Harcourt, Brace.

———. 1929/1957. *A Room of One's Own*. New York: Harcourt Brace Jovanovich.

———. 1938/1939. *Three Guineas*. New York: Harcourt, Brace.

Wordsworth, William, and S. T. Coleridge. 1969. *Lyrical Ballads, 1798*. Ed. W. J.
B. Owen. 2d ed. London: Oxford University Press.

Yaeger, Patricia. 1988. *Honey-Mad Women: Emancipatory Strategies in Women's Writing*. New York: Columbia University Press.

Yorke, Liz. 1991. *Impertinent Voices: Subversive Strategies in Contemporary Women's
Poetry*. London: Routledge.

Yu, Anthony C., ed. 1973. *Parnassus Revisited: Modern Critical Essays on the Epic
Tradition*. Chicago: American Library Association.

Zanker, Graham. 1987. *Realism in Alexandrian Poetry*. London: Croom Helm.

About the Contributors

Eavan Boland is Professor of English at Stanford University. She lives in Dublin for part of the year with her husband and two daughters. Her most recent books include *Object Lessons: The Life of the Woman and the Poet in Our Time* (1995) and *An Origin Like Water: Collected Poems, 1967–1987* (1996).

Angela Bourke is Lecturer in Modern Irish and director of the M. Phil. in Irish Studies at University College Dublin. She is the author of *Caoineadh na dTrí Muire: Téama na Páise i bhFilíocht Bhéil na Gaeilge*, a study of women's religious poetry in Irish (1983), and of a short story collection, *By Salt Water* (1996), as well as numerous articles and reviews on Irish oral tradition.

Olga Broumas and T Begley have been collaborating in poetry, translation, performance, photography, and mixed media since 1989. They received a Witter Bynner Translation grant for their translation of *Open Papers*, essays of Odysseas Elytis, which was published in 1995. They have published three chapbooks, *Unfolding the Tablecloth of God, Helen Groves*, and *Ithaca: Little Summer in Winter*, as well as *Sappho's Gymnasium: Collaborations, 1989–1994* (1994). They live in Brewster, Cape Cod, where they teach Body Sound and Text classes and intensives.

Anne Carson is a poet and Professor of Classics at the University of McGill. She is the author of *Eros the Bittersweet* (1986), *Plainwater* (1995), and *Glass, Iron, and God* (1995).

Rita Dove, U.S. Poet Laureate from 1993 to 1995, is winner of a Pulitzer Prize and has published six poetry collections, most recently *Mother Love* (1995), as well as a volume of short stories, the novel *Through the Ivory Gate* (1992), and essays under the title *The Poet's World* (1995). Her first full-length play, *The Darker Face of the Earth,* opened at the Oregon Shakespeare Festival in July 1996. Ms. Dove lives with her husband and daughter near Charlottesville, where she is Commonwealth Professor of English at the University of Virginia.

Rachel Blau DuPlessis has published *Writing beyond the Ending: Narrative Strategies of Twentieth-Century Women Writers* (1985), *The Pink Guitar: Writing as Feminist Practice* (1990), *The Selected Letters of George Oppen* (1990), and poetry collected in *Tabula Rosa* (1987), *Drafts 3–14* (1991), *Drafts 15–XXX, The Fold* (1997).

Susan Stanford Friedman is the Virginia Woolf Professor of English and Women's Studies at the University of Wisconsin–Madison. She is the author of *Psyche Reborn: The Emergence of H.D.* (1981) and *Penelope's Web: Gender, Modernity, H.D.'s Fiction* (1990), the editor of *Joyce: The Return of the Repressed* (1993), and co-editor of *Signets: Reading H.D.* (1990). She has published articles on the women's long poem and feminist theory and is at work on books on modernism and on identity in feminist multicultural theory.

Kathryn Gutzwiller is Professor of Classics at the University of Cincinnati. She is the author of *Studies in the Hellenistic Epyllion* (1981), *Theocritus' Pastoral Analogies: The Formation of a Genre* (1991), and *Poetic Garlands: Hellenistic Epigrams in Context* (forthcoming), as well as articles on Greek and Latin poetry, literary genres, and women in ancient literature.

Marilyn Hacker is the author of eight books. Her *Winter Numbers* (1994) received both a Lambda Literary Award and the Lenore Marshall Prize of the Academy of American Poets and *The Nation*, both in 1995, and her *Selected Poems* (1994) received the 1996 Poets' Prize. *Edge*, her translations of the French poet Claire Malroux, was published in 1996 by Wake Forest University Press. She lives in New York and Paris.

Joy Harjo is a poet and musician whose group, Joy Harjo and Poetic Justice, has released a CD titled "Letter from the End of the Twentieth Century" (1996). Her publications include the award-winning *In Mad Love and War* (1990), *The Woman Who Fell From the Sky* (1996), and a collection of interviews called *The Spiral of Memory* (1996).

Diana E. Henderson, Associate Professor of Literature at MIT, is the author of *Passion Made Public: Elizabethan Lyric, Gender, and Performance* (1995) and of articles on early modern drama, Spenser, and Joyce.

bell hooks (Gloria Watkins) is a writer and teacher who speaks widely on issues of race, class, and gender. She is the author of *Ain't I a Woman: Black Women and Feminism* (1981), *Feminist Theory from Margin to Center* (1984), *Talking Back: Thinking Feminist, Thinking Black* (1989), and *Yearning: Race, Gender, and Cultural Politics* (1990). Her column "Sisters of the Yam" appears monthly in *Zeta* magazine, and she writes poetry and creative prose as well.

Susan Howe is the author of *My Emily Dickinson* (1985), *The Europe of Trusts* (1990), *Singularities* (1990), *The Birth-mark: Unsettling the Wilderness in American Literary History* (1993), *The Nonconformist's Memorial* (1993), and *Frame Structures: Early Poems, 1974–1979* (1996) She is a professor of English at the State University of New York at Buffalo.

Romana Huk is Associate Professor in the Department of English at the University of New Hampshire. She has published essays on contemporary poets, has co-edited a collection, *Contemporary British Poetry: Essays in Theory and Criticism* (1996), and is currently editing a book of proceeds from *Assembling Alternatives*, an international conference she ran on experimental poetries in 1996. She is also the author of a forthcoming monograph on Stevie Smith.

Akasha (Gloria) Hull is Professor of Women's Studies and Literature at the University of California, Santa Cruz. She has published many books and articles on black women's literature, including *Color, Sex, and Poetry: Three Women Writers of the Harlem Renaissance* (1987), and a volume of her own poetry, *Healing Heart: Poems 1973–1988* (1989). She is currently working on a study of spiritual consciousness in African American women's writing.

Virginia Jackson is Assistant Professor of English at Rutgers University. Her forthcoming book on Emily Dickinson is entitled *Dickinson's Misery*, and she is currently at work on a manuscript titled *Longfellow and the Institution of Poetry*.

Jayne Elizabeth Lewis is Associate Professor of English at UCLA. She is the author of articles on Samuel Richardson and on eighteenth-century women writers, and *The English Fable: Aesop and Literary Culture, 1651–1740* (1995). She is currently writing on Mary Queen of Scots.

Alicia Ostriker, Professor of English at Rutgers University, is the author of eight volumes of poetry, among them *The Imaginary Lover* (1986), which won the William Carlos Williams Prize; *Green Age* (1989); and *The Crack in Everything* (1996), which was nominated for a National Book Award. Her prose work includes *Stealing the Language: the Emergence of Women's Poetry in America* (1986) and *The Nakedness of Fathers: Biblical Visions and Revisions* (1994).

M. Nourbese Philip is a poet, writer, and lawyer who lives in Toronto. She has published four books of poetry, *Thorns* (1980), *Salmon Courage* (1983), *She Tries Her Tongue: Her Silence Softly Breaks* (1988), and *Looking for Livingstone: An Odyssey of Silence* (1989), a poem in prose and poetry. Her first novel, *Harriet's Daughter*, was published in 1988. Her two collections of essays are *Frontiers: Writings in Racism and Culture* (1992) and *Showing Grit* (1995).

Yopie Prins is Assistant Professor of English and Comparative Literature at the University of Michigan. She is the author of the forthcoming *Victorian Sappho: Declining a Name* and has published various articles on classical Greek literature, Victorian poetry, and nineteenth-century Hellenism.

Maeera Shreiber teaches in the English Department at the University of Southern California. Currently a fellow at the Stanford Humanities Center, she has published essays on various modern and contemporary women poets and on cultural poetics. She is co-editor of a volume of essays on Mina Loy and is completing "Dwelling and Displacement: The Genres of Jewish American Verse."

Karen Swann is Professor of English at Williams College. She has published articles on Coleridge, Wordsworth, Burke, and Keats, and is currently completing a study, *Lives of the Dead Poets*, on the riveting deaths of English Romantic poets.

Eleanor Wilner is a poet who teaches in the MFA Program for Writers at Warren Wilson College. Her books include *Reversing the Spell: New and Selected Poems* (1997), *Otherwise* (1993), *Sarah's Choice* (1989), *Shekhinah* (1985), *Maya* (1979), and *Gathering the Winds* (1975), a book on visionary imagination.

Index

Alexiou, Margaret, 140, 207, 303
Altieri, Charles, 301, 309–10
Anyte, 212
Anzaldúa, Gloria, 9
Apollonius, 209, 211
Aristotle, 39, 177, 214, 224, 226–27
Asclepiades, 210, 212, 215, 220
Auden, W. H., 193, 311
Austen, Jane, 58

Baker, Houston, 336
Bakhtin, M. M., 6, 148–53, 330
Barthes, Roland, 13–14, 255
Begley, T, 7–9, 252–59
Behn, Aphra, 57, 172–73, 176
Benjamin, Walter, 155, 166–67
Blake, William, 151, 159, 162, 263
Bloom, Harold, 14, 18, 220
Boland, Eavan, 7, 9, 187–92
Boswell, James, 70–75
Bourke, Angela, 6, 9, 135, 138, 140, 142–
  44, 146
Bradley, Katherine. See Field, Michael
Bradstreet, Anne, 42, 47
Brontë, Charlotte, 97
Brooks, Gwendolyn, 17, 23, 31, 194,
  279
Broumas, Olga, 7–9, 252–59
Browning, Elizabeth Barrett, 16, 38, 58,
  97–99
Browning, Robert, 91–92, 97, 161–62, 231–
  34, 240
Butler, Judith, 46, 88

Callimachus, 209–13, 220
Carson, Anne, 7, 9, 223–28, 248
Case, Sue-Ellen, 46
Catullus, 211
Cecil, Anne, 44–46, 49, 58
Cixous, Hélène, 31
Clifton, Lucille, 8, 30–31, 273–95
Coleridge, Samuel Taylor, 41, 74
Colonna, Vittoria, 43–45, 47
Cooper, Edith. See Field, Michael
Croft, Herbert, 70, 72–75, 77
Culler, Jonathan, 3, 14, 88

De Lauretis, Teresa, 53, 337
De Man, Paul, 88
Derrida, Jacques, 4, 13–14, 16, 18, 36, 88,
  177
Dickinson, Emily, 1, 5, 7, 9–10, 18, 30, 37–
  38, 80–82, 85–90, 92, 96–108, 151, 196,
  263, 296, 320, 332–33
Dillon, Wentworth (Earl of Roscommon),
  171–72, 177–78
Donne, John, 40, 45
Dostoevsky, Fyodor, 164–65
Dove, Rita, 6, 9, 23, 111–15, 195
Dowling, Linda, 233
Dryden, John, 170–71, 174–75, 177–78
DuPlessis, Rachel Blau, 8–9, 17, 20, 30–
  31, 147, 150, 327–43
Duras, Marguerite, 53

Edelman, Lee, 238–39
Eliot, George, 16–17, 57–58

Eliot, T. S., 19, 27, 36, 147, 198, 328
Elizabeth I, queen of England, 48–49
Elytis, Odysseas, 252–54
Erinna, 7, 203–11, 214, 220–22
Euripides, 209, 221–22

Faderman, Lillian, 236, 246
Field, Michael, 7, 229–51
Finch, Anne, 6, 56, 166–70, 173, 175–84
Foucault, Michel, 307
Franklin, R. W., 80–82, 101
Freccero, John, 41, 48–49
Freud, Sigmund, 33, 62, 68, 334
Fried, Michael, 95–96
Friedman, Susan Stanford, 5, 8–9, 13–17, 23, 26–27, 305
Fuller, Margaret, 92

Gallop, Jane, 10
Gambara, Veronica, 43–45, 47
Gascoigne, George, 39–40, 56
Gilbert, Sandra M., 9, 14, 42, 47–48, 103, 145, 155, 220
Glazener, Nancy, 152–53
Goethe, Johann Wolfgang von, 91
Grahn, Judy, 18–19, 22, 27–31, 35–36
Greenblatt, Stephen, 4
Gubar, Susan, 9, 14, 42, 47–48, 103, 145, 155, 220, 236
Gutzwiller, Kathryn J., 7–9, 211–12, 218

Hacker, Marilyn, 7, 9, 17, 193–201
Harjo, Joy, 6, 9, 126–31
Hart, Janet, 254
Heilbrun, Carolyn, 41
Henderson, Diana E., 5, 8–9
Herbert, Mary Sidney (Countess of Pembroke, 42), 45–46, 52
Hesiod, 210, 213
H.D. (Hilda Doolittle), 15, 17, 26–29, 263, 334
Higginson, Thomas Wentworth, 81–82, 89–92, 96–97, 100
Holst-Warhaft, Gail, 208, 303–4, 317
Homans, Margaret, 9, 14, 101
Homer, 26, 203–4, 207–8
hooks, bell, 8–9, 296–300
Horace, 177, 180–82, 196–97
Howe, Susan, 5, 8–9, 17–18, 30–31, 80–84, 101, 320
Hughes, Langston, 36
Huk, Romana, 6, 8–9, 154
Hull, Akasha (Gloria), 8–9
Hutchinson, Lucy, 173, 176

Irigaray, Luce, 31–33, 88

Jackson, Virginia, 5–6, 8–9
Jacobus, Mary, 62, 70
Jameson, Fredric, 4, 317
Jardine, Lisa, 42, 47
Johnson, Dianne, 278
Jones, Ann Rosalind, 38, 40–41, 43, 47, 52, 58
Jonson, Ben, 40–41, 45, 56–57
Joyce, James, 21–22

Kaye/Kantrowitz, Melanie, 270
Keats, John, 16, 107
Keller, Lynn, 9, 13–14, 16–17, 301
Koestenbaum, Wayne, 236
Kristeva, Julia, 14, 35
Kruchenykh, Alexei, 329

Labé, Louise, 43–44
Lacan, Jacques, 33, 35, 42, 154, 159
La Fontaine, Jean de, 166–69
Lanyer, Aemilia, 38
Leighton, Angela, 235–36, 246
Leonidas, 210, 212, 214, 220
Levi, Primo, 197–98
Levinas, Emmanuel, 313, 315
Lewis, Jayne Elizabeth, 6, 9
Loeffelholz, Mary, 9, 17, 88
Lord, Albert B., 132–33
Lorde, Audre, 31
Loy, Mina, 17, 19–22, 26, 35–36

Marlatt, Daphne, 31–32
Meleager, 215–16, 221
Melville, Herman, 319
Memmi, Albert, 141
Merwin, W. S., 256
Michaels, Walter Benn, 95–96
Mill, John Stuart, 231
Millard, Elaine, 149–50
Millay, Edna St. Vincent, 17, 58
Miller, Nancy K., 41, 168, 178
Milton, John, 170–71, 173–75
Mitchell, Adrian, 117
Montefiore, Jan, 9, 42, 53, 148, 155
Moody, Ellen, 44–45
Moraga, Cherríe, 9
Morrison, Toni, 273–74

Neely, Carol Thomas, 57
Ní Chonaill, Eibhlín, 132, 134–46
Nossis, 7, 203, 211–22

Ong, Walter, 133, 145
Ostriker, Alicia Suskin, 8–9, 19, 22–26,
    31, 35–36, 263–72, 276–77, 287, 312–13
Ó Tuama, Seán, 134–36, 139–42
Ovid, 168, 170
Oxlie, Mary of Morpet, 46–47

Parrish, Stephen M., 62, 66
Peirce, Charles Saunders, 92–96, 99–100
Perloff, Marjorie, 329
Petrarch, 5, 38–43, 47–49, 52–58, 176, 303,
    305
Philip, M. Nourbese, 6, 8–9, 116–25
Pinch, Adela, 79
Plath, Sylvia, 23, 31, 154
Pound, Ezra, 15, 19, 27, 36, 193, 196, 198,
    333
Prins, Yopie, 7–9, 236

Racine, Jean, 176, 179–80
Rich, Adrienne, 8, 17–18, 23, 26, 30, 58,
    254, 301–17
Rossetti, Christina, 38
Rukeyser, Muriel, 195, 311, 323

Sanchez–Eppler, Karen, 93
Sand, George, 92
Sappho, 7, 90–92, 188–91, 196, 202–4, 206–
    8, 210–11, 213, 215–16, 219–51, 253–59
Scarry, Elaine, 100, 306, 320
Schenck, Celeste M., 4, 14, 45, 147
Schiesari, Juliana, 302–3, 316
Sedgwick, Eve Kosofsky, 3
Sexton, Anne, 22, 30, 263
Shakespeare, William, 41–43, 50–51, 89,
    111–13
Shange, Ntozake, 17, 31
Shelley, Percy Bysshe, 98–99
Showalter, Elaine, 2–3
Shreiber, Maeera, 8–9
Sidney, Sir Philip, 39–41, 47, 51–52
Sidney, Robert, 52, 54–55

Silverman, Kaja, 316
Skinner, Marilyn B., 203, 207, 210, 212–
    13, 216–17, 220
Smith, Stevie, 6, 147–65
Sollers, Philippe, 329
Spalding, Frances, 148, 156, 158, 163
Spenser, Edmund, 41, 52, 134
Stein, Gertrude, 17, 30–31, 33, 35, 149,
    151, 153–54
Stevens, Wallace, 36, 310
Stuart, Mary, 43, 47, 49–51, 55–58
Swann, Karen, 5, 9

Tasso, 178–79
Theocritus, 207, 211, 218
Thomas, Dylan, 161–62

Vendler, Helen, 195, 309, 313–14
Vicinus, Martha, 234, 236
Vickers, Nancy, 40–41, 327
Virgil, 47, 188–89

Walcott, Derek, 117, 194
Walker, Alice, 274
Waller, Gary, 40, 42–43, 52, 55–56
Warland, Betsy, 19, 31–36
White, Chris, 235–36, 240–41
Whitman, Walt, 16, 312–14
Wiesel, Elie, 269
Williams, William Carlos, 15, 36, 333
Wilner, Eleanor, 8, 318–26
Wittig, Monique, 38
Woolf, Virginia, 19, 23, 38, 43, 56, 133,
    150, 169, 175–76, 314, 335
Wordsworth, William, 5, 16, 41, 60–79,
    169–70
Wroth, Lady Mary, 38, 42–43, 45–49, 51–
    58

Yaeger, Patricia, 149–50, 152
Yeats, William Butler, 154

Reading Women Writing

A SERIES EDITED BY

Shari Benstock and Celeste Schenck

Tainted Souls and Painted Faces: The Rhetoric of Fallenness in Victorian Culture
by Amanda Anderson

Greatness Engendered: George Eliot and Virginia Woolf
by Alison Booth

Talking Back: Toward a Latin American Feminist Literary Criticism
by Debra A. Castillo

Articulate Silences: Hisaye Yamamoto, Maxine Hong Kingston, and Joy Kogawa
by King-Kok Cheung

H.D.'s Freudian Poetics: Psychoanalysis in Translation
by Dianne Chisholm

From Mastery to Analysis: Theories of Gender in Psychoanalytic Feminism
by Patricia Elliot

Feminist Theory, Women's Writing
by Laurie A. Finke

Colette and the Fantom Subject of Autobiography
by Jerry Aline Flieger

Autobiographics: A Feminist Theory of Women's Self-Representation
by Leigh Gilmore

Going Public: Women and Publishing in Early Modern France
edited by Elizabeth C. Goldsmith and Dena Goodman

Cartesian Women: Versions and Subversions of Rational Discourse in the Old Regime
by Erica Harth

Borderwork: Feminist Engagements with Comparative Literature
edited by Margaret R. Higonnet

*Narrative Transvestism: Rhetroic and Gender in the
Eighteenth-Century English Novel*
by Madeleine Kahn

The Unspeakable Mother: Forbidden Discourse in Jean Rhys and H.D.
by Deborah Kelly Kloepfer

*Recasting Autobiography: Women's Counterfictions in
Contemporary German Literature and Film*
by Barbara Kosta

Women and Romance: The Consolations of Gender in the English Novel
by Laurie Langbauer

Nobody's Angels: Middle-Class Women and Domestic Ideology in Victorian Culture
by Elizabeth Langland

Penelope Voyages: Women and Travel in the British Literary Traditions
by Karen R. Lawrence

Autobiographical Voices: Race, Gender, Self-Portraiture
by Françoise Lionnet

Postcolonial Representations: Women, Literature, Identity
by Françoise Lionnet
Woman and Modernity: The (Life)styles of Lou Andreas-Salomé
by Biddy Martin
In the Name of Love: Women, Maochism, and the Gothic
by Michelle A. Massé
Imperialism at Home: Race and Victorian Women's Fiction
by Susan Meyer
Outside the Pale: Cultural Exclusion, Gender Difference,
and the Victorian Woman Writer
by Elsie B. Michie
Dwelling in Possibility: Women Poets and Critics on Poetry
edited by Yopie Prins and Maeera Shreiber
Reading Gertrude Stein: Body, Text, Gnosis
by Lisa Ruddick
Conceived by Liberty: Maternal Figures and Nineteenth-Century American Literature
by Stephanie A. Smith
Kassandra and the Censors: Greek Poetry since 1967
by Karen Van Dyck
Beyond Consolation: Death, Sexuality, and the Changing Shapes of Elegy
by Melissa F. Zeiger
Feminist Conversations: Fuller, Emerson, and the Play of Reading
by Christina Zwarg